India Working
Essays on Society and Econ

CW00410015

By drawing on her extensive fieldwork in India, and on the adjacent theoretical and empirical literature, Barbara Harriss-White describes the working of the Indian economy through its most important social structures of accumulation: labour, capital, the State, gender, religious plurality, caste and the economic organisation of physical space. The author's intimate knowledge of the country enables her to convey vividly how India's economy is being socially regulated. Her conclusion challenges the prevailing notion that liberalisation releases the economy from political interference, and leads to a postscript on the economic base for fascism in India. This is a sophisticated and compelling book, by a distinguished scholar, for students of economics, as well as for those studying the region.

Barbara Harriss-White is Professor of Development Studies at Queen Elizabeth House, and Fellow of Wolfson College, University of Oxford. Her recent publications include *Globalisation and Insecurity: Political, Economic and Physical Challenges* (2001), and *Sonar Bangla: Agricultural Growth and Agrarian Change in West Bengal and Bangladesh* (with Sugata Bose and Ben Rogaly, 1999).

V

Contemporary South Asia 8

Editorial board
JAN BREMAN, G.P. HAWTHORN, AYESHA JALAL,
PATRICIA JEFFERY, ATUL KOHLI

Contemporary South Asia has been established to publish books on the politics, society and culture of South Asia since 1947. In accessible and compehensive studies, authors who are already engaged in researching specific aspects of South Asian society explore a wide variety of broad-ranging and topical themes. The series will be of interest to anyone who is concerned with the study of South Asia and with the legacy of its colonial past.

In memory of Gordon White

India Working

Essays on Society and Economy

Barbara Harriss-White

University of Oxford

CAMBRIDGE
UNIVERSITY PRESS

PUBLISHED BY THE PRESS SYNDICATE OF THE UNIVERSITY OF CAMBRIDGE
The Pitt Building, Trumpington Street, Cambridge, United Kingdom

CAMBRIDGE UNIVERSITY PRESS
The Edinburgh Building, Cambridge CB2 2RU, UK
40 West 20th Street, New York, NY 10011–4211, USA
477 Williamstown Road, Port Melbourne, VIC 3207, Australia
Ruiz de Alarcón 13, 28014 Madrid, Spain
Dock House, The Waterfront, Cape Town 8001, South Africa

http://www.cambridge.org

First published 2003

Printed in China by Everbest Printing Co.

Typeface Plantin 10 (*Adobe*) 10/12 pt. *System* QuarkXPress® [PK]

A catalogue record for this book is available from the British Library

National Library of Australia Cataloguing in Publication data
Harriss-White, Barbara, 1946– .
India working: essays on society and economy.
Bibliography.
Includes index.
ISBN 0 521 80979 7.
ISBN 0 521 00763 1 (pbk.).
1. India – Economic conditions – 1947– .
2. India – Social conditions – 1947– . I. Title.
(Series: Contemporary South Asia (Cambridge, England); 8).
338. 954

ISBN 0 521 80979 7 hardback
ISBN 0 521 00763 1 paperback

Contents

Preface and acknowledgments

This book has developed from the Cambridge Commonwealth Lectures that I gave in 1999 under the title, 'India Working: Working India'. This was a cryptic label with two sides to it. First, there was 'India Working', in which the economy and society were imagined as pieced together as a watchmaker might assemble a watch – with the difference that the economy is an organic social machine with 'agents' that affect its own working. Second, there was 'Working India', an interaction between theoretical ideas about the economy and field evidence of it, applied rather as a stand-up comedian works a club – provoking responses from the audience and 'interpreting' them. There is an enormous amount of material 'from the audience' for this book. I sought to limit it by celebrating the contributions to our understanding of the economy made by what its great exponent in Africa, Polly Hill, called 'field economics'. Fieldwork on the Indian economy is carried out by surprisingly few economists, some anthropologists and students of politics, and many geographers. The project required an interdisciplinary approach and draws on anthropology, economics, gender studies, geography, politics and the sociology of law.

The result is a set of essays – which are just that – attempts and experiments. They are limited in their scope and none of them are to be considered complete, for doing justice to any of them would take several lifetimes.

I am very grateful to the Smuts Memorial Fund Trustees of the University of Cambridge for the honour of their invitation to give the Commonwealth Lectures, originally for 1998, and for the humane way they responded to the circumstances that delayed them by 18 months; and to Cambridge University Press, especially the CUP readers, and Marigold Acland for her patient support. At CUP, Paul Watt and Edward Caruso have seen the book through its production with expert efficiency. I am also grateful to the President and Fellows of New Hall, Cambridge, for making me a Visiting Scholar, and to the British Academy and Queen Elizabeth House, Oxford, for their grants towards research assistance.

The project would not have survived its gestation were it not for more than a little bit of help from my friends and my family. Chapter 1 has been improved by information kindly provided by Graham Chapman and Anushree Sinha. Chapter 2 is adapted from a paper by Nandini Gooptu and me entitled 'Mapping India's World of Unorganised Labour', published in the *Socialist Register, 2001: Working Classes, Global Realities*, pp. 89–118, and published here with permission from Nandini and from the editors of the *Register*. Jairus Banaji, Rohini Hensman, Leo Panitch and Ben Rogaly also helped give it shape; Gerry and Janine Rodgers supplied useful literature and Danny Sriskandarajah collected statistical information. I am also very grateful to Judith Heyer for many wide-ranging conversations about the Indian economy and rural labour. The draft of Chapter 3 on class was commented on by the following scholars: Venkatesh Athreya, Jairus Banaji, Jan Breman, John Harriss, P. S. Jha, Jos Mooij and Ben Rogaly. Matthew McCartney lent his very able brain to the project and was funded for this purpose by Queen Elizabeth House, but Conrad Barwa, Diego Colatei and Danny Sriskandarajah have also helped.

Chapter 4 on the State has been presented to seminars on Contemporary South Asia at Queen Elizabeth House, on Commonwealth History at Oxford, on the Anthropology of the Indian State at the London School of Economics, on South Asian Politics at the School of Oriental and African Studies, on the Informal and Expolary Economy at the Moscow School of Social and Economic Sciences, at the Centre for Development and the Environment at the University of Oslo, and the Centre for Development Research in Bonn. I am grateful for discussion to Venkatesh Athreya, Dan Banik, Elisabetta Basile, Sheela Rani Chunkath, Stuart Corbridge, Sarita Das, Hans-Dieter Evers, Nandini Gooptu, John Harriss, Sudipta Kaviraj, Mushtak Khan, Martin Lau, Jos Mooij, M. S. S. Pandian, Rathin Roy, Subir Sinha, Anasuya Sengupta, Teodor Shanin, S. Subramanian, David Washbrook and Andreas Wimmer, and the late S. Guhan, Indrani Sen and Gordon White.

Chapter 5 on gender has benefited from reactions from presentations at the Department for International Development, London; at Cornell University and Oberlin College (USA); from comments by Cecile Jackson, Karin Kapadia, Irene Tinker and Alice Thorner; from prices provided by Venkatesh Athreya and M. S. S. Pandian; and from data on livelihoods teased from my field notes by Elinor Harriss.

Chapter 6 depended on Pauline von Hellermann, who provided intelligent research assistance, and Arvinder Singh, who shared his research. I am grateful to them and to the British Academy for having funded them. Alice Thorner kindly let me have the run of her library and disagreed with parts of the first draft. John Harriss was generous enough to give constructive criticism and let me see his paper, 'When a Great Tradition Globalises' in draft. Gunnel Cederlof, Nandini Gooptu, Patricia Harriss, Judith Heyer, Pierre Lachaier, Linden Moore, Ben Rogaly, Mary Searle Chatterjee and Pritam Singh were all good enough to react critically to the early version. I was glad to have responses from members of the Contemporary South Asia Seminar at QEH, Oxford, and participants at the Cambridge Advanced Programme in Development Economics Research, 2001.

Chapter 7 on caste summarises the first results of a much larger project on the political role of civil society in the regulation of business originally energised in conversations with Gordon White (see *IDS Bulletin*, 24, 3, 1993, 'The Politics of Markets'), and carried out in collaboration with Elisabetta Basile, whom I wish to thank for her friendship and intellectual solidarity. The draft also profited from responses by Neil Armstrong, Chris Fuller and M. S. S. Pandian. I wish to thank for their help with fieldwork: Paul Pandian, P. J. Krishnamurthy, M. V. Srinivasan and hundreds of citizens of Arni who spoke to us over the period 1993–97. Kaveri Harriss extracted details on caste from some of her parents' field schedules from 1983 and 1973.

Chapter 8 on space involved Elisabetta Basile, Jo Beall, Claudio Cecchi, Graham Chapman, Sharad Chari, Biplab Dasgupta, John Harriss, Doreen Massey, Kate Meagher, Khalid Nadvi and Anasuya Sengupta. They pointed me to literature, helped with data or commented on the early version. Lastly, the conclusions fetched helpful responses from Jairus Banaji, Bob Benewick, John Harriss, Rohini Hensman and Gilbert Sebastian. Roger Crawford scanned maps and diagrams and helped behind the scenes. Julia Knight made sure I had secretarial support when it was most needed. Imogen Hood and Maria Moreno helped prepare the typescript, and Maria and Kaveri Harriss consolidated the bibliography. Gilbert Sebastian drafted the index. I am, as A. K. Bagchi once put it, 'non-incriminatingly' grateful to them all.

In September 2001, the month of crisis in which this book was finished, my two daughters let me soak in work in so far as this was possible, and they willingly helped in the many practical and professional ways for which writers so often thank their parents, partner or copy editor. Thank you Kaveri and Elinor. In this final month I also discovered a tribute by Marc Galanter in his acknowledgements in *Law and Society in Modern India*. He says this: 'Everyone who writes, dreams of a reader who reads one's work with an intensity that matches its writing and who delights in friendly argument that reveals to the writer more than he knew was there.' He was 'extraordinarily fortunate' to have such a reader and friend. I could not put it better and my good fortune is even greater for I have been blessed with two. They are P. J. Krishnamurthy from Arni and Raja Annamalaipuram and Colin Leys in Toronto. Every draft chapter provoked great batches of reactions hand-written on foolscap airmail paper from P. J. K., with many more examples of the economy I am describing than I could include in the book. Colin Leys pretended to know little about India in order to draw this project out. He then insisted that it was readable and accessible to a wider audience than I had originally intended. I am deeply grateful to them both for the interest they took and the support they gave. The faults and limitations that remain are mine.

Maps, figures and tables

Maps

Figures

Tables

Glossary

Indian terms

Ajlaf low-status Muslim

Amir rich and educated Muslim

Arora Hindu trading caste in Punjab

Ashrafi high-status Muslim

Baniya/bania Hindu trading caste

Benami a transaction or property right made out in a false name

Bharat India

Bhil tribal people

Bidi a country cigarette

Bidri ornamental metal work inlaid with silver

Biradari Muslim industrial/occupational 'guild'

Brahmin Hindu priestly caste

Caste defined in three ways: (1) *varna* – pan-Indian status divisions (*brahmin* (priests)); *kshatriya* (warriors and rulers in charge of order); *vaisya* (landlords, traders, liberal professions); *shudra* (agricultural producers and performers of services); (2) 'community'; (3) *jati* – a lineage/a subdivision of a caste, exclusive units for marriage and commensality (eating)

Chakkiliyan scheduled caste cobblers

Chettiars a south Indian trading caste

Crore unit of 10 million

Dalit literally 'the oppressed' in Marathi, a category for low- and scheduled-caste people

Darzi Muslim tailor

Digambara one of two major Jain sects (sky-blue clad)

Gharib (the) poor

Gounders a strongly upwardly mobile south Indian agricultural caste

Grama sevak village level worker (government official)

Harijan literally 'children of god', Gandhi's term for untouchable castes

Harijan pallar ex-untouchable agricultural labouring caste

Harijan paraiyan ex-untouchable agricultural labouring and drum-
    beating caste
Havala money-laundering
Hindutva literally 'Hindu-ness', Hindu national identity
Jains a south Asian religion in the Hindu family
Jajmani the system of unequal exchange of goods and services between
    upper and service castes
Jatis caste; a kinship group defined by birth, endogamy, commensality
    and (especially for lowest castes) occupation
Jats north Indian dominant Hindu agricultural caste
Kabadi low caste re-cyclers in north India
Kaikkoolar south Indian weaving and trading caste
Kallars upwardly mobile formerly 'criminal' south Indian caste
Khatik north Indian sanitary workers
Julaha Muslim weaver
Lakh unit of 100 000
Lohana Sindhi merchant caste
Lohar Muslim blacksmiths
Madrassa Muslim religious school
Mahajan big trader
Mahavir janam Jain festival
Marwari business caste with its epicentre in Rajasthan, but which has
    dispersed throughout India, some members of which are Jain and
    some Hindu
Mazhabis Sikh scheduled caste
Mughal era time of Muslim emperors who ruled between 1526 and
    1858
Mundy agricultural wholesale shop/wholesale market
Nadar highly entrepreneurial south Indian business caste, originally
    toddy tappers
Naickers south Indian agricultural caste (see *Gounders*)
Naidus south Indian agricultural and trading caste, originating from
    what is now Andhra Pradesh
Pannadi scheduled caste agricultural labour
Pothohari Sikh merchant class
Qassab Muslim butchers
Ramgharias artisanal engineers
Ryotwari owner-occupancy land tenure system of small peasant
    proprietors
Sangam organisation
Sangh parivar family of Hindu nationalist organisations
Saurashtrians migrant weavers and silk merchants

Shvetambar Jainism   one of the two major Jain sects (white-clad)

Scheduled caste (SC)   constitutional term for untouchable castes entitled to positive discrimination

Scheduled tribe (ST)   constitutional term for tribal or *adivasi* people entitled to positive discrimination

Shia   major Muslim sect

Sunnath   the custom of Mohammed the prophet

Sunni   major Muslim sect

Swadeshi   economic nationalism, 'self-provisioning'

Toddy   an alcoholic drink fermented from palm sap

Tulluva vellala agamudaiya mudaliars   south Indian agricultural and trading caste

Unani   Muslim system of medicine

Vaisya   merchants, one of the four *varnas* or major social groups

Waqfs   Muslim charitable organisation

Zamindari   rentier landlords and tax collectors

Technical terms

adaptive efficiency   loose definition of efficiency in terms of the flexibility of the norms and institutions shaping economic growth and development

affines   people related by marriage (generally through the female line)

agnate   relatives through the male line

allocative efficiency   the maximisation of output from given inputs at a point where marginal costs equal marginal returns

chit fund   a rotating credit association

clientelism   a comprehensive relation of dependence upon a patron

co-parcenary property rights   equal shares in, or rights to inheritance of, a jointly owned property

liberalisation   removal of restrictions to trade and investment

rent-seeking   the seeking of private gains from public office

rurban   pertaining to small towns and their rural hinterlands

sharecropping   a form of land tenure in which land is rented out on the basis of a set proportion of the harvest

structural adjustment   a set of reforms to 'structures' of prices, subsidies and exchange rates to bring domestic prices in line with international ones and therefore to change the structure of production

Exchange rates   in the mid 1990s the Rupee was approximately 44 to the US$, 60 to the £. By 2002 the Rs was 50 and 66 respectively.

Abbreviations

APL	person/household above the poverty line
BJP	Bharatiya Janata Party
BPL	person/household below the poverty line
BSP	Bahujan Samaj Party
CITU	Confederation of Indian Trades Unions
CPI (M)	Communist Party of India (Marxist)
CPM	popular abbreviation of CPI (M)
CSO	Central Statistical Organisation
ECA	Essential Commodities Act
ENRON	a multinational power company
FCI	Food Corporation of India
FPS	Fair Price Shop
GVA	gross value added
IAS	Indian Administrative Service
IC	intermediate class
IIFT	Indian Institute of Foreign Trade
ILO	International Labour Office
IPS	Indian Police Service
IR	intermediate regime
IRDP	Integrated Rural Development Programme
IRP	Indian Republican Party (*Dalit* political party)
NCAER	National Council for Applied Economic Research
NDP	Net domestic product
NGOs	non-governmental organisations, also known as voluntary organisations
NIE	New institutional economics
NPE	New political economy
NSS	National Sample Survey
PDS	Public Distribution System (of food and essential commodities)
PMK	caste-based south Indian party (*Gounders*)
RSS	Rashtriya Swayamsevak Sangh
UNDP	United Nations Development Programme
UNRISD	United Nations Research Institute for Social Development

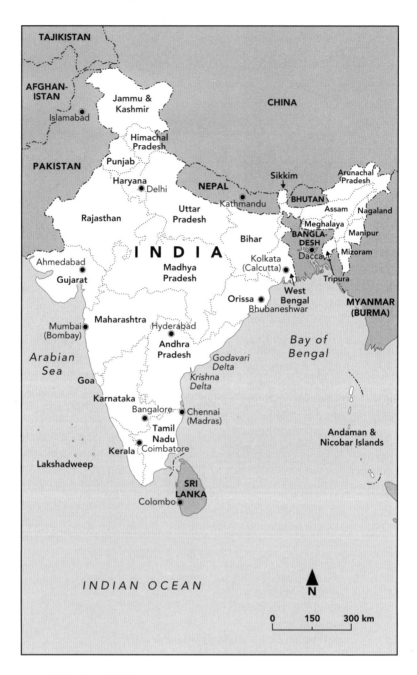

Map 1.1   India

1 Introduction: the character of the Indian economy

Development, however it is defined, requires the production and distribution of a surplus. The character of capital, its conflicts and collaborations, shape the way this surplus is accumulated, distributed, saved and invested, and the way different parts of society respond to these processes. To understand the economy we have to understand how accumulating classes are able to exploit others and to 'induce other classes to accept as in their interests the requirements for continued capital accumulation'.[1] In this book we explore the process of accumulation in rural and small-town India. From the 1991 Census we know that fewer than 12 per cent of the population lived in metropolitan cities, the headquarters of corporate capital, the 'habitus' of the globalised economic, technological and political elites (see Figure 1.1 and Table 1.1). Over 74 per cent of the population were rural, and a further 14 per cent lived in towns with populations under 200,000: a total of 88 per cent.

This is the India faced day to day by the vast mass of the population, and our aim is to describe how it works. We will pass through the corrugated iron gates set in the high walls that conceal the industrial compounds with their mills, looms, lathes, stores, drying yards, parboiling tanks and hoppers, dyeing vats, ginning hangars and yarn-twisting

Table 1.1 *India: population and settlement size (1991 Census)*

	Total population	%
Urban class I	139 226 559	16.6
Other urban	76 806 225	9.1
Total urban	216 032 784	25.7
Rural	623 968 414	74.3
Total	840 001 198	

Source: G.P. Chapman

[1] Leys 1996, p. 183.

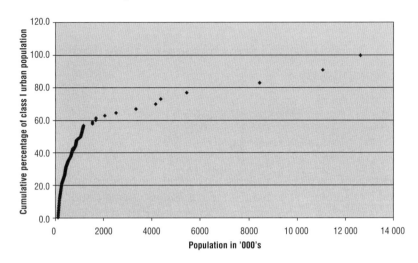

Figure 1.1   Dispersion of class 1 urban population, 1991

factories. We will stoop under low-thatch awnings and adjust our eyes to the gloom of traders' and money-lenders' offices, with their large safes, banks of phones, gaudy calendars and pictures of the gods. We will see local businessmen stuffing rolls of banknotes into the hands of election candidates, visit an agricultural extension officer moonlighting in his pickle firm, see the leader of a business association fingering the automatic rifle always close to hand in his reception room, and hear the grossly overladen buses lumbering through the dust over molten and pitted tarmac, taking workers home. The bus and factory owners, traders, officials and politicians are key players in India's accumulation process – together with the workers and other people engaged in a vast range of small-scale production and trade.

Of course, some of the goods sold by local traders are the products of 'big' business, located in the cities far away (although the well-known corporate brands of toothpaste and shampoo sold in remote tribal villages are quite often counterfeit and locally produced). But corporate, 'metropolitan' India, the India of the 12 per cent, lies outside the scope of this book, for reasons that must be made clear at the outset. First, although metropolitan India features so centrally in much of the literature on Indian development, its true significance is impossible to grasp unless the economy of the 88 per cent in which it is embedded is adequately understood. Second, an adequate analysis of the economic relationships between 'metropolitan/corporate' India and the India of small towns and villages, grounded in detailed empirical work, has yet to be undertaken.

The India of the 88 per cent – its many labels

Field researchers have given various labels to the economy we will explore. Each of them has specific purposes and strengths and we will use them whenever they seem appropriate, but most of them also have weaknesses and their very proliferation indicates that there is no good theory around which to build a consensus.

The India of the 88 per cent is sometimes called 'local', as opposed to national, or state-provincial; but 'local' is often also used to refer to the detail of activity carried on in cities. It has been called 'real', 'actually existing', and even 'authentic', to distinguish it from the imagined economy that is so often inferred from official data in a selective way to support orthodox economic theories. However, 'real' is also a term used to distinguish productive activity from financial capital; and the implication of 'authentic' – that the top of the economy is *in*authentic – is unacceptable.[2] Its markets have been called 'mud-floored' and indeed many are, but this does not mean that none are marble-floored.[3] Its economy is sometimes called 'unorganised' – to distinguish it from the 'organised' and registered economy; and this is useful, so long as it is clear that 'unorganised' does not mean 'unregulated'.[4] Sometimes it is called the 'bazaar' economy, but this term tends to play down the scale of capitalist accumulation involved. Elsewhere, the terms 'lower' or 'bharat' are used to distinguish it from the modern, planned political society of 'India' – but we will see in this book how crucial 'India' is to the economic functioning of 'bharat'.[5] It could well be called 'mofussil' ('upcountry'), but this is a Tamil word not widely used elsewhere. It certainly includes 'Malgudi', the Tamil town in which the novels of R.K. Narayan are set, but although Narayan's 'painters of signs' and 'vendors of sweets' are to be found in it (not to mention one or two 'financial experts'), it involves larger scale activities as well as petty production. Two other labels, however, are particularly influential, and must be considered in slightly more detail: the 'informal economy' and the 'black economy'.

[2] See de Alcantara (1992) and the discussion of terms in Jeffrey (2001, p. 222).
[3] Crow 2001, p. 4.
[4] Though this has no implications for the organisation of labour, or for the regulation of governance or contracts in the informal economy.
[5] Kaviraj 1991.

The informal economy

The informal economy is the economy not covered by official data on registered enterprises. It is useful to think of it as having two different though related meanings.

The first meaning of 'informal economy' is the economic activity of firms and individuals that is not registered for the purpose of taxation and/or regulation by the State.[6] The fact that it is not regulated by the State does not mean that it is not regulated at all, for there are many non-state means of regulation, which we shall be exploring in this book. There are four main reasons why an economic activity is not registered or regulated by the State:

1 it involves production or exchange that does not take the form of market transactions (for example, non-capitalist production, household production, reproductive work; non-monetised market exchange such as barter or payments in kind; and non-market exchanges such as those of clientelage and patronage, and some kinds of collective action)[7]

2 it consists of market transactions by units or firms that fall below the size threshold for direct taxation or licensing – generally where the revenue collectable would be less than the administrative costs of collecting it. In this respect virtually the entire agricultural sector is informal, being untaxed and neither accounted for nor accountable; but because we shall argue – perhaps controversially – that local *accumulation* takes place in towns, not on farms, agriculture itself will largely be the backdrop to most of the economic activity examined in this book. In the untaxed, small-town sector, the State may conceivably keep some records – for example, of residential and commercial sites – or may auction a marketplace to a manager who, in turn, keeps records of site fees, but the State has no further records. And most of the labour 'market', including the entire domestic service sector, hardly enters the State's records at all

3 it involves various kinds of mobile exchange and production – from rag-picking and recycling (much of which is either below all tax thresholds or concerns untaxed products) to rural 'home-working' financed from towns (in this case it is capital and commodities rather than people which are constantly moving)

---

[6] Breman 1976 was an early dissenter, arguing that India's informal economy included production and exchange of a substantial scale and was capitalist in nature, but under conditions where the social relations of the labour process were highly personalised. The activity might indeed be registered, but its key defining characteristics were the informality of its social relations.

[7] These are the kinds of exchange that Offer 1996 has called the 'economy of regard'.

Table 1.2   *Share of the formal and informal sector (%)*

	Informal			Formal			
	Rural	Urban	All	Rural	Urban	All	Source
Employment							NSS 93–94
Female			92			8	
Male			80			20	
Population	68	14	83	6	11	17	NCAER
Income	48	20	68	7	25	32	(94–95)
Savings	41	18	60	9	31	40	
Exports							IIFT
Agricultural			31			69	(96–97)
Manufacturing			41			59	
NDP			60			40	CSO (95–96)

For abbreviations, see p. xix
Source: Sinha et al. 1999

4   it is criminal business activity (for example, adulteration, forged brands and labels, and so on).

By definition it is not possible to know the size of the informal economy, and estimates vary considerably according to their differing methodologies and databases. One may work in both the formal and informal sectors in different seasons or times of day, and households cannot be neatly classified as 'formal' and 'informal' on the basis of occupations. One influential estimate of the 'unorganised' sector, published in 1996, was that it accounted for 90.3 per cent of all livelihoods.[8] In 1999, the National Council for Applied Economic Research, using a process of plausible inferences from data on a survey of households, also estimated that the registered, formal, 'organised' economy accounts for the major component of the livelihoods of less than 9 per cent of rural households, and only half of urban ones.[9] Approximately 83 per cent of the population work wholly in the informal sector (in the sense we are discussing here): 92 per cent of women workers, 80 per cent of men. Accounting for an estimated 60 per cent of net domestic product, 68 per cent of income and 60 per cent of savings, the informal economy is thus anything but marginal (see Table 1.2). On the contrary, it is predominant. It is also far from being unsophisticated. It does not consist mainly of the urban equivalent of peasant households (though household production and domestic reproductive work are surely much more significant, in terms of

[8] Breman 1996, p. 4, Table 1.1.
[9] Sinha, Sangeeta and Siddiqui 1999.

the numbers of people involved and livelihoods they provide, than they appear to be in India's GDP as it is currently calculated). And it is certainly *not* outside the ambit of market exchange or capitalist accumulation; it is an intrinsic part of both.[10]

The second meaning of 'the informal economy' is a particular type of behaviour *within* the 'formal economy' as defined above, a kind of activity whose significance has been seriously neglected in social and economic theory. It refers to economic activity practised by firms in the formal economy, and even in the interstices of the State itself, which is itself not covered by state regulation or record-keeping. Some of it is needed to make complex organisations work efficiently – the kind of activity whose cessation gums up any organisation on the rare occasions when people decide to 'work to rule'. These informal practices – and the informal rules that govern them – are therefore accepted as legitimate. But they also commonly create rents – rents extracted from corruption, which are typically devoted to unproductive purposes, but also rents essential for productive accumulation; for instance, rents obtained from the exclusive informal links that exist between state banks and industrial companies.[11]

So informal economic activity in this second sense also escapes state regulation (particularly taxation, but also health and safety, labour and land-use regulations). It includes fraud and theft from the State, the corrupt abuse of public office, the illegal privatisation of public property rights, the theft or privatisation of public time (moonlighting). The social legitimacy of corrupt and fraudulent activity is less secure than informal economic activity, and it is increasingly contested.[12]

Neither of the two ways of distinguishing between a 'formal' and an 'informal' economy yields clear boundaries between the one and the other. Laws and policies regulating the economic exchanges between the State, the formal sector and the informal economy are continuously changing. Further, while institutions may exist to enforce such regula-

---

[10] In the Indian literature, the informal economy tends to be defined as *urban*. Much effort has been devoted to isolating and quantifying it and to examining the relationship between the informal and formal, the unorganised and organised, and the unregulated and regulated sectors of the economy (Breman 1996; Sanghera and Harriss-White 1995). This academic work has been prompted by the political problems of rural–urban migration, and its resulting pressure on urban infrastructure and utilities, and by conspicuous urban poverty. Initially preoccupied with the classification of what was rapidly realised to be a highly complex sector, scholars conducting urban surveys and ethnographic research have exposed the reductionism of dualistic models of formal and informal labour market behaviour. Their work has also forced us to recognise the extreme diversity and segmentation that marks relations of production, employment, technology and of product markets in sectors outside agriculture.

[11] Khan and Jomo 2000b, pp. 1–3; Khan 2000a, pp. 66–8; Banaji and Mody 2001.

[12] See Guhan and Paul 1997; Visvanathan and Sethi 1998.

tions, they are often ineffective, lacking suitable agents with adequate material resources. While the informal economy in the first sense is typically the domain of the politically weak, the second can be the domain of the powerful. In the latter case, their exercise of power will be almost by definition 'quiet' and to the best of their ability 'not visible'.

The black economy

As we have seen, elements of both kinds of informal economy are 'black';[13] but the size of the black economy is unknown.[14] Arun Kumar, after an exhaustive review of concepts, arrives at a definition that copes with the problems of legality, taxable thresholds and unaccounted data: the black economy is all factor incomes other than labour (profit, interest and rent) that should be but are not reported (Kumar 1999, p. 54). Erring on the side of caution, and going sector by sector, he arrives at an estimate that in 1990–91, 30 per cent of the economy was 'black' and that by 1995–96 it was 40 per cent.[15] If 60 per cent of the economy is informal (according to NCAER's estimates for 1999), and if at the very least 40 per cent of the economy is black, then it is possible that over half of the informal economy might be black. So the second definition of the informal economy given above, to which far less attention has been paid, may point to a larger sector than the first.

A sector of this magnitude cannot be strictly 'invisible'. The causes of the ballooning black economy lie in an increasingly illegal and criminalised political process, in the service of private accumulation: a nexus in which politicians, officials, criminals, and businessmen and their (often poor and dependent) 'runners' and fixers are bound together in a mutually protective embrace. These, in fact, are the real forms of 'collective action' that dominate much of the economy, a development catalysed by the liberalising economic reforms of the 1990s.

The impact of the black economy on the macro-economy is serious. Economic policy levers have been abandoned in order to entice capital out of the black economy into productive – and taxable – activity. But this 'deregulation' also makes capital flight much easier. At the same time, the

[13] In the West, at least, the word 'black' may no longer be quite politically correct but it is the adjective commonly used and understood, and its dictionary definitions stress aspects of wickedness as much as colour. While formerly it may have taken place in the depths of darkness, now it goes on in broad daylight.

[14] Arun Kumar's deconstruction of Indian national accounts in order to build an estimate of the black economy shows as a by-product that official data consists of many gross estimates (Kumar 1999).

[15] Roy's estimate (1996) is of a similar order of magnitude. A simple extrapolation would make the black economy 53 per cent of NDP by 2000.

closing of certain legal loopholes and the creation of incentives to repatriate capital from abroad have resulted in a fictitious spurt to growth rates caused by the reporting of previously undeclared production. Yet foreign exchange losses and corruption intensify.[16] Lack of demand leaves an excess capacity, a capacity that is in any case based on uncompetitive technology. The foreign element in many joint ventures beats a retreat, and foreign capital seeps back instead in relatively small quantities through the capital markets.[17] International capital invests in big Indian companies only gingerly,[18] with the result that speculative activity proliferates (for example, in real estate and the stock market), and new opportunities are created for concealing profits. Budget and trade deficits are exaggerated as a result, as is the interest burden in the budget. Regular 'formal' interest rates have to attract savings back from the black sector, so profits have to rise to cover the resulting higher interest component in costs. They tend to do so at the expense of labour. Kumar therefore sees unorganised – non-unionised – labour as a separate 'shock-absorbing' class, one that is comprehensively subjugated, such that the politics of accumulation hinges *not* on the conflict between capital and labour so much as on one between different elements within the propertied classes: the black and the not-so-black. These competing fractions of capital are further split in a multiplicity of ways between different sectors, regions and nexuses of co-operation and interest at the political centre in New Delhi and Mumbai and in the States.

While Rathin Roy has found that 'black' assets are dispersed all over India in real estate, plant and machines, inventory and trade stock, films, precious metals and criminal kinds of commerce and illegal commodities,[19] Kumar reckons that black *incomes* are highly concentrated in the top 3 per cent of households – some 10 million – distributed 60:40 between the private informal sector and the public sector, although this estimate relies heavily on assumptions rather than evidence.[20] We will not contribute to the debate on quantities, but we shall encounter the question of black incomes and assets again when we examine fractions of capital in Chapters 3 and 4.

[16] See Harriss-White and White (eds) 1996.

[17] Total portfolio investment between 1991–92 and 1997–98 stood at $15 billion and foreign direct investment at $10 billion, about one-fifth of planned goals (Athreya 1999, *Frontline*, 26 November, p. 109).

[18] Banaji and Mody 2001.

[19] Roy 1996, p. 26.

[20] Kumar 1999, pp. 80–104; 135–40. According to official statistics, in 1994–95 out of 6.7 million income tax assessees, only 5543 individuals (from a population of well over 950 million) declared incomes in excess of Rs 1 million (then about £18k equivalent). The modal class of income taxpayers was Rs 50 000–100 000 (£900–1800). In and under this class were 90 per cent of all taxpayers, owning 86 per cent of all taxable income and paying 72 per cent of all tax (Government of India 1997, p. 73).

Unlike the informal economy, which can be studied by sustained field-work, the black economy cannot be directly researched. Evidence of it is usually encountered as the accidental by-product of fieldwork devoted to other purposes, and all such evidence is heavily problematical. But Arun Kumar's deconstruction of the national accounts shows that even the most fundamental of official data may be false, and false in unknowable ways, too.

Fieldwork

A great deal of the evidence used in this book is drawn from *field economics*. The working of the Indian economy is pieced together from remarkable studies undertaken on a small scale, at a micro level, with long field exposure; from results that are by their nature difficult to aggregate for a scaled-up interpretation.[21] Although, as we will argue below, alternative approaches present other problems, some words of warning are in order about the one used here. The impact on accumulation of the social institutions revealed by fieldwork is likely to vary with the local and historical context. Some of the material used here comes from one town in south India whose business economy has been studied at first hand in every decade since 1973,[22] and from three villages in its environs, similarly studied in detail, from a set of 11 in the region of northern Tamil Nadu.[23] Chapters 5 to 7 rely most on this pin-point of evidence, though supplemented by data from elsewhere whenever possible. The other chapters draw on a much wider range of literature also grounded in fieldwork.

The case for relying on field economics, however, is strong. First, the huge territory and the high proportion of the population (see Table 1.1) cannot be generalised about without a reliable basis in local research. Field economics is an indispensable starting point for studying the India in which four-fifths of Indians live. Second, the structure of demand and supply cannot easily be got hold of any other way. The goods and services consumed by the vast bulk of the '88 per cent' are income-inelastic basic wage goods, among which the only conspicuous product of corporate capital is clothing. Household budgets are dominated, even in the upper deciles of the 'rurban' (rural and small town) population, by food, though the shares of meat, dairy and horticultural products, vegetable oils and spices have increased in recent years. The budget items that have

---

[21] The problem is discussed in Chapter 3.
[22] See Harriss and Harriss (1984); Harriss (1991a); and Basile and Harriss-White (2000) for previous analyses.
[23] See Farmer 1977 and Hazell and Ramasamy 1991.

increased most rapidly are consumer durables (but from minuscule percentages), health expenditure, transport, cinema and social-cum-religious functions.[24] In 1984 in northern Tamil Nadu, such items formed 9.3 per cent of the total expenditure of rural elite households, 12 per cent of the budget of small farmers and 11 per cent of the spending of landless agricultural labourers. Similarly, in Punjab – one of the most developed states – in the late 1980s, the proportion of total expenditure very likely to have been on goods that are *not* basic wage goods was 11 per cent for rural people and 14 per cent for those in towns.[25] It is impossible to identify how much of total expenditure was for the products of the corporate sector, or metropolitan India, and therefore it is also impossible to track the extent to which the India of the 88 per cent is implicated in the economy of the 12 per cent, though there is no doubt that it is. In 1989 the all-Indian average share of total expenditure that went on all non-food items was 36 per cent in rural areas and 43 per cent in urban ones.[26] Table 1.3 ranks Indian states according to the proportion of rural household expenditure on goods likely to have been produced in the corporate sector. Though dated, the evidence here shows that most expenditure, even in the richest rural areas, is on basic wage goods that are distributed through regional markets. Since official statistics for local trade are extremely poor there is no alternative to field research to find out how it works.

The third point about relying on field economics is the question of defining the appropriate level at which to study accumulation. Although much analytical energy has been spent on examining the concentration of assets (that is, the class structure) in villages, and the degree of asset mobility (that is, class formation) within them, the concentration of assets held in local *towns* is incomparably greater. Table 1.4 shows that in one region of northern Tamil Nadu in 1993–94, the coefficients of concentration of *land* vary between 0.53 and 0.61 and of total rural assets between 0.62 and 0.75.[27] (These indicate high inequality in the control of land; they have also been on the increase over the last two decades). But the coefficient of concentration for businesses in the *town* (not including the small stocks of assets of wage-working households) is *0.89*. Rural assets are very rarely as unequally distributed as this. Furthermore, as Table 1.5 reveals, the average incomes of urban labour were double that of rural labour and the aver-

---

[24] Hazell and Ramasamy 1991, pp. 45–9.
[25] We identified beverages, tobacco and all consumer durables as being in such a category. 'Miscellaneous goods and services' add a further 18 and 19 per cent.
[26] These data are from the Centre for Monitoring the Indian Economy, 1997.
[27] The Gini coefficient ranges from 0 (perfectly equal distribution) to 1.0 (perfectly unequal distribution). Values of over 0.5 for economic distributions are not common.

Table 1.3 *Regional variations in rural consumption of corporate goods*[a, b]

State	Total consumption expenditure (Rs)	Consumption of corporate products (Rs)	% of total consumption expenditure
Assam	160	10.1	6
West Bengal	170	13.8	8.1
Gujarat	171	14.8	8.6
Karnataka	158	13.8	8.7
Bihar	152	13.8	9
Kerala	216	20.4	9.4
Tamil Nadu	171	16.5	9.6
Orissa	147	14.7	10
Uttar Pradesh	165	20	12
Maharashtra	171	21.1	12.3
Haryana	245	34.6	14
Andhra Pradesh	183	26.5	14.4
Madhya Pradesh	153	22	14.6
Punjab	265	40.9	15.4
Rajasthan	219	36.6	16.7

[a] The latest raw data are for 1988–89.
[b] Corporate goods is a category comprising liquor, clothing, footwear and all consumer durables. Although not all of these products are from the corporate sector, the category of corporate goods will still be underestimated here.
Source: Raw data in Centre for Monitoring the Indian Economy 1997

age incomes of firms in the different sectors of the urban economy, while being extremely varied, were many multiples of those on the average farm. By the mid-1990s, the average value of assets per business household in the local town had reached 20 times the average value of household assets in three nearby villages. If one wishes to see capital accumulation and class formation at work, then, it is necessary to examine a region and the relations between the villages and towns within it. Here too, there is no substitute for field research.

So although general statements of a quantitative sort about accumulation in the India of the 88 per cent cannot be based on the kind of evidence assembled here, it is only through fieldwork that they can be known at all. Evidently, as Ron Martin put it recently, any theorising from this kind of material is 'discursive persuasion', in the attempt to make 'richer maps of reality'.[28] This is exactly what is aspired to in this book.

[28] Martin 1999, p. 82.

Table 1.4 *Rural and urban concentration of assets: south India*

Gini coefficients	Urban business	Villages					
		Nesal		Vinayagapuram		Veerasambanur	
		Excluding zero values	Including zero values	Excluding zero values	Including zero values	Excluding zero values	Including zero values
Land ownership		0.51	0.81	0.46	0.62	0.46	0.66
No. zero values		208		79		51	
Asset value	**0.89**	**0.75**	**0.76**	**0.63**	**0.63**	**0.62**	**0.63**
No. of observations	196	339	339	259	259	136	136
No. zero values		11				4	
Land		0.61	0.85	0.55	0.69	0.53	0.71
No. zero values		208		79		52	
Other agricultural assets		0.81	0.84	0.71	0.72	0.66	0.71
No. zero values		48		15		18	
Non-agricultural assets		0.67	0.70	0.55	0.55	0.59	0.61
No. zero values		24		4		7	

Source: Field surveys 1993–94, Harriss-White and Janakarajan et al. 2002

Table 1.5 *Rural-urban income differentials: south India, 1983–84*

Type of firm/household	Average income per capita as multiple of poverty line[a]	Household Size
Silk – factories	95.0	13.0
Rice – mills	36.0	8.5
Rice – wholesalers	20.0	6.5
Other foods – wholesalers	10.0	6.0
Fuel and energy – retailers	5.6	9.0
Non-food agric. products – workshops	5.3	6.5
Farm inputs – retailers	4.6	7.3
Other goods – wholesalers (1 firm)	4.4	7.0
Other goods – retailers	4.5	6.5
(Other goods – retailers: exceptional firm)	15.7	6.0
Other foods – retailers	3.0	6.8
Non-food agric. products – retailers	2.4	7.9
Transport repairs and services	2.4	4.5
Financial services	2.2	8.5
(Financial services: exceptional firm)	226.0	6.0
Other foods – workshops	2.0	7.0
Other goods – workshops	1.6	6.0
(Other goods – workshops: exceptional)	85.0	4.0
Other repairs and services	1.4	6.4
Rice mill labour (male)	0.49	4.0
Rice mill labour (female)	0.38	4.0
Twisting factory labour (male)	0.45	4.0
Twisting factory labour (female)	0.38	4.0
Paddy firms >1 ha	1.85	n.a.
Paddy firms <1 ha	0.92	n.a.
Agricultural labour (male)[c]	0.28	4.0[b]
Agricultural labour (female)[c]	0.18	4.0[b]

[a] Rs 48/capita/month (Dandekar and Rath 1971), all deflated to 1973 prices.
[b] Simulated household size, not real averages.
[c] Data for this calculation from J. Harriss (1986).
Source: B. Harriss, 1991a

Social structures of accumulation

Each of the chapters that follow focus on a different dimension of the matrix of social institutions through which accumulation and distribution take place. This has been the particular focus of Gordon and Kotz and their colleagues in the United States, who have coined the term 'social structures of accumulation' (SSA) to describe it.[29] Whereas orthodox economics treats the regulative environment in which production and distribution take place as lying outside its scope, the social structures of the accumulation school insists on its centrality. This approach also challenges the reductionism of conventional economics in which capitalism is first reduced to markets, then markets are reduced to the purely economic domain, and further to the simple intersection of supply and demand. The crucial significance of social structures of accumulation emerged from the work of these researchers on long waves, business cycles, instability, crises, uneven macroeconomic development and diverse trajectories of capitalist development in the industrialised world, yet their central ideas are no less relevant to the study of capitalist accumulation taking place over a relatively short period of time and in a 'late-developing' economy such as India's.

The SSA school focuses on the social institutions chiefly involved in the process of assembling factors of production and then converting the resulting products back into money. The general hypothesis is that this complex of institutions emerges and gradually becomes consolidated, but the very fact that it becomes consolidated eventually tends to block and undermine the accumulation process that it initially promoted. At the core of this ambitious intellectual agenda is the question of how such a continually changing set of institutionalised structures ensures or undermines stability, by shaping both class conflicts and conflicts between competing concentrations of capital.[30] No general hypothesis is advanced about the relative importance of the different elements of the structural matrix, there is no privileged list of 'crucial' institutions or forces. On the other hand, some institutions are always seen to be involved; in particular, those that structure the relations between labour and management, and regulate competition and conflict in production; those that determine the pattern of demand; and those that shape the character of industrial organisations and the institutions of finance. Among the institutions that perform these functions the State is always found to be crucial, as it regulates capital and labour, transfers resources between different social groups, shapes political space and reinforces ide-

---

[29] Gordon, Edwards and Reich 1982; and Kotz, McDonough and Reich 1994.
[30] In this it differs from regulation analysis, which posits crisis as being the result of the internal dynamic of accumulation itself – at its loosest, the mode of regulation is no longer adequate to the accumulation process. The social structures school would argue that there is far less determinacy in such a process. A great range of mechanisms relate accumulation to its institutional matrix. Crises may involve the collapse and destruction of social institutions (Kotz 1994). Crises will be resolved not only (as in regulation theory) by capital's finding new ways of organising labour, but also through political innovations resulting from struggles between capital and labour, and between capital and labour combined ('the economy'), and other social institutions.

ology. Political parties are also seen to be crucial. Besides the State, certain other social institutions shape accumulation: the SSA school has particularly emphasised race, gender and the cultural means by which the division of labour and the distribution of the surplus are legitimated.

In contemporary India, the State's role in private accumulation is clearly no less fundamental. In Chapter 4 we will look critically at its capacity to overcome obstacles to accumulation (including the obstacle posed by the State's own redistributive projects), and at its power to regulate the accumulation process, compared with the regulative power of market forces and of other dimensions of social organisation, with their often conflicting rationalities. In the India of the 88 per cent, however, it is clear that a range of non-state social structures, and the ideas and cultural practices attached to them, are even more crucial for accumulation than they are in industrial societies. Six, in particular, are explored in this book: the structure of the workforce and social classes (the subjects of Chapters 2 and 3) and gender, religion, caste and space (the subjects of Chapters 5 to 8). In most of the literature on India, class, gender, religion and caste are typically understood not as social structures of accumulation but as components of 'civil society', and are often lumped together as networks or as 'social capital'.[31] However, this misses the point that each of the elements of the social structure of accumulation works in a specific way and it is this specificity that is the focus of this book. In addition to the structures commonly viewed as elements of 'civil society', when we look at the important determinants of accumulation in rural and small-town India we see that the territorial dimension is highly significant, too. Although hardly ever considered as such, the way *space* is structured is therefore as relevant a social structure of accumulation as the others, and we shall see that regional and local differentiation and specialisation is a highly defining – and perhaps limiting – feature of the Indian economy.

While the primary objective of this book is to describe and analyse the economy of India's 88 per cent, it has a wider aim as well: to contribute however modestly to the analysis of contemporary capitalism. This is urgently needed if it is to be tamed to serve social objectives that are necessary for human fulfilment, if not for survival itself, but which markets under capitalism simply cannot meet and often crudely prevent. In particular, it seeks to be a sustained interrogation of the now commonplace notion that economic 'liberalisation' means that the economy is released from political control. If the detailed study of India's economy reveals

---

[31] As in 'a durable network of more or less institutionalised relations of mutual recognition' (Bourdieu 1992, p. 63, quoted in Jeffrey 2001, p. 222). See Fine (2000) and Harriss (2001a) for critical treatments of the depoliticised umbrella concept of 'social capital'.

one thing more clearly than another, it is that 'liberalisation' means a change in the character of this control, not a release from it. This change owes much, paradoxically, to historical continuities in India's social structures of accumulation. It is a change that is not as self-evidently beneficial as those who have unleashed liberalisation would have us believe.

2 The workforce and its social structures

Nothing is ever produced without labour. In a capitalist economy labour is taken and turned into labour power; so the way this power is organised and disciplined shapes the accumulation process. In this chapter we will see how social and political institutions that discipline and regulate labour and labour power fuel accumulation and contain the conflicts generated by capitalist growth. Even trade unions play roles that facilitate backward forms of accumulation and the practices of 'flexible employment' which characterise advanced capitalism have long been established in India and are crucial to accumulation.[1]

India's economy is about the size of Belgium's, but for every Belgian there are a hundred Indians competing for livelihoods. Out of the country's huge labour force of over 390 million, only 7 per cent are in the organised sector (that is, are workers on regular wages or salaries) in registered firms and with access to the State's social security system and its framework of labour law. Even the term 'organised' is seriously misleading because only about half of that 7 per cent are unionised,[2] and we will see later that in India unions are deliberately *dis*organised. The rest – variously estimated at between 83 and 93 per cent of the workforce – labours in the 'unorganised' or 'informal' economy.[3] In fact, India's economy *is* 'unorganised'. All this 'unorganised' labour is unprotected by the regulatory regime of the State because what little exists is not enforced. It is thereby deprived of rights at work. 'Unorganised' firms are supposed to be small. In fact, they may have substantial workforces, occasionally numbering hundreds, but where workers are put deliberately on casual contracts. There is no neat boundary between organised and unorganised labour. Some sectors, notably mining and dock labour,

---

[1] Albeda and Tilly 1994; Kotz 1994.
[2] Bhowmik 1998.
[3] Eighty-three per cent is the NCAER estimate, Sinha et al. 1999. Ninety-three per cent is the residual from organised-sector statistics. Most of the agricultural sector is included, even though land is registered, because of the small and fluctuating size of labour forces on the vast bulk of individual holdings.

straddle the divide. In practically every 'organised' firm, including state-run corporations, unorganised labour is selectively incorporated into the labour process.[4]

From 1977–78 to 1993–94, while the economy grew at 5 per cent and the population at 2.2 per cent,[5] employment in the organised, corporate sector grew barely at all at 0.1 per cent. Despite the official discourse of compressing the State, public-sector employment continued growing at 2.2 per cent. Meanwhile, unorganised employment expanded at 2.6 per cent.[6] The discrepancy between the growth of the economy and that of employment is explained by the fact that growth has become increasingly less labour-absorbing. The fastest growing industries – engineering and software – are those with the highest labour productivity. Over this same period (1977–94), the organised sector shed an estimated *half* of its labour force. Small-scale production has been adversely affected by credit-rationing and by stagnant domestic demand. That left agriculture, the construction industry, quarrying and petty trade to act as shock-absorbers, but they too have increasingly weak elasticities of employment.[7] Investment in public infrastructure (irrigation, roads, stores, electricity, industrial estates) works in synergy with private investment but it has atrophied.[8] As a result, unemployment and underemployment are on the increase, and the real wages of workers in the unorganised sector have begun to stagnate and in some areas have declined. All this was clearly foreseen in 1989 by the World Bank, which predicted that some 8–10 million of extra unemployment would result from the 'stabilisation' phase of the reforms alone.[9]

Nowhere are these trends more evident than in manufacturing where the unorganised state of the workforce is 'over determined' by a variety of converging forces. For most of the twentieth century – and long before the era of flexible specialisation or economic liberalisation – a process of decentralised agro-industrial mercantile accumulation gave rise to a numerically powerful stratum of small-scale capitalists with low managerial costs and flexible labour practices, a stratum that (as we will see in Chapter 3) was almost literally a law unto itself.[10] The regulation of work-

---

[4] One recent study of corporate capital put the proportion of unorganised labour in different corporations at between 40 and 85 per cent (Davala 1992, in Bhowmik 1998).

[5] This is well over the Hindu rate of growth (3 per cent), the famous phrase of Raj Krishna's.

[6] Guhan and Nagaraj 1995, p. 9. Organised employment for women grew at three times that for men, fastest in the urban tertiary sector (Srivastava 1999).

[7] Ghose (1999), using National Sample Survey Organisation data; Olsen (forthcoming); Bhalla (1999).

[8] See data in Harriss-White (2002a).

[9] World Bank 1989.

[10] Gooptu 2001; Baker 1984; Harriss-White 1996a.

place relations by the State was not imposed on capital after industriali-sation, but was put in place as industry developed. From the very start, strong incentives were created for capital to evade these laws, and the State has tended to act in the interests of capital whenever organised labour tried to get the law enforced. From the 1970s onwards, the employers' response to trade unionism ensured that in India labour was *informalised* through subcontracting, putting-out, and casualisation even in so-called 'organised' firms. Informalised labour not only lacks rights, it lacks stability of income and occupation.[11]

Indian capitalism has developed in distinctive eras, strata, sectors and regional blocks. The tiny minority of labour in the corporate and public sector – the so-called 'commanding heights of the economy', the heights that confront the mountainous orogenies of global capital – now pro-duces about 20 per cent of GDP.[12] Its standard of living depends, how-ever, on wage goods produced by the much cheaper labour in the informal economy. The informal economy has now been estimated at 60 per cent of GDP.[13] Agriculture is still the largest single sector. While its share in the economy shrank from 41 per cent in 1965 to 29 per cent in 1994, during a period when both its technologies and its relations of production were transformed,[14] its share in total employment has hardly changed – from 73 per cent to 67 per cent. Its labour productivity remains stagnant, currently at around one-third of that in manufacturing and services.

The biggest component of the unorganised workforce (363 million strong) consists of the catch-all category of the 'self-employed'. Although 'self-employed' may cover small family businesses, for the most part people classified this way are semi-independent peasants with small assets, petty commodity producers and traders. They exploit their own household members and often both hire in and hire out labour according to seasonal peaks; their 'independence' conceals 'sundry forms of wage labour'.[15] One recent estimate is that 56 per cent of all Indian workers are 'self-employed' in this sense, 29 per cent are casual wage labourers and just 15 per cent are in any kind of regular waged or 'salaried' employment, whether organised or not.[16] Of late, 'self-employed' people have entered wage labour markets

---

[11] Deponte 2000.

[12] Mani 2000; Kaplinsky 1999.

[13] The other estimated 20 per cent is formal sector, non-corporate production. See the estimates of Sinha et al. (1999), based on classifications of occupations and households from National Sample Survey Organisation data.

[14] Byres 1981. With the exception of services, the distribution of employment between sectors of the economy has hardly changed in the last two decades.

[15] Breman 1996, p. 12.

[16] Ghose 1999.

in droves, chosen by employers in preference to the third of the Indian population who have no assets at all because they are seen as more knowledgeable workers.[17] Having minuscule assets means being able to manage the trade-offs between the calendar of demands from petty production and trading and those of waged work. The implication of casual employment is that while employers will stop employing wage labour beyond the point at which marginal returns and costs are equalised, employees themselves will seek to maximise work days.[18]

The large-size, relatively high growth and labour-absorptive capacity of the unorganised economy are distinctive features of Indian capitalism. How these workers are disciplined is a key part of the social structure of accumulation in India. Another feature is the unskilled nature of much of this work, reinforced by the use of casual labour and flexible employment practices, so that little importance is attached to training and the development of skills.[19] A further distinctive feature is the absolute poverty of the workers. While organised workers receive a third of all wages and incomes, 36 per cent of the population survive on incomes below the stingy, nutrition-based official poverty line, a number far in excess of the official estimates of the number who are unemployed or underemployed.[20] In 1995, an average agricultural labouring household of two adults and two children earned about $130 a *year* between them. Two-thirds of all landless agricultural labourers live below the poverty line, and many of these labouring households are caught in a 'standard of living paradox' in which real wages rise and state benefits (such as subsidised food, clothing and housing) may percolate down, but nutrition does not improve and debt mounts up. This paradox is explained by reductions in labour demand – in days worked by such households.[21]

Most work is unregulated by the State, but labour arrangements are far from 'unstructured'.[22] Indian labour markets are much more complicated than can be modelled using supply and demand alone.[23]

---

[17] Bhalla 1999.
[18] This latter practice is known in the literature on peasant economy as 'self-exploitation' (Ellis 1993).
[19] Desai 1999.
[20] Poverty varies according to harvests and food grains prices. Two-thirds of those said to be living on under $1 a day in the world today are in South Asia. The official Indian rural poverty line is set and revised at a rural income allowing for the consumption of 2400 calories per day, together with 20 per cent for shelter, clothing and medicine. By this account poverty was at 28 per cent in 2001–2 (Shariff 2002). Fifty-seven per cent of India's poor live in the poverty belt covering east and central India, inland Maharashtra and eastern Madhya Pradesh, a diverse and scarcely urbanised region. The intransigent persistence of poverty masks a massive increase in inequality (Bhalla 1999). Official poverty lines vary for policy purposes. In the mid-1990s the poverty line for Tamil Nadu, for example, was doubled from Rs 5000 per household ($113) to Rs 12 000 ($272).
[21] The standard of living paradox is Heyer's term – see Heyer (2000).
[22] Bhowmik 1998, p. 149; Shah 1999.
[23] Binswanger and Rosenzweig (1984); and see the model of caste and the labour market by Akerlof (1984).

Labour is controlled not only through the manipulation of various non-class social identities but also through the segmentation and fragmentation of labour 'markets'. For instance, the blurred boundary between the organised and unorganised sectors is also a division of castes and gender.[24] These social identities still affect the tasks most people do – the kinds, terms and conditions of contracts they are offered, and either settle for, or refuse. They make for significant differences to the terms and conditions of work. In a recent study of two villages in West Bengal, for example, 12 different types of wage labour contracts were found. There was no single village wage for casual labour. For any one kind of contract there was a great diversity of detailed terms and conditions, including pay. In very few households did every working member have the same type of contract such as 'casual labouring' or 'permanent labouring' (though households are conventionally classified using such labels). Labour contracts were affected by gender (women had more open-ended obligations and less power to choose), caste (which affects the tasks available to members of a given household), age, and household composition. All these factors led to variations in the earnings of landless labourers.[25] Multiple solidarities tend to make collective, class-based action much harder to achieve.[26] Under capitalism, gender, caste and household structures are modified slowly, unevenly and in a great diversity of ways. These different kinds of social identity generate the volatile political forces – the struggles *over* class – that overlay the glacial development of the conflict *between* classes.

In the rest of this chapter I describe the way capital manipulates key social institutions in order better to control labour; the weakness of labour politics that results and the Indian State's limited response to the needs and interests of labour.[27] The politics of labour are also expressed outside the workplace. Here there is an important distinction to be made

---

[24] In 1991 a mere 4 per cent of the female workforce was in the organised sector. Women were 12 per cent of the organised workforce but 33 per cent of the unorganised workforce, and that is likely to be a gross underestimate. Scheduled caste workers are heavily concentrated in the unorganised workforce (Bhalla 1999).

[25] Rogaly 1996.

[26] Dreze and Sharma 1998.

[27] The mapping of the social structures enveloping Indian labour cannot be carried out, quite literally because the work on India's regions of accumulation has not yet been done. It is a daunting task because India's regions are an amalgam of agro-ecological, agro-structural and politico-administrative areas. There are huge regional variations in the composition of capital that affect options for labour. While in the so-called Bimaru States (after the Hindi for 'sick') less than 20 per cent of rural jobs are not in agriculture; 54 per cent are in the rural non-farm sector in Kerala and 30 per cent in West Bengal. Yet, the latter relatively advanced States – and those with active Communist Parties – have high levels of unemployment, while the reverse applies to Bimaru States. It is the persistence of petty production and artisanal work in poor States, together with the decline of petty production as a safety net and the inability of the economy to absorb labour at the wages offered, which explain this paradox. Other States such as Maharashtra have developed with relatively low levels of unemployment, relatively tight labour 'markets' and an employment guarantee scheme run by the State (Thorner 1995; Nagaraj 1999; Banaji 1999).

between the politics of labour and the politics of the poor, as Nandini Gooptu has now shown.[28] Poverty is the significant reality for poor labouring people. It is most unlikely that any significant transformation of the conditions that cause poverty could happen without initiatives by poor workers.

Labour–land relations

The labour and land relations of Indian agriculture, expressed in the detail of the labour process, reflect local class configurations and, through them, the locally dominant mode of appropriation and accumulation of surplus. Capitalist landowners set the terms and conditions of work, most important of which is a socially determined wage.[29] The size of their holdings, their production decisions (crops, technologies) and their investment decisions (particularly in irrigation and in the non-farm rural economy, in sectors like trade, finance, construction, mills, looms, processing industry and transport) determine the demand for labour.[30] Their economic power is bolstered by caste authority and political clout.

The technologically precocious region of north-west India is a case in point. The early stages of the green revolution were highly labour-absorptive. Large landowners responded by luring some labour into permanent contracts to tie them, while shifting others to piece work and gangs ('contract' labour) to reduce labour costs. They also subdivided tenancies to reduce the costs of supervising labour and to ensure that unwaged family labour contributed to production. Later, employers started to mechanise to cram an extra season of rice or cotton into this wheat-producing region. The capacity of agriculture to mop up labour while production was growing fell, and labour even began to be displaced. Large landowners casualised their labour. Real wages fell. Employers turned to migrant labour, not to compensate for local shortages, but to ensure control. A striking increase in reverse tenancy (in which small owners rent out land

[28] Gooptu 2001.

[29] The economic power of employers is bolstered when they enter local agribusiness: their pre-harvest loans can be interlocked with post-harvest sales, thereby indirectly controlling the markets that shape the production of their creditors.

[30] The wage has been hypothesised as set at a level at which the efficiency of output from nutritional inputs is maximised (Rodgers 1975). Several factors make this implausible: the wage is not instantaneously translated into work, it may also have to feed more mouths than that of the employee alone, and casual contracts in which labour is free to change employers prevent the latter from linking payment in one period to effort later on.

to large operators) was engineered to concentrate holdings and reap rents from economies of scale. Militant agitations in the name of all agrarian interests have consolidated gains for the local elites at the expense of landless labour, which has been kept quiescent and controlled by permanent contracts and by threats to demand for their work.[31]

By contrast small peasants and landless agricultural labourers who form the great mass of the rural workforce[32] are obliged to provide for their dependent family members, to work to honour consumption loans (often at usurious rates of interest) and, wherever there is no alternative, by the coercive power of dominant landowners to respect rental contracts yielding low returns to tenants. They are effectively reduced to being wage workers in thin disguise. Average landholdings have fallen dramatically. In cases where small-sized families have small-size farms, the smaller the holding the greater the proportion of the household that has to work for wages – including children, sick or disabled and elderly people.[33] Wage dependency is increasing inexorably in agriculture. In 1961 there were three cultivators for each landless labourer, by 1991 the proportions were almost equal.[34]

The compulsions of labour have never gone without challenge, although the political agenda of the mass of labourers who are low caste may put food security (mediated through the State) and dignity (especially rights to use village space and public wells) ahead of contracts and pay. Labour scholars of northern India have recorded a flurry of strikes in the 1990s over wages, the length of the working day and humiliating treatment by employers; and the *dalit*[35]-based Bahujan Samaj Party has been voted into power in the State of Uttar Pradesh. The counter-tactics of employers, including the formation of private armies to coerce labour through brutal suppression, reflect their power over aspects of life outside the wage relation. Employers have also denied recalcitrant labour access to common property resources and space in order to force them into submission.[36]

---

[31] Jha 1997; Bhalla 1976 and 1999.
[32] Some 60–80 per cent in one recent study in south India (Colatei and Harriss-White 2002a).
[33] See Jha (1997) Table 3. On- and off-farm work is not directly substitutable. Either work on the small plot owned comes first and so wage work is a residual, irrespective of the pay, or off-farm activity determines the crop choice and labour inputs on a small farm and cultivation is the residual (Bharadwaj 1985).
[34] Varma et al. 1997.
[35] '*Dalit*', literally meaning the down-trodden, refers to untouchables and other low castes.
[36] Srivastava 1999; Lerche 1999.

Coercion in contracts: Patronage and debt-bondage

To reduce costs, capital has a powerful interest in labour that is flexible. Flexibility is commonly achieved by capital through casualisation and by labour through its physical movement. Yet many employers (be they agricultural, rural or urban) want people to work at their literal beck and call: to work with cattle, irrigation, monitoring consignments of grain in town, shifting between workshop/firm and farm, between farm and family. Although outright, permanent, inheritable bondage is illegal and increasingly rare, labour is commonly tied not only by site but also by debt, by contracts that link in a single-agreement the terms and conditions for labour with those on land, money or product markets, and by the non-contractual obligations of patronage that may also require the work of the women and children of a male labourer. Such ties have thrived on the lack of symmetry of power associated with customary rights, particularly with rights of employers to command family labour and rights to terminate the relationship. There is no archetype for such arrangements, much regional variation in their incidence and much debate about their significance in the process of capitalist transformation.[37] They are widely argued to be breaking down thanks to migration that offers alternative work; new technology that reduces demand for labour; struggles by labour for contracts less encumbered by customary notions of dependence, inferiority and obligation; and other efforts towards emancipation, sometimes organised along lines of caste.[38] Yet the skein of patronage may uncoil only to recoil in the form of debt-bondage and labour attachment. Throughout South India, for instance, the refusal by labourers to perform collective, unpaid irrigation 'duties' as 'clients' of a new stratum of lower caste landowners – work their fathers performed for *brahmins* who have since sold their land – has contributed to ruining the longstanding system of tank-fed agriculture and forced landowners to invest in (or rent) private wells. The provision of accommodation and/or debt can then be used to force labour to operate electric pumpsets at night or whenever rationed electricity is available. On advanced cotton seed farms, even pre-pubescent girls are being bonded into labour. At one and the same time such practices reduce costs and assist agrarian accumulation, while at home they shift the consequences of male refusal to work

[37] See Lerche (1995) and Breman (1999) for the argument. Most notably Tom Brass (1993) has argued for the term 'deproletarianisation' to cover new relations of 'unfreedom' that buttress accumulation by holding down the price of labour, controlling its movement, forcing debt, and manipulating the social identities of workers. Rather than deproletarianisation, these practices can be seen as the tactics of a savage form of proletarianisation, since wage labour is never free.

[38] Lerche 1999.

on to ever younger women, while boys are educated to escape agriculture.[39] Further north in Andhra Pradesh the refusal by men to accept this sort of contract means that women have graduated from being the assumed adjunct to permanently employed ('attached' or close to bonded) male labour to having such contracts in their own right.[40] In Gujarat, studied by the anthropologist of labour, Jan Breman, 'neo-bondage is less personalised, more contractual and monetised, while also the elements of patronage have gone, which provided some protection and a subsistence guarantee, however meagrely defined, to bonded clients in the past'.[41]

The consequence of neo-bondage is that labour politics has had to be focused 'upwards', towards and against local patrons. Resistance usually consists in violating debt obligations and escaping, though it can also take collective forms.[42] Where bondage is now largely 'economic' (enforced with physical violence, when necessary) and not based on social (and indeed legal) legitimacy, or on workers' acceptance that employers are socially and ritually superior and have the right to extract labour, workers are found to resist coercive arrangements, even though they are still forced to enter into debt relations for job security or from sheer poverty. Some even choose the more risky option of wage labour on piece rates, rejecting the security offered by debt-bondage. While this may not improve their economic condition, Breman concludes that it 'might benefit the dignity of labour' and signal an emancipatory move.[43]

The spatial unit for labour

The social construction of the spatial unit for labour varies hugely in India. Rural workers have begun to migrate seasonally on a large scale. 'People who migrate this way are not "just" migrants. They may also be own-account farmers, petty traders, school students, gatherers and priests.'[44] Buses designed for 50 people can be found transporting 190 on peak days. New sources of demand for labour for harvests hundreds of miles away or in seasonal 'mud work' (construction) enable migrant

[39] Mosse 1997; Janakarajan 1997.
[40] da Corta and Venkateshwarlu 1999; Venkateshwarlu and da Corta 2001.
[41] Breman 1996 p. 169.
[42] Workers have attempted to turn debt relations to their advantage. In the power loom industry in Kumarapalayam town in Tamil Nadu, for example, employers debt-bonded labourers when they were in scarce supply but soon found that workers proceeded to dictate terms of employment, realising that employers were not in a position to dismiss them while the latter still owed money to the former (de Neve 1999).
[43] Breman 1999, pp. 423–5; Breman 1996, pp. 237–9.
[44] Rogaly et al. 2000.

labour to raise agricultural wages and to break free from debt relations and other demeaning practices in their villages of origin.[45] Nevertheless, the village still tends to be the key unit for the organisation of rural labour, particularly for women workers who are stuck with the prior requirements of housework and children. Familiarity counts in employers' decisions whether or not to spend time supervising operations. Both employers and employees have expectations about future work based on compliance and loyalty. The structures of differentiation in land relations, through which demand for labour is organised, vary village by village. So in the absence of highly developed rural transport (which is very far from universal in India), even if daily casual wages are known to be higher in the next village, labourers, especially women, often do not seek them. In turn, this generates a fundamental lack of symmetry in the relations between agricultural employers and casual labour. While employers may not always maximise profit, they are able to use non-economic means to exploit workers; meanwhile, workers are unable to maximise wages.[46] Since those who do travel to get better wages are mostly men, it is hardly surprising either that the gender differential in wages is widening.[47]

Outside agriculture, even though the distribution of non-agrarian castes may still shape recruitment, sometimes being based on networks, routes and towns rather than spatial territory, in urban areas as in rural ones the geopolitical unit for a given labour market may be small.[48] Individual small capitalists can set the terms and conditions of their labour contracts. Even when casual wages are 'agreed' across a sector within a town (imposed by associations of employers, often without any consultation with labour) the implicit terms for 'casual' labour (which may include hours, bonuses and perquisites) can be altered individually.[49] The breakdown between the cash and kind (food) components of wages can vary from firm to firm. Such practices prevent easy comparisons – either by labour itself or by scholars of labour.

So the small-scale and fragmented nature of labour markets restricts collective action on the part of workforces encompassing several villages or a segment of the non-farm or urban economy. The excess supply of labour also puts limits on negotiations for fear of dismissal. Despite these

[45] Rodgers and Rodgers 2001. Most rural migrants, especially women, remain within the same district: <http://www.panasia.org.sg/nird/rds2.thm#2.20 to 23>.

[46] Rudra 1992.

[47] Though *within* the agricultural sector it is converging (Unni 1999).

[48] For linear and network territoriality, see Mines (1984). Even in the organised sector 'sheer physical concentration or dispersal affects the capacity of workers to sustain strikes and the aggressiveness of employers' (Banaji and Hensman 1990b).

[49] Perquisites include clothing, loans of cash, help towards the school fees of children, medicines and medical fees; see Harriss-White (1996b, p. 255 and Chapter 7) on caste.

constraints, small groups of workers do try to negotiate their terms of employment at the level of the individual village or firm, and at times achieve wage increases or changes in employers' practices by 'formalising' terms of employment.[50] Their action, however, is focused on individual employers in the locality and is rarely of long duration, with the possibility of reversals and with few implications for the wider labour market. Breman has argued that the movement of labour between firms or over short distances to get other jobs 'must ... be explained as a deed of protest'[51] – an expression of class consciousness, showing workers' increasing refusal to accept their conditions passively. The fact remains that these attempts at wage negotiation or escape have no general impact on the relations between capital and labour, and fail to be enlarged into collective class-based resistance. The problem is not that workers lack political consciousness or the willingness to resist their exploitation, but that the structural constraints are too severe. Where resistance occurs, employers often resort to force and violence, often with the complicity of the local State and the police.

The gendering of work

Domestic labour produces new labour power for the wage labour market and protects and sustains it when it is unemployed, incapacitated or past coping with the physical toil. This labour is female. It has long been appreciated that the process is not a straight subsidy between the genders because unpaid domestic labour cannot be reduced to a money equivalent. Reproductive strategy also varies with class position. In households with few, if any, assets, people are compelled to work to reduce dependency, so it is not surprising that the highest proportions of female and child employment (euphemised as 'participation'!) are found here. By contrast, as we will see in Chapter 5, educated women in the propertied classes are frequently 'withdrawn' (another euphemism because they are never allowed to work in the first place) and effectively secluded. They thereby waste the economic potential of their education.[52] Where the material conditions of individuals have been researched, women are found to own and control so remarkably fewer assets and income than men, and are so significantly less educated that it has been suggested that their class positions are uniformly lower than men.[53]

[50] Breman 1996, pp. 248–54. The *Labour File* vol. 5, no. 12 noted four large co-ordinated protests against the state and landlords in 1999 (pp. 26–8).
[51] Breman 1996, pp. 255–6.
[52] Clark 1993. The wastage even extends to having adverse implications for the life chances of their girl children (see Chapter 5).
[53] Papola and Sharma 1999; da Corta and Venkateshwarlu 1999.

Though the gender division of *paid* work is more flexible than used to be thought, the division of domestic labour has proved extraordinarily rigid. The very rare case where an elderly man cares for children to liberate adult women for fieldwork is the exception that proves the rule that even disabled women must cope with the 'domestic' priorities: collecting fuel and water, washing clothes, cleaning the interiors of houses, child care, care of the elderly and sick, post-harvest processing, and the preparation of food.[54]

Women work longer and harder than men[55] and their wage work is what is available when the tasks are done. They face discrimination in every conceivable respect. Over two-thirds of women have no money returns from their work, though the proportion of wage workers among those working is higher than it is for men. Female labour is heavily concentrated in rural sites, in agricultural work, on casual contracts and at wages bordering on starvation.[56] Women's wages are practically everywhere lower than those of men, irrespective of the tightening effect of male migration or of the development of male jobs in the non-farm economy. In agriculture in the 1990s, women's wages were on average 71 per cent those of men.[57] In non-farm work, women are likely to be concentrated in the lowest grades and stages, on piece rate rather than time rate, and with earnings much lower than men.[58]

Women's wage work is not necessarily empowering for them either at work or at home. In Andhra Pradesh – as we saw – while the feminisation of the gender division of tasks has enabled men to refuse work, their employers have been able to impose attached contracts on wives. Increases in women's absolute or relative income do not necessarily

[54] Gillespie and McNeill 1992; Erb and Harriss-White 2002.
[55] Jackson 1999.
[56] The average daily wage for rural women is 47 per cent of the official nutritional poverty line. For urban women it is 44 per cent. The average wage for rural men is 66 per cent and for urban men 79 per cent of the poverty line (Ghose 1999).
[57] Ghose (1999); the data are the latest for 1994. The logic of wage work may differ according to gender. When women have a target income, they are still prepared to work until their marginal productivity approaches zero (and therefore to accept very low wages) while men will strenuously resist attempts to lower wages below a 'reservation'. The question is whether women are low paid because they are forced into tasks of low productivity consistent with their prior obligations (which are the result of patriarchal power relations within households), *or*, because jobs bear social meanings, low-status jobs attract low-status people, and women are ascribed with low status as people, *or* because women's wage work is also at the mercy of patriarchal discrimination on the 'market'. The jury is still out. The facts that women can be paid less than men where tasks are directly comparable, that women are being forced into attached contracts and that employers regularly refer to women's wages as 'pocket money' need setting against the successful struggle for gender parity in minimum wages in parts of the rice bowl of West Bengal and in Kerala.
[58] Deshpande 1999; Iyer 1999.

increase the power they have over domestic resources, budgets, decision-making and spending, despite – or because of – the fact that women's expenditure decisions are more likely to benefit the entire household.[59]

Whereas the workforce as a whole is becoming more masculine, the agricultural labour force becomes more feminine as women take on (or are forced by men to take on) most tasks except for ploughing and work with engines and mills. Despite serious under-reporting, many millions of women have entered the workforce over the last three decades. 'Participation' – largely distress-induced – went up from 16 per cent in 1971 to 32 per cent in 1988. With this proletarianisation of women, however, comes female unemployment. As with domestic work, female unemployment is hidden. One careful study puts it at six to seven times that of men. One million jobs may have been lost in the 1990s. Female under-employment (women looking for more work) is also increasing at a faster rate than for men.[60]

The literature gives an overriding impression that women are as docile politically as they are reputed to be economically. However, the support of women (taking the form of unpaid work, or even willingness to bond their own labour) has sometimes been important to struggles by men. In Bihar, women who are not bonded and who have employment options outside agriculture have taken the lead in strikes.[61]

Age and work capacity

Child labour has always been part of the family labour force. Nearly two-thirds of child labour is of this sort. It is the continuity between this and paid work on the one hand, and the State's egregious neglect both of education and of any means of implementing the existing limited law banning child labour in hazardous industries on the other, which penalise the children of labourers.[62] The most recent estimate is that while 40 million children work, 13 million or 6 per cent of the 215 million children aged between 5 and 14 work for wages. The casual component of this

---

[59] Male consumption has been shown in a number of studies not only to be biased towards the provision of investment goods but also to male adult goods: liquor and narcotics (Ghosh 1999).

[60] Ghose 1999; Varma et al. 1997; da Corta and Venkateshwarlu 1999. In urban areas, while men are casualised, the proportion of women workers on regular wages has actually increased, though there is little opportunity for upward mobility and regular work is now threatened again by 'flexibilisation' (Visaria 1999; Kundu 1999).

[61] Wilson 1999; Kapadia and Lerche 1999.

[62] Education is still not mandatory and in the only State where it was made mandatory (Tamil Nadu in 1995) it has not been implemented. The law on child labour is the Child Labour (Prohibition and Regulation) Act of 1986 (Dhagamwar 1992).

young army – one-third – is slowly rising and being feminised. 'It is not that the economy cannot do without child labour, it is rather that many children cannot do without employment' comments Ajit Ghose (1999, p. 2604). This begs questions about why this should be so. If they are orphans or escaping abusive families, if their parents are sick or disabled, then they lack access to social security. If their parents are underemployed and looking for work, then employers' cost-cutting may account for it. If their parents are employed, then their low wages, and sometimes their 'selfish' consumption patterns – especially that of alcohol and narcotics by men – explain why children work and why they may still be malnourished when they do.[63] When adults are unemployed or mired in debt-bondage, children have to join the labour force.[64] Apart from domestic reproductive work, agriculture and animal husbandry, there are certain industries where children are extensively used in preference to adult labour, the Sivakasi match-making 'cluster' being a notorious case. Controlled by influential business families, it is organised at home or in sweat/workshops. The State turns a blind eye in various ways – from exemption from the Factories Acts to not enforcing the Minimum Wages Act.[65] Child labour is only slowly on the decline as (non-mandatory) primary education diffuses at a snail's pace. Illiteracy and poor levels of education are means to reproduce casual labour, with predictable consequences generation upon generation.[66]

There is, of course, no age of retirement for 'unorganised' labour. Instead, people are incapacitated from the labour market by the physical insults of old age, by deteriorating eyesight and eye defects (in agriculture after decades of staring at the reflected sun in wet fields, in weaving by years of close work in dim light), and by occupation-related accidents and diseases. There is increasing evidence that employers will screen labour according to physique, and pay differential piece rates according to each worker's physical condition.[67]

---

[63] Harriss 1991b; Heyer 2000.

[64] Chandrasekhar 1997.

[65] The carpet industry in Uttar Pradesh and Jammu and Kashmir is another example. It is known that many of the children here are virtual slaves, purchased with lump-sum payments to parents by agents for carpet manufacturers. Most of these children come from the lowest castes and tribes, agricultural labouring families in Bihar, subject to fierce oppression from private armies of upper caste landowners.

[66] Yet secondary education produces a peculiar paradox for workers because it behaves as a luxury good, allowing young educated people, especially women, *not* to enter the labour market. Argument and statistics here are from Ghose (1999).

[67] See the study of rural adult incapacity and disability in Erb and Harriss-White (2002).

Caste and class

Caste still shapes ideologies of work and status. It makes for compartmentalised labour 'markets', 'with non-competing groups whose options
are severely constrained'.[68] It stratifies pay. By means of caste, entry into
the non-farm economy is screened.[69] Caste ideology also affects whether
women work at all, what work they can do, and how far from home they
may move. In particular, to be in the 'scheduled castes' (SC) (the lowest
castes, mainly untouchables and 29 per cent of the population) makes a
person twice as likely to be a casual labourer, in agriculture and poor.[70]
SC women are also more likely to be in low-paid menial labour, thus
reinforcing the gender division. In towns, all the work connected with
sanitation and public health infrastructure, without which the economy
cannot function, is entrusted to 'scheduled castes'. Even when employed
by the State, these workers face routine harassment and contemptuous
treatment. Elsewhere as labourers, they are often still found doing physically dirty jobs, or handling food still to be stripped of its protective
husks and shells. As petty traders they have entered markets for commodities with certain physical properties; for example, fruit with skins or
vegetables – or recycled materials – that need further physical transformation before being consumed. In these cases, entry to even petty trade
is a struggle: carving out and defending physical territory previously
occupied by others or encroaching on congested public space.

Scheduled caste and tribal people are constitutionally entitled to
positive discrimination ('reservations') in the public sector to redress
their social and economic 'backwardness' and deprivation, but the consequences have been uneven and paradoxical. Reservations have helped
to entrench the importance of caste as a social institution for access to
higher education and to jobs in the administration and public-sector
enterprise. But they have also reinforced the caste-based segmentation of
the labour market[71] and have turned the reserved castes into an interest

---

[68] Harriss 1989.
[69] See Jeffrey (2001) for Uttar Pradesh (UP) and Heyer (2000). In the villages near Coimbatore, which were studied by Heyer, scheduled caste agricultural labourers – *pannadis* –
enter the non-farm economy as wage labour, while 'cobblers' – *chakkliyans* – cannot do
this. *Pannadis* ensured the physical protection of caste Hindus, while *chakkliyans* were
bonded to them. The latter's main achievement is to be less bonded.
[70] Scheduled in the constitution to receive positive discrimination: a term for untouchables,
Gandhi's *harijans* ('children of god') and now self-termed '*dalits*' (the oppressed). For
analyses of workforce data and data on the many dimensions through which scheduled
caste (SC) and scheduled tribal (ST) people are still viciously discriminated against, see
Nagaraj (1999); Jayaraj and Subramanian (1999); Ahmed (1999).
[71] Mendelsohn and Vicziany 1998, chapter 4.

group when the original intention had been to dissolve caste differences. Reserved jobs are limited (sometimes by retaliation from those implementing them). Reserved posts commonly absorb only a fraction of those who qualify. The market for jobs for low-caste people is therefore segmented between those who do and do not benefit from reservation.

Castes have indeed become interest groups with reaches way beyond that of reserved jobs. Workers themselves sometimes enforce the stratification of occupations by caste so as to maintain their hold over enclaves of the labour market or sectors of petty trade. Caste is also the basis from which urban, occupation-based, trade associations have evolved (see Chapter 7). These are developing powerful corporatist regulative roles, substituting for the State and unambiguously supporting local capital in a way that limits class conflict. Their collective political agendas push labour issues low down. Through collective action based on 'occupation', decisions are taken to lengthen working days, flout other aspects of the labour laws and ignore safety provisions. Even when employers and employees belong to the same caste, terms and conditions can be imposed on labour, and attempts by labour to unionise can be collectively resisted by upholding caste solidarity. Ways of organising labour can be encouraged that disempower workers: associations of 'textiles workers' are actually (caste-based) master weavers. Organisations representing yarn twisters, marketplace porters and handcart pushers entirely managed by bosses have also been found.[72]

Yet, while caste is used by employers to exploit labour and keep it fragmented, labourers, too, deploy caste identities to organise and, often, to enhance their status in the face of exploitation. Workers may emphasise caste linkages to maintain their hold over a particular enclave of the labour market (for a ubiquitous example, scheduled caste municipal sanitary workers). When employers and labourers belong to the same caste (for example, in the diamond-cutting industry in Surat (Gujarat), or in the industrial district making cotton knitwear in Tiruppur (Tamil Nadu)),[73] labourers often emphasise their caste solidarity with employers, thereby ensuring the exclusion of other caste groups. This has ambivalent effects. While such a monopoly benefits labourers, their reliance on vertical caste ties undermines their ability to challenge exploitation by employers. (There has never been a strike in the Surat diamond industry, despite extreme exploitation and physical abuse.)[74]

[72] Basile and Harriss-White 1999.

[73] *Saurashtra patels* are owners, commission agents and traders, and they employ labour from the same caste. In Tiruppur a significant part of the entire cluster, both owners and workers, are *vellala gounders*.

[74] For the Surat case see Engelshoven (1999). For Tiruppur, see Chari (2000); also Cadène and Holmstrom (1998).

No less importantly, but far less instrumentally, however, caste plays another role in labour politics. It has provided an important idiom for many sections of the labouring poor, especially lower castes, to organise politically, although not always within the context of work or labour relations.[75] Social movements and the political mobilisation of untouchables (or *dalits*)[76] in India in recent years have gained momentum in their search for respect and social status. They have turned to the State for protection of their rights and for preferential access to public employment and education. Caste-based social movements have developed in synergy with the workplace-based politics of lower castes. For instance, scheduled caste municipal sanitary workers have organised to improve working conditions and wages, and at the same time have established caste associations for the internal reform of their caste, demanded recognition and respect and challenged the legitimacy of ritual subordination. Lower caste groups have also attempted to forge horizontal linkages with cognate castes of labourers and thus expanded the scope of mobilisation. That lower caste labourers in both rural and urban contexts now more actively contest the power of their employers can be understood only within the context of a wider process of political mobilisation. In rural Bihar, the struggles of scheduled caste/untouchable landless labour, at times in alliance with radical left-wing political organisations, against their 'clean' upper or middle caste landowners–employers, have led to violent confrontations, caste battles reflecting class conflict.[77]

In her book on the political history of poverty in north India, Nandini Gooptu argues that it would be wrong to interpret such political mobilisations of labour and expressions of collective identity in the language of caste as a form of false consciousness, not least because caste and class exploitation interpenetrate in the strategies deployed by employers, and because exclusion from, or inclusion in, particular sectors of the labour market rests very significantly on caste status. If the labour market continues to be embedded in institutions of caste and if caste still determines relations between labour and capital, then it would be misleading to dismiss the politics of caste, when it operates outside the workplace, as being irrelevant to the politics of labour. In fact the former is central to the latter. Caste consciousness and *class* consciousness are not mutually exclusive, but can reinforce each other. The growing power of lower caste politics, involving its institutionalisation in political parties and increasingly successful electoral participation, may have little *direct* impact on labour relations. For Gooptu, it forms a very significant aspect of the

[75] Gooptu 2001.
[76] The word *Dalit* means the 'oppressed' (see footnote 70) and encompasses a wider category of low-caste people than does 'ex-untouchable'.
[77] Omvedt 1993. Clean castes are those not ritually polluted.

politics of the labouring poor, even if not of the politics of labour *qua* labour. It also enhances the capacity and willingness of labour to contest the power of upper caste employers and their exclusion from various segments of the economy and the labour market.

Workforce insecurity

Workers in India are insecure. The coexistence of open unemployment with positive wages has proved hard to explain unless the continual resistance by employees to any reduction of the real-food equivalence of the wage is factored in. Open unemployment (at 12 per cent) is not such a feature of work as intermittent, insecure and poorly productive underemployment. Over a quarter of the casual labour force at any given moment is looking for more work and the proportion is growing. Seasonal unemployment and employment overlap and coexist. Even industrial and commercial capital operates seasonally, with periods of idleness dotting the weeks of peak labour demand.[78] Employers use many ploys to make labour insecure. Payments are withheld. Contracts and debt are manipulated so as to ensure the availability of labour at peak periods of demand (at below the going rate) while at other times, labour is dumped or made to work at below-market rates.[79]

These tactics are certainly not confined to agriculture. In small towns dominated by agro-processing, there is not one but several fault lines in the security of labour. The typical 'unorganised' firm (tightly controlled by hierarchised male family members in order to concentrate accumulation – see Chapter 5) has a labour force divided by its extent and kind of security. Being part of the permanent labour force is here a condition to be aspired to, in contrast to being permanent labour in agriculture. Labourers are selected by origin (local), caste (usually not scheduled), and gender (male). Permanent work offers a diversity of livelihoods, all requiring individual trust. Contracts are individualised and verbal. They vary in their periods of payment and of notice of dismissal, the one delayed (sometimes pay is yearly) and the other instant. Some permanent jobs can be part-time, some seasonal. Many bosses agree to time off for employees to work their own land or to do periodic trade, or they make working on the owner's land integral to the factory or workshop 'contract'.

---

[78] Purchases and sales avoid astrologically inauspicious days and times; the entirely secular flow of salaries surges once a month; the agricultural harvests produce gluts two and sometimes three times a year; religious festivals and one or two major marriage seasons are interspersed.

[79] Kapadia 1995a.

A primitive and personalised form of occupational welfare is usually extended to this part of the labour force. Employers will give loans and also 'gifts' of petty cash for purposes such as medical expenditure, education and marriages. At one and the same time these acts parody state social protection and reveal how capital acts opportunistically to tie up labour it does not wish to lose. In stark contrast, the casual labour force is characterised by low and fluctuating pay, higher turnover and no security. While labour recruiters may be given annual bonuses and lent small sums of money, attempts are made to turn labour over so as to reduce its customary entitlement to annual gifts and to avoid protective obligations.

Male casual labour is occasionally unionised.[80] Yet the multiplicity of unions invites the political mediation of disputes, which are rarely resolved in favour of labour. The labour laws tend not to be enforced by unions but by the State Factories Acts inspectors with huge territories to cover and few resources with which to enforce the law are more often than not found to be implicated with bosses in a nexus of corruption around the evasion of labour protection laws and the erosion of labour rights.

Female casual labour is subjected to extremes of casualisation, negligence and harassment, and to unsafe and unsanitary working conditions, their wages often being reported by bosses as 'pocket money'.

In such firms, work has for decades been subcontracted, often exported to rural sites to avoid inspection and to profit from cheap or unwaged family labour, from low rents and from the ease of evasion of any 'welfare' obligations and taxes. So capital uses informal practices and the idiom of social protection highly selectively, thus rendering the majority of the workforce insecure and a small minority less insecure. But employers' philanthropy works in ambivalent ways, which not only protect but also bind the beneficiaries. As a result, the politics of labour within a firm may be fractured and complex.

The State and labour

India has two forms of state-mediated social protection. In the first, the State favours its own employees. 'Public employees are served best or rather have ensured that they are best served' with respect to pensions, provident funds, sickness, maternity and unemployment benefits.[81] Twelve per cent of the workforce is covered (overwhelmingly male). The State also gives persistent subsidies to the highly regulated 'market' for

---

[80] Workers in the unorganised sector are under 1 per cent of all members of trade unions.
[81] Guhan 1992.

social insurance (covering at best 8 per cent of (male) lives) and experiments endlessly (but with few successes) with ways and means of increasing the coverage of social insurance. The idea that a welfare state or 'protective social security' is a luxury India cannot afford is contested by few. It then becomes possible to argue that the ramshackle and leaky raft of anti-poverty policies, targeted development schemes, employment guarantees and food security measures managed through the public distribution of grain (all of which have their own histories and politics) are the appropriate, 'promotive' forms of social security.[82] Certainly, they are the unsystematic ways in which the State 'protects' labour. They are all that capital allows the State to achieve in this direction. Critics have observed that rather than promote labour they subsidise it for capital.[83]

The second system of social security, set up in Tamil Nadu in 1989 and copied in New Delhi in 1995 (so that the legal framework exists for other States to implement),[84] is a major departure from this orthodoxy. Consisting of pensions for the aged, widows, agricultural labourers and physically handicapped people, survivor benefits, maternity assistance, marriage grants and accident relief (to those under a poverty line set by local States, in this case set at twice the national level), it amounts to 1.5 per cent of state expenditure.[85] In the late 1990s, the pension was Rs 125 ($2.5) per month plus one free meal a day and two sets of clothing a year – in total, in the region of Rs 5000 ($100) per year. It is not a luxury. In the State where it was first implemented, old age and widows' pensions were most consistently claimed, with one evaluation showing that a third of those eligible were included after five years of operation.[86] Many old people are found unsupported by their relatives, contrary to widespread assumptions. One recent study shows that 7 per cent of rural households are 'collapsed' units consisting of single individuals.[87] Local discretion proves kinder than the official eligibility guidelines that have proved harsh and restrictive. Even so the majority of those eligible are not covered, particularly women.[88] Long delays qualify this benefit. Bribes involving sums equal to 18 months' benefit neutralise it for some and act as a barrier to access for others. While the impact of this rough but unready safety net on the lives of claimants may be very significant, its all-India impact on the security of workers' lives is negligible.

[82] Ahmed et al. 1991.
[83] Olsen, forthcoming.
[84] This was in a highly opportunistic last-ditch attempt by the then ruling Congress Party to drum up pre-electoral support.
[85] 0.4 per cent of state domestic product (Harriss-White 1999a, p. 316).
[86] Guhan 1994.
[87] Colatei and Harriss-White 2002a.
[88] Harriss-White 2002b.

The case of social security makes a wider point worthy of a little elaboration. Just as the politics of labourers differs from the class politics of labour, so state interventions that significantly affect the world of labour are far from confined to one department of government. Conversely, the work of the Labour Ministry may have a limited, or even backhanded, impact on workers.

Take the labour laws.[89] Their loopholes are big enough for the proverbial bus to be driven through them. The Trades Union Act *allows* registration but does not *require* recognition of trade unions as agents of collective bargaining. While the Industrial Disputes Act curbs the rights of employers, their powerful tool – the lock-out – is hardly penalised and the State is empowered to conciliate through a judicial maze that makes workers dependent on highly qualified, legally knowledgeable representatives. Any union, however small, can intervene in labour disputes, thereby creating a field day for manipulation by employers.[90] The Minimum Wages, Contract Labour and Child Labour Acts declare entitlements that actually have to be struggled for by labour organisations. Further, without reforms to give access to the courts and make their decisions binding, these laws are toothless. Labour organisations asserting claims to entitlement are, moreover, dealt with under criminal procedure. At best, all these laws have a normative role: to provoke – and act as a rallying point for – mobilisation.[91] At worst, the very laws supposedly protecting labour encourage capital to informalise it.

The State-in-action also reveals itself as profoundly ambivalent towards the assetlessness of labour. On the one hand, it lends support to business at labour's expense, all the way from the ring-fencing of unorganised labour to the close relations between the promoter families dominating big business and the nationalised banking institutions.[92] Elsewhere there are mighty subsidies to those with property, however 'small scale', in the shape of cheap or free electricity, fertiliser, credit and food, all ineluctably resistant to blandishments from Washington.[93] The first three can intensify the pace of differentiation, while cheap food slows it. The public distribution system of subsidised food grains (and up to 59 other essential commodities) is broad-based, broadly redistributivist and

---

[89] The 1926 Trades Union Act, the 1947 Industrial Disputes Act, the 1948 Factories Act, the Employers' State Insurance Act, the 1961 Maternity Benefits Act, the 1965 Payments of Bonus Act, the 1972 Employees' Provident Fund, Miscellaneous Provision Act, and the Payment of Gratuity Act; not to mention those affecting the unorganised sector: the 1970 Contract Labour (Regulation and Abolition Act), and last and least the 1986 Child Labour (Protection and Regulation) Act (Bhowmik 1998).

[90] Bhowmik 1998.

[91] Dhagamwar 1992.

[92] Banaji and Mody 2001.

[93] Bardhan 1998.

very hard to fine-tune.[94] In Kerala and West Bengal, leftist parties have achieved land reforms and laws securing tenancies, thereby consolidating a decentralised base for petty accumulation.[95] Yet throughout India, the nexus of tax evasion and bribery results in gains to capital that are more substantial than those accruing to labour, from the petty livelihoods brought into being by this nexus (see Chapter 4 on the State). On the other hand, the beneficiaries from land or tenancy reforms, from the distribution of house sites and from periodic amnesties on encroachment, are but drops in the ocean. State-directed commercial credit which might enable landless people to buy patches of land and join the micro-propertied classes is deliberately denied them. The negligent enforcement of the social wage also weakens labour. The river of revenue from tax on liquor is at the expense of widespread domestic violence, pauperisation and food scarcity in the households of drinkers.[96] And the many nutrition and employment schemes, fuelled by the massive buffer stock of food grains that the Government of India is obliged to replenish (as much for political as technical reasons), often do little more than see labour through the hungry season, thereby subsidising (female) labour for capital. Only in those rather rare places where the wages on employment schemes exceed the ruling swathe of rates for agricultural labour may such schemes have an empowering knock-on effect on claims for wage increases. Only when the public works created by such schemes prove to be public goods relevant to the mass of the rural 'public', then the spatial and social mobility of workers – out of bondage and into towns and the non-farm economy – may be given a boost.[97]

Labour politics

The character of work – contracts and debt that are imposed and coercive, the migration and movement of labour, the segmentation of markets, the idiosyncrasy of employment practice – interacts to thwart concerted action by labour and to enhance the appropriation of surplus. So how does unorganised labour contest the power of capital? At one end of the spectrum, everyday forms of resistance prevail, including non–co-operation with employers in periods of peak demand for labour, reneging on debt repayment, or simply escaping and leaving a job; at the other end of the spectrum, wage bargaining, protests and even strikes.[98] Yet while instances of large-scale labour agitation are not hard to find, they are best understood

[94] Mooij 1999.
[95] See Mooij (1999); Herring (1983) for land reforms.
[96] Manor 1993.
[97] Srivastava 1999; da Corta and Venkateshwarlu 1999.
[98] Breman 1996 chapter 8; Omvedt 1993. A case in point is the unionisation of informal sector women workers through the Self Employed Women's Association (SEWA), discussed by Hensman (2000).

as exceptions to the general trend. Labour protests tend to remain small-scale, local and focused on particular employers. The possibility of enlarging their scope remains severely restricted, and frequent changes of employment and employers aggravate labour's political difficulties.

As Gooptu has shown, much of the political expression of Indian labour is to be found outside the context of work, in non-class modes of action and in the arena of democratic politics and social movements. The mobilisation of lower castes (those usually located at the lowest end of the labour market) and landless workers into political parties has already been discussed. The labouring poor may also forge solidarities in the neighbourhood. Their experience of control or exploitation is not confined to the workplace: they are also disciplined by the State, notably by the police, especially in urban areas where the labouring poor are the most usual targets of police action and brutality. Increasing urban violence and the mobilisation of poor people in urban neighbourhoods against the police reflect the State's control over labour's public spaces. The oppression of labour also involves their lack of urban housing, essential services, utilities and infrastructure. In this, the local and national States and the local propertied elites are all complicit. Not only is there completely inadequate provision of public housing, but local councils also systematically fail to raise taxes from those with property to extend the provision of services (a point developed in Chapter 4).[99]

Problems of housing and lack of urban services for workers have crucially shaped their politics, with violent clashes in urban neighbourhoods over changes in the use of space, territory and services, both among the poor themselves and between the poor and local propertied classes or agents of the local State.[100] While the shortage of housing and infrastructure is a predicament shared by all workers, the competition for them undermines class solidarity.[101] The Shiv Sena for instance has been notably successful in using local infrastructural deprivation in poor parts of Mumbai to mobilise low-class workers and their wives, and to incorporate them into their violent, xenophobic, patriarchal movements.[102]

[99] Capital has a conflict of interest. On the one hand, it is in the interest of employers to ensure housing for workers so as to reproduce the labour force. On the other, when labour is in excess supply, and indeed in order to reinforce its mobile and flexible character, local capital helps to prevent the creation of permanent 'habitats' for labour by avoiding investment in housing directly and by evading the taxation that would generate resources for it. The direct exploitation of labour at the workplace is all of a piece with the indirect exploitation of labour through the lack of provision of essential infrastructure (see Chapter 8).

[100] Cadène and Holmstrom, 1998. In Deponte's study of informalisation in Kanpur (2000), laid-off textiles workers are shown to have exchanged forms of subordination based on caste and labour struggles through trade unions for subordination based on insecure livelihoods and poverty, and struggles through faction and patronage.

[101] Narayanan 1997

[102] Deshpande 2001

India's formally organised labour unions have a number of features that need to be introduced here because they accentuate the weakness of India's unorganised labour. First, organised labour has no coherent project for unorganised labour. Indeed, unorganised labour may be seen as a threat to organised labour. To reach out from the organised fortresses of comparatively privileged work – only 4 per cent of the labour force – to labour scattered far beyond the ramparts has proved extremely difficult. Second, the union movement is itself fragmented. With the exceptions of employees' unions organised around individual industrial units, unions set up by individual corporates, public-sector unions and unions formed around individual charismatic leaders, unions are by and large organised by competing political parties. When parties split, unions split; when regional political parties develop, unions regionalise; and they are also starting to be organised along communal and caste lines (see Chapters 6 and 7). Third, unions are, therefore, an important part of the politics of electoral mobilisation and party political rivalry. It is quite common for unions to be captured by bosses who fund political parties. When such unions do represent the interests of labour, they do this through party politics. As a result, unorganised workers cannot look to most trade unions for representation, let alone support.[103] Fourth, the elaborate regulative framework for labour contains trade unions politics within a legal strait-jacket dominated by lawyers, bureaucrats and politicians, who in practice rarely find in favour of labour when it comes to adjudication. These are formidable distractions not only from taking up the cause of unorganised labour, but even from seeking redress for the grievances of the more vulnerable sections of unionised labour; for example, for women and for low-caste workers threatened with arbitrary and illegal dismissal.[104]

Moreover, since the 1980s, the corporate sector, determined to secure flexibility and to control pay, have worked their way down a 'menu' of tactics to fracture the workforce, reduce numbers and erode workers' legal rights: lock-outs (in which employers use labour law to prevent the workforce from working – a practice that is lumped together with strikes in official police statistics![105]), voluntary retirement, violation of settlements and changes in job specifications (and therefore their work and social security rights), not to mention the violation of ILO conventions. In addition, production units have been relocated to geographically dispersed sites, and out-sourcing or subcontracting has become increasingly commonplace. The expansion in the ranks of unorganised labour has

[103] Jhabvala and Subrahmanya 2000.
[104] Hensman 2000.
[105] Justino 2001

thus been undercutting the existing base of the trade unions movement. Liberalisation has added considerable impetus to this process, but it is clearly not a cause of it.[106]

Instead of the industrial, class-based labour politics now unravelling in the West, in India the struggle between capital and labour is being played out in the arena of democratic party politics. The 'democratic upsurge' has elicited from the propertied, upper and middle classes and upper castes a 'conservative revolution',[107] the most dominant institutional expression of which is the Hindu nationalist political party: the Bharatiya Janata Party (BJP). The study of election statistics has shown quite conclusively that the poor and lower castes rarely support the BJP, whose core constituency is the upper and middle classes and castes. Sociological research has revealed the strong participation of commercial interests, business castes, and rural and urban capitalist classes in the activities of the BJP and its affiliated organisations. These interests are drawn to the party because it pledges its commitment to the increasingly expansionist ambitions of Indian capital, and because it espouses ideologies of caste and patriarchal subordination, as well as a strong, militarised state, capable of enforcing political stability, public order and discipline. In their quest for economic security, and to prevent the democratic political mobilisation of the poor, the propertied now look to the BJP. There is ample evidence that militant, Hindu-chauvinistic, right-wing organisations, like the Shiv Sena in Mumbai, have been instrumental in undermining labour militancy and strikes since the 1980s – with their own trade unions acting in cahoots with employers to emasculate militant employees' unions.

Conclusion

If class struggle is first a struggle over class and only second a struggle between classes, we might say that the overwhelming majority of the Indian workforce is still engaged in the first struggle while capital, even though stratified and fractured, is engaged in the second. If one thing is clear from the complexities of India's workforce it is that its social structure makes labour easy to control and hard to organise. Liberalisation intensifies the struggles for, and between, class.

[106] Bhowmik 1998, pp. 158–62; International Labour Office (ILO) 1992; Banaji and Hensman 1990a, 1998. However, when it comes to *strikes* there is evidence that it is not the intrinsic characteristics of given industries, or their components (plants), but it is the history and experience of bargaining at the plant level that explains industrial conflict. See Banaji and Hensman (1990b).

[107] Hansen 1999.

Liberalisation involves an assumption on the part of employers that India's comparative advantage lies in the indisputably low cost of labour. But India's large reserves of cheap labour cannot constitute the foundations of a modern, globally competitive economy. Not only does such a strategy entail the suppression of political and trade union rights for the majority of wage-earners, and the deliberate fragmentation of the labour force, but it also presumes a poorly educated, semiliterate (and poorly nourished) mass of labourers. Such a workforce will not provide the necessary mass demand for the goods and services produced by a modern economy integrated into the global system.

3   Indian development and the intermediate classes

Scholars have long sought to explain Indian development through the use of class analysis.[1] Exactly how the dominant class coalition is composed has been heavily contested (like the question of whether agricultural workers and petty producers make a working class, which we discussed in Chapter 2), but few have ever doubted that 'monopoly capital', 'big business', rich agricultural capitalists and landlords, and the technocratic administrative-cum-political elite have been of crucial importance.[2] An earlier idea that a loose coalition of 'non-monopoly' or 'regional' capital, or 'auxiliary classes' consisting of 'small landowners, rich and middle peasants, merchants of rural and semi-rural townships, small-scale manufacturers and retailers'[3], might be the class elements that mattered most for the direction and pace of development has been almost entirely out of court. That idea was first proposed in 1967 by Kalecki in his theory of the 'intermediate classes'. Then, after some very lively debate about its relevance to India, it was refined and applied rather convincingly to India's conditions of economic stagnation by P.S. Jha, who focused on the specific role of scarcity in this dispersed kind of accumulation.[4] Since the mid-1980s, however, the predisposing conditions for the hold on power of the intermediate classes are thought to have disappeared, and it is evident that liberalisation is not a project of theirs. If our focus is the India of the 88 per cent, however, we need to question the

---

[1] Every class analysis has specific objectives. For Mitra (1977) it was to establish the reasons for the long-term price relationships between agriculture and industry encapsulated in the terms of trade, which govern the transfer of resources between sectors of the economy; for Thorner (1982) it was to clarify the mode of production in agriculture; Bardhan's analysis of class coalitions helped to explain mediocre growth and the proliferation of subsidies (1984); Byres (1996a) pursued the power of the capitalist coalition controlling the process of planned development; Roy (1998) has examined the class interests responsible for fiscal failure; and Herring (1999) sought the class roots for the failure of India's developmental state.

[2] Rudra 1989; Mitra 1977; Bardhan 1998.

[3] The terms used here are more recent and from Ahmad (1996a, p. 44); Baru (2000, p. 208).

[4] Kalecki 1967/1972; Raj 1973; Namboodiripad 1973; Byres 1996a, b; Jha 1980.

received wisdom about the dominant coalition. What are we to make of the fact that the intermediate classes are both still very numerous and locally very strong in both political and economic terms? Mushtak Khan, in his painstaking and original review of rent-seeking in both markets and States throughout Asia, goes so far as to take their role as prime movers of development as being entirely self-evident and not requiring any special defence.[5] Does their continuing weight in the economy, and their distinctive mode of operation, cast doubt on prevailing expectations about the prospects for India's development along neo-liberal lines? Is class analysis, in this distinctively Indian variant of Kalecki's 'theory', still important for understanding the process of accumulation in India? Unpacking and answering these questions is the main aim of this chapter. While predicting the long-term influence of the intermediate classes may be difficult, we find that they still constitute at the very least a powerful structure of accumulation that analysts of India's macroeconomic prospects ignore at their peril.

Intermediate classes and regimes – the ideas

Why was it thought necessary to distinguish the 'intermediate classes' in the first place? To answer this question we cannot avoid a brief excursion into the history of ideas about the development of the Indian economy. The story begins with six lucid and provocative pages by the Polish economist, Michal Kalecki (1972).

Kalecki was trying to understand the role played by social classes in economies and States that were in transition to mature capitalism, and in which the majority of people were not yet wage-earners. He had Egypt and Indonesia in mind.[6] In such conditions, Kalecki argued, a grouping of the self-employed and small farmers forms a distinct 'class force'. They are 'intermediate classes' (IC) and their predominance gives rise to an 'intermediate regime' (IR). The defining characteristic of the classes composing an intermediate regime is that there is no contradiction between labour and capital or between labour and management. Their 'earnings can neither be classified as a reward for labour, nor as a payment for risk-taking (that is, profit) but are an amalgam of the two. The self-employed thus lie midway between the large-scale, professionally managed capitalist enterprises of the private sector, and the working classes' (Jha 1980, p. 95). Family labourers (including women and

[5] Khan (2000b) – see especially pp. 90–5.
[6] They are late starters in industrialisation, quite large economies with aspirations to self-sufficient development and with natural resources that make such a path appear reasonable.

children) are not paid any wages. Production rather than profit may be what people aim to maximise, or 'target incomes' may be their goal. The bureaucracy comprises salary earners, but since officials are also assumed to derive income from bribes, fraud and the private sale of state goods such as licences and sanctions, they are *de facto* self-employed and earn a fee from the provision of their services.

Kalecki's 'intermediate classes' do not correspond to the Marxian definition of class, the key distinctions not being discrete positions in relation to the means of production but essentially one of scale and of occupying a 'contradictory class location' (to adopt E. O. Wright's term) in relation to capital and labour.[7] But note that in the formulation we quote, Jha allows space for the self-employed themselves to employ wage labour (that is, for owner-managed firms to join this coalition) and it is his formulation that we will follow here.[8]

For Kalecki, these classes are 'not necessarily rich'; but they constitute a very large crowd.[9] Yet while they are extremely dispersed compared with big business and the public sector, they appear as 'masters of the countryside'[10] when they confront the mass of the small peasantry and the agricultural labour force. Jha estimates that in India in 1980 there were 30 million 'intermediate' income earners with eight to 10 times as many dependants – some 250 million. These people are able to come to dominate the political economy, according to Kalecki, because of the small size, regional isolation and entrepreneurial weakness of what he terms the 'native upper middle-class'. Burdened with capital constraints

---

[7] In this, intermediate classes resemble peasants who typically hire in labour at certain seasons and may hire themselves out at others. They may also simultaneously lend and borrow money. Some of the ICs depend on merchants' and usurers' capital for reproduction, as do peasants. ICs differ from peasants in that they are unable to retreat from markets and survive at all. They also develop pre-emptively or collusively around the State's structure of regulation. They will both be an intended outcome of state action and the unintended outcome of struggles between the State and other classes.

[8] See the earlier discussion of the 'informal' and the 'black' economy (Chapter 1). Many of these enterprises are in the informal economy because they are small; sometimes they are illegitimate. Small-scale enterprise or industry does not necessarily mean small capital, as shown by industrial field-research on the development of branch firms, of putting-out and of subcontracting. By these tactics, large firms gain eligibility for subsidies and pre-empt protective labour legislation (J. Harriss 1981, 1985, 1989).

[9] It may be objected that trying to locate ICs in databases will be like searching for needles in haystacks, and that the concept is excessively loose and might be better replaced by 'small capital'. The point is that small capital has not been theorised while ICs have. Like ICs, small capital is also vague, compatible with rents, surplus value, own labour product and redistribution through the market. Ironically, given the significance attached to classification in studies of the peasantry (well reviewed in Thorner (1982) and Athreya et al. (1990)), the importance of the ICs is not to be found in a mechanical classification but in this class force *in action*.

[10] Lenin 1960 p. 186.

and facing imperfect and fragmented markets, their debility has to be substituted for by a State that 'leads directly' (through various economic interventions, to be described next) 'to the pattern of amalgamation of the interests of the lower-middle-class with state capitalism' (1972, p. 163).

Their amalgamation creates an intermediate class regime with interests at variance with the enormous army of the land-poor or landless rural and urban workers (Kalecki calls them 'paupers'). Wage workers have a vital interest in keeping the price of wage goods low against their wages, while the intermediate classes[11] have an interest in keeping such goods scarce, their prices high relative to wages; and in profiting from that scarcity.[12]

Preconditions

Kalecki then argued that there were specific conditions peculiar to less-developed economies that might allow an 'intermediate regime' to perform the role of a ruling class.

1   An incomplete land reform that deprives the feudal class of its position in economic life and benefits the self-cultivating middle peasant. With respect to India, Byres has convincingly argued that middle peasants or small agrarian capitalists were the principal beneficiaries of the abolition of large-revenue farmers – zamindars – and the subsequent very incomplete land reform programmes.[13]

2   Non-alignment in international relations, so as to utilise credit from the socialist countries that existed then as a counterweight to foreign capital. 'Such a position in international relations defends the intermediate regimes ... against the pressure from imperialist powers aimed at restoration of the "normal" role of big business in which the foreign capital would play an appreciable role' (Raj 1973, p. 1191). In a word, the Cold War was helpful. It allowed non-alignment from 'capital' without the constraints of autarchy. Thus, the Germans, British and Soviets all provided aid for steel mills, while the United States gave aid for the purchase of American food grains.

3   A developmental State. The weakness of the 'native' upper middle class leaves them unable to perform the role of the dynamic entrepreneur. The State therefore takes an active role in accumulation. The

[11] Which, from the perspective of the class of paupers, seems a small proportion of the population and also exceptionally powerful at the local level.
[12] Jha 1980.
[13] See Byres 1981.

social overhead capital needed to provide the foundations for more directly productive investment has two characteristics that make state involvement essential: first, a high minimum efficient scale, relative to the small domestic market; and second, a long gestation period prior to returns. The intermediate regime 'nationalises' economic development via a developmental State in preference to using the only other alternative: foreign capital. International capital would be expected to enter specific sectors, such as railways, in order to facilitate the extraction and export of resources rather than to integrate and develop the national economy. It will only create infrastructure if it can get private competitive advantage from it.

These features characterise the 'intermediate regime' – a regime based on the intermediate classes – which erect a form of state capitalism, distinct from classical capitalism, to promote and nationalise economic growth in a way that specifically benefits them. This mode of accumulation and regulation depends on politics. Since the State plays a vanguard role in the economy, the struggle among the various classes is focused on the penetration and control of its institutions. Private (middle) caste and class accumulation is enhanced to the detriment of 'collective' or more broad-based growth and development. The State is used by the intermediate classes for accumulation rather than for legitimation. And as we show here, their politics and power are exercised informally.

Intermediate class power

While Kalecki enumerates the political strategies by means of which such a State would remain in power and continue to benefit the intermediate classes, he is vague in his explanation of how these classes come to be the major political players over the heads of the two classically antagonistic classes (labour and, particularly, big capital). He simply asserts that 'representatives of the lower middle class rise in a way naturally to power' (1972, p. 162) and that small businessmen defend themselves (by means not specified) against displacement by unfettered capitalism. And later he also asserts quite blandly that the 'state capitalist road' encourages the expansion of the productive potential of this intermediate class and gives employment opportunities in the state apparatus for its children.

These questions concerning the way an intermediate regime acquires and holds on to power were therefore not convincingly answered. When in 1973 K.N. Raj grasped the nettle and declared that Indian political and economic development could be understood in terms of Kalecki's theory, he was promptly and sharply challenged by E.M.S. Namboodiripad on the simple grounds that both he and Kalecki had underestimated the pivotal role of the domestic big bourgeoisie.[14] Most significant among the factors undoubtedly neglected by Kalecki is the potential *synergy* between large and small business. On the one hand, the state provision of social overhead capital in the era of the green revolution – in the form of irrigation, roads, power and essential agro-inputs like diesel, credit and fertiliser – did indeed benefit agricultural capital. On the other hand, in urban areas the State was simultaneously providing inputs complementary to big business through its policy of public-sector investment in key upstream industries (iron and steel, coal, transport, power, minerals, atomic energy, arms and ammunition), while also providing big business with cheaper labour through subsidised wage goods. In reality, 'state capitalism' is far from sufficient a concept with which to link the elements of an avowedly heterogeneous ruling alliance of intermediate classes if big business is ignored. We need to trace the process by which policy is initiated by, and benefits, a particular class fraction.

This is the objective of P.S. Jha's political economy of the period of stagnation in Indian development between 1965 and 1980. For Jha, the sole necessary precondition for ICs to flourish is the existence of pervasive *shortages* and consequently inflationary conditions. The response of ICs distinguishes them from the big bourgeoisie. ICs seek rent while the big bourgeoisie seek profit. Under conditions of 'shortage', the ICs can engage in mark-up pricing of their products. Small-scale business and traders can avoid central price controls by engaging in parallel trade and speculation, and by siphoning resources into the black economy. The small entrepreneur can gain directly from such activity, unlike the shareholder – or the manager – of a professionally managed company. Besides, the rich peasantry and proto-capitalist farmers who dominate the supply of the marketed surplus of food and agro-industrial raw materials manipulate the timing of their sales so as to benefit from shortages. Those who control that surplus are *also* the most self-sufficient households in terms of subsistence. In years of drought, peasants and their creditors make an absolute income gain from increases in official procurement prices and the even greater increases in the residual 'open' market prices due to the inelastic nature of demand for food grains, especially cereals. Meanwhile, public goods and services can be informally privatised as 'nice little earners' for public-sector employees. The numerically vast intermediate classes can thus direct state expenditure so as to favour their interests.

[14] Raj 1973; Namboodiripad 1973.

Jha gives policy examples from licensing and price controls.[15] Licensing (which was explicitly intended to prevent the excessive concentration of economic power, along with anti-monopoly provisions, reinforced by capacity constraints in the consumer industries) generated a bias against large-scale investment. Price controls on crucial intermediate goods such as cement, steel, non-ferrous metals, cotton textiles, coal and chemicals, and necessities such as food grains and edible oil, helped perpetuate the very shortages that originally inspired state intervention in price-setting, both by reducing supply incentives and by increasing leakages to the black market. The stage was set for smaller firms to proliferate. Meanwhile, the public sector, which suffered from chronically low-capacity utilisation (partly as a result of this informal competition), saw its profitability and thus its growth constrained by its high fixed costs.

Another example is directed credit. After bank nationalisation in 1969, lending was directed to 'priority areas'. By 1974, 33 per cent of bank advances were directed to 'agriculture, small-scale industry, small transport operators, small business and professional and self-employed persons' (Joshi and Little 1994, p. 134). These categories are almost identical to the 'intermediate classes' described by Jha. By 1985 the proportion had risen to 40 per cent. The beneficiaries of directed credit enjoyed subsidised interest, easy recourse to default and periodic, election-inspired loan write-offs, to such an extent that by 1994 three-quarters of regional banks had negative net worth.[16]

The State's policies systematically diverted investment away from areas of government control, from public and large-scale private enterprises, to small-scale industry and trade. Systematic biases in tariffs,

---

[15] Licensing created reservations exclusively for over 100 industries in the small-scale sector. Since bank nationalisation in 1969, credit and raw materials were targeted to the small-scale sector. The combination of striking over-achievement in targeted credit disbursement to a residual category of 'other', and virement from the remaining sectors of directed credit worked to the advantage of smaller and/or unregistered businesses. The prices of 84 major commodities were controlled, which reinforced the drift of capital from large- to small-scale industry and from industry to (parallel or black) trade. Rising costs squeezed formal sector profits and prevented an adequate provision for depreciation. Controls on steel, fertiliser, bulk drugs, shipbuilding and oil refining were based on 1971–72 prices and costs. Subsequent high inflation meant that by 1974 no single plant in these sectors was capable of earning even a 10 per cent return on capital. Inevitably, production was siphoned into the black market and to smaller scale production. Investment was diverted from productive activity to 'financing smuggling and into cornering stocks of goods in short supply' (Jha, 1980 p. 60). Another well-studied area where there is contradictory evidence for the capture of subsidies to small-scale industry by large capital in disguise *and* the successful dispersal of capital is the case of industrial estates – see the research on Vapi's engineering and chemicals cluster by Gorter (1997); see also Saith (2001) for a comprehensive historical analysis of policy for 'small-scale industry'.

[16] Joshi and Little 1994, pp. 34–6.

price controls and licensing affected the pattern of economic activity and the consequent distribution of economic gains. Licensing benefited small enterprises at the expense of the large business houses (such as the Birlas and Tatas). Price controls weighed down like heavy anticyclones on the commanding heights of the economy, but were easily avoided by small producers and traders in the less-pressured foothills. Government policy thus openly and systematically favoured the self-employed classes and they subsequently subverted policy to their further benefit through more or less organised and politicised corruption and clientelism. Borrowing from Kalecki, Jha concluded 'It is the rise to dominance of an intermediate class or stratum consisting of market orientated peasant proprietors, small manufacturers, traders and other self-employed groups which benefited from economic stagnation and had a vested interest in its perpetuation' (Jha 1980, p. vii).

Still pursuing Kalecki's model, but seeking to repair one of his omissions, we may say that the means whereby the intermediate classes achieve economic and political power are far from 'natural', but on the contrary are highly contrived. They rise to dominance not only through a marriage of convenience with the State but also through the particular way power is practised in and through markets.[17] Of all the groups listed by Jha, those making the highest rates of return are invariably merchants and trader–money-lenders.[18] We can take examples of elements of agricultural trade that are common to three different agrarian regions in India[19] to describe the politics of markets.

The politics of markets

A major political weapon is *non*-competition. Market structures that constrain competition are ubiquitous, masked by the appearance of crowding. Commercial capital is more highly concentrated than are agricultural assets. Taking agro-commerce; for example, the Gini coefficient for assets in the Coimbatore district in south India was found to be 0.66, for gross output 0.82 and for storage 0.92, whereas for land it was only 0.48.[20] An oligopolistic elite coexists with petty trade in complex marketing systems littered with brokers and giving a superficial impression of competitiveness. In reality, significant capital barriers, as well as

---

[17] See Chapter 5, on gender, for the governance structure and relations of firms.
[18] Harriss 1981, 1993; Harriss-White 1996a; Singh 1999.
[19] The paddy belt of West Bengal (Birbhum and Bardhaman Districts (Harriss 1993)), the Coromandel Plain of northern Tamil Nadu (North Arcot District (Harriss 1981)) and the precociously advanced agrarian region surrounding Coimbatore in south-west Tamil Nadu (Harriss-White 1996a).
[20] The index of inequality of distribution where 0.0 is equal and 1.0 completely unequal. See Harriss-White (1996a).

social barriers, deter entry to key points in these marketing systems.[21] Large firms generally *start* large. Traders compete over the exclusion of others, the defence of market shares and access to the State. *Non*-competition is effected by many other means. Network contracts, co-ordinated and repeated over time, lower risk and reduce the quantities of working capital needed. They are a non-competitive form of exchange. Sellers can also be tied by credit obligations, and by spatial micro-monopolies. Interlocked and triadic contracts (contracts between three parties)[22] limit or even exclude choice in the markets that are linked in this way.[23] Large firms may keep petty ones alive while at the same time preventing them from accumulating by controlling the terms and conditions of their acquisition of information, contacts, credit and storage.[24] Firms also reduce the transaction costs of making contracts by vertically integrating activities needed for inputs into the company. And whereas the everyday vernacular classification of firms according to their functions – for example, transport, ginning, wholesaling or whatever – might suggest that the activities fall into standard patterns, whenever they have been examined this has proved not to have been the case.[25] Instead, what we find is diversity, complexity and a tendency to *uniqueness*, so that the very notion of a 'market system' composed of comparable units becomes problematic. Indeed, this complexity and specificity may be understood as a form of reputational 'branding', an extreme form of market segmentation. However, by its means the marketing system as a whole is endowed with plasticity and resistance to environmental uncertainties and political or economic shocks.[26]

A second aspect of market politics is that the intermediate classes which operate in markets actively defend themselves against 'unfettered'/ bigger capital, sometimes openly aided by the State. One ploy is to concentrate on servicing separate, 'niched' product markets (for example, handloom textiles). Or, if they must compete directly in a given market (say rice, oil or tobacco), intermediate classes carve out one or more subsystems segmented by quality, itself the result of the alternative technologies used for processing the commodity in question. Local producers

---

[21] See Chapter 7.

[22] For instance, a water-seller forces a producer buying water to repay in rice to a trader who reimburses the water-seller in cash – see Janakarajan (1993).

[23] Their implications for efficiency, the main objective of the theoretical literature on contractual interlinkages, will be touched on in the conclusion to this chapter (and see Olsen 1996 for a review).

[24] Dasgupta (1992 pp. 166–7, p. 206) shows how *mahajans* – big traders – in West Bengal tie petty traders to specific sites that they control, thereby enabling them to reproduce their firms from day to day but not to accumulate.

[25] Harriss 1993; Harriss-White 1995a.

[26] Harriss-White 1995a.

can also undercut the costs of big capital by super-exploiting labour: both wage labour (by means of casual contracts, negligent health and safety conditions, long working days) and family labour (see Chapters 2 and 5). In other words, in many sectors of the Indian economy – in, for example, machine tools, textiles, carbonated soft drinks and most food staples – product markets are comprehensively sliced up by different technologies of production, different modes of organisation of labour, the size distribution of firms and by product type and quality.[27]

The power of the local elite is also consolidated by their manipulation of party politics. Political parties have rarely had consistent positions on private trade so it is more rational for merchants to fund all parties that are likely to achieve power (or to challenge merchants by trying to organise their labour) than to commit themselves to the politics of any one party. The intermediate classes do not hold themselves aloof from politics, but the way they exercise power is for the most part *not* through belonging to parties. They wield power collusively, in overlapping organisations of diverse kinds: cultural, co-operative and philanthropic, as well as trade associations. The latter are often organised in response to threatening changes in policy by the State. Having been called into life, they can develop a vital self-regulatory role and can enforce the selective exclusion or participation of smaller traders (see Chapter 7). They can wring concessions from the State. Their politics is reactive, defensive and opportunistic, and, when federated, their elastic reach extends to the state and national capitals.

A fourth kind of market politics is that the contracts on which local market operations are based are largely enforced by social rules rather than state sanctions. The family is one arena of rules and control. Locally specific ethical values also underlie the norms of the commercial economy[28] and are able to exclude outsiders from it (see Chapter 6). The vast majority of contracts are still oral, cemented through tight networks based on repeated transactions and protected by high non-economic barriers.[29] Ascribed characteristics (family, caste and locality) are only slowly being replaced by acquired characteristics (efficiency and reliability), most obviously among the local agents of global capital and in long-distance trade, though even the latter may be struc-

---

[27] J. Harriss 1980, 1981; Harriss-White 1996a; Silberstein 1997; Sriskandarajah 1997.

[28] Generalised morality is not necessary for trade. See the debate between Platteau (1993, 1994) (who argues it is) and Moore (1994); on socially specific ethics see Ramanujam (1990), and on case material from agro-commerce for context-specific ethical norms see Harriss-White (1996b and c).

[29] Repeated transactions and delays in payment require trust. Relations of individual trust between trading parties are found to be associated with risk-taking and expansion of business territory. Widespread trust in political institutions is associated with co-operative activity and use of state development institutions. Failures of either kind of trust jeopardise their outcomes (Dasgupta 1992; Luhrmann 1979, pp. 39–61).

tured by interlocking networks. Reputation is an indispensable political resource in both the informal and the black economies; and since the reputation of a trader can be inherited by his sons, they may prefer to accept quite oppressive relations inside a family business rather than leaving and thereby risking a breach with the father that forfeits the legacy of his business reputation. Oppressive relations may be preferred to the consequences of its loss. Contract enforcement also takes the form of sheer physical coercion. The use of this crude form of power has expanded noticeably in the 1990s, and takes forms ranging from mobile loan-enforcement agents, who use motorbikes to cruise the country-side, to armed squads and organised criminal protection forces with international scope.

There are, then, very good reasons to reject Kalecki's assumption that the rise to power of the intermediate classes is 'natural'.[30] The interface between the State and the economy is not a neat fault line but a 'spong-iform' terrain in which the intermediate classes consolidate themselves, above all in the informal and black economies. It has been objected that ICs show no signs of concerted class action, relying instead on particularistic tactics.[31] But the mass reliance by this class coalition on such tactics *is* a generalised characteristic of their politics. The outcome threatens and redefines the State's official development project. The State's bureaucratic elites, where not themselves implicated in similar systems of tribute, investment and consumption, have distractedly overlooked the political accommodation between intermediate classes and the huge mass of their local 'subalterns'.[32] The State is accountable, certainly, but accountable to local capital.

Shortcomings of the 'intermediate classes' analysis

The Kalecki–Jha analysis of classes in Indian development has two kinds of weakness: empirical and theoretical.

Historical shortcomings

First, on the historical and empirical side, Jha, like Raj, may have underestimated the importance of big capital in the Indian economy, though the data are not conclusive. Between 1972 and 1978 the top 20 Indian business houses appeared to increase their control of 'total productive capital'

[30] See McCartney and Harriss-White (2000) for an elaboration.
[31] Streefkerk (1978, p. 306), quoted in Gorter (1997, p. 83).
[32] In India, then, intermediate capitalists therefore do not have to enter politics directly in order to protect their portfolios and privilege themselves. Elsewhere in Asia – for example, in Thailand – it has been necessary for capitalists to protect themselves through formal entry into party politics (Khan 1997, 2000b; Rutten and Upadhya 1997).

in the private sector from 61 per cent to no less than 87 per cent.[33]
Between 1980–01 and 1990–01, however, according to data gathered by
the Centre for Monitoring the Indian Economy (CMIE), while the gross
value added (GVA) by the entire factory sector rose from Rs 12.6 crores to
28.5 crores, that in the non-factory sector rose from Rs 9.5 to 17.6 crores.
Throughout this later period the non-factory sector amounted to roughly
40 per cent of total industrial GVA. Within the factory sector, firms with
more than 1000 workers contributed only about 25 per cent of its GVA. So
firms with under 1000 workers, many of which have *far* fewer than 1000
workers, may contribute as much as 85 per cent of total industrial GVA.[34]
A further set of questions about big capital's party and non-party politics,
about the tensions over market shares where intermediate classes compete
directly with big national capital, and about how their mutual interests are
accommodated are left unresolved in IC theory.

Second, Jha ignores the paradoxical politics of policy implementation
in which policy may be transformed out of all recognition.[35] One example
is policies officially aimed at protecting specific subsets of small industry
through planning, capacity controls and licensing. On the ground, this
policy is frequently emasculated through the 'indirect power of quiet sabotage and everyday forms of resistance by local power groups'[36] (Bhagwati 1993, p. 329). The implementing and regulatory agencies may be
captured to establish unplanned or 'less small' industry; or to let the sub-
sidiaries of big companies grab state-subsidised infrastructure; or to
divert subsidies to trade and money-lending; or by using persuasion to
prevent enforcement and vigilance; or by simply evading the law and
securing *ex post* amnesties for doing so.[37] This kind of politics works in
favour of Jha's case in the short term, but against it in the long term, since
the 'nutrient base' devoured by it is not infinite.

Third, Jha does not sufficiently explain why – as he sees it – corruption
reduces growth. It is clear that it must do so primarily through causing
inflation and stagnation; second, through fraud and tax evasion that
deprive the State of developmental resources; and third, through the lack
of any necessary correlation between capacity to bribe on the one hand
and productive, growth-inducing efficiency on the other.[38] Yet the case of
the East Asian 'tigers' shows that this is not necessarily true everywhere,
at least not in the short term. Khan, reviewing the record of South Korea,

---

[33] Sandarasa 1991.
[34] CMIE 1994, Tables 8.14, 8.6 and 8.7. I am grateful to P.S. Jha for pointing these tables
out.
[35] The phrase is Kaviraj's (1988).
[36] A theme developed in Chapter 4 on the local State.
[37] Bardhan, 1998 p. 43; Byres 1996a, p. 67.
[38] Guhan 1997, p. 14.

concludes that corruption will speed growth if dysfunctional economic regulations are evaded or if productive rights are transferred to those able to invest efficiently.[39] So the undoubted corruption of the intermediate classes in India is not a *sufficient* cause of stagnation.

Theoretical problems

First, with respect to the theoretical difficulties with a ruling coalition of intermediate classes, Jha analyses these disparate forces but ignores conflict within the coalition. He also ignores the economic consequences of such conflict. The tremors, earthquakes and faults *within* the dominant classes have been dissected by Bardhan.[40] His conception of how the dominant class coalition is composed differs from Kalecki–Jha's, being made up of the proprietary class of the State/intelligentsia, the industrial bourgeoisie and rich farmers. Bardhan also draws important inferences from the fact that their interests conflict: '(w)hen diverse elements of the loose and uneasy coalition of the dominant classes pull in different directions and when none of them is individually strong enough to dominate the process of resource allocation, one predictable outcome is the proliferation of grants and subsidies to placate all of them' (1992, p. 321). This is a useful connection to the thesis of the 'intermediate regime', because whereas regulatory intervention was a striking characteristic of the period before the 1980s, Bardhan's focus is on the later period in which the growth of subsidies became a marked and growing characteristic of Indian state expenditure. Yet it is easy to forget that the huge raft of regulative intervention floated on in this latter period, and much floats on to this day. Bardhan's 'proprietary class' does exercise an important control over parts of the national economy but is a tiny minority, whereas Jha focuses on the numerical majority and its influence on the practice of politics. Bardhan, for his part, ignores class struggles taking place outside the ruling coalition. Furthermore, he does not explain why the State does not use what he has suggested is its relatively autonomous position *vis-à-vis* the industrial bourgeoisie and the big farmers to promote an independent developmental project, and indeed even ignores some evidence that it has done so.[41]

---

[39] Khan 2000b, pp. 95–8.

[40] Bardhan 1984.

[41] Evidence for the developmental nature of the India State would include the Green Revolution in the 1960s, the rise in savings and investment ratios since Independence, the maintenance of low inflation, and the autonomy of top leadership, which was able to shift regulatory ideology as early as 1985. Jha also ignores the evidence. For both protagonists in this later round of the debate ignited by Raj and Namboodiripad, the (weak) existing evidence does not help their cases.

Second, while the contradiction between interests of the 'intermediate classes' and those of working people in the examples we have mentioned is consistent with Jha's analysis, the contradiction between the interests of the 'intermediate' classes and those of big capital is not what Kalecki imagined. In India, as we have seen, the economies of scale achieved in large enterprises do not threaten petty capitalists unless both fractions of capital produce the same or closely substitutable commodities. Only where such direct competition is unavoidable does the coalition of the intermediate classes appear to be a potential constraint on the accumulative drive of large-scale capital.

Yet ICs are not big businesses in miniature and big capital may still be challenged by intermediate capital for several reasons. First, economies of scale accrue at high levels of capacity utilisation and big business has found these extremely difficult to achieve. By contrast, the intermediate classes use technologies that break even at much lower capacity, and they are in the position to organise the often-seasonal supply of agricultural raw materials in such a way as to enable higher capacity utilisation (if necessary breaking storage control laws in the process). In so doing they deprive larger capital of capacity-increasing supplies.[42] Second, the numerical significance and far more extensive spatial dispersion of intermediate capital allow it to accommodate itself more easily to, and to gain more concessions from, the State than big capital can.[43] Small capital is also often found acting as the agent for either large capital or the State under advantageous contracts that significantly reduce the risk to the agent. Operating 'passively' as an agent allows them to shift their working capital between a range of alternative uses and thus expand output, essentially financed by those they are contracted to.[44]

Third, even though big/corporate capital undeniably evades tax, it is easier to locate for tax purposes than are millions of scattered businesses. Fourth, there are economic sectors where big business, employing unionised labour with enforceable rights at work and rights to social security, is comprehensively undercut by the labour forces of ICs, which have no such rights and are even more undercut by unwaged family labour.[45] Fifth, the self-employed and small businessmen can evade

[42] Mani 1991; Harriss 1993.
[43] Baru argues a strong case for the reverse, that 'regionally based' capital suffers from lack of access to the key resources of licences and permits doled out at the Centre (2000, pp. 222–3). Our evidence here and in Chapter 4 shows that the regional and local State has had, and still has, many controls and powerful incentives to be receptive to lobbying by ICs.
[44] Mooij 1999.
[45] Indeed, since the 1970s big business has been hell-bent on informalising its labour through casualisation and subcontracting to ICs (Harriss-White and Gooptu 2000).

central price controls and reap direct gains from speculation (in the black economy). Retail shareholders and professional managers of an incorporated company cannot do this.[46]

In the intermediate classes, accumulation is paradoxically both highly dispersed and highly concentrated. It is highly dispersed when judged by the capital concentrations in the formal economy and in the public sector. It is this high degree of dispersal of capital and technology that enables intermediate classes not only to be functionally useful to big capital, but also and more seriously to constrain it. It is highly concentrated when judged by the distribution of assets *within* the intermediate classes, not to mention in comparison with assetless labour.

The relevance to the economy of the 88% of the theory of intermediate classes

One more criticism of Jha's combination of Kalecki's theory of the intermediate regime with the analysis of India's 'scarcity' is that it is ultimately merely a special case of the so-called new political economy (NPE),[47] which seeks to identify economic distortions, and then the interest groups that benefit and subsequently have a built-in incentive to perpetuate and propagate them, at the expense of collective rationality and efficiency, or the 'public good'. It is true that NPE economists such as Jagdish Bhagwati can sound very much like Jha. For them, the villains are 'the politicians who profit from the corruption, the bureaucrats who enjoy the power, the businessmen and workers who like sheltered markets and squatters' rights' (Bhagwati 1993, p. 53). The fact is that in a polity as complex as that of India it is not possible for a single political economy to account for every question. In the face of this critical fire, the Kalecki–Jha theory has a phoenix-like resilience. Let us examine some of the reasons why.

Unlike the mode of reasoning deployed in NPE, in which political and social factors are treated merely as given parameters of the economic system, Jha's approach is historical and dialectical. Not only does he link policy outcomes to vested interests but he also shows how policies react back on the relative power positions of these fractions;[48] and further, how

---

[46] Promoter families reap other kinds of primitive gain (see Banaji and Mody 2001).

[47] Toye 1993. Indeed, Toye dismisses Jha's evidence as having done no more than added price controls to fine-tune Krueger's framework of rent-seeking.

[48] The case study is of the power loom sector, gaining from a loophole of regulations to protect small-scale weaving. Power loom interests and Jat farmers from Uttar Pradesh infiltrated the Congress Party, who generated a political representative in Charan Singh who continued to protect them under the Janata regime (1977–80).

unintended outcomes (or even – those taboo subjects – outright policy mistakes) can lead to the defence and protection of the distorted incentives that created them.[49] Moreover, Jha's State and markets are *real:* embedded in class configurations that have been welded together by shortages. They are not the abstract autonomous entities that figure in the formulations of writers on India's political economy, all the way from Bardhan (1984) to Joshi and Little (1994).

Jha's political economy also gives rise to two important hypotheses. First, it implies that the precondition for liberalisation must be the formation of a new class alliance stronger than that of the intermediate classes. Second, it suggests a plausible explanation for Indian inflation paranoia.[50] If the structure of regulation established under the 'intermediate regime' is broken, then inflation will no longer be offset by a growing budget deficit. Rising levels of inflation will have to be accepted by vulnerable segments of the population for a reason much more convincing than those proposed by either orthodox Marxists or orthodox development economists.[51] The orthodox Marxist explanation for the budget deficits that threw India into the arms of the IMF in 1991 is that the State was unable to impose direct taxes on property owners.[52] Conversely, liberal economists argue that the deficits reflected sheer demand overload and the breakdown of 'accommodative' politics.[53] In these explanations, inflation is an *outcome.* Jha's mode of analysis reverses this line of causation. Inflation causes the deficit to increase *because of* the structure of policy-making in an intermediate regime. Inflation results from *scarcity-inducing* shocks of various kinds (the droughts of 1964–66, 1973–77, 1979–80; the oil price rises; and the radical rightward ideological shift in policy in 1989–90, which has its own semi-autonomous history).[54]

Nowhere can the mechanism be better seen than in the foundation of the Indian economy; that is, staple foods. The fact that the demand for food grains is inelastic means that in years of scarcity both state procurement and state expenditure on the public distribution system rise disproportionately while there are also hikes in open market prices.[55] Inflation

---

[49] See Toye 1993, p. 160. The evidence is for responses to unexpected shocks – controls on essential commodities and on exchange deadlines in the 1950s resulting respectively from an ideological shift and an international trade shock – after which the patterns of profits gave intermediate classes a vested interest in the perpetuation of the system.

[50] With its 10 per cent critical threshold.

[51] See McCartney and Harriss-White (2000) for a critical treatment of the evidence for this argument.

[52] Patnaik 1997.

[53] See the discussion in Roy 1996.

[54] Pedersen (2000) is useful on this history.

[55] Most grain, when procured by the State, is purchased from traders not farmers (to reduce the costs of acquisition). Traders make losses on sales to state trading corporations. They sell their residual grain at higher prices, legitimately to compensate (see Harriss, 1984a).

follows these price rises. Black-marketing and tax evasion follow the widening gap between state-administered fixed maximum prices and open market ones. A rise in prices causes a disproportionate increase in government expenditure not only because of the size of the food subsidy but also because the State is the employer of last resort and state employees are protected by 'dearness allowances' to offset inflation in the cost of living.[56] Revenues are pinched while expenditure is forced to expand. Subsidies on electricity, fertiliser, diesel and food cannot be easily abolished. Inflation is a lesser evil than mounting debt. The State reacts to the deficit by cutting capital expenditure or allowing inflation free rein, or both.

This *real* structural adjustment long preceded the IMF-imposed one of the 1990s (see Chapter 4). The casualties of this inflation-induced process are state accumulation and economic growth. The intermediate classes are enabled to go on feeding off the conditions created by scarcity and encouraged by the structure of regulation, but in constantly aggravating scarcity they bring about an eventual crisis in the economy. Scarcity becomes a luxury no one else can finally afford. Kalecki saw the intermediate regime as vulnerable to pressures from foreign capital or feudal elements, rather than to the self-defeating nature of its own economic strategy, but Jha's judgement is explicit: 'the intermediate class fattens on the debilitation of the economy' (Jha 1980, p. 121).

Structural threats to the 'intermediate regime'

Now we turn to the role of the 'intermediate classes' in the recent era of unprecedented challenge to their power. By 1990 India had already lost all of Kalecki's preconditions for the intermediate classes to rule: the collapse of non-alignment (following the collapse of the USSR in 1989); the inexorable pressure from global market forces and the 'Washington consensus' from the early 1980s onwards, to dilute state capitalism, transform the structure of regulation, and to compress state spending; and, finally, also to abandon the 'developmental state'.[57] The State reeled *not* so much from strangulation by poor revenue mobilisation (though the structure of revenue is odd – with a slender direct tax base and only 8–11 million out of an eligible pool of about 200 million actually paying income tax through the last 15 years of the century). Instead, it was fatally hobbled by debt and the growth of unproductive expenditures, prominent among which were interest payments.

---

[56] Public-sector employment rose from 7 million (58 per cent of the organised sector) in 1960–01 to 18.3 million (71 per cent of the organised sector) in 1998, and was 17 million in the late 1990s (Panini 1996, pp. 48–9; Banik 1999, p. 5). Capital-intensive, heavy-industrial, planned growth has a low employment elasticity.

[57] Kumar 1999, p. 77.

Other factors *not* theorised by Kalecki, however – structural changes in the Indian economy – had also created a set of new class forces with the potential to challenge the power of the still numerically dominant 'intermediate classes'. The Gulf War oil shock of 1991, which initiated the switch to liberalisation, was simply a contingent trigger that these underlying structural changes made effective.[58] Three of the most important changes can be noted here:

International capital

It is generally argued that India's fiscal deficit led to its current account deficit; that is, in the 1980s the growing balance of payments deficit was generated domestically.[59] But international capital played a role that is neglected in this account.[60] In the 1980s access to international finance became easier, so that non-inflationary growth could be financed by borrowing abroad. Global institutions with growing volumes of money to lend were looking for areas into which to spread their portfolios. Their willingness to finance the current account deficit encouraged liberalisation and *this* encouraged financial profligacy.[61] As a result the balance of payments became more complex (it was no longer just the difference between imports and exports, but now included the disequilibrium between foreign debt and current income as well). As capital expenditure – and interest rates – became increasingly affected by international confidence in the exchange value of the rupee, the writing was on the wall for state capitalism and national planning, as the downgrading of India's credit rating in early 1991 confirmed.

'Marketising' India

Under an 'intermediate regime', markets come to be regulated in the interests of its heterogeneous classes through state capitalism (in Kalecki's model) or through the creation of shortages (in Jha's) or both. A new wave of marketisation, by challenging both of these mechanisms, also challenged the interests they served. As early as the late Indira period, the early 1980s, marketisation had been initiated (for example, through the delicensing of 32 groups of industry and the removal of investment limits, the reduction of domestic entry barriers and increased competition in domestic industry) and the proprietorial use by pro-

[58] The shock of the Gulf War on oil prices amounted to some $3.3 billion, jerking the balance of payments deficit to $8–10 billion (Herring 1999).

[59] See Joshi and Little (1994) for an influential example.

[60] See, by way of contrast, Amin (2002); Chandrasekhar and Ghosh (1993, p. 667).

[61] The 'Rajiv boom' of the 1980s in which foreign credit was not always put to productive use.

moter-families of their so-called corporate capital had received its first international challenges. Technology imports were liberalised and indicators of efficiency (particularly the productivity of labour) perked up.[62] A dramatic shift – already well advanced in the 1980s – was consolidated in the focus of investment towards industries in which India was seen as having a historical comparative advantage, in skill- and labour-intensive industries such as clothing, jewellery, gems, handicrafts, agro-industries, computer software and light engineering.

The consolidation of the 'middle class'

The 'middle class', a fashionable category defined by relatively high income, 'modern professions' and their correlates – mainly import-intensive, high-tech/highly branded private consumption goods[63] – swelled from an estimated 60–80 million urban people in the mid-1980s to a (probably overestimated) figure of about 300 million in the mid-1990s.[64] The expansion of the stock market in the 1980s[65] created an important structural link between these middle classes and the big bourgeoisie, the professional intelligentsia and the cream of the agricultural capitalists, who all shared a common interest in consumption and were united in opposition to the tricks of scarcity creation at which the intermediate classes were so adept.

These powerful countervailing forces would seem to spell the end of the 'intermediate regime'. However, although there is some important evidence which suggests that the relative economic power of the intermediate classes has weakened, it would be premature to organise a wake for them.

State resources

If 'intermediate classes' thrive on a structure of regulation that has a heavy emphasis – in practice if not in theory – on trade and distribution, its dismantling should lead to a shift away from trade and towards production. Profits and revenue will rise as a result not only of 'informalisation' (that is, the movement of formally regulated activities into the

---

[62] Ahluwalia 1992; Jalan 1992; Nagaraj 1994.

[63] Chandrasekhar and Patnaik 1995. Other correlates are 'lifestyle' and attitudes (Sunder Rajan 1993), consumption patterns and the possession of modest consumer durables (Shurmer-Smith 2000, pp. 28–46) and 'entrepreneurship' (Panini, 1996, p. 47), though Panini attributes these traits to socialist development and the leading role of the public sector.

[64] The three estimates are, respectively, from Kohli (1990); Dubey (1992), quoted in Corbridge and Harriss (2000) and Stein (1998, p. 394). They contrast markedly with NCAER's 1996 estimate that only under 1 million are in the market for BMW and Mercedes cars and that some 75 million alone have incomes in excess of Rs 70 000 a year (Shurmer-Smith 2000, pp. 30–1).

[65] Baru 2000, pp. 222–3.

informal sector), but also of the incorporation of unproductive and black activity into new recorded and taxable forms. And in the early 1990s part of the regulative structure – that of tax – was altered; tax rates were cut across the board.[66] Indeed, there was a persistent rise in the share of revenue from direct taxes (though not enough to compensate for the cuts in indirect taxes). But revenue elasticities do not necessarily relate directly to income tax cuts. The effect of tax cuts on revenues in India was not necessarily through increased effort (as is theorised for OECD countries). Revenue growth in India is at least equally attributable to policy changes that enabled the reclassification of some of the undeclared productive industrial activity to contribute to statistics on growth.[67]

Countervailing forces

New fractions of capital gained strength relative to the intermediate classes: through liberalisation, tax cuts, privatisation, reforms to the external accounts, the enmeshment of the State in markets (notably those for money), stagnation in public investment, the shifting of basic infrastructural provision to the (increasingly international) private sector, and stagnation in employment creation. The tax system was changed so that small businesses and the self-employed were now presumed to have a tax liability, at a fixed rate, so as to reduce non-compliance and detection costs. This was a direct attack on the 'intermediate classes'.[68] The limited attempts made to reform the agricultural sector[69] constituted another, very much less powerful, but nonetheless direct attack.

Inflation

Once the structure of policy that supported the 'intermediate classes' had started to be unwound, inflation was tolerated. By 1994–95, prices were still rising at about 10 per cent, despite a run of average-to-good monsoons and 30 million tonnes of food grains in reserve. Inflation ran at perhaps as much as 11 per cent for agricultural labourers and 13 per cent for industrial workers.[70]

[66] See the data in Bagchi (1994) and Chakraborty (1997).
[67] Kumar 1999, pp. 130–4.
[68] A formula was applied to the section of the salariat owning a house, car, telephone and/ or credit card to draw them into the tax net.
[69] Cuts in public infrastructure, fertiliser subsidies and directed credit intending to remove the cushion to agricultural capital by removing price distortions, but, except the first, hedged and mitigated in practice.
[70] Government claims that inflation was reduced to 2–3 per cent per annum by the end of 1999 came in for severe criticism on grounds of selectivity, both of evidence and of base lines. See Venkatesh Athreya (reporting in *Frontline*, 20 November 1999, p. 109).

What is striking about the effect of each of these changes is that they could all be predicted from the Kalecki–Jha theory. Although it certainly does not account for all the power relations underpinning national capitalist development, it does account for much of the class nature of the Indian local economy over several decades, and also yields a series of successful predictions, including that of the conditions of its own destruction. But what do the intermediate classes look like now in their new situation of what at first sight seems to be one of political and economic decay?

The demise of the 'intermediate regime'?

There are several ways of looking at this process, and all have some merit. For a start the formal institutions of Indian democracy and the State have experienced – as a result of the processes described above – what has been variously called 'political decay', 'fragmentation', 'cleavage', 'refracturing' or 'political awakening'.[71] We saw that the economic idiom of political appeasement in the 1980s, 'the proliferation of subsidies and grants' (Bardhan 1988, p. 218), is conventionally invoked as the reason for the problem that is now said to be 'solved' by liberalisation. The 'solution' can be seen as a *reduction* in the rewards to political power, replacing both state-led 'development' and patronage by a lean, technocratic, night-watching, minimally regulative State that diverts entrepreneurship and accumulation away from 'the State' and back to 'the market'. This is what is meant by 'removing the economy from politics', stopping the State from being used as a means of accumulation. But political parties, mobilised around language, caste, religion and region, now compete for what is left. Where lower castes have gained through education, job-reservation and employment in the public sector or through employment in the non-farm economy (operating in some places according to new social rules), local propertied elites mount a political reaction to their disenfranchisement, in some cases openly resorting to violence.[72] Further, there is a mass of case material showing the many ways that fall short of open, organised violence, yet that are suggestive of local regimes of intensified accumulative pressure during the era of liberalisation.

[71] The phrases are respectively from Kohli (1990); Stein (1998); Yadav (1996).

[72] See the Chunduru case study in Andhra Pradesh in 1991 (Kannabiran and Kannabiran 1991). See also the caste-based violence in southern Tamil Nadu and regular outbursts in Bihar. Other kinds of political reaction to disenfranchisement have high developmental opportunity costs: the cost to the State of maintaining a substantial part of the Indian army 'on alert' in Kashmir and the north-east States. Some Marxists see in such violence the failure of prevailing values and ideologies to legitimise the existing division of labour. Political parties have failed to accommodate the social classes generated by economic development. Other sites of politicised mass violence are in cities and industrial areas – epicentres of big capital and organised labour (Mukhajan et al. 1994, p. 1112).

Where liberalisation threatens the nexus between local capital and the local State, or makes it no longer such a generous source of rents, there are many signs that it is replaced by primitive business practices. Of course, the evidence for this, drawn from 'field economics', cannot sustain arguments about its quantitative importance. Nor is it clear whether these new processes of accumulation are frittered away in consumption, or fuel new production. But the evidence is very extensive. Our particular list comes from businesses in a small south Indian town between 1994 and 1997:[73]

1   economic misdemeanours of all sorts: adulteration, arbitrary deductions, tampering with weights, measures and quality standards, forging price or brand labels, forging tickets of all sorts; the under-declaration of turnover to owners by managers, the appropriation of returns, false muster rolls;

2   economic crimes such as theft, fraud, unlicensed activity, tapping of electricity and TV cables, grossly physically polluting activity;

3   'mafianisation': organised crime based on the privatisation of physical security measures concentrated in sectors such as finance (in the black economy), the wholesaling of food grains (in which credit is subject to complex contracts festooned with extra-economic, intangible conditions) and transport (now needing personal protection services for owners);[74]

4   the evasion of tax by a great variety of means (under-declaration, under-billing, unlicensed operation, collective negotiation, pre-emptive investment (in firms that fall below the tax thresholds, using untaxed spare parts, and so on). This type of loss to the State has been estimated as being about 20 times more important quantitatively than are leakages due to corruption;[75]

5   the continual oppressive treatment of labour (through wage rates; the composition and timing of wages; the casualisation of contracts; the extension of the working day; the use of children; the poor quality or non-provision of basic sanitation, health and safety precautions) and the weakening and crushing of their organisations.[76]

Braudel dismissed these kinds of tactics as 'elementary fraud' (1982, p. 55). Other writers on accumulation (such as those of the 'Emilia-

---

[73] Harriss-White 1996d; Basile and Harriss-White 2000.

[74] See Janakarajan (1993). Note that interlocked/triadic contracts are not an exclusive character of backward agriculture. More generally, the economic role of a contract cannot be deduced from the mere fact of its existence (Harriss-White 1996c).

[75] Roy 1996.

[76] See Harriss-White and Gooptu (2000) for a review.

Romagna' school, which studies industrial districts, and which we will meet in Chapter 8) ignore such practices, celebrating instead the indispensability of the factors of trust and reputation in the operation of local economic elites. Yet elementary fraud and trust are not incompatible, just as competition is not incompatible with collective action. Trust and reputation may be enjoyed among peers, while 'elementary fraud' and crime are practical weapons used against the State, labour and poor consumers.

In practice, control of the economy is being wrenched with the greatest difficulty from the 'intermediate classes'. There is, for example, considerable inertia and indecision in tackling the very largest state transfers – the subsidies on fertiliser, food grains, electricity and credit – regardless of whether the subsidy is controlled by the central or state governments.[77] And even if the economy *were* being effectively removed from control by elected politicians by liberalisation, this does not mean that it would be removed from *politics* – if by 'politics' is understood the real power relations at work in the economy. In reality, the market economy seethes with non-party politics, at the least in four interrelated ways.[78] First, the politics of market structure has been discussed earlier (pp. 50–3). Second, the politics of organisation – both formal collective institutions and informal networks – which will be discussed in Chapters 6 to 8 on religion, caste and space. Third, the politics of 'social embeddedness' – that is, the influence on market structure and behaviour of the social order and ideology – will be the focus of Chapters 5 and 6 on gender and religion. The last is state power, which is the focus of the next chapter, but is so crucial to an understanding of the persistence of intermediate classes under threat that some elaboration is needed here.

The State 'saturates' markets in two ways. One is directly through state production, trading, storage, transport and credit.[79] This is the part of the State most vulnerable to privatisation. Research on every kind of

---

[77] The slow and erratic nature of the process of liberalisation has been explained in at least five ways: (1) the politically unstable conditions in which it has taken place with direction from several parties/coalitions; (2) resistance from the States to reforms in sectors under their constitutional control; (3) coalition politics that sets constraints on action other than issues on which there is a consensus (that is, low-priority issues move to the top of the political agenda); (4) liberalisation as a symbolic mask for another political project – a Hindu nationalist one that requires liberalisation to move slowly; (5) deliberate stealth given the interests squared against it (see Corbridge and Harriss 2000, chapters 6 and 7). In this process the economic has been removed discursively from politics in the sense that election agendas prioritise identity, national security and control over the means of repression to the neglect of infrastructural resources, water, food scarcities and the gap in development between the north and the south. But the economy, and the role of the public sector in it, then become arenas of *non*-party politics.

[78] We are using the classification of the politics of markets developed first by Gordon White (1993).

[79] Harriss 1984a; Harriss-White 1996c.

state intervention affecting agricultural trade and agro-industry in two districts in south India showed that all these measures, from the 1940s to the present, were officially intended to reduce the power of private capital. Each institution established for this purpose then expanded in regulative scope, resources and manpower, became puffed up with technological gigantism and finally settled into position in the hierarchy of bureaucratic power. Some were intended to make profits and have not (famously, co-operatives, textile mills and trading corporations); others have made profits for unintended reasons (for example, storage corporations and regulated marketplaces).[80] The outcomes of this direct state trading have rarely been as predicted. Liberalisation, however, has hardly touched these institutions and organisations.

The second way the State 'saturates' the markets is by means of regulative law and institutions, which set long, crenellated boundaries between State and market, boundaries that involve almost every department of government. This arena of market politics is even less vulnerable to reform. The State defines goods that can and cannot be traded (so that new goods and services – such as courier services, computer keyboard skilling centres, cable TV installation – are often temporarily outside the regulative law). It regulates technologies that may or may not be used, for instance, in food-processing.[81] It controls the rights to exchange property by means of trade and also price ceilings for some essential commodities (including basic food, drugs and freight).[82] It sets quality and safety standards, identifies sites and times for market exchange to take place and on paper it ensures the public health environment. It sets eligibility criteria for actors, can legitimate contracts, set rules for liability and penalties for delinquency. It regulates information and advertising, and last but not least, the terms and conditions of work. Every one of these aspects listed can be and is actively contested. This regulative kaleidoscope is implemented in a myriad ways that distort the officially intended aim – with neglect (for example, in overlooking the exploitation of child labour), extreme regional unevenness (for example, agricultural market regulation), with sabotage and capture by traders (for example, with respect to storage, co-operation, targeted credit, or the Factories Acts labour laws), the exchange of threats for bribes (for example, in the case of licensing), with evasion by powerful traders and the selective imposi-

---

[80] Harriss 1985.

[81] See Harriss and Kelly (1982) for rice and oil. For rice the technology most appropriate for rural conditions has been outlawed for the last quarter century – see Pacey and Payne (1984) for the reasons why.

[82] See Mooij's (1999) study of the Essential Commodities Act.

tion of the law on weak ones (storage controls again), and with the co-option of private capital by the State (for example, in agro-processing).

Often regulative law is successively amended in ways that throw up contradictions and that, in an effort apparently to increase its transparency, actually increase its opacity.[83] Anyway, the law is better specified than enforcement agencies are resourced. Direct state participation and regulative law are thus not parametric frameworks (as mainstream economics assumes), they are arenas of political contest that can weaken the administrative legitimacy of the State. As a result, hybrid property relations and forms of enforcement proliferate, not only benignly through kinship, collective action and social networks, but also savagely, via novel contractual arrangements involving private protection forces. And, in the absence of state regulation, other institutions step in. At the level of the firm, for example, the family form of organisation and local contractual routines protect it against external threats. Collective action by traders or producers ensures the collective ownership and maintenance of sites, insurance, protection of property, economies of scale, the reduction of transaction costs and the resolution of disputes (see Chapters 6 and 7 on religion and caste). At the same time, collective action can erect barriers to entry and foster collusion, and can impose extra-legal and oppressive penalties on outsiders. Registered or unregistered, these practices and institutions exist in profusion. Regulation is, then, multi-layered, unsystematic and idiosyncratic, and often serves narrow institutional interests. Mushtak Khan has termed it all a *clientelist* State, in which the power of political and bureaucratic patrons to create developmental rents is still continually contested by more powerful clients representing local capital and – in his formulation – riddled with factions. The outcome is the political preservation of a structure of rents, in markets and in the State, which do not serve the developmental purpose for which they were intended.[84]

The disentangling of regulative politics from the management of the economy can benefit big capital at the apex of the economy.[85] This policy line has been favoured by all the major party political alignments (except the left) at the centre. Lower level fractions of capital, which have been able to secure these forms of collusively implemented 'partial intervention', have no interest in liberalisation. They do not benefit directly from liberalisation, do not get liberalisation and do not need political parties as

---

[83] See Harriss-White (1996c) for the Regulated Markets Acts, and Mooij (1999) for the Essential Commodities Act.

[84] Khan 2000b, pp. 91–5.

[85] But not in cases such as fertiliser in which production has benefited from subsidies at the same time as suffering from controls on capacity, quantities and technologies.

their instruments. 'It does not matter whether Ravana rules or Rama rules', goes the saying. They play their part in qualifying liberalisation by diverting resources into the black economy.[86] It is hardly surprising that with the exception of aerated cool drinks, certain medical drugs, cosmetics (much subject to counterfeiting) and transport, liberalisation has been slow to take root in these sectors of the economy. Even if it were to take root and even if local firms were to develop as agents of multinational capital, the non-party-political nexus of local economic power would still survive in most of the ways we have described. Unless deregulation were to be accompanied by countervailing forces capable of regulating capital in the interests of society at large, deregulated markets could well become more rather than less unruly than 'regulated' ones.[87] It is also hardly surprising that research showed that the bulk of the Indian population at the turn of the millennium did not know that the economy was being reformed.[88]

Upper fractions of the ICs and regionally based 'non-monopoly' capital may develop a new set of interests – in regional stock exchanges, regional lobbies and regional political parties – in order to compete with apex 'monopoly' capital. In seeking foreign collaboration above the heads of 'monopoly' capital, they are assisted by liberalisation.[89] These interests do not harm those of the lower fractions of the ICs.

Although the homogeneity of interest and the relative strength of the composite 'intermediate classes' decline as the economy grows, becomes complex and globalises, the ICs are still a numerically powerful coalition. While the economy changes around them they persist. It is wrong to assume them to be 'transient' or 'transitional'.[90] Their ranks are perpetually renewed by entrants drawn from lower and lower castes (see Chapter 7 on caste). While some members of these classes may support the casteist and economic-nationalist project of *Swadeshi* (against international capital, against wage labour and consumers) and the ambivalently casteist and Hindu supremacist project of *Hindutva*, neither *Swadeshi* nor *Hindutva* are *necessary* to the 'intermediate classes'. They are simply *consistent* with their interests (see the Appendix 1 for an elaboration of this point).

Since the 1990s, a new wave of 'primitive' accumulation has swept through the local economy. It is primitive in two senses of the term: first, although capitalist production relations have long been entrenched, each

[86] The size of which increased by 33 per cent in the first half of the 1990s (Kumar 1999).
[87] See Chapter 6 on religion for the interest of Hindu nationalists in a 'Hindu' public order.
[88] Varshney 1999.
[89] Baru 2000, p. 223.
[90] Ahmad 1996a, p. 49; Baru 2000, p. 208.

individual capitalist has to develop his or her own starting point for accumulation, historically prior to and necessary for capitalist enterprise. Second, a significant element in these initial resources, even now, is obtained through fraud, corruption and economic crime against labour, consumers, weaker competitors and the State. This new wave of accumulation therefore takes place in a moral environment in which trust is less and less systemic and more and more individuated.[91]

'Primitive accumulation' is therefore to be understood as a process that not only *pre-exists* the era of productive capital, in the macro-historical way described with great vividness by Karl Marx,[92] but one that *coexists* with it. Spaces for small capital are continually created even in the era of globalisation, alongside more advanced forms of corporate capital. However, while Marx theorised the necessity for the continual replenishment of petty production in the interstices of capital, and even allowed for the possibility of the working labourer to transform himself to a small and on occasion a full-blown capitalist, he did not theorise, as he did for agrarian and industrial capital, the extra-economic pathways whereby such – as he saw it – 'minor' forms of accumulation would take place. He merely concluded what is so amply demonstrated in the workings of the Indian local economy, that 'Force itself is an economic power' (Marx 1976, p. 47). It is therefore possible that what Marx himself took to be preconditions for accumulation may instead be the features of certain trajectories of accumulation.[93]

At the local level, then, the intermediate classes are not so much in decay as cornered and fighting. This was also predicted, not for India by Jha but in a general way by Marx: 'The lower middle classes, the small manufacturer, the shopkeeper, the artisan, the peasant, all these fight against the bourgeoisie, to save from extinction their existence as fractions of the middle class' (1967, p. 91). In a country as big as India, with a GDP on a par with that of Belgium and in which resources *remain* exceedingly scarce relative to its population, this fight can be prolonged and draining. It is also marked by great unevenness. In cities like

---

[91] In the same way, the origins of the capital of the propertied elite of Dhaka, Bangladesh, has been traced back to money-laundering, black-marketing, smuggling, embezzlement, fraud, default on loans, illegal commissions, forced occupation of land, the deliberate creation of scarcity and sales of permits and licences (Silberstein 2000).

[92] Marx 1976, chapter 28. First, Marx catalogues the 'reckless terrorism' with which labour was dispossessed and 'transformed into mercenaries' and land for agrarian capital was engrossed. Then he describes the process of enslavement and looting of colonies together with the State's complicity through protectionism, the creation of the national debt and the fiscal system by which the class of capitalists was consolidated.

[93] This is a point also made by Timberg from his research into the role in the Indian economy of Marwaris (1978, p. 170).

Mumbai and Coimbatore it has taken the form of organised riots and turf wars.[94] The intermediate classes have been fighting against entrants from lower ranked castes – and religious minorities – and smaller units of accumulation with lower costs. Elsewhere the 'intermediate classes' are clawing at the State for both subsidies and concessions, and surfing their new wave of primitive accumulation whose victims are labour and consumers (see Chapters 4 and 7 on the state and on caste).

The case of bus transport in south India illustrates these points (in this case through the allocation of rationed route concessions). It also shows how bureaucratic corruption has been politicised over time and how the autonomy of the public sector is compromised.[95] Bus transport has to be state-regulated in the public interest, and private- and public-sector companies compete.[96] Routes are supposed to be allocated bureaucratically according to transparent tender proceedings. Bus fares are also capped by administrative fiat. Over time, however, administrative corruption has ensured a prioritisation of routes according to returns, net of wear and tear, which broadly matched the ranking of bribes. In the 1980s this administrative rent-seeking discretion was politicised. Politicians captured the process of regulation, seizing and sharing the rents formerly collected by officials. Routes were doled out periodically at a 'public' meeting of politicians and bus owners according to the latter's roles in electoral and party political funding. Even more recently, in the 1990s, bribes were collectively organised and these *collective* political investments by bus owners reaped returns in the form of policy changes timed to disadvantage the State's own public-sector bus transport organisations in favour of private owners. This is a more subtle form of corruption,[97] whereby the State's development project is subverted by powerful economic interests.[98]

The *quid pro quo* for the tribute received by officials and politicians is a blind eye turned towards primitive and illegal business practices. The illegal practices necessary to raise the funding for securing route allocations affect the profitability of firms very directly – and also their size. Illegally poor standards of maintenance, severe overcrowding, predatory poaching of routes and the illegal extension of routes are routinely toler-

---

[94] Hansen 1997; Bardhan 1997; People's Union for Civil Liberties 1998.

[95] Cinemas and liquor shops and agencies have a similar politics.

[96] In Tamil Nadu, the State owns 17 000 busses and private operators manage some 5000. By contrast, in each of Kerala and West Bengal, the State owns about 4000 busses, while private operators run 20 000.

[97] Theorised by Khan (1996) and by Roy (1996).

[98] In theory, political corruption may bypass the bureaucracy entirely, the implementation of favours from corrupt alignments being administered according to political command in a 'legal' manner.

ated by the State. Tax is evaded in part through collective negotiation. The bus owners' collective fixing of the pay of their workforce overrides any countervailing power on the part of organised labour, and this in turn sets up incentives to employees to tolerate free-riding quite literally, and to practise free-riding themselves by under-declaring ticket returns. They also fail to issue tickets or to remit undocumented payments, in return for further illegal payments by bus users. The owners' imposition of terms and conditions of work also masks routine illegal extensions to the working day. There is a saying: 'what *thangam* (gold/bribes) cannot do, *Sangam* (organisation) can do'. In deploying both forms of politics, bus owners can hedge their bets. Labour and consumers suffer. So does the public interest, and so in turn does the legitimacy of the State, a subject to which we turn next. Even when the State is not controlled by 'intermediate classes' they remain very important players, contesting and often neutralising its regulative capacity.

The 'intermediate classes', then, show every sign of a resilience unanticipated by either Kalecki or Jha. They are not a transitional phenomenon. While India is fast being reinvented discursively,[99] there is a great deal of continuity in the real economy at the local level. Whether 'intermediate classes' are losing the struggle to 'roll-back the wheel of history', as Marx supposed of what he called the 'lower middle class',[100] or whether they still have the capacity to slow down and even halt its advance in India, are questions not yet easy to answer.

---

[99] See Das 1994; Khilnani 1997; Corbridge and Harriss 2000; and the BJP website: <http://bjp.org/news>.
[100] Marx 1967, p. 91.

4   The local State and the informal economy

The balance between state and market has changed over time, from a relationship of control and antagonism to one of partnerships and complementarity. In solving the problems of market failure and helping markets to grow ... (g)overnment intervention can be market enhancing (Chhibber 1996, p. 15).

The World Bank's vision of the State, captured in this quotation from the Staff Director of the Bank's 1997 *World Development Report* on the role of the State, could hardly be more different from the reality of the actually existing State in the India of the 88 per cent. The aim of this chapter is to bring out this difference, its causes and potential consequences, and to grasp the role of the State as a structure of accumulation at the local level. We will find that while corruption, which the Bank sees as the central problem of the State, is indeed commonplace, a deeper and more quantitatively important phenomenon is fraud. Of particular significance is the complicity of the State in tax evasion; indeed, the development of tax evasion is the real 'structural adjustment' that has occurred in recent decades, a structural adjustment more significant and profound than the set of reforms implemented under that title from 1991 onwards.

The actually existing State

Few terms in social science are as contested as that of the State, but this chapter deals with it at a much lower level of abstraction than that at which most of the debate has taken place. For our purposes, 'the State' will be defined rather pragmatically as a set of institutions of political and executive control, 'a palpable nexus of practice and institutional structure centred on government'.[1] We have encountered it already, as a direct economic

---

[1] After Abrams (1988). Indian scholarship, being of scant importance to mainstream political science, was able to preserve a significant body of work on the State throughout the period of the Cold War when the important debates about the nature of the State by Poulantsas (1980), who saw it in structuralist terms, and Miliband (1983), in instrumentalist terms, could be ignored by mainstream political science until Scocpol et al. 'brought the State back in' (1990).

actor in industry and trade, as a regulator of markets (and having powerful interests of its own in such interventions), and as a provider of the infra-structure without which a market economy cannot function at all.[2]

Most of the empirical literature on the Indian State focuses on three main contradictions or tensions. The first is (or was) a contradiction or tension between planned (socialist) development and an accommoda-tive, formally democratic kind of politics that leads politicians to adopt populist measures favouring current consumption at the expense of invest-ment and future consumption (what Myrdal meant by 'the soft state').[3] These measures contribute to low growth and the income transfers involved have to be rationed, which in turn creates incentives for corrup-tion. The second major tension is between democratic politics, based on universal suffrage, and the politics of a not-quite-big-enough bourgeoisie proper, who have to co-opt other important classes (notably those dom-inating the marketed surplus). This means continual policy negotiations and compromises, and a ragged process of policy implementation, lead-ing invariably to policy-dilution and the proliferation of subsidies.[4] These too often have to be rationed and access to them is again sought through bribes and nepotism.[5] The third major tension is between planned devel-opment and the interests of private capital. This is complicated. The State provides the infrastructure that supports private capital, but also regu-lates private capital and even substitutes for it where capital will not or cannot go, or where it cannot be trusted. The scale of the funds involved gives rise to increasingly massive acts of fraud, accentuating the distor-tions caused by tax evasion.[6]

There are also tensions of a different kind between the central govern-ment and the federated States over their respective jurisdictions, power and

[2] India's State has been analysed in terms of its developmental autonomy, the class coali-tions it expresses, and its class embeddedness – in an inconclusive literature driven by paradigm wars. That the Indian State consists of coalitions protecting the capitalist class (Bardhan 1984, 1998; Byres 1996a) ignores the role of the developmental State in projects of non-capitalist social transformation (for example, anti-poverty policy and caste reservations). That the State is autonomous and developmental (Kohli 1990; Her-ring 1999) ignores its private interest nature. That the Indian State is embedded in class (Evans 1995) ignores its role as an arena of social contestation along other lines; for example, patriarchy. That it is dominated by private interest or dyads of principals and agents, apart from being inherently implausible and positing an impoverished repertoire of human motivation, ignores the evidential base for all these other characterisations. Herring (1999) and J. Harriss (2000) both review the many dimensions through which the State has been characterised and report no consensus.

[3] Myrdal 1968; 1973.

[4] Bardhan 1984.

[5] Up to the point at which the total cost of the bribe exceeds the subsidy or the market alternative.

[6] Byres 1996a; Roy 1996.

resources – and over their respective degrees of autonomy[7] and between the different levels within each jurisdiction. The local level of the national State cannot be assumed to be a 'simple' microcosm of the centre.[8] Last but not least, there is the pervasive and massive tension (introduced in Chapter 1) between the 'black' and 'white' economies, the growth of which has serious implications for fiscal success, and hence for development; that is, for sustainable growth, efficiency, emancipation and well-being.

Most commentators argue that the black economy is driven by corruption and focus on its implications for efficiency. The 'new political economy' sees corruption as a 'clearing response to the inefficient distribution of free public goods'.[9] On this view, both the traditional revenue collection and registration functions of the State, and its more modern developmental functions, operate in conditions of 'institutional scarcity'. State officials become discriminating monopolists who can in effect sell informally privatised state property rights. They can also defraud the exchequer. The resulting 'economically irrational' outcomes overwhelm 'good policy advice'.[10] The solution, according to the 'new political economy' school, is deregulation; that is, to get the incumbents to abolish the positions from which they engage in this systematic exploitation of illegal income-earning opportunities in the public sector.

In all of this discourse the State is seen as an institution with boundary lines.[11] Civil society is something separate. On this political theorists and policy advisors agree: the State is one thing, markets are another. But at the local level we find no such clear separation. When we look at the local State, the actually existing State below the level of the State capital, as we follow policies down the hierarchy of levels, we soon find ourselves in an economy that is on the edge of – or frankly outside – the ambit of state regulation (despite what is laid down in official statements of intention, and in legislation and orders and institutions); that is, in the informal economy.

How is the informal economy actually regulated? How is order enforced? We have already looked at some of the *non-State* means involved: the use of trusted family labour; bilateral and multilateral contracts, especially repeated and interlocked contracts, usually through networks; the

---

[7] Guhan in Cassen and Joshi (1995); Landy (1998).

[8] Respectively Roy 1996, p. 28; Kumar 1999, pp. 71–9.

[9] Jagganathan 1987, p. 110. Public goods are non-excludable and non-rivalrous. Very few goods have both these qualities. For the most part public goods are the result of a political consensus and many reasons other than non-excludability and non-rivalry are given for the public provision of 'actually existing' public goods, notably strategic importance and social essentiality.

[10] Krueger 1974.

[11] Khilnani 1997; Das 2001; Corbridge and Harriss 2000.

importance of individual and collective reputation; regulation through collective institutions; through an often inconsistent normative pluralism; and through private protection forces.[12] However, there remains a great deal of disorder in such markets. Significant commercial profits are made from the manipulation of regulative shortcomings, and disorder can be a tactic in the struggle to increase and protect both product market shares and distributive shares (the balance between wage costs and profits). It is not for nothing that rent-seeking was first recognised in markets rather than in the State. In practice, state and non-state institutions of regulation interact, so that market and State are not separate.

Most research on the local State looks at access and coverage. Much of it deals with numbers – quantifying the eligible 'targets' and contrasting them with the actual 'beneficiaries' – utterly leached of social characteristics. It rarely shows how access is shaped by everyday forms of communalism, for example, or by the gender discrimination practised by state officials. And on the few occasions when the social character of the local State has been studied, the focus has tended to be on law and order and on extreme events, not on 'quotidian practice'.[13] When reviewing this body of work Akhil Gupta noted that 'surprisingly little [research] has been conducted in the small towns where ... a large number of officials live and work' (1993, p. 376). As we have already stressed, the field material produced by such research offers many small and partial insights. Whether such insights represent exceptions or the norm – whether they should be treated as models, or just anecdotal footnotes – is always a matter of judgement. But as we also insisted earlier, without work at this level, unavoidably limited as it may be, no worthwhile account of the State is possible at all.

The local State in action: five case studies

The World Bank's 1997 *World Development Report* on the State concludes: '(t)he challenge is to identify a menu of regulatory tools from which countries can select those most likely to yield benefits in their specific country settings'.[14] Faith in free choice and 'markets' is very deeply

---

[12] See pp. 34–5, 50–3 in this book. See also the elaboration in Harriss-White (1996d).

[13] Wade's study of the irrigation bureaucracy has been exceptional in this respect. For examples of studies of access and coverage, see Harriss, Guhan and Cassen (1992); for the daily practice of communalism by the local State, see Jeffery and Jeffery (1998); for an unusual analysis of state failure in a range of village-level institutions, see Dreze and Sharma (1998); for the functioning of the irrigation bureaucracy see Wade (1985) and Mollinga (1998); for ethnographies of 50 years of Indian corruption, see Visvanathan and Sethi (1998).

[14] Chhibber 1996, p. 15.

entrenched inside the Bank. By the end of the twentieth century the menu of regulatory tools selected by a country had come to be known as its 'product'.[15] How far this represents a meaningful, let alone useful, way of conceiving the State in the India of the 88 per cent is what we want to ascertain. To do this we first set out five case studies of the local State in action, based on fieldwork. We then review some of the chief determinants of this actually existing local State, before summarising the consequences for development.

Three of our case studies concern state regulation of markets and infrastructure, one concerns the state promotion of 'human development', and one deals with the State as a fiscal agent. The case of state food grains trading in Karnataka shows how the State may actually create informal (even black) markets.[16] The second case study, of land market relations in Karachi, Pakistan, was the unintended consequence of survey research on legal access to environmental justice.[17] We have included it as the result of its great relevance to our problem; in no sense is its inclusion intended as an act of provocation. While there are hints of parallel developments in India,[18] Martin Lau's study of Karachi is the most explicit analysis of how informal markets create informal States. The third case is drawn from a collection of life histories of junior officials in Tamil Nadu.[19] It shows some of the developmental pathologies resulting from 'institutional scarcity' – the State's shortage of people and resources. The fourth case study concerns officials in an unnamed State in south India that was trying to improve opportunities for women.[20] It became apparent that the identities of officials shaped the effectiveness of the State. The fifth case concerns the State's fiscal performance in a town in Tamil Nadu. It shows that the lack of state resources, and the distribution of what it did collect, reflected quite precisely the pattern of class power relations, not official development policy.[21]

When we contemplate the actual results of applying various 'regulatory tools' as revealed in these cases we are prompted to question the

---

[15] See Kay (2002) for a general analysis of national competitive advantage.
[16] Mooij 1999.
[17] Lau 1996.
[18] See, for instance, the two studies of the politics of (metropolitan) industrial districts: Gorter (1998), and Benjamin and Bengani (1998).
[19] Harriss-White 2002e.
[20] Sengupta 1998.
[21] In all five studies, insights from structured field surveys of a type where the researcher conducts the research at first hand are combined with the fieldworker's insights from accidental and unstructured encounters. The labels 'participant observation' or 'ethnography' would be attributing to such crucially important, but unpredictable research events, systematic attributes they do not have. Mooij (1998) is most useful on this eclectic field method.

extent to which any State can choose its toolkit, or freely select its 'product', the choice implied by the quotation from the World Bank at the beginning of this section. We also see the blurred nature of the boundaries between the State and the intermediate classes; between the official State and a very large 'shadow' State; and between social identities and official state roles. Above all, the cases refute the idea that in the India of the 88 per cent there is a separation between State and society.

The regulation of commodities: The Essential Commodities Act and the Public Distribution System in Karnataka

The Indian State, declaring itself to be constitutionally obliged to guarantee food supplies, confronts, and attempts to provide a legal framework of regulation for, one of the most fundamental sectors of the economy: the production and distribution of food grains. Through its own control over food distribution it also successfully regulates and formalises a substantial economic subsector, which accounts for some 13 per cent of the supply of grain. The law (the Essential Commodities Act of 1955 (ECA)) is complex and inconsistent, covering 60 commodities and implemented in Karnataka by means of 70 government control orders. There is no simple correspondence between its far-reaching equity goals and anti-trader discourse, on the one hand, and its rules and procedures on the other. This law and the institutions implementing much of it – the Public Distribution System (PDS), comprising central and state government trading corporations and a network of fair price shops (FPS) and co-operatives – are the subject of a unique, rich, comparative ethnography in two south Indian States by Jos Mooij.[22] We will tease out some of her observations about the relation between the food administration and the informal economy.

In Karnataka the State procures a set fraction of the output of licensed grain mills at prices *below* the ruling post-harvest levels. On the residual free market this leads to wider profit margins than would otherwise be obtained, in order to compensate for these losses. These wide margins attract a mass of small-scale traders and processors, many of them unlicensed.[23] Furthermore, illegal sales of state-procured and subsidised food generate illegal livelihoods for ration-shop dealers,

---

[22] Mooij 1999. This research is comparative, examining the operation of the Act throughout the food bureaucracies and at the interfaces with non-state production, marketing and consumption in a surplus district in a surplus State with a 'vertical' politics of patronage (Karnataka) and in a food deficit district and a food deficit State with a 'horizontal' politics mobilising the labouring classes (Kerala).

[23] See also Harriss (1993) for West Bengal.

warehouse managers, transporters, and so on, and the profits made from these fraudulent activities are shared with officials in the food administration. In addition, to reap excess profits from grain smuggled in defiance of movement restrictions requires the active connivance of both lorry drivers and checkpost guards, which also has to be paid for. Thus the State generates interwoven, parallel, informal and illegal grain markets, ensuring that a larger number of intermediaries and a greater range of interests in grain markets exist than would be the case *without* the PDS.

As a result of the ECA, the residual open markets are characterised not so much by price competition as by a jostling for access to the food bureaucracy, with whom there are accommodative relations of black-marketing, fraud and corruption. The food bureaucracy shares in the rates of return to private trade, which are far greater than they would be in 'equilibrium' conditions. There are two reasons for this. First, since food controls reduce the volume of flows, prices in deficit areas are higher, and in surplus regions lower, than if controls were lifted. Profits on the former are shared with food administration officials. Second, state-administered procurement requires the concentration of supplies at a few points (usually big mills) to minimise transaction costs. These are oligopolies, maintained and protected by the rationing of licences and by relations of patronage and accommodation between individual millers and the officers of food departments and corporations.

This nexus of interests sets entry barriers to the commercial economy and has differentiating impacts. The tender procedure gives advantages to those bidding for contracts to mill state-procured paddy (unmilled rice) who enjoy economies of scale. The continual threat of prosecution of successful contractors encourages compliance with the state grain levy and its administration. This has differentiating consequences. First, in order to simplify procurement the State has effectively created a collusive oligopoly, through its rationing of licences. Second, a firm appointed to mill and transport grain on contract to the State can then switch its working capital to expand other operations. Third, as the official milling out-turn standards (66 per cent of rice per unit of paddy) usually enable an efficient miller-cum-trader (who can get an out-turn of 68 per cent or more) to reap a few incremental percentage points of grain in excess of standards, this officially non-existent grain can be siphoned from the public system into the private one. Trader-millers able to use these tactics profit at the expense of those not contracted to the State.

The corruption that has developed as a result of the creation of informal private markets is not a question of individual profit-maximisation and 'market-clearing', but an aspect of a social structure governed by rules and norms. These set the going prices of bribes, the terms of access and the distribution of returns. Flows of tribute parallel to the financial flows of the formal system of taxation work their way upwards to politicians and administrators who redistribute it (in acts of political patronage), or consume or invest it.[24] People are fully capable of identifying 'excessive' levels of predation and of imposing sanctions on non-compliance to the norms of corruption. Locality, gender, caste and party politics are crucial to the operation of these rules.[25]

The PDS is intensely politicised in three ways: through the self-interested patronage of politicians, through political monitoring of performance and through political brokerage between enforcers and traders. The latter is at the behest of private capital. Bribes may be involved but in return for these, the State is defrauded of much larger quantities of resources in cash or grain.[26] Part of this stream of fraud finds its way to politicians as a return on the large investments required to get elected.

It is actually misleading to call this a 'soft' State, as Myrdal put it, 'in that policies decided on are often not enforced ... and that the authorities, even when framing policies, are reluctant to place obligations on people' (1968, p. 66). Mooij's research shows that there are now quite rigid and 'hard' social relations of *both* a developmental and a rent-seeking kind that constitute obstacles to reform. These lead to a kind of development that pre-empts regulation. In the case of the PDS, these relations give rise to pressures to phase the liberalisation of the grain trade in such a way that provisions which regulate *private* trade are the first to be dispensed with. Ceilings on quantities and periods of storage and restrictions on the movement of goods are consequently the first regulations to be removed, while the removal of those that reduce risk or subsidise private trade (the use of private firms as agents, the subsidising of credit, the targeting of food distribution) is delayed.

The regulation of land use and land 'markets' in Karachi, Pakistan

In the case just described the State generates informal markets. In our second case informal markets generate an informal State. Unfortunately, while the phenomenon of the 'shadow' State is known to be both

---

[24] Whether these flows are generalised to patrimonial, populist or clientelist forms of state politics depends first on the relative status of bribers and second on the need to purchase votes. Here may be extensive political (or political-cum-administrative) leakage (either privately appropriated or partly redistributed downwards) at every stage of the trajectory of money (Harriss-White 1996e). See also Wade 1985; Gupta 1993).

[25] There is a substantial literature showing the ways in which market exchange (land, labour, money and commodities) is embedded in institutions of class, ethnicity, locality, gender and age (see Harriss-White 1995a for a review), but there is strikingly little research asking what difference these social institutions make to the operation of actually existing States. Ramamurthy (1995) and Mooij (1999) hint at the roles played by caste and gender, respectively. Jeffery and Jeffery (1998) examine gender and communal identity in relation to the local State.

[26] Mooij 1999, p. 232.

common and important in India, to our knowledge it has been described only very elliptically in the scholarly literature, so case material from a very big city in Pakistan is used to illustrate it here.[27]

Within half a century, Karachi has progressed from being a pleasant, planned colonial port of some 400 000 people to a multi-ethnic megalopolis of 12 million, the biggest city and the commercial hub of Pakistan. In the face of pounding waves of migrant squatters, the regulation of land use has been the responsibility of a series of state agencies, the last but one of which managed to plan a ring of lavish satellite settlements. These, however, were rapidly engulfed by illegal squatter workshops and homes. Half the population of Karachi has seized the land it lives on illegally and has gained access to water and electricity[28] 'by stealth'; that is, by means of an elaborate set of social relations of corruption and fraud. These relations re-ration and re-order state provision. They also require continual payments in order to remain 'informally legitimated'. These informal markets have created and paid a parallel or 'shadow' State. In so doing they also feed and informalise a privatised development project. Eventually official agencies capitulate to this *fait accompli*, and being empowered to legalise these slums, attempt to obtain payments from settlers for long-term leases and utilities. Settlers meet these demands with violent resistance. Meanwhile, excluded from access to legal protection by a lack of formal property rights, residents are subject to arbitrary or politicised harassment, and eviction by political officials and the police. The patently weak developmental State has been transformed into a highly oppressive one.

This does not mean that the 'imported' institutions of law and State are unimportant.[29] But instead of being merely bypassed or ignored, formal state law and institutions now form the basis for a regime of private extortion. Indeed, in this case the local State was poised for a second phase of capitulation in which even the private armies protecting the 'informal' construction sector were to be recognised as legitimate. Additionally, the formal State and law now indirectly regulate the informal property market. An illegal developer will follow the land-use guidelines of the current Karachi Development Authority because he will thereby

---

[27] One such is the study of civic politics in industrial districts in Delhi (Benjamin and Bengani 1998) where illegal workshops have proliferated on residential land deficient in infrastructure and services, and requiring the same regularisation of title (converting real estate into industrial land) as described for Karachi. In the Delhi case, there are three kinds of politics spawning shadows: the networks surrounding upgrading of services; the networks binding the authoritarian and entrepreneurial Development Authority to large contractors; and the alliances, mediated by mafias, between corporate giants and the State to convert industrial land into real estate and to develop it. We use Lau (1996) here.

[28] Though not to sewerage.

[29] Griffiths 1979.

avoid the threat of penalties other than those for the illegal seizure of land, and will charge higher rents as a result.

The parallel system of taxation and provision that 'shadows' the State in cases like this is hard and dangerous for researchers to penetrate. While public officials mostly play their shadow roles using resources stolen from the State, there is another set of intermediaries who ensure that the informal economy is supplied cheaply with goods, rights or favours from the State (or who simply steal them), and who can sell goods and services to the State at higher prices than would be the case in an 'open' market. These intermediaries fetch and carry, and perform various necessary technical activities (such as tapping electricity supply cables). They provide protection, adjudicate disputes and enforce the rules and norms of the 'shadow' State. While the 'shadow' role of state officials is derived from their public positions, the intermediation of shadow agents depends on other social structures such as ethnicity, religious affiliation or locality. One ironic result is that these 'shadow state' structures have succeeded in providing cheap housing for the poor (many of whom in turn provide domestic and other services for corrupt official patrons). There is no guarantee, however, that this would still be the case if the property rights of the informal land sellers and developers were to be legalised.

Institutional scarcity and development in Tamil Nadu

According to the World Bank's State, 'introducing greater contestability (through decentralization, delegation and participation) improves the operation of state institutions'.[30] It is part of a process of 'streamlining' the State. The next case of decentralisation and participation in Tamil Nadu shows a State that is depleted rather than streamlined. At the local level the general state administration has two wings – developmental and revenue – the social relations of which were studied by collecting life histories from a total of 35 local, low-level officials in northern Tamil Nadu in 1994–95.[31] Most of these local development officials do not live in the localities they administer, but in the local town. As a result, they had limited access to the dense web of information that characterises village society. The great majority of them were of higher caste and (to judge from their property) class status than those they were employed to serve, though their comparative affluence did not prevent them from demanding bribes. Their private political and social status was significant in explaining what the local State did, and the limits of its capacity.

In 1994–95 there were too few development officials to perform their developmental roles effectively; in this respect nothing had changed over

[30] Chhibber 1996, p. 16.
[31] Harriss-White 2002e.

the previous two decades.[32] For instance, the lowest level development official, the *grama sevak* (village-level worker), for instance, administers (as a minimum) small savings schemes; the Integrated Rural Development Programme (IRDP) loans and their recovery; unemployment schemes; bio-gas and smokeless stove programs; eye camps; and street-lights, as well as the chores connected with drinking water – the maintenance of hand pumps and overhead tanks. The authoritarian nature of the development wing of the local State is evinced by the heavy load of targets placed upon officials.

Furthermore, the scarcity of supporting resources means that wealthier officials may even borrow money privately in order to achieve their targets. For instance, a private loan might be obtained to cover transportation 'out' to a series of scattered villages for purposes of agricultural extension. On one occasion a large private payment was made to the police to encourage them to investigate a theft of state property; on another private funds were used to rent a store for the safe-keeping of state property. Officials from poor backgrounds were clearly less likely to be able to meet their targets. Any official borrowing money privately to perform his or her duty has a very strong incentive to extort bribes from clients. Extreme resource scarcities also result in 'participation' in the form of collective social action by clients. Piped drinking water, for instance, is commonly maintained by collective action when state-provided supplies break down (water pumps fail, pipes leak). Such ad hoc collective responses are notoriously conflictual. Structured by caste and locality, groups repairing drinking water infrastructure are often involved in disputes. Women and low-caste users of water are often discriminated against and excluded. A bureaucracy weakened by a lack of resources experiences these kinds of 'collective action' as defiance and often regards the groups as undemocratic and unaccountable.

The local developmental State in northern Tamil Nadu was highly politicised. Administrative duties were vulnerable to political interference. Transfers of posts were influenced by party political affiliation, as well as by bribes.[33] Not only did party politics influence who got to the front of the queues for access to state resources, they also structured the administrative response.

The developmental State thus gives rise to a distinctive sector of the informal economy that emerges in response to its failures and incapacities. State duties are commonly best seen as a risk-reducing residual activity for state officials – for example, one Agriculture Department official derived his main income from exporting pickles – and a niche in the

[32] Chambers and Wickremanayake 1977.
[33] See the corroborative evidence in Banik (1999).

bureaucracy offers private returns from bribery that reward the initial investment needed to get the position. Conversely, parts of the informal economy can sometimes be informally 'taxed' to achieve state objectives. For example, some illegal industrial units that were causing severe environmental pollution and notoriously avoiding or evading commercial taxes were threatened with sanctions by a district collector *unless* they funded and maintained a sterilisation ward in the local hospital – which they did. More insidiously, given the growing importance of the informal economy, state effectiveness increasingly depends on the private status of public officials – on their class backgrounds, their caste and their gender – further blurring the boundary between State and society.

And in the local revenue wing of the State, the slow flow of information, extraordinary procedural complexity and wide discretionary power create incentives for private intermediaries to make informal livelihoods by interpreting the rules and negotiating access for clients.[34] The 'shadow' State exists at the most local level of all.

Social identity and the local State

Anasuya Sengupta has studied the impact of the gender, caste, religion, age and locality of origin of officials on their ability to implement official goals. A department in a south Indian State has been entrusted with the task of improving opportunities for women, and, if measured by outcome indicators (with some slightly heroic assumptions about cause and effect), has been quite successful.[35] Sengupta found, however, that personal identities and the ideologies through which they are construed profoundly influenced performance. Gender, caste and region of origin affected recruitment, transfers and promotion in predictable ways.[36] The programme in question was required to employ mainly female personnel

---

[34] See Erb and Harriss-White (2002) for the devastating barriers of access faced by disabled people to their state entitlements where bribes are commonly equivalent to 18 months of disability benefit.

[35] Sengupta 1998.

[36] Vacancies have become a political resource (Banik 1999). On the one hand, transfers were thought to prevent staleness or corruption, to place appropriate competencies, to keep distance and to allow the accumulation of a repertoire of skills and knowledge. But they have come to enable some of the very dysfunctions they were intended to prevent. Transfers are subject to political control so as to locate compliant civil servants in networks of power that determine the flow of good within the political system, and to encourage or quash political competition (Mathur 1996, p. 16). The velocity of transfer increases with expected or speculated elections (for which large funds are required). Bribes depend on the 'wetness' of the sectors of the State (the wettest being industry, commerce and finance) and the characteristics of individual posts (the implications of the location for the standard of living of quantities of public money commanded, opportunities to raise money from clients, and risk and visibility (Wade 1985; Banik 1999)).

– it did, at the top and at the base.[37] But the influential middle level of officials, who had to be peripatetic and mobile, were mainly male, since women are not allowed to stay away from home alone overnight. The domestic work burdens of female officials, the practice of paternalism, sexual harassment (both inside and outside the State) and gendered differences in the understanding of the gender-based project by officials all affected performance. For instance, the men understood the programme to be about the nutrition and education of women, while women understood it to be about mothering and mentoring. The power of young, female officials was lower than that of male and/or older individuals. At the same time, younger, urban, educated women were preferred for promotion over older, rural women whose local knowledge and experience would have improved the programme's performance.

Caste is, of course, equally influential in determining state performance, and better known in this respect than gender. The policy of reservations of jobs for people in backward and scheduled castes shapes public-sector behaviour through interests and groupings within government departments. There is a wide variation in departmental compliance with reservations policy, though generally it is poor.[38] Freezes on the number of reserved posts intensify caste-based pressures for preferential access. The official system then begins to be parodied. Patronage and payment structures lead to an entirely informalised system of 'reservations', which is independent of those for backward and scheduled castes and tribes, and not based on merit either.

Religion also has an impact on the State. The public adoption of caste Hindu rituals inside a department has the effect of excluding Muslim officials from the core group and is said to structure the timetable of work.[39] Even at its most innocent, this contradicts the State's official secularist project. The use, for lack of alternative buildings, of temples and Muslim prayer houses as sites of service delivery is undertaken as proof

---

[37] About 20 per cent of the IAS are women while 25–30 per cent are scheduled caste (Banik 1999, p. 5). A highly placed informant in a north Indian state bureaucracy has noted that while gender is more of an impediment to promotion than caste status, there are no female IAS officers of scheduled caste or scheduled tribal origin. He notes that female IAS officers are very rarely promoted to positions of power in the Home, Commercial Taxes, Finance, Commerce and Industry ministries or state departments. Nor are they made Chief Secretary. High-ranking female officials rarely choose to put special effort on account of their gender into development policies that seek to transform the status of women. Scheduled caste politicians 'deal awkwardly' with high-caste female IAS officers, across barriers of class, caste and culture, as well as gender, and, in power, they seek to influence promotions and transfers so that they do not have to deal with them at all.

[38] *Frontline* 1999, 26 November.

[39] We have other case material for Muslim and Hindu religious observance taking precedence over work during office hours.

of the secular character of government, but it also leads to systematic differences, based on religion and caste, in access to state-provided services.

Locality is always loaded with the connotations of a moral unit, of fictive kinship and of solidarity.[40] But locality is also an instrument of efficiency, for it reduces the information costs of state activity and makes it easier to monitor and publicise opportunistic behaviour. The higher the officials are in the administrative hierarchy, the less embedded in their locality they are, even while the scale of what they regard as their locality expands. Further, local bureaucratic involvement is in tension with the need for educated officials. To get and retain educated officials, locality becomes less and less significant in recruitment, yet local knowledge is more and more crucial to development outcomes. Yet even local knowledge is ambivalent in this respect. For instance, it is very difficult for local-level workers to be 'neutral', in the manner expected by higher level officials, towards local caste and community norms.

The depletion of municipal finance

The south Indian market town of Arni, which became a municipality in 1951, has already engulfed 11 villages. The population directly associated with Arni's urban economy is about 100 000, inflated by transients and by regular commuting from its ring of satellite villages. These suburbs resist incorporation into the municipality because of the increased local taxes this would involve. Such resistance is widespread and makes local urban government in India chronically under-funded. For nine years (from 1987 to 1996), local municipalities were not democratically managed; instead, they were run by political appointees from the state capital. There was a brief interlude of democratic governance between 1986 and 1991. During this period, inflation and a tax revaluation greatly increased *potential* municipal revenue. Table 4.1 shows selected elements of local revenue and expenditure. Under democratic rule, revenue from property taxes and from the tax on municipal market traders increased, as did expenditure on salaries.[41] Under the undemocratic and politicised rule of the early 1990s, duties on property transfers were better enforced than they were under the elected local government. Throughout the period for which we have data, 1983–84 to 1992–93, professional tax paid by the local elite fluctuated wildly, but the trend was towards the

[40] See Lambert (1996) for an important deconstruction of the political meaning of locality.
[41] These data are incomplete because the municipality does not account separately for salaries. The headings aggregated here are those categories indicated by the Municipal Commissioner as being dominated by the salary component. They show how salaries are protected in the structure of expenditure.

evasion of payments. The contribution to local revenue by citizens with taxable property and incomes fluctuated significantly, but rose in absolute current terms by a factor of 3.5 from 1983–84 to 1992–93 while their proportional share of revenue increased by 35 per cent. More significantly for our argument, the very poorest firms in the municipal markets, 'platform' traders doing business at the entrance of established shops or from mobile stalls, or those with wares displayed on gunny bags and sacking beside the roads (with typical gross outputs per firm well under 0.5 per cent of those of the 15 top firms), contributed 4.5 times more in absolute terms by the end of the period than they did at the start. Their share in the municipality's total revenue doubled. The municipality proved to be better at taxing people earning less than its own employees than it was at taxing the elite.[42] The entire municipal budget for 1993 equalled the gross output of just one of the most substantial businesses in town. Three interpretations suggest themselves: (1) a class conspiracy (between officials and the commercial elite) to exploit other classes; (2) a class battle, given the political weakness of local government in the face of the local elite (since the tax collectors have lower social status than those being taxed); and (3) lack of state legitimacy (tax evasion representing a 'principled protest' by the elite at the high expenditure on salaries and the low expenditure on infrastructure). The last set of circumstances is likely to be self-perpetuating.

While the town has been upgraded as a First Class Municipality for tax purposes, for other purposes it has not. Its population figures, conditioned by an increasingly irrelevant administrative boundary, are a severe underestimate. This anomalous situation prevents the appointment of officials by the Public Service Commission so that the entire staff of the town administration consists of appointees of the Special Officer (from the time of direct rule) or the Commissioner (democratically elected since 1996). Hence, most of the appointees are said by key informants to be the clients of local economic notables, through their influence with one or other of these two officials.

In this case, tax evasion fuels a black economy, characterised first by the informal privatisation of local government services. This is as characteristic of schooling as it is of refuse disposal, and it leads to double standards in performance (poor public standards and better private ones). Second, corruption is systemic. Third, a black financial sector balloons. This is composed of funds not declared to the tax authorities, which nonetheless must be invested or banked. It reinforces tendencies

---

[42] The Jha Committee (Govt of India 1983) reports that with the efforts of 95 per cent of staff in the Revenue Department a mere 5 per cent of income tax is collected, disproportionately from the lowest and most numerous category of assessees, mainly in the salariat.

Table 4.1 *Municipal receipts and expenditure^a*

Source	1983–84	1984–85	1985–86	1986–87	1987–88	1988–89	1989–90	1990–91	1991–92	1992–93
Total Receipts^b	77.9	102.2	94.8	166.7	139.3	133.3	190.6	180.1	165.0	199.9
of which:										
Fees, rents and income from services	8.0	7.1	8.1	11.8	20.6	19.5	18.9	21.8	24.1	29.8
Taxes from propertied classes:										
Property	7.4	8.8	9.1	9.8	13.3	19.3	17.5	18.8	22.4	22.4
Professional	1.1	1.5	1.2	2.0	1.2	0.8	0.9	0.7	3.6	0.8
Duties on property transfers	2.5	2.5	2.5	5.4	5.5	5.9	6.4	6.9	11.5	16.0
% of total receipts	14	12.5	13.5	8.6	14.3	19.5	13	11	22	19.6
Taxes and levies from poorest traders:										
Municipal market	2.3	2.4	2.5	4.7	11.5	11.8	11.5	12.1	11.5	15.0
Cart stand	1.4	1.5	1.8	2.8	2.0	2.6	2.5	3.3	2.4	3.0
Fines on encroachment	0.2	0.2	0.2	0.2	0.1	0.1	0.1	0.1	0.1	0.1
Slaughter house fees	0.1	0.1	0.1	0.3	0.1	0.2	0.2	0.8	0.3	0.2
% of total receipts	5.0	4.1	4.8	4.7	9.8	11.0	7.5	9.0	8.6	9.0
Total expenditure	62.2	99.9	102.6	105.1	119.1	128.7	205.0	183.6	164.2	201.3
of which:-										
selected staff^c	19.8	22.1	27.0	29.8	31.7	44.8	108.0	87.7	85.5	96.2
% of total expenditure	32	22	26	29	27	35	53	47	52	48

^{a} Arni Municipality, current Rs, lakhs (00 000).

^{b} Major sources of revenue are regular Government of Tamil Nadu allocations, deficit grants, loans and advances.

^{c} Staff of municipal office, tax collectors, public works staff, employees in water supply, public health, sanitation and inspection, market and cart stand management, urban lighting and town planning. See footnote 41 on page 85.

Source: Raw Data provided by Commissioners, Arni Municipality, 1984 and 1994.

to unproductive investment, oppressive labour relations in the informal economy and to short-term finance and investments.

The local State and the accumulation process

What generally significant features of the actually existing local State, relevant to India's accumulation process, can we extract from these examples? A longer list based on some of the available secondary literature is provided in Appendix 2. Here somewhat arbitrarily we highlight six: the porous nature of the boundary between the State and civil society; the significance of the 'shadow' State; the importance of the private status of officials; the consequences of liberalisation at the local level; the depletion of the local State's resources; and fraud and tax evasion. Finally, we will look briefly again at the difference between these features of the existing Indian State, and the conception of the State used by the World Bank.

Porous boundaries

The material summarised in Appendix 2 shows time and again the 'patterns of amalgamation of the interests of the lower middle classes with state capitalism' (Kalecki 1972, p. 163). These examples are not mistakes, accidents or aberrations, although they are often evaluated as if they were. Nor can they be considered as pathological. They add up to a particular kind of development politics and capitalist development. This gives rise to distinctive property relations and class forces, a distinctive wide-based, meshed distribution of private wealth and public resources for development, the result of which is to enhance and protect the power of a coalition of interests or classes organised around local agrarian and mercantile accumulation and politics. This coalition is large and significant. It not only redefines the official development project, but also consumes the resources with which it is meant to be prosecuted. As Rajiv Gandhi once had cause to exclaim: 'There can be no protection if the fence starts eating the crop'.[43] Trimming the State, as the World Bank urges, will not curb this behaviour.

The 'shadow' State

The concept of the 'shadow' State has already been applied to Sierra Leone in the context of civil war.[44] It is also irresistible as a label for the

---

[43] In Herring (1999).
[44] It is also a relevant concept for conditions such as those in Afghanistan and Somalia where the formal State collapsed.

kind of State we have described. Whereas the Sierra Leonian 'shadow' State was a wholly 'informal' entity, and whereas some informal economies are only very loosely connected to their respective formal economies, the 'shadow' State we have described here comes into being because of the formal State and it coexists with it. It can be defined as that part of the informal, 'real' economy that cannot operate without the particular form taken by the State. While it might be considered to be analytically separate from the definition of the State as a set of institutions of political and executive control centred upon government, with which we embarked, *the 'shadow' State is part of the actually existing State.* The 'shadow' State is big, yet it is ignored in development discourse.

Some roles in the 'shadow' State are played simultaneously by the bureaucrats of the official State; for instance, accepting tribute, patronage and/or clientelage. Other 'shadow' state livelihoods are a form of self-employment, although they depend on state employees, politicians and other interested social forces for their incomes; for example, private armies enforcing black or corrupt contracts, intermediaries, technical fixers, gatekeepers, adjudicators of disputes, confidants, contractors and consultants. Hence, the real State, including its shadow, is bigger than the formal State, and has a vested interest in the perpetuation of a stricken and porous formal State. Informed estimates of the resources leaking from anti-poverty programs and from the Public Distribution System of food grains in the early 1990s put them at between 15 and 20 per cent of their budgets.[45] But by the end of the 1990s in some parts of India, notably Bihar, up to 40 per cent of the development budget was said to be creamed off by contractors.[46] The 'shadow' State spills into the lanes surrounding state offices and into the private (some would argue, the 'female') domestic space of officials' residences. This must be the most vivid image of the blurred boundaries between State and society.

The norms of the 'shadow' State may become society's norms, as these proverbs show: 'deliver us from justice', and 'an honest man is he who does not know how to live'. There are severe penalties for not playing according to the 'shadow' State's rules. And as a result of the operation of the 'shadow' State and the informal economy, as a result of the use of the State for accumulation, the formal State loses legitimacy.

Even the official State's famous monopoly of coercion may be challenged. Private armies, security forces and mafias proliferate, either because the State is no longer able to guarantee property rights, because powerful elements in the local economy seize property rights from the State that they need to protect, or because state officials can raise private resources for their own protection from the pay-offs they get for diverting

[45] Copestake 1992; Saith and Harriss-White 2002.
[46] Corbridge and Harriss 2000, p. 171.

the threats to private property rights posed by the State in the cause of its development efforts.

The private status State

When the State's legitimacy weakens, its capacity may come increasingly to depend not only on formal bureaucratic procedures but also on the *personal social identities* of state officials. The consequences of this – or even of a tendency towards it – are far-reaching. One example occurred in the early 1990s; the scene is a small yarn-twisting factory where an income tax officer barges in and demands that the owner pay income tax of Rs 2000.

The officer: 'For a minimum gross output of Rs 1000 a day, the profit is at least Rs 200, so you must have a monthly income of Rs 6000. A government servant on Rs 5000 a month pays income tax, so you should pay'.

The owner: 'You get pensions, subsidised loans for houses, group insurance and a one-month bonus a year, so get out!'

The tax collector, lacking the social standing to insist, left.

The State is thus, first, subordinated to the accumulative zeal of local capital. Second, caste, religion, gender and locality significantly influence access to the State, to its allocations and its social transfers, in ways that tend to exclude women, scheduled castes and Muslims, enforcing a dull everyday communalism and thwarting people's capacity to mobilise across these social divisions.[47] Third, the characteristics of state officials shape the performance of the local State, while the State in turn transforms these social identities (both inside the State and in society at large). At the local level, *private status* is likely to determine the State's operation as much as or even more than does *private interest*, which has been so central to the thinking of the new political economists.

Fourth, as Andre Béteille says: 'in all public institutions, those in superior positions are likely to be of higher, and those in inferior positions of lower, caste'; and when 'personal relations are considered to be the basis of trust ... it is difficult to see how they can be excluded from professional and business activity. The case of public institutions is different, but even here some legitimate grounds exist for the use of recommendations based on personal knowledge ... One can easily see that ground will be repeatedly crossed in a society in which family and kin ties have compelling force and where at the same time independent or private enterprise is progressively displaced by governmental organisation' (1997, pp. 444 and 446). As examples, Craig Jeffrey chronicles the two routes by which

---

[47] Jeffery and Jeffery 1998; Lerche 1998.

rich male *jats* in UP convert their agricultural wealth into power in the State, first by getting state jobs (in the bureaucracy, police and army) via education, tactical marriages and bribes, and second by corruptly co-opting state institutions to the point where intermediaries routinely police established norms of tribute (bribes) that vary according to 'gender, status, caste, kinship and a host of personal considerations'.[48]

Liberalisation, actually existing structural adjustment and institutional scarcity

In the World Bank's thinking, 'The great (and false) debate between state and market seems to be over for now. There is growing realisation that a more credible – not larger – state is needed to create the institutional infrastructure for markets to flourish. A more agile, information-intensive state [will be needed to work] in concert with the international community'.[49] In theory, therefore, India's economic reforms should legitimate black and parallel markets, work to eradicate the distinction between formal and informal, and put paid to the 'shadow' State. The vitality of the market should remove the shortages and scarcities on which the intermediate classes thrive. The removal from state control of goods and services that create opportunities for rent-seeking should reduce corruption. This in turn should strengthen good governance and state legitimacy, encouraging compliance with tax laws and fiscal discipline.

But the last chapter showed that the reforms of the 1990s have mainly been confined to the advanced industrial sectors and to those at the global interface. Even if in the year 2001 there was a 55-million-tonne mountain of grain in reserve, the reforms had not eliminated scarcities in many essential commodities and political manipulation still ensured that grain remained scarce for people below the poverty line.[50] The prediction that deregulation will reduce corruption can be confounded by many factors. Partial changes in ownership may multiply sites for corruption by complicating lines of accountability and diluting enforcement

---

[48] C. Jeffrey 1998.

[49] Chhibber 1996, p. 16.

[50] Grain is given a 50 per cent subsidy to citizens now called 'BPLs' (those with ration cards identifying them as 'Below the Poverty Line') but, in an apparent act of generosity, the quota, doubled in mid-2000 to 20 kilograms per month and increased in 2001 to 35 kilograms, is not allowed to be purchased in units less than this amount. It therefore cannot be purchased by poor people at all. That unmanageable grain stocks have accumulated may be a quite deliberate action to discredit the PDS and the public body administering it – the Food Corporation of India (FCI), the largest state corporation in Asia. It could equally well result from disincentives to States to incur further debt from distributing grain procured in north-west India by the FCI.

capacity. There will be no change in corruption under a regime of privatisation if the State continues to regulate market structure and conduct directly or indirectly through quasi-state organisations. Some business interests will use corrupt means to maintain access to resources or exemptions, while others will use bribes to enforce deregulation and increase the scope of market exchange. Officials may seek bribes against promises of future economic rents, given that their tenure outlives that of politicians. This form of privatisation long preceded the contemporary reforms. As Mushtak Khan has argued, powerful clients/capitalist accumulators continue to hold the keys to the economy so that fiscal reform is met with the now familiar recourse to legal or discretionary loopholes and informal pay-offs.[51]

Legal deregulation might be significant if law and the institutions of law enforcement were effective, but where exchange is regulated by reputation, norm, collective action and private force, changes in the law will not necessarily affect market performance very much. Certain commodities will always have to be state-regulated, if only to ensure the State's capacity to distribute essential commodities in emergencies. Others cannot be left to self-regulation either *de jure* or *de facto* because politically sensitive 'collective' interests will not be served by the market, even if they are not well served by the State either.[52]

In fact 'liberalisation' in the form of a contraction of the state is not a new phenomenon, or the product of a sudden ideological change of face in 1991 by the then ruling party. It has really been going on informally for a long time by starving the local State of revenue, sometimes in very acute forms. For example in Arni, which we visited above, roughly 90 per cent of municipal taxes are said to be paid in the last month of the fiscal year. This 'seasonality' can cause the state to teeter chronically on the brink of fiscal collapse. As the fiscal hungry season lengthens and the fiscal famine intensifies, capital expenditure is cut and its ratio to current expenditure declines; then, within 'current expenditure', materials, goods and services are reduced relative to salaries; finally staff are not replaced and recruitment is frozen. In services provided out of state rev-

---

[51] Khan 2000b.

[52] Industries that remain regulated by the Government of India are: (1) commodities reserved for production in small-scale industries; (2) commodities covered by the Essential Commodities Act of 1955, plus its special provisions; for example, agricultural produce such as food grains, sugar, edible oil and pulses, cement and kerosene, and so on. Industrial licences are still (2001) required for coal and lignite; petroleum (other than crude) and its distillation products; the distillation and brewing of alcoholic drinks; sugar; cigars and cigarettes made of tobacco; electronic aerospace and defence equipment, industrial explosives (for example, detonating fuses, gunpowder); hazardous chemicals; drugs and chemicals (Reserve Bank of India 1999).

enue, we then encounter half a fire brigade (and even half a fire brigade dependent on informal patronage for access to water, in the absence of a budget for well-deepening); sweepers waiting months for their pay; and a police force at half strength.

Tables 4.2 and 4.3 provide some evidence of trends in public spending at the all-India level. In one crucial respect these differ from those that cause this sequence of state contraction at the level of a small municipality. Over the last 30 years, even during the period of liberalisation, the public sector has increased inexorably as a share of GDP, from 12 per cent in 1968 to 28 per cent in 1998, whereas the reverse is true at the level of the town and its municipality. Nevertheless the growth of current public expenditure – through revenue, debt and transfers (from the Central Government to the States) – has outstripped that of capital expenditure.[53] In Table 4.2, periods of shortfall in revenue receipts due to shocks have been identified. These shocks are almost invariably due to drought, which continues to have severe ramifications on most sectors of the economy whenever it happens (though the era of liberalisation has been spared the most severe episodes, which were in 1966–67; 1972–4; 1980–81 and 1983–84). Table 4.2 shows the adverse repercussions of drought-induced shocks on revenue as a proportion of GDP. Tables 4.2 and 4.3 show that when this happens, public-sector capital investment is stalled to protect current expenditure. Within the latter, salaries (on a long-term upward trend in terms of their share of gross domestic product)[54] tend to be protected at the expense of purchases of goods and services.

The consequences of state depletion

The effect of what the new political economists call 'institutional scarcity', but which we see as state depletion, is the destruction of institutions needed by the mass of the workforce to redress the 'hidden injuries of class'.[55] Although understaffing reinforces bureaucratic incentives for rent-seeking, such corruption, which is at the centre of the concerns of the new political economists, is really only the tip of the iceberg. There has been a rise in the discretionary powers of officials, and also of their patrons and minders in civil society. Discretion and foot-dragging in conformity with the desires of a political patron and private paymaster are

---

[53] Bhatia 1996; Reserve Bank of India 1999. During this period, capital investment has drifted away from agriculture towards commerce and manufacturing (see Central Statistical Organisation 1999, Tables 2.7B and 2.8B).

[54] From 9.6 per cent during the period 1985 to 1989 to 12.1 per cent in 1997–98 (Reserve Bank of India 1999, Statement 151, p. 183).

[55] Corbridge and Harriss 2000, p. 171.

Table 4.2   *Tax: GDP ratios (1965–66 to 1995–96) and the ratio of factor income of public employees to NDP (1965–66 to 1984–85)*

Year	Total tax revenue (All India)			Compensation of public employees (CPE) as % of NDP	CPE as % of govt contribution to NDP
	Direct	Indirect	Total		
1	2	3	4		
1965–66	2.81	8.37	11.18	10.6	80
1966–67	2.59	8.43	11.03	10.3	81
1967–68	2.25	7.73	9.99	10.1	83
1968–69	2.29	7.96	10.25	11.0	81
1969–70	2.38	8.02	10.40	11.3	81
1970–71	2.34	8.67	11.01	11.7	81
1971–72	2.53	9.52	12.05	12.3	81
1972–73	2.64	9.98	12.62	12.5	82
1973–74	2.50	9.41	11.92	12.9	84
1974–75	2.50	10.09	12.59	13.1	82
1975–76	3.17	11.03	14.20	14.6	80
1976–77	3.04	11.48	14.53	14.7	74
1977–78	2.79	10.99	13.78	14.2	74
1978–79	2.74	12.17	14.90	14.8	75
1979–80	2.71	12.76	15.46	15.6	75
1980–81	2.40	12.19	14.59	15.7	77
1981–82	2.59	12.52	15.11	15.9	73
1982–83	2.52	12.77	15.29	16.8	71
1983–84	2.36	12.82	15.19	16.6	72
1984–85	2.30	13.18	15.48	17.7	72
1985–86	2.38	14.11	16.50	n.a.	n.a.
1986–87	2.35	14.56	16.91		
1987–88	2.25	14.85	17.10		
1988–89	2.47	14.44	16.91		
1989–90	2.44	14.56	17.01		
1990–91	2.29	14.09	16.38		
1991–92	2.70	14.03	16.73		
1992–93	2.75	13.43	16.17		
1993–94	2.68	12.36	15.04		
1994–95	3.00	12.35	15.35		
1995–96	3.20	12.47	15.66		

Years underlined are those of drought and its immediate impact.
Sources: Bhatia 1996; Chandok 1990; Government of India 1997.

Table 4.3 *Fiscal expenditure of the Government of India*

Year	1980–81	1985–86	1989–90	1990–91	1991–92	1992–93*	1993–94	1994–95	1995–96	1996–97	1997–98**
Total expenditure as % of GDP											
a. Wages and salaries	10.9%	9.6%	9.6%	12.0%	9.8%	9.9%	9.2%	8.7%	9.2%	9.2%	12.1%
b. Commodities and services	12.1%	11.5%	12.4%	9.3%	11.9%	11.4%	12.7%	12.2%	13.4%	12.9%	11.3%
c. Gross fixed capital formation	7.8%	8.4%	8.3%	7.8%	8.0%	8.9%	9.0%	8.9%	9.1%	8.8%	9.0%
d. Increase in works stores	0.7%	0.2%	0.3%	0.4%	0.2%	0.4%	-0.2%	-0.3%	-0.1%	0.0%	0.0%
e. Financial resources provided to the rest of the economy (transfers, loans and investments)	68.5%	70.3%	69.3%	70.5%	70.1%	69.4%	69.4%	70.5%	68.4%	69.1%	67.6%

* Revised estimates.
** Budget estimates.
Source: Reserve Bank of India 1999, statement 151, p. 183.

Table 4.4 *Two global point estimates of black income generated in India (Rs million)*

Item	1975–76	1980–81
Tax-evaded income	37 410	98 130
Illegal activities	33 180 to 49 780	57 130 to 85 700
Under-declared immovable property values	22 560	36 640
Leakages from the public sector	1540 (maximum)	4190 (maximum)
Leakages from the private corporate sector	2530 (maximum)	3250 (maximum)
Under-invoicing of exports	1390	2350
Global black money estimate	99 580 to 118 700	203 620 to 236 780
As a percentage of GDP at factor cost, current prices	15 to 18	18 to 21
Leakages total (and as % of black income)	4070 (4.09)	7440 (3.66)

Source: Roy (1996)

widespread. Selective (and often politicised) undermanning is normal.[56] The pattern of vacancies has less and less to do with the difficulties of fill-ing reserved posts;[57] there is intense pressure from all kinds of social organisations for preference in recruitment. Havoc is caused to lines of accountability because lay-offs are not systematic, and there is a reduced capacity to enforce regulations. Departmental memories exist only in the lower ranks of the bureaucracy, if anywhere. The terms and conditions of bureaucratic service deteriorate, raising incentives to moonlight and to supplement salaries in other ways.[58] The quality of state-provided goods and services deteriorates, encouraging private or black alternatives. Queues lengthen with increasing incentives to 'exit', so that only the need-iest clients remain queuing: the State tends to be aggravating inequality, the very opposite of its constitutional mandate.

As the State becomes weaker, so elements in it attempt to buy off pow-erful challenges from the informal economy by selling rights to the State's political transactions. Politicians have long realised this and have inserted themselves as brokers, paid by powerful interests to *prevent* regulation and taxation, and paid by officials to influence their transfers and promotions. These payments are returns to investments in the electoral process, and they also reinforce a politician's capacity to see off challenges. Payments from officials lead in turn to an acceleration in the velocity of their post-

[56] Exacerbated by increasing velocities of transfer (Noorani 1997a and b; Banik 1999).
[57] In 1999 a special Commission of the Government of Tamil Nadu exposed the lie that the supply of suitably qualified candidates for reserved posts was in any way constrained.
[58] The salary rises recommended by the 5th Pay Commission have diffused from central to state administrations and are slowly being claimed by parastatal organisations. As a consequence, administration costs rose from Rs 31 821 *crores* in 1996–7 to Rs 106 521 *crores* in 2001–2 (*Indian Express*, August 21st, 2001; *Deccan Herald*, May 1st, 2002).

ings. The result is a '*spinning*' senior administration. Between 1977 and 1999, for instance, in UP there were 13 governments, interspersed with President's Rule. The six-monthly rotation of the BSP and BJP in 1997–98 led to over 1000 transfers in the UP of cadres of the elite Indian Administrative Service (IAS) and Indian Police Service. Under Mayavati, transfers ran at an average of seven per day. Under Kalyan Singh they had risen to 16. Over half the corps of IAS officers are transferred within 12 months of posting.[59] This 'spinning' State has a severe impact on economic regulation. As the bureaucracy is politicised, morale plummets. The costs in the loss of quality of administration are significant. Incompetence increases, if only because the time is lacking to acquire the informal knowledge and to develop the informal relations that make institutions work – not to mention corrupt preferment. Incompetence at the top leads in turn to acts of passive resistance by subordinates. Since the quality of supervision declines, other kinds of disruption are possible. Disincentives to innovate are built-in. State capacity to achieve goals slows down as the velocity of transfer speeds up. Planned projects are subject to time and cost overruns; Robert Chambers calls these effects a 'slipping clutch'. Public information becomes less systematic and abundant. Poor quality, easily sabotageable law raises questions about the intentions underlying the law and the possibility of corrupt coalitions between the administration and the judiciary. The prevalent lack of experience of legislators suggests incompetence rather than conspiracy. But the resulting skeins of corruption satisfy a broad set of interests so effectively that the consequences of incompetent law-making are very similar. The State loses legitimacy, revenue compliance weakens, and the contradiction between rights, obligations and resources intensifies. This is hardly what is envisaged in the World Bank's demands for civil service reform.[60]

The developmental failure of fraud and tax evasion

Tables 4.4 and 4.5, for the all-India level, reproduced from Rathin Roy's research, show that the great bulk of black income is due to the lack of capacity of the Indian State to tax effectively. A questionnaire supplied to all Income Tax Commissions to provide information for the last Government of India report on *Aspects of the Black Economy in India* (1985) is the source of the latest data on the origins of black income. Black income is generated primarily in 'areas of petty bourgeois activity – the domain of the trader, contractor and (real) estate agent. This points to the build-up of a significant wealth owning and wealth generating constituency *outside*

---

[59] Banik 1999, pp. 34–5, footnotes 69 and 70.
[60] See Das (1998).

Table 4.5 *Aspects of the black economy in India: selected data from the NIPFP qualitative study*

Sectors/Activities	Significance rating (%)
Sectors generating black income	
Construction	77.6
Professionals	77.9
Film industry	91.1
Trade	69.2
Large-scale manufacturing	89.5
Hotels, restaurants, etc.	43.6
Road transport	50.0
Illegal activities generating black income	
Smuggling	90.8
Selling of licences and permits	48.4
Kickbacks, bribes, etc.	57.4
Capital gains on real estate transactions	92.4
Methods of black income generation	
Suppression or understatement of gross receipts	96.1
Exaggeration of expenses	83.6
Under-valuation of assets	83.6
'*Benami*' business	51.5
Forms in which black wealth is held	
Shown as income deriving from agricultural activity	93.7
Under-values real estate	96.0
Held in precious metals or jewellery	74.6
Under-valued business equipment, stocks, etc.	65.1

the dominant coalition identified by Bardhan' – of big business, the agrarian elite and the professionals.[61] The mechanisms are under-declaration of receipts, under-valuation of assets and exaggeration of expenses. The form taken by black wealth is not cash (the medium of corruption) but real estate, wholesale and retail trade stocks, and precious metal (although gold is less significant than land and real estate). Leakages from the private and public sectors due to corruption amount to merely one-twentieth of the losses from tax evasion and the black economy. Tax evasion and crime do not always require corruption.

The consequences of the loss of state control over such a large part of economic activity have been well elaborated by Arun Kumar. They can be summarised as a loss of control over development policy because of inadequate funds and leakages in expenditure. He highlights social infra-

---

[61] Roy (1996), tables and quotation from pp. 28–9; Bardhan (1984, 1998, pp. 40–53).

structure, education, health, housing and civic infrastructure, which are under-provided and of poor quality; environmental degradation and waste; and an overblown tertiary sector. The internationalisation of the economy is 'unplanned', in a way that marginalises the mass of the population; and the institutions of democracy are increasingly subverted. Resources are laundered abroad. 'Paradoxically, the interest of those who have benefited most from the black economy has also been hurt the most since growth has been stunted.'[62] The appearance of resource shortages and poverty weakens India in international fora. 'This has led to the voluntary acceptance of an unequal globalisation on the terms laid down by outsiders ... Indian politics ... has even less space to represent the interest of the weak in society, weakening its democratic fabric'.[63]

Finally, consider a simple calculation. Using data on poverty indicators, assuming the constancy of all the relevant parameters and making allowance for inflation, it appears that the aggregate annual 'poverty deficit' in the mid-1990s amounted to about Rs 12 500 crores. This is the annual expenditure deemed necessary for the Indian State to eradicate poverty. Now the stock of smuggled gold alone that was accumulated in the six years from 1990–95 has been carefully and conservatively estimated to be about 1300 tonnes, valued at international prices as US$15 billion in 1998 (Rs 52 500 crores). If this entire stock could have been impounded and made to yield a modest, stable return of 15 per cent per annum, it would have generated a stream of Rs 7875 crores in perpetuity, or over 60 per cent of what is estimated to be required to wipe out the entire scandal of income poverty in India.[64]

The Indian State and the World Bank's State

I have tried to describe some of the forms taken by the local State, most of which are not so much market-friendly but market-abused. They are the self-reinforcing product of a pervasive reluctance to comply with regulative law. It is reform to non-compliance that ought to be at the heart of the new international project of capitalist development in India – just as accountability ought to be at the centre of development policy.

Other students of the local State have written of 'ontological incoherence', 'multiple-layering', 'negotiated grids', 'normative pluralism' and 'the coexistence of predatory and development States and fractions

[62] Kumar 1999, p. 191.
[63] Kumar 1999, p. 192.
[64] Subramanian and Harriss-White 1999.

within States', of 'the domination of the developmental State at the centre and the predatory State lower down', the State's 'dissolving into the
tissue of society at the local level', of 'multiple manifestations and inter-
penetrations' and 'particularistic embeddedness'.[65] The keys to an understanding of the local State suggested here are the plurality of state forms
and the meshing of State and society, such that the line between the official, but 'private status' State (in which officials bring into active play
their social identities derived from outside the State), and the private
interest 'shadow' State (in which a much larger proportion of society
gains livelihoods dependent on the form of the State than is employed
directly by the State), is hard to draw.

The World Bank's project for the State is the opposite of what is
needed. First, according to the World Bank, a better set of regulative policy tools needs to be developed from which 'governments' can select
those they need, according to criteria of efficiency. What we see, however,
is that a very impressive mass of regulative tools is already available to the
Indian State, but that in the cases reviewed here those that are selected,
used and transformed in use are those that foster the accumulation of the
local capitalist class.

However, instead of counterpoising the State and market, as the World
Bank used to, it now speaks of a partnership between them in order to
provide the institutional infrastructure for market exchange; that is,
India's 'product'. But India's distinctive 'product' at the level of the local
State is a basis for widespread fraud, springing from social unaccounta-
bility. Corruption is the surface phenomenon, the way most people
encounter, visualise and discuss the local State.[66] But tax evasion is the
much more important state and social failure. The evasion of tax is not
only a matter of accumulative greed, it is also the most obvious sign of a
distinctive conception of accountability and morality that focuses on
close kin and immediate locality, and excludes the generation and redistribution of resources through the State to society as a whole.

Anti-corruption campaigns have more of a history than anti–tax-evasion campaigns. Anti-corruption campaigns are championed by civil
society organisations, while the most successful anti–tax-evasion campaigns have taken the form of state amnesties for the declaration of
previously concealed income. Their politics is under-researched and conditions for the success of either seem to be rather limited. An evaluation
of Indian anti-corruption campaigns by Anne-Marie Goetz and Rob

---

[65] J. Harriss 2000; Sengupta 1998; Gupta 1993; Mooij 1999; Landy 1998; Jeffrey 1998;
Herring 1999.
[66] Gupta 1993; Guhan and Paul 1997.

Jenkins identifies one such necessary condition: the need to avoid safe compromises of the sort commonly made by NGO-style civil social organisations as agents of the State if people's rights to audit and to information are to be asserted.[67] To do this successfully a resolutely independent and persistent process of contestation was required. However, the World Bank, in its pragmatic, authoritarian and discursive incoherence, and in its practice of financial patronage (that is, its highly discriminatory patterns of 'aid') has taken the opposite stance. 'Broad political contestability, however, appears to be neither necessary nor sufficient for sound economic and social policies.'[68]

The World Bank also wants to have States redesign their apparatuses to be information-intensive agents of globalised capital, providing abundant, continually updated data and indicators, not only of the condition of the economy but of many other parts of society too, including non-governmental organisations and the 'social sector'.[69] The impressive on-line data service produced at all levels by the Indian State serves as a high-tech mask behind which the political and social relations described here continue to operate.

Contemporary calls for the radical privatisation of the State, from what is rather comically termed the 'international development community',[70] ignore the effective radical privatisation, informalisation and now mafianisation that south Asian States have been undergoing for much longer than the era of liberalisation of the 1990s. Even in the corporate sector, which is not the concern of this book, the absence of enforceable state regulation conforming to the standards of governance of global corporate capital has lured international (finance) capital into the fray as a regulator. It is international capital, rather than the State or labour, that is currently exerting the most active pressure to reform degenerate patriarchal, authoritarian and familial governance structures and non-compliant contractual behaviour at the apex of Indian capitalism.[71] Even in the corporate sector its success is very limited and there is absolutely no reason to suppose it capable of being extended into the informal economy.

[67] Jenkins and Goetz 1999; see also Noorani 1997b.
[68] Chhibber 1996, p. 16.
[69] Wolfenson 1999.
[70] An absurd if not hypocritical community, given the divergent sets of interests involved (ranging from intensely competitive NGOs, via the individual bilateral aid donors competing for niches and distinctive missions, to the major fault lines between the neo-liberal project of the World Bank and the IMF (via the UNDP's rights and redistributivist agenda), and to the possibly more critical and toothless projects of UNRISD and the ILO, and so on).
[71] Banaji 2000; Banaji and Mody 2001.

Governments like that of India resist the Bank's procrustean reforms, not only for reasons of electoral politics, but also because in reality States do not take the form assumed by the World Bank. The Indian State is protean; its form is complex. Although the local State's capacity to protect and to deliver has degenerated during the 1990s, we have suggested that there is patterned structure to this process of degeneration. The pattern underlying the turbulent relations surrounding the State's competence, autonomy and accountability is the drive of capital for a regulative environment in which it can maximise and stabilise its returns, and minimise both its costs and its obligations and accountability.

Any useful reform, whether to market regulation, to infrastructure for development or to the social sector, must start from these sets of material interests. Most suggestions for reform do not do this and they are cooped up in statements of good intention. Reforms to the policy agenda (and to the priorities of policies on that agenda) will be of little consequence without careful attention to two other kinds of politics of policy. These operate simultaneously with the politics of the agenda, but in the less publicly visible processes of 'policy implementation'. One is the realm of procedure in which policy intention is translated into laws and rules. The evidence in this chapter has shown two salient features of the politics of procedures. The first is the slippage between rhetoric and rules; the second is that the arena of rules is a set of political resources for the control of which there is competition inside and outside the State. The other kind of politics of policy involves the power struggles over the raising and allocation of resources by the State and over access by those allocated such resources. In this chapter it has been shown that this complex and degenerate State is locked into relations of accumulation with intermediate classes (as well as with corporate capital).[72] It has a large shadow of informal livelihoods capable of exerting much more pressure on state performance than has generally been recognised. It is most unlikely to be the instrument of its own reform. In the search for reformist social forces it would seem that those interests that are capable of manipulating the politics of procedure (for instance, by public interest litigation) and the politics of resources (for instance, by reform to public finance) in the interests of a socially encompassing accountability are less evident than are the reformist social forces operating at the discursive level (putting forward policy ideas), or those working for improvements in popular access (helping disadvantaged people to know their rights and – sometimes – to get them).

[72] Mukherjee and Kundu 2000.

5   Gender, family businesses and business families

In this chapter we turn to a less well-publicised social structure of accumulation – in all countries, but not least in India – the social construction of gender relations. This affects much more than the position of women in the *economy*, but we can usefully begin there. The economic position of women is institutionalised in many different ways: in the types of firms they mainly work for (petty, undercapitalised, illegal/informal, domestic), in the sectors of the economy where they are concentrated (notably agriculture), in the types of task they are assigned (particularly tasks with limited or no upward mobility, and those that require skills achieved with little or no formal education) and the types of contract they are given (casual). The proletarianisation of women has resulted in distinctive 'segmented labour market opportunities, largely different work rules and means of control, patterns of participation, compensation for skills and education and lower pay' (Albeda and Tilly 1994, p. 216). This affects the prospects for increasing female employment in secondary labour markets (that is, for services and clerical work and in the female professions such as teaching and nursing), and suggests the likelihood that increasing demands will be made on the State to regulate the terms and conditions of female participation. All of this narrative has been lifted from the 'gender history' of the pre- and post-war *American* economy. The eerie relevance of this to contemporary India testifies to the basic fact that patriarchal relations have always been a prominent feature of capitalism.[1]

But this is *not* to subscribe to the fallacy of 'viewing modernisation everywhere in the world today as essentially a replication of what happened ... in Western Europe ... and North America' (Madan 1997, p. 418), and for good reasons: India is different in many crucial respects,

---

[1] It is thus of lesser relevance to the mainstream project of the social structure of accumulation school in which the role of social structures in the periodisation of capital is stressed, and more relevant to our less ambitious project of characterising Indian capital.

and not just as regards the prospects for women's advancement.[2] Gender is integral to the economy in other ways, too, and it is not merely a labour market phenomenon.[3] For example, there is a hierarchy of power based on the male control of sexuality, which shapes the social structures of accumulation in ways that both cut across class *and* define the *capitalist* class. In this arena of power, young men are subordinated to older men – patriarchy in its original sense, the governance of male society by its elders. These 'male relations of patriarchy' – relations among men in which gender identity is important – have developmental and welfare consequences that actually reinforce the marginalisation and subordination of women in various ways.[4] By tracking these male relations of patriarchy we can better understand India's contemporary paradox of gender, involving the increased participation of women in the economy, and increased household assets, and yet at the same time, *increased excess female child mortality*. For this we need to describe the gender relations by means of which capital is controlled, and their implications for both development and well-being.

Just as feminist discourse has had to tread its way through the legal, political and analytical minefields of gender-essentialism,[5] so the study of male relations of accumulation cannot avoid a confrontation with both *essentialism* (the notion of an inherent 'masculinity') and *naturalism* (the idea that such relations are given by nature and biology). If the question of the impact of male relations of patriarchy on the economy has been posed at all, it has been done implicitly as part of a defence of the adaptive efficiency of the Hindu *family* against an occidental critique of it, based in turn on an orientalist ideology of the Hindu family as a developmental obstacle.[6] This defence has stressed the adaptability of the

---

[2] This has been the object of much high-quality research. Any selection is invidious but see Agarwal (1994); Bardhan (1993); Baud (1983); Kapadia (1995b), Krishnaraj and Deshmukh (1993); Mies (1986); Mencher (1988); Saradamoni (1985) among many others. Walby (1990) identifies six arenas through which patriarchal relations are construed and maintained: household production, wage work, the State, male violence, sexuality and cultural institutions. The sphere of the firm and of capital accumulation, the object of this chapter, is entirely missing.

[3] Clark 1993, p. 10.

[4] See Jackson (1999) for a general analysis of masculinity and work.

[5] See Chowdhury (1998) for her lucid exposition of the trade-off for political mobilisation between, on the one hand, unessentialist and nuanced conceptions of the female gender – and their consequence, which has been to fracture the Indian women's movement – and, on the other, the analytical impasse of an essentialist conception of gender as a homogeneous category, under which women could mobilise to claim basic rights.

[6] Madan (1997, pp. 422–6) calls it a 'deductive argument', but it is also a tangled one: economic growth is thwarted by, on the one hand, the disincentives to investment, work and discipline of co-parcenary property ownership, and on the other by the opposite – by the fragmentation of co-parcenary property. Less ambiguously, growth is threatened by the stunting effect of the non-meritocratic inheritance of occupational skills and the likely rise in the risk of failure, and also by the brake applied to the development of impersonal forms of trust (though this argument is set against one stressing the value of family support in risky ventures). More ambiguously, growth is threatened by the 'irrational' nature of either collective *or* authoritarian decision-making.

Hindu household to new combinations of capital and labour, and to the management of unindividuated property rights. While it has been sensitive to the role of the Hindu household in the reproduction of social inequality,[7] this defence has been gender-blind. It can be used as a 'text' that describes the roles of men.[8]

The Indian economy, however, is not organised only through households and markets, it is also organised through firms. The firm has been called an 'island of planned coordination in a sea of market relations' (Hodgson 1988, p. 178). If we dispense with 'supertrader' theories of firms as bundles of quasi-market contracts (as Amartya Sen does with consummate ease for Beckerian theories of that other non-market institution, the family),[9] we are left, according to the new institutional economics, with three other possibilities. The firm can be seen as either (1) a unit of authority in which principals devise optimal contracts for agents to maximise work in their own and their managers' interests at minimal supervision and transaction costs; (2) a social space where the entire calculus of transaction costs is not necessary; or (3) a set of norms and institutions to minimise uncertainty and opportunism. These rationales are not mutually exclusive, nor are they really empirically testable, or capable of being compared – a common fate of explanation in the new institutional economics. In all of them, however, something real – the firm – is dissolved into an abstract social space, a set of norms. It is as though firms did not exist as the building blocks of capital. Yet this is what they are, and they have a distinctive gendered character. In small-town India, firms are the concrete extensions into market exchange of the household – the unit of production and reproduction, which is *also* the unit of control over technology and money. As Gordon White put it, the firm is: 'a combat unit designed for battle in the market' (1993, p. 8).[10]

The links between this combat unit's gender relations at work and home have to be made empirically, and we will use material from the town of Arni in Tamil Nadu and from its surrounding villages.

---

[7] Madan 1997; Béteille 1997.

[8] The question of deconstructing 'hegemonic masculinity' has been recently answered (in an innovative way) by Jackson (1999) in relation to subaltern men and women and their work. Her arenas are labour markets and households.

[9] On the grounds of being simultaneously oversimplistic and based perversely on an assumption that markets are actually redundant. For, in expecting market-like equilibria of prices and quantities *without* all the institutional arrangements that go to make markets, markets are *both* central *and* redundant (Sen 1997, p. 454)!

[10] For Béteille 'the family has replaced caste as an agent of social control' (1997, p. 448). This is an assertion we would wish to dispute if 'society' is understood to include the economy – see Chapter 7. The family firm is as significant an arena for social control as are its kinship arrangements; the latter commonly being arranged to serve the former. Moreover, just as this unit of people may have a complex composition, so its associated unit of capital may proliferate into a complex portfolio of firms, mini-conglomerates with a rich taxonomy of forms of control and management. Their tactics of accumulation may not be fully understood from the analysis of any one of their components (an error not infrequently committed by field economists and revenue authorities alike).

Arni is 150 kilometres south-west of Chennai; still four hours by bus! Its official population in 1991 was 55 000, up from 39 000 in 1971 (but in the previous chapter we saw that the population of the 'organic' town is much larger, possibly double that). Five per cent of its population is agricultural and works its land from town. The economy is dominated by retail shops, mills (for rice and silk), by the workshop manufacture of gold ornaments, by the sale of fuel, by industries transporting people, by trade in commodities and by banking and informal finance. Its large firms have proved durable. The level of concentration in Arni's businesses is dramatic (see Table 1.4, p. 12). In 1973–74 the gross output of the top 10 per cent of firms (measured by their assets) was 13 times larger than that of all the firms in the bottom 50 per cent. The top firm had an output 4.5 times greater than that of the smallest 50 per cent of firms put together. By 1983–84 the figures were 66 times and 9 times, respectively. Ten years later they were 117 and 43 times; that is, an entirely different scale of local capital was being accumulated at the top.

But the vast mass of businesses are family firms with small labour forces (see Table 5.1). The average number of livelihoods (seven to eight per firm) has not changed much over the period 1973–93. The proportion of *purely* family firms (petty commodity producers and traders, key components of the intermediate classes) has risen from 28 per cent to 35 per cent over the 20-year period, while the proportion of family labour in the entire labour force has remained static at around a quarter.[11] The workshops and mills, however, have become increasingly 'satanic' over time, through the remorseless casualisation of the wage labour force. Between 1973 and 1993, casual labour increased from 23 per cent of all jobs to 57 per cent.

Patriarchy and Accumulation I: Men[12]

Patriarchy among the business elite of Arni (made up of firms with (under)estimated present values of between Rs 33 lakhs (£50 000) and Rs 33 million (£500 000) in 1994) may be described well enough for our

[11] While all owners of capital are active workers, the composition of this workforce has changed with the entry of a small number of female family members of low caste.

[12] The field material used here comprises the 20 firms of the business elite (including rice and silk, fuel and transport) from a random stratified 6 per cent sample of 253 businesses, interviewed in 1994–95. The elite subset comprises forward and 'upper' backward castes: mainly *tulluva vellala agamudaiya mudaliars, saurashtrians, jains, naidus* and *chettiars*, and is disproportionately important in terms of assets, employment and gross output. We also use field material on nearly 100 leaders of institutions of collective action or trade associations interviewed in 1997.

Table 5.1 *Caste and gender in the business economy of a town in south India, 1973–93*

1973	No. of firms sampled: 93		workforce: 664			
	Family labour		Permanent		Casual Wage	
CASTE	Male	Female	Male	Female	Male	Female
Forward caste/other	9	0	4	0	0.7	0
Backward caste	6	0	15	5	0.1	0
Most backward caste	6	0	14	8	6	4
Scheduled castes	3	0	0.1	0	3	6
Muslims	3	0	2	0	2	0
	27	0	35.1	13	11.8	10
1983	No. of firms sampled: 126		workforce: 1037			
Forward caste/other	3	0	2	0	0	0
Backward caste	12	0.3	17	3	3	2
Most backward caste	4	0	17	3	5	3
Scheduled castes	1	0	2	0	10	2
Muslims	3	0	3	0	2	0
	23	0.3	41	6	20	7
1993	No. of firms sampled: 253		workforce: 1955			
Forward caste/other	3	0.6	0.1	0		
Backward caste	10	3	7	2		
Most backward caste	5	2	4	0.5		
Scheduled castes	2	0.4	0.6	0.1		
Muslims	1.5	0.2	0.7	0.1		
Caste + gender unknown					57	
	21.5	6.2	12.4	2.7	57	

Figures in percentages of total workforce
Source: Basile and Harriss-White, 2000

purposes without needing to deconstruct either capital or men further. We start by focusing on them.

Table 5.2 models the life-cycle of members of a family business. Young boys are actively socialised into the management of capital from early ages. Not so girls. Though the business day peaks early, it has a sizeable stretch that is literally (and may be also figuratively) black, lasting into the night (long after school hours) to take advantage of the cheaper telephone rates after 9 p.m. Commercial contracts may also be made in special rooms at home – as happens, for example, in the silk trade. In this way the

Table 5.2 *Gender roles in family businesses*

Males	Females
Firm	*Household*
Management and control by male family members	Strategic control by men
	Tactical control and socialisation by women
Permanent labour force (clientelised, males)	Female/child wage labour in domestic service
Casual labour force (sometimes unionised, males)	Occasional male labour in domestic service
(largest single element of productive labour, deliberately casualised, female)	
Life-cycle	
Youth	*Formation*
(Work) shop and home-based socialisation into management of capital and labour	Home-based socialisation into management of household (children, food, ceremony)
Apprenticeship	Educated for marriage alliance
(sometimes elided with schooling)	
Skills, contacts, networks, individual and collective elements of reputation	
(higher education may be threatening)	
Entry in business	*Marriage*
As member of family firm, with division of tasks based on male authority	Durables in dowry crucial to groom's status in family firm
As 'independent' firm closely financed and controlled by male elders	Fungibles in dowry contribute to groom's starting capital
	Household reproductive labour
Death of patriarch	Production of male labour crucial (1) to power relations in division of property and (2) to size of family firm
Splitting of family firm	
Vulnerability of property rights, finance, conflict over sites and rights	
Consolidation of business	*Consolidation of household*
Growth of firm	Social work
Formation of conglomerates with brothers and sons	Management of household
Complex overlapping forms of ownership	Reproductive work
Subcontracting, casualisation of labour (especially female labour)	
Amassing of dowries for daughters	
Investment in land	

public political arenas of 'market' and 'State', conventionally considered as male space, are able to penetrate to the heart of domestic territory conventionally considered female.[13] Boys are allowed to watch contract-making there and to witness the compliant behaviour that reaps big returns later on, but girls are discouraged. The effects cannot be costed but we can see how implicitly costly it is in cases when fathers have died young. Not only is the household given an economic shock, but young sons are also deprived of this basic socialisation, and the upward track of the family's accumulation trajectory is jeopardised. Other kin or caste members sometimes substitute, but this is no longer seen by them as a duty; its costs make it increasingly dispensable. Youths serve apprentice-ships with their fathers, or more commonly with their uncles. Unpaid over a period of years, they are gradually recognised to have gained skills, networks of contacts, and individual and collective elements of reputa-tion (the lubricants of power that Bourdieu[14] has called social and cul-tural capital) in ways that reinforce the continuity of caste-based business. This is the more important because the crucible of the modern business network – school and college – does not yet perform this role. Young men's education is then sacrificed to the control of capital. Arni has been a good laboratory in which to see this process at work because, until 1999, it lacked further education facilities and young males had to migrate elsewhere for them. Only 6 out of 82 male members of business-elite family workforces had been allowed to gain degrees. There are two reasons for low levels of male education in the local capitalist class. One is that those who do have degrees are not seen to be using them in their family businesses. As pure investments, the returns are not obvious to elders. 'Will education mean bread?' they ask. The other is the risk of higher education to the integrity of family capital when young men in whom property has already been vested, so as to avoid tax, migrate out of family control to get a college education, thanks to the State's failure to provide higher education locally. This is what Sen might call an 'allo-cational error' (1997, p. 455), because the business elite is thereby seri-ously under-equipped for the technologies (information and other electronic technology) required for the next scaling-up of capital.

---

[13] See Chapter 4. So much for one of Weber's conditions for capitalism – the separation of the household from the place of work (1970/1994, p. 356). Just as domestic space is not exclusively private and female, so 'outside' is far from being exclusively public and male. The space of a town devoted to public activity is also gendered: within temples and cinemas, even within institutions of the State such as hospitals and schools, space is gendered to the point of segregation.

[14] Bourdieu 1984.

In this necessarily somewhat stylised account, young men have two alternatives: to be allowed to start on their own or join (part of) a jointly operated firm. Partnerships are still rather rare (and cross-caste partnerships are rarer) and when they occur they are temporary, one partner tending to supply labour and the other capital. It is extremely rare for fathers or elder brothers *not* to provide an enabling part of the starting capital and to have an influence on the management of capital afterwards. Subsequently, money is made available on privileged terms (often without interest) and swung between male family members' firms. This finance is important not only in itself but also as a credential and collateral for further informal and commercial credit arrangements. For these reasons, the partition of joint businesses can deprive firms of access to large pools of credit. Partition makes firms vulnerable: the business equivalent of the newly incoming north Indian bride. Bitter feuds can also erupt between brothers over the clarification of hitherto fuzzy property rights and component firms, and occasionally 'conglomerates' can crumble in their entirety. Just as important as finance is control over the rights to rent – or the transfer and 'inheritance' of – exact sites. Location is as significant an element in profit as are the labour process, repeated contracts and the prices of commodities.

Although the dowries of incoming brides have been very important to the capitalisation of the largest local units of capital – two generations ago[15] – their importance can be exaggerated. Dowries include substantial components of consumer durables or status goods such as *sarees*, which complement more fungible forms of capital like gold.[16] While marriage alliances do enable the transfer of resources, usually to bride-receivers, the cementing of business alliances with sons-in-law and other affines is less common, happening in only 20 per cent of the elite firms in Arni.[17] Even though tax law offers incentives for single, male ownership, and even though firms comply with those incentives on paper (to avoid tax and to profit from subsidised credit that is available to single-owner firms), the actually existing control of capital is through flexible cross-

[15] So the dowry is not a recent practice in this region.

[16] Dowries in the form of consumer durables are economic multipliers creating demand for these lumpy items and generating a system of market exchange in advertising, credit and trade to provide the goods concerned.

[17] Women are vehicles for the transfer of assets. It is illegal for women not to inherit ancestral property, but the law is ignored. Dowry (also illegal since the Dowry Prohibition Act of 1948) has been slowly but inexorably replacing bride price, and is being notoriously masculinised (the dowry controlled by bride-receivers rather than by the bride). However, this transfer of assets still does not usually lead to business links between givers and receivers. Increasing numbers of girls are being educated, even though this increases the size of dowry necessary. In elite firms almost as many girls as boys have university degrees. The reasons given for female education are to enable upwards mobility in status through strategic alliances (see also Heyer 1992), but also 'progress' and 'shame at our ignorance'.

generational configurations of agnates,[18] an average of four men in all. Usually they live in a single household, though a few work jointly but live separately. Irrespective of living arrangements, men negotiate authority based on the division of tasks and skills among them, while also deferring to authority based on age. Tasks are divided; they include accountancy, purchase, sales (and the negotiation and enforcement of contracts and credit relations) and the supervision of labour. Money and investment are supervised by the oldest family member. There has been little change since the 1960s when M.N. Srinivas (1966) observed of industrial entrepreneurs near Delhi that it was usual for a man to recruit his partners, managers and technical experts from among his close kindred, implicitly male kin. Part of the elders' task of managing the family firm involves 'guaranteeing the male line for at least three generations' (Dorin et al. 2000, p. 8).

These joint firms *can* be explained in transaction costs terms: as lowering the costs of acquiring, and the risks of keeping, trade secrets, information, accounts and trustworthy relations. Some business heads can actually calculate the transaction and opportunity costs of their male-family-based forms of management, and know how much cheaper they are than market alternatives. At the same time, family firms are *authoritarian* hierarchies of capital and labour. Information cannot be assumed to flow entirely freely inside such a firm. Nor can opportunism (at any point in the hierarchy) be assumed to be non-existent.

However, it is hard to rationalise in terms of transactions costs the practice of equal (implicit) returns to brothers regardless of their productivity, especially when reinforced by a hierarchy of rituals and a language of respect at work and by unequal status at home. The individual is subordinated to the family business at work and to the business family at home. Nevertheless, the gains from co-operation and compliance prevail, or else jointly managed male firms would not be so common. Factors such as a collective and individual interest in accumulation across generations, the security of employment, non-economic gains, and the deterrent effect of social and economic sanctions on alternative wage work combine to explain the prevalent supply of male labour at notional nominal rates, which are well *below* those of the labour market.[19]

The stylised firm we are considering here is often part of a small conglomerate in which a father and his sons, or a set of brothers, will jointly control and individually manage several firms or kinds of capital: land, trade, finance, property and transport – and these are all local. The 20 elite firms in Arni, from which this material is drawn, control between them the following assets (see Table 5.3): 19 textiles firms, 25 other trading

[18] That is, males related through the male line.
[19] Harriss-White 1996a, pp. 243–5.

Table 5.3   *Elite portfolios (assumed to be under-declared)*

West Bengal (1990) Bardhaman (largest 8 agribusinesses)*	Tamil Nadu (1994) Arni (largest 20 businesses)
140 acres of land	319 acres of land
15 large rice mills	17 rice mills
12 cold stores	19 textiles firms
2 oil mills	(>1000 looms)
13 trading firms	25 trading firms
? urban property + storage	>30 houses
8 non-agricultural industries (nails and	>30 shops
screws/cardboard boxes, etc.)	3 cinemas
12 lorries	2 hotels (one with swimming pool)
	wedding hall
	35 lorries/buses
	12 cars
	all have satellite/cable TV

*Their subsidised loans from nationalised banks for technical upgrading are equal to 20 000 anti-poverty (IRDP) loans

enterprises (not including literally thousands of handlooms located in the environs), 17 rice mills, 319 acres of land, at least 30 houses and at least 30 shops, 3 cinemas, 2 hotels and a wedding hall, 35 lorries/buses and 12 cars. All had satellite or cable TV. One-fifth also acknowledged having 'substantial' investments in permutations of dowries, jewellery, finance companies (black), stocks and shares, and (international and male) travel and education. In contrast to the pattern of a quarter of a century previously, the elite of the 1990s did not use agricultural profits for their starting capital. However, they remain fascinated by land, which is largely exempt from tax and whose value appreciates inexorably in real terms. Many business families purchase comparatively large holdings, often managed professionally. While the transition from agricultural trade and agro-industry to non-agricultural trade does not pose insuperable obstacles, the transition from agricultural trade to non-agricultural *industry* is rare. This is a persistent failure we have found elsewhere in India throughout the last two decades.[20]

Combinations of family, firm(s) and farms are quite commonly organised in different ways. Where possible they are controlled by men. Land will be controlled by the oldest male. The tendency to diversity, complexity and uniqueness in the way portfolios of assets are arranged strength-

[20] See Harriss 1981 for North Arcot in the early 1970s; Harriss-White 1996a for Coimbatore in the early 1980s; Harriss 1993 for West Bengal in the early 1990s; and see Chapter 8 for an expanded discussion of this obstacle.

ens the resilience of local-level capital with respect to shocks and risk. It serves a similar purpose to tendencies to uniqueness in the activity combinations of individual firms (which was discussed in Chapter 3).

Over the last 15 years, two major changes in these little conglomerates have strengthened the networks in which male members are positioned. One is the strategic placing of members of trading households in the professions and the bureaucracy – from clerks in the Electricity Board to officers in the IAS – depending closely on the scale of the family's capital. A selective approach to education has proved tactically important, for almost all of these relatives have higher education attainment than those in trade. As a result, practically no firm of any economic significance is today unconnected to people with a direct personal stake in the State. Such a tactic involves surmounting entry barriers that take the form of 'fees' or 'deposits', often totalling several years of salary equivalent.[21] The low but stable (and stabilising) incremental income that a bureaucratic salary brings to the investing household is a less convincing explanation for such investments than one that points to the status it brings, and one that sees the relatively large investment as justified by the expectation of future returns from bribery. Trading families that position themselves for the latter reason then have access to a wide range of forms of 'primitive' accumulation (see Chapter 3), exploiting labour, consumers and symbiotic economic relationships between business, and the administration and the ruling political parties.

The local business elite has also come to be tenuously integrated – largely through professional employment – with the global diaspora (with kin in the United States, United Kingdom, France, Australia, Hungary, Sri Lanka, Malaysia and Saudi Arabia). But these are exceptions that prove a rule, for the elite's investments are mostly risk-averse and localised.

An increase in the age at marriage, and a general halving of completed family sizes within the space of a generation, have given rise to a *shortage of brothers*. This acts to hinder accumulation. The brother-shortage makes itself particularly felt in the length of time it takes to build a reputation with a network of contacts and therefore gain access to credit and set up a firm.[22] The lack of brothers will be particularly felt in young adulthood,

---

[21] See Jeffrey (1999) for examples among *jat* capitalists in Uttar Pradesh.

[22] It is also a complete recasting of the (admittedly inconclusive) argument that nucleation is associated with industrialisation and urbanisation (Madan 1997, pp. 428–34). Of the 20 elite firms, five are run out of nuclear households, averaging five members while 13 are controlled by joint households, with an average population of nine. The average household size in the rural region is 4.9 (Nillesen 1999). It is unclear why, when male family labour is so important, so many of the local elite business households have behaved, demographically, like the average unless the (low) possibility of business failure persuades families to be cautious in their fertility while success enables families to bring in more male distant relatives. There is scant evidence for this and much for joint families with components consisting of sons, their wives and two or three children.

often at the start of the life of a new firm. The largest of local firms are those based on households or families well stocked with sons or brothers.[23] It is likely to be this shortage of brothers that is driving new relations of governance in family businesses which involve the inclusion of affines (sons- and brothers-in-law) and their skills and money.

How do male relations of patriarchy affect markets and the local processes of accumulation? They are mutually reinforcing. Figure 5.1, the employment structure of a model family business, shows how labour 'markets' are structured to enforce the capacity to accumulate through patriarchal arrangements. There are three components of wage labour in a typical firm. Two are male: the permanent labour force or 'salariat' and male casual labour. The male salariat is *minimised* so as to limit employers' obligations towards labour under the Factories Act. Salaried work and permanent status are associated not with skill or even higher levels of pay, but with the level of trust involved in a task (for example, nightwatchmen), with caste (closer in rank to the owners' than is the casual labour force's) and location of origin (close-by).[24] This is the labour customarily entitled to primitive, arbitrary and paternalistic forms of 'occupational welfare' (feebly imitating formal sector welfare, for example, by helping with expenses for weddings or with the costs of sickness and sometimes with the cost of educating a worker's bright son). This labour has customary rights to annual perquisites and sometimes even a stake in the firm (parodying a dividend). At the same time, credit and debt are used to *immobilise* valued permanent employees, and to enforce loyalty. This male labour is never unionised. Theirs is a politics of patronage. The second component of the wage labour force, casual male labourers, relates to employers in a variety of ways. They may be seasonal commuters from their own land. Frequently, they are not really 'casual' at all, but they are not treated as permanent labour in the legal sense. Perquisites are rarer. The only advantage of casual labourers is trade union organisation, which employers try to resist, though (as we learned in Chapter 2) not always successfully. Owners can, however, weaken unions by encouraging the formation of a number of them, or by managing their agendas or deliberations (as we will see, in Chapter 7 on caste). Certain heavy and regular tasks, like loading and unloading, are invariably out-sourced and are provided collectively by men (described by one trader as 'ruined farmers') organised into work-groups according to their caste (low) and locality (nearby).

The third component of the labour force, casual female labour, contrasts strongly with all this. There is none at all in pure trading firms,

---

[23] While a household is a unit for commensality, a family is a property grouping of households of men related by a common male ancestor.

[24] Particularly noteworthy in the case of clerks dealing with accounts who are the most likely to be locked into subordinate relations of patronage.

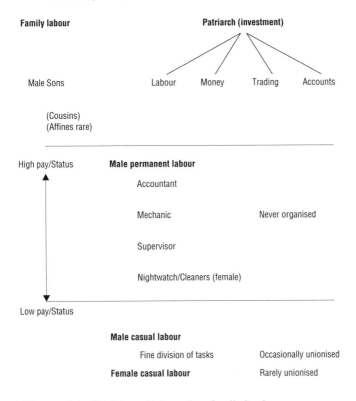

Figure 5.1 Division of labour in a family business

although they amount to 38–75 per cent of the workforce in businesses involving the processing of products.[25] They are, and have always been, quite deliberately casualised. Attempts to organise women politically (in ways other than caste, locality and kin, which structure recruitment) are ruthlessly squashed. Very few indeed are allowed to belong to trade unions.[26] As well as being subordinated politically, they are subordinated economically (through lower wages unjustified by any gendered productivity differentials) and sometimes physically (through sexual harassment). In another field study we found that the larger the firm, the higher the proportion of the total labour force composed of female casual labour. And the larger the firm, the more biased towards profit is the distributive share. Labour organisation and casualisation were heavily structured around gender. Both could be happening simultaneously in a given firm. In firms where female labour was concentrated, the largest relative

[25] Between 1997–99 about 10 women were recruited as permanent salaried labour in retail shops in this town.
[26] See also Baud 1983, p. 132.

wage share nevertheless still went to men. We also found male solidarity (organised through a plurality of unions) had more visible outcomes on pay and conditions than either female solidarity (organised around recruiters and supervisors), or male–female solidarity (organised, if at all, through each factory).[27]

Markets other than labour also operate to the disadvantage of women. Women are debarred from access to formal bank credit, both by explicit bank rules and by other barriers; for example, not owning appropriate collateral. Male control of capital and property is underwritten by the State. The licensing of a female trader requires not her name in the State's register of licences, not even that of her husband, but that of her *father*. Furthermore, incremental change in techniques and technology tends to displace female labour,[28] though computing may yet prove exceptional in this regard.

Patriarchy and Accumulation II: Women

While female agricultural labour is being increasingly proletarianised, and as agriculture is being feminised, real female agricultural wages have not tightened in the way male wages have, because women are unable to commute to wage work in town (see Table 5.4). They are prevented from doing this by their prior responsibility for domestic work at home. As a consequence, women's wage rates in town are considerably higher than are women's agricultural wages, because the supply is drawn from within a tight radius. Just under half the urban wage labour force is female and is restricted to weaving, yarn-twisting, rice-milling, construction, sanitary work and waste disposal.[29] Drawn from the lower castes, female wage workers are often the principal income earners (despite the employers calling their wages 'pin money'). Women's wages for jobs with the same kind of effort and skill as those done by men vary from 40 per cent lower (in thread workshops), through to 60 per cent lower (in rice mills), to 75 per cent lower (in twisting factories).[30]

---

[27] The distributive share is the relation between total wage costs and profits. The study was in Coimbatore District (Harriss-White 1996a).

[28] See Harriss and Kelly (1982) for all-India evidence in rice and oil-milling. With respect to silk, the evidence is much more place-specific. Many thousands of livelihoods have been created in handloom weaving over the last 15 years, but loom technology has *retrogressed*. Labour is biased towards men and children (increasingly prised away from schooling) who can put in the long hours, free from the mandatory call of household maintenance work (Nagaraj et al. 1996).

[29] This varies greatly across India. According to the 1991 Census, however, in north-west India in intermediate-sized settlements like this one, female participation amounts to only 5 per cent of the population (Kashyup and Guha 1997, p. 89).

[30] Since the labour process is sex-sequential (male and female tasks being interdigitated, or sequenced), rather than sex-segmented (goods produced by either male or female labour), it is difficult to calculate the separate productivities of each sex. (In fact, I do not know whether this has ever been done.)

Table 5.4   *Casual labour rates: northern Tamil Nadu: 1973–74 to 1993–94*

| | 1973–74 Rs | | 1993–94 Rs | | | |
| | | | Current Rs | | Constant Rs | |
	M	F	M	F	M	F
Av. daily agricultural wages (weeding/ transplanting)	2.7	1.4	20	8	3.4	1.4
Av. daily urban wages (rice milling)	3.3	1.7	30 to 35	20	5.1 to 5.9	3.4

Deflator: 0.17 (consumer price index for agricultural labour).
Sources: Hazell and Ramasamy 1991, p. 201 for 1973–4; field surveys for 1993–94

Educated women have economic niches in clerical jobs in local government and a toehold in the professions (medicine and teaching). It is very rare to find a woman lawyer or member of the police force, and there is just one female supervisor to be found among the 20 elite firms. Those with other skills such as accountancy and computing work in other towns in organised-sector firms (in Vellore and Ranipet) but not in local businesses, where being female is the greatest entry barrier of all (the rare exceptions are always mentioned as flouting norms). Since fieldwork was finished in 1997, at least two training centres in computer keyboard skills have arrived, creating a significant demand for training the daughters of rural elite families. This is indeed a silent revolution, at present connected with status enhancing hypergamy and exogamy on the marriage 'market',[31] not with demand for local labour.

From 1983 to 1994 the contribution of unwaged female family members to the total workforce rose strikingly, from 0.3 per cent to 6 per cent (see Table 5.1). This trend has been confined to women from Backward and Most Backward Castes, especially those over 40, who have embarked on the part-time management of small businesses (such as fruit and vegetables, meat and gold). Widows and abandoned women leave trade as soon as their children leave home or enter the labour market. While a few of the wives of agrarian capitalists have created – and dominate – a surreptitious subsector of rural chit fund credit specially for women,[32] in the elite urban family businesses there is little evidence of female entrepreneurship over the last 25 years. One business is formally owned by a woman but managed by men. Another woman has been foiled by the

---

[31] Hypergamy means marriage to someone of superior status. Exogamy means marriage outside the community or village.
[32] See Colatei and Harriss-White 2002b. Chit funds are rotating credit institutions where the manager takes a commission and where members contribute regularly, with one member taking the fund each round.

State in her attempts to become a silk merchant. Both a licence and bank credit were refused on the grounds of her sex.[33]

Women in business families perform three kinds of unremunerated reproductive roles. First they reproduce, and look after capital-managing male labour. Second, though increasingly rarely, they help to provide food as part of the wage paid to labour in kind. Third, daughters are married strategically to fix commercial contacts (see pp. 160–1 in Chapter 6).

As we concluded in an earlier study of intra-household food allocation,[34] women are positioned according to a paradigm of service and subordination through work. Not only do men have direct control over female labour and bodies within the household, but also the extraction of surplus through labour 'markets' is intensified by female subordination. The differentiated forms of this subordination were put to us vividly by a local CPM leader: 'Well-to-do women watch TV and do some welfare. Only in this generation can a mother-in-law and daughter-in-law sit together to watch TV. Working-class women toil in the factories. There is no interaction' (from an interview in 1997).

Nor do women play a role in public culture or local collective life, except at the very margins, in the sex-segregated international social service clubs (such as the Lionesses – the women's wing of the Lions Clubs). There, the material resources they handle are not abundant. Instead, their role is modest: buttressing the prestige of male Lions and Rotarians by acts of cross-class philanthropy (for example, school uniforms and kits for poor children). Women are but tiny minorities in just a few caste and trade associations and trade unions. Where women form an important minority in the workforce (as in tailoring, sanitary work and to a lesser extent in goldsmithing) their corporate affairs are managed by men, just as the interests of labour are frequently managed by capital. Leaders of all the caste associations in Arni declared that the laws providing for the female inheritance of property were honoured in the breach and 'over-ridden'. We heard of five cases of property inheritance by women reported from among about 50 000 women and girls. The way urban civil society is organised reinforces patriarchy in the market economy.

It is the State, not the market, that has provided opportunities for the relative economic empowerment of women, through education and through employment as clerks,[35] (elementary) teachers and sanitary

---

[33] Although we were unable directly to research the gender ideologies underpinning the gendered institutions of accumulation, we encountered the notion of male responsibility entitling men to specific kinds of male indulgence (see Jeffrey (1999) on 'whisky and chicken' get-togethers in north India).

[34] B. Harriss 1990.

[35] There is a 'kind of quota' for women here. At the national level, in the public sector, 16.5 per cent of jobs were held by women in 1997 (Reserve Bank of India 1999, pp. iv–46).

workers. The importance of the last category accounts for the fact that no less than 45 per cent of employees in the municipality are women. Yet, women are still conspicuous by their absence from the higher echelons of the administration. There is a very live tension in low-caste families between the education of girls (in order to prise open public-sector employment and enable upward mobility), and the costs of providing dowries for educated girls together with the income forgone while a girl is being educated above the fifth standard (year). The net result of this tension is to make scheduled caste adults increasingly 'anti-girl'.

Does the State pose a challenge to patriarchy? Not a big one. As Agarwal shows (1994), employment by itself is a weaker element in the economy than command over assets. But it is the only thing to which all but the most exceptionally placed women may aspire.

So the role played by gender in the accumulation of capital involves power based on the male control of both male labour and male and female sexuality. This patriarchal power cements the division of male family labour in the firm and ranks their status in the family. It shapes individual rights to property and collective access to the state. It is a significant force for wage labour at work and controls its entitlement in times of need. Patriarchal power structures the entry into markets and the roles played by women as producers and traders. The exercise of this power meshes with that expressed in other social structures of accumulation, with important consequences for development.

Implications I: Development

The way family businesses are controlled has a number of consequences for development, both in the sense of growth and accumulation, and in the sense of well-being. First, the specialised set of male authority relations through which the managerial labour-owning capital is socialised tends to suppress competition between firms, and the pattern of control of branches by brothers qualifies non-competition further. Local purchasers are well aware that they face at best a collusive oligopoly in important sectors of the urban economy and the oligopolists are quite frank about it; for example, 'We co-operate. We have separate networks but we run the x business together here'; 'Our relatives control all the prices of q in this town'. The capture of a market, or of a sector of labour, avoids intra-family competition and conflict. Second, small units, umbilically attached to others by kinship and finance, use labour that is unprotected and exploitable, just as it is in putting-out arrangements, job-working and subcontracting, which are all commonplace contractual arrangements. These forms of production and trade are ways of avoiding both the Factories Acts' regulation of labour and the Commercial Taxes' regulation of output. So accumulation is enhanced at labour's expense and tax obligations to the State are minimised, depriving it of resources.

Hence, patriarchal control of business is not allocatively efficient. Amartya Sen has theorised households as sites of 'co-operative conflict',[36] suggesting that the co-operative element is productive while the conflictual element is distributional and takes place primarily between the genders. But both co-operation and conflict are actually at work in production, and conflict between male management is threatening. Partition is as vulnerable a moment in the development of a firm as is start-up, because of the problems presented by the equitable division of property, finance and market shares. So, within the business family, relations between men are carefully, almost naturally, constructed so as to nurture co-operation and *control* – control over other, mostly younger, men. It is by means of this control over men that control over capital is concentrated. This patriarchal governance is *allocatively* inefficient, with contradictory and complicated consequences. First, capital is controlled, but less efficiently than it might be if women were able to work on terms commensurate not even (yet) with men, but merely with their education. Meanwhile, under-educated sons are put in charge of computers and use them suboptimally, and highly computer-literate, young local women are not employed. Technical change is discouraged. Yet the result of this allocative and technical inefficiency may be *adaptively* efficient because the local economy is more labour-intensive than it otherwise might be.[37] The need to keep capital under tight patriarchal control leads to only low-risk diversifications, local in space and narrow in their commodity composition. Strangers are generally still not welcome to co-operate.[38] Yet there is nothing much in the competitive environment to require the professionalisation of management, which family labour can easily undercut.

As a result, local capitalists are generally successful in keeping women economically disenfranchised as owners of the means of production or

---

[36] Sen 1990, 1997.

[37] As Esther Boserup noted in 1970, and still now, technical change in a given sector is masculinising. Skilled categories of work are dominated by men (Boserup 1987, pp. 69–76). Boserup argued that both demand and supply factors play their roles in this. Employment regulations for women increase their cost while the inflexibility of modern industrial discipline is incompatible with the rearing of children (1987, pp. 110–17). See Harriss and Kelly (1982) for all-India evidence of (subsidised) technological upgrading, increased operational scale, concentration of ownership and the masculinisation of wage labour in rice and groundnuts; Harriss and Harriss (1984) for common consumer goods; and Stanley (2002) for a case of the mechanisation of gold ornament-making in Arni. With respect to handloom silk-weaving, even though loom technology has *retrogressed*, labour is biased towards men (Nagaraj et al. 1996).

[38] Fukuyama 1995, p. 336.

trade, except on a petty scale.[39] By contrast, the State plays an ambivalent role. On the one hand, it empowers women (as it empowers scheduled castes) through offering them livelihoods. On the other hand, it prevents women from owning the means of production and entering business, and denies them access to formal credit. Change in all these respects is complex and its direction appears to be dominated by men.

We would not wish to do more than speculate on how distinctively 'Indian' these male patriarchal arrangements are. In his treatise on *Trust*, Fukuyama distinguishes France, Italy, Taiwan and Hong Kong from the United States, Germany and Japan on the basis of general levels of trust. The first group, being societies with *low* levels of trust, have economies with a preponderance of relatively small-scale firms based upon male family labour. Even in large corporations and public companies, the promoter family's shares constitute a large proportion, indicating their influence over management, and professional managers are comparatively rare. The 'glass ceiling' on accumulation constituted by family forms of accumulation is associated with decentralised and flexible, network-based forms of economic organisation. India is very conspicuous by its absence in *Trust* but would belong to the low-trust group.[40] With respect to the Chinese commercial diaspora, Greenhalgh (who examined family firms as part of her critique of the revisionist emphasis on (Confucianist) culture to explain rapid capitalist development in East Asia) found *inter alia* the same kind of structuring of male family labour as we have described here. Authority is vested in male 'elders' with females severely subordinated and exploited in the effort to keep production costs low, confined to non-managerial and part-time work and excluded from inherited property relations.[41] So in neither of these respects is India distinctive, even if the complex and dynamic outcome of the workings of all the significant social structures of accumulation gives the Indian economy its character. India's distinction relates to the demographic consequences of family businesses.

Implications II: Well-being

Male relations of patriarchy did not at first sight seem a *development* issue, and certainly do not seem directly an issue of *well-being*. However, we have seen that the former notion was false, and the latter is also false, on two counts. First, the reinforcement of patriarchal relations in the class

---

[39] As with the entry of low-caste women into part-time management of fruit and vegetable stalls, and of widowed or abandoned women as petty traders in the Municipal Market.
[40] Fukuyama 1995.
[41] Greenhalgh 1994.

controlling local capital has effects on the welfare of women. These effects are theorised as positive for women workers (in the upwardly mobile subaltern classes) but negative in the heart of the business class. Second, this male-biased concentration of capital with adverse implications for female welfare has a class logic to it which is obscured by the analytical attention paid to income.[42] Let us explore these issues.

The patriarchal governance of small-scale capital has consequences for the most extreme aspect of well-being – life chances themselves. What is without doubt a demographically audacious extrapolation is entirely consistent with a growing literature in Indian economic demography. The under-15 sex ratio (female/male (FMR))[43] for the 66 children of the elite firms in Arni is 784 (*including* five households with a combined total of nine boys and 23 girls). In other words there are fewer than eight girls for every 10 boys. If these households were statistically representative, it would seem that one in five girls from the town's elite have been denied life. This is an extremely low FMR. The 2001 Census, while reporting a reduction in anti-female sex bias in the population as a whole, finds that the juvenile sex ratio has deteriorated dramatically from 947 in 1991 to 927 in 2001, and in the most prosperous States of the north-west it has dropped to exceedingly low levels: 820 in Haryana and 792 in Punjab.[44] Sex-selective scanning and abortion (unreported in the rural environs) was mentioned matter of factly in the town as an ingredient of modernity by 1997. Prior to the late 1990s the mechanism of culling would have been neglect in infancy rather than infanticide, which has never been reported there.[45]

Satish Agnihotri, who has investigated the effect of 'prosperity' on the differential well-being of the genders in a compendious study of the sex ratio at the district level throughout India, gets close to the materialist argument being put forward here in his charitable observation that elite female disadvantage is more a case of 'men gaining more in the wake of prosperity than females being discriminated against'(1997, p. 250); that is, before he himself shows this interpretation to be false at the all-India level. In fact, we are witnessing what I have elsewhere called 'gender-cleansing'.[46]

There are three economic explanations for gender-cleansing. They rest on the assumption of utility-maximising families (households) allocating resources between the genders purely according to differential returns. The

---

[42] This class logic can operate irrespective of other ways in which the economy is regulated; for example, by religion and caste.

[43] Females per thousand males.

[44] Athreya 2001.

[45] See George (1998) on infanticide generally and George et al. (1992); Chunkath and Athreya (1997) on its practice in Tamil Nadu; and *Frontline* vol. 16, no. 23, 19 November 1999 for evidence of the growing incidence of female foeticide in Tamil Nadu.

[46] Harriss-White 1999b.

three factors stressed are female labour participation (for which there is systematic data); dowries (for which there is hearsay evidence), and changes in marriage patterns (for which there is only case material from field economics). We will look at these competing explanations.

Taking *labour market participation* first, the *orthodox* hypothesis explaining the paradox of 'gender-cleansing' in wealthy families is that wealth is associated with the withdrawal of women from economic participation (first from wage work and then from the external sphere altogether). This double seclusion is said to be in the interest of the status of the household. Wealth and seclusion are then accompanied by an increase in the incidence and the size of dowries, and – in the 'female-friendly' south – by the diffusion of north Indian marriage patterns. As a result, the economic costs to families of women rise, going up the scale of family wealth, and their economic benefits fall. With this changed equation, so does their relative status,[47] and so do their chances of being allowed to be born, to live at all or to live to adulthood. Agnihotri assumes such a logic at work; he recasts this process, cross-sectionally as a 'Kuznets curve' with a U-shaped relationship between adverse female life chances and household wealth.[48] *Improvements* in FMRs associated with increasing wealth are supposed to be reflected in the reinsertion of women into upper professional segments of the labour market (from the returns from which women are expected to gain increased intra-household entitlements). Though this is testable on an all-India scale with the help of proxy variables (land) for 1961, 1987–88 and 1992–93, the results have cast doubt on the Kuznets relationship hypothesised by Agnihotri. In 1961[49] in north India alone, female disadvantage intensified with increasing wealth until the FMR reached a minimum of 870, after which it began to be reduced; and renewed female labour participation was significant in the explanation of reduced female disadvantage among the elite (see Figure 5.2). However, the scale of landownership at which female disadvantage started to be reduced was 24 acres (10 hectares) – above which we are talking about only a minute fraction of the population. In south India in 1961, though the lowest FMR was higher – at 930 – there was no U-shaped relationship at all, and female labour participation (which is higher than in north India) did not explain the change in the FMR. In the two more recent periods[50] there are no

---

[47] See evidence for rural elite female disadvantage in Heyer (1992), Kapadia (1994) and Wadley (1993); and for urban evidence see Vera Sanso (1995).

[48] After Kanbur and Haddad 1994.

[49] From 1961 Census data on household composition and landholdings (Agnihotri 1997, pp. 250–93).

[50] Using NSSO round 43 for 1987–88 and round 50 for 1992–93 for per capita expenditure and adult and child FMRs (Agnihotri 1997).

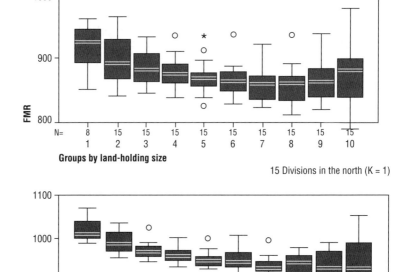

Figure 5.2   Female–male ratio by landholding groups
Source: 1961 Census, Household Economic Tables, Part III: Tables B-X to
B-XVII: FMRs for all–age groups for households engaged only in cultivation
(Agnihotri 1997, 2000, p. 282).

U-shaped curves to be found; instead, there are continuously negative
relationships for both urban and rural sub-samples (see Figure 5.3). A
steeper slope characterises urban subsets compared with rural ones and,
in the highest per capita expenditure category in south India, a very low
local FMR of below 900 is found.

The relative impacts of female labour participation and wealth have
been modelled for rural south India.[51] Landless labouring households are
hypothesised to strategise their gender composition according, first, to
the marginal costs of rearing a girl, and second, to differentials in labour

---

[51] Nillesen and Harriss-White 2002.

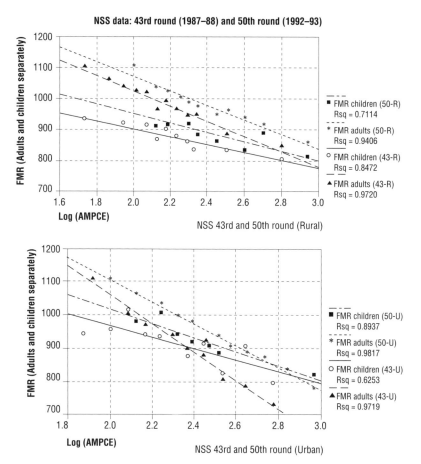

Figure 5.3   Female mortality rate–per capita expenditure relationship
Rsq = 'R squared'. This is a common index of the explanatory power of a
regression line.
NSS refers to the 'National Sample Survey'.
FMR is the female-to-male sex ratio.
AMPCE is average monthly per capita expenditure.
Source: Agnihotri 1997/2000, p. 293

market returns. Often girls are at a survival advantage in labouring
households, but in landless households in 8 villages in northern Tamil
Nadu, all within two hours' bus drive from Arni, the survival differential
between the genders converges with increases in assets. It would appear

Table 5.5 *Child sex ratios in villages in the Ambedkar and Tiruvannamalai districts (girls under 7 per 1000 boys) 1993–4*

	8 villages: 1993–95		4 villages: 1981–82	
Aggregate	856	(n = 1030)	1013	(n = 463)
Scheduled caste	886	(n = 413)	982	(n = 123
Caste	750	(n = 399)	1007	(n = 269)
Landless	952	(n = 397)	969	(n = 192)
Landed	730	(n = 633)	1053	(n = 271)
Landed caste	645	(n = 352)	1100	(n = 231)

The data have been tested for age misreporting. It is assumed that random error is insignificant. Summing the disaggregates will not equal the totals because of the category 'other' (Muslim, Christian, etc.).

that households without land, but with other kinds of assets do provide unwaged domestic productive work for which women are valued.[52] But in landed households the *opposite* obtains; as total assets increase so too does the survival differential (see Table 5.5). Not only has the sex bias appeared in villages where it was absent 10 and 20 years ago, but child sex ratios are lowest in the *landed* caste households of the local non-scheduled, agricultural castes.[53] Reports of the recent emergence of infanticide have organised their explanation around caste (either 'traditional' infanticidal castes – scheduled castes and *kallars* in Tamil Nadu, for instance – or upwardly mobile 'backward' agrarian castes (for example, *gounders* and *naickers*)).[54] But in the villages around Arni, caste does not furnish the explanation of excess female child mortality – the key factor is assets. Prosperity reduces the survival chances of girls, not when it is in the form of income but when it takes the form of property.

Another economic explanation concerns *dowry*, widely thought to be a disabling economic burden. In the absence of systematic widespread evi-

[52] In this instance agricultural work by itself does not tilt the survival chances towards women and girls (Nillesen and Harriss-White 2002). Mothers may take male children to work with them, leaving girls neglected at home (Nagaraj 1986). Or, if female labour force participation is complementary to demand for on-farm or domestic (weaving) labour of sons, then increases in female labour unaccompanied by increased returns may result in drops in the relative mortality of boys, thereby widening the differential (Foster and Rosensweig 1999).

[53] See Nillesen 1999. The lowest child FMRs at the block level in Tamil Nadu – which is a microcosm of India – is 645 (Harriss-White 1999b). These are compensated for by blocks with 'Keralan' ratios exceeding 1000.

[54] Even research that puts caste as central has an economic explanation at its heart, see respectively Sundari and Thombre (1996), Visvanath (1996) and George et al. (1992).

dence on dowries or dowry-related savings, at best it is possible to infer from differences in the amounts of expenditure and savings following the births of male and female children that reductions in current expenditures are made when girls are born (see Subrahmaniam 1996, for instance). Parents of girls start to save in the anticipation of future lumpy expenses. The greatest of these is the transfer of property at marriage. Some arguments relating dowries to the economy are entirely speculative. For example, the idea that the dowry is the price for scarce men under conditions of population growth[55] assumes men cannot take brides of ever younger ages and lower castes. The idea that it is the price for the groom's education[56] assumes that elite grooms have a costly education, which we have seen is not always the case. The notion that the dowry is a productive resource in investment tactics ignores its common form of consumer durables. Locally it is justified as an insurance premium for the services provided by kin to ensure marital 'harmony' or dispute resolution.

On *changes in marriage patterns*, Judith Heyer, in her analysis of the reproductive strategies of rural elites in the region of Coimbatore, shows how hypergamy, dowry and open-ended gifts connected with the bride's reproductive cycle are deployed to establish connections and contacts useful for agriculture and trade. The system, she concludes, is 'driven by brides' families' in a micro politics of interest. Further north, another village study has revealed how the landowning elite has selectively adopted certain features of the north Indian kinship system (not only dowry, but also hypergamy and exogamy) while retaining the distinctively south Indian feature of consanguinity.[57] Consanguinity makes sure accumulation is kept within a very close circle of kin. Village exogamy means a reduction in the close and immediate support that can be given to a young bride. Within one generation, dowry has risen from being a feature of 45 per cent of marriages to 80 per cent of them. Dowry was concluded to be part of a 'pick-and-mix' tactic of kinship consistent with growing female disadvantage.

In north India, the combined use of hypergamy and dowry in accumulation long predates the modern era, and was seen, together with female infanticide, as an attribute of caste.[58] But hypergamy and dowry are now

---

[55] See Pisani and Zaba 1997, in Agnihotri 1997, p. 275.

[56] See Kapadia 1999, p. 15.

[57] Consanguinity in south India involves marriage between cross-cousins or uncles and nieces. In the same region, SC marriages are increasingly taking a distinctly more Dravidian form over time. See Harriss-White 1999b.

[58] Clark 1983. That castes use female infanticide, hypergamy and dowry for advancement is evinced by the Rajput village of Devra in Rajasthan, where, according to the Times of India News Service (June 1999), *all* female infants have been killed at birth for the last 110 years, one who escaped rendering this practice newsworthy.

extensive, rampant and linked to class. The south is following suit. In the booming knitwear industrial cluster of Tiruppur in south-central Tamil Nadu,[59] the ideal in male behaviour is the self-made man, unfettered by shackles of kin and caste, whose reputation is based on acquired rather than ascribed qualities and whose profits are based on skill. There the dowry is deployed as a substitute for the capital a man would hope to get from his father. On this, Karin Kapadia comments that dowry 'is the most public acknowledgement of a man's worth that he is likely to experience', a public calculation of his 'achievements' (although marriages actually take place in the anticipation of achievements – at least in business); 'it *is* modernity'(Kapadia's italics, 1999, pp. 17–18). If *this* is modernity, then the public signalling of the economic status of bride-givers is *also* modernity. Kapadia concludes that 'forms of modernity' (in this case gender discrimination through dowry) 'may appear to be continuations of tradition when they actually are new meanings' (1999, p. 10) (in this case the appropriation of the kinship system of north India in the interests of capital accumulation).

Although it is hard to demonstrate these relationships rigorously on a large scale, it is clear that a range of material patriarchal logics is likely to be relevant to the life chances of women. From the perspective of the class interests of business families, however, two qualifications need to be added.

First, consider the relation of women's dowries to the total assets controlled by males. Among the rich, if income is derived from a *salary*, the ratio of a given dowry (to be paid for daughters) to *assets* is likely to be relatively high, and the conventional cost/benefit calculus may indeed account for sex discrimination. However, in a propertied household, the ratio of dowry to assets is likely to be lower to the point that it is implausible as an explanation for gender-cleansing.

Indeed, we find that in Arni the escalation of dowries is *not* commensurate with the escalation, entirely uncelebrated in the literature on sex bias, in the value of property accumulated and controlled by males. Elite households in Arni would rather betray the value of their total investments than give systematic information about dowries given and received – and the former was a well-guarded secret. However, we do know the range and types of investments and major acts of consumption – enough to know that the firm we studied was in most cases merely a component in these families' portfolios. Leaders of local caste associations gave us dowry norms and we can take their upper limits as characteristic of the dowries of the elite. We also have estimates (which are without doubt on

[59] Studied by Chari 2000.

Table 5.6 *Arni: dowries, 1994*

Caste/trade	TVAM[a]	Saurash-trian	Barber	Tailor	Auto-rickshaw driver	General
Gold Sovereigns	20–70	10–50	3–10	7–10	5	
(Upper Rs value)	260 960	186 400	37 280	37 280	18 640	
Fridge						12–23 000
Scooter						22–36 000
TV (black and white)						10 000
TV (colour with home theatre)						15–30 000
Motorbike						60–70 000
Moped						15–25 000
Low-estimate consumer durables						49 000
High-estimate consumer durables						103 000

Note: A 'large dowry' is therefore estimated at Rs 260 960 + 103 000; that is, Rs 364 000
[a] TVAM = *Tulluva vellala agamudaiyar mudaliar* (dominant backward caste)

the low side) of the present net value of the firm we studied from the elite household's investment conglomerate.

The dowry norms are caste-specific. Local leaders of several caste associations – notably castes that Mattison Mines (1984) terms 'artisan merchants' (*senguntha mudaliars, lingayats* and *naidus*) – denied that dowries were given, though individual members of these castes acknowledged the practice. The dowry norms for the merchant elite specify combinations of gold sovereigns and consumer durables (such as a fridge, scooter or moped, and a TV with 'home theatre' (video)). In Table 5.6 details for dowries in the mid-1990s have been listed. A 'large' local dowry in 1994 might have comprised Rs 2.6 lakhs in gold and Rs 1.03 lakhs in kind: Rs 3.6 lakhs in total (then over £7000). If we apply these dowries to the daughters of present elite owners and divide the current (low estimate of) remaining assets between the total sons of the elite, we find that the *average (low-estimate) value of inheritable assets per male is 12 times the value of the average (high-estimate) value of transferable assets per female.* This puts paid to the widely held idea of dowries as being in any sense economically equivalent pre-mortem inheritances.

There is a further irony. Acts of male agency (for instance, deciding to let girls achieve high levels of education, refusing the duty to maintain unmarried daughters, encouraging them into employment and into undowered marriages, actively supporting a wife to enter trade, and so on) are unusual, secular kinds of market engagement. They could well intensify rather than neutralise the gender imbalance in the control of capital. With the reinforcement of male control over capital as it grows, the greater the absolute size of the unit of capital and thus the smaller the ratio of dowries to business assets. The smaller the ratio between dowries, plus the costs of female education on the one hand, and productive, commercial and finance capital on the other, the relatively less of a liability are women. When class is factored in, in the propertied elite, the larger the dowry, the less powerful the case for dowry as the material explanation for gender-cleansing.

Second, consider the capital-managing labour requirements of the family firm. As fertility rates fall, the need for male family members in these family-managed capitalist firms persists and intensifies, and the relative economic usefulness of their women declines. This is another material disincentive for daughters in business families. However, although this seems a powerful explanation, it is always possible to use daughters and sisters to draw male in-laws into firms with a male deficit. Alternatively, professional managers can be hired, though the latter's costs are greater than any kind of family labour. It has to be concluded that in the absence of *ideology*, neither the gendered transfer of assets between generations nor the gendering of the division of labour explains such acute female disadvantage in life chances.[60]

We are left with the argument that although the severity of bias in the juvenile sex ratio is quite class-specific, gender-cleansing has to be accounted for by gender ideology. This is also Agnihotri's conclusion. The north Indian 'pattern' of anti-female discrimination is spreading southwards by means of 'cultural circulation', rather than through changes in the economy. It is taking the 'prosperity route' (that is, it is occurring first in a class that can deploy the psychologically distancing 'technical' mechanism of sex-selective abortion,[61] as opposed to the malign neglect or deliberate culling of girls after birth). From this class it 'seeps into the substratum', where children are beginning to be reported in the records of primary health centres as dying from 'social causes'.[62] These are agrarian classes where girls have never been culled before.

[60] Further factors are possible. While education and dowries are calculable expenses, business assets can fluctuate, especially after their partition. The need to cushion this element of uncertainty could be yet another justification for the unequal control of capital between the genders. Another explanation impossible to verify *ex ante* and therefore tending to be circular, is the lack of female support when 'hard times' threaten the business of brothers.

[61] Estimated to now account for 0.5 per cent of potential births in India (and as many as 5 per cent in Korea) (Dasgupta and Bhat 1995).

[62] See Chunkath and Athreya 1997.

To conclude, it is not just trends and terms of male and female participation in the economy here, but the position of women in the gendered structure of productive assets and the gendered process of capital accumulation – resulting from what appears to be an intensification of male-patriarchal relations – that is associated with their mortal loss of relative status. This intensification may be due to the halving of completed fertility within a generation, but of even greater importance is the independent diffusion southwards of a culture of female inferiority. Dowries can then be seen as an opportunistic means of accentuating male control by appearing to compensate women for it.

In *the absence of* a quite fundamental delegitimation of male and male–female relations of patriarchy, and of changes to the control of capital,[63] and given that labour markets are heavily segmented *within* each gender, for work alone to empower women from wealthy households, it has to involve that kind of social interaction that is 'an antidote to seclusion and its adverse consequences' (Agnihotri 1997, p. 285). Work will not even be a palliative if it is not outside the domestic arena. Glove-stitching at home will not do. In towns like Arni and in its environs, it is 'the State' rather than 'the market' that has supplied such work, though the State's longstanding and limited emancipatory role in this regard is now threatened by liberalisation.[64] It is now not Indian kinship practices, so much as Indian capitalism mediated by ideology, that endangers women. Women are statistically most at risk in the richest households, and have become more at risk as time has passed. The increasing relative exclusion of women from the ownership of capital is perhaps the greatest and most far-reaching irony in India's economic development.

---

[63] Bina Agarwal has argued both carefully and controversially that they are necessary for *rural* India. See Agarwal (1994) and Razavi (1999) for summaries of the arguments for and against.

[64] Between 1994–97 (the latest figures), while employment in the public sector contracted by 2 per cent on aggregate, the loss of jobs in central government, local bodies and parastatal institutions concealed a 15 per cent increase in employment in state governments. So far, employment for women has held up, growing from 15 to 16.5 per cent over this period (Reserve Bank of India 1999, pp. 20, iv–46; tables IV–36).

6 India's religious pluralism and its implications for the economy

India is by any standards a highly religious country, but by no stretch of the imagination is it purely Hindu. It has sizeable minority religions that have evolved, alongside the dominant Hindu religion, over many centuries.[1] Some of these other religions are conventionally seen as members of the 'Hindu family', having been created on south Asian territory: Jainism, Buddhism and Sikhism. Others are extremely long-established in the south Asian peninsula: the religions of tribal people, the religions of the scheduled castes (whose separate existence from brahminical Hinduism remains controversial),[2] Christianity, Islam and the Parsi faith.[3] In total, counting in Scheduled Castes and Tribes, minorities practising religions other than mainstream brahminical Hinduism may well comprise as much as 45 per cent of India's population.[4] Even if we exclude the scheduled castes and tribes, 17 per cent of the population belonged to minority religions in 1991. Yet, while the relation between religion, poli-

---

[1] Minorities is a crude category. In practice the differentiation of sects in certain 'minorities' is so intense that some amount to minorities within minorities; for example, the *memons* of Hindu origin within the Sunni sect of Islam; the Ghogari Lohana within the Gujarati merchant branch of the Lohana caste originating from Sindh (Pierre Lachaier 2001, personal communication).

[2] There is evidence from the ranking of *dalits* of their being a subordinated but assenting part of the Hindu universe. There is also evidence of their being defined in opposition to Hinduism (as a 'folk culture' and as propertyless people), of their being distinct from Hinduism (in egalitarianism, gender roles, attitude to defilement, governance and political mobilisation), and of their being a complex mixture, the balance depending on context. The interpretation of much of the ethnographic evidence is contested. These controversies are well reviewed in Armstrong 1997.

[3] Varshney (1993, pp. 230–1) suggests that the Hindu nationalist criteria of Hindu-ness as embodying territory, a concept of fatherland and holy-land, means that Christians, Muslims, Parsees – and Jews – with holy lands outside south Asia meet only two of the three criteria. It is certain that Hindus, Jains, Buddhists and Sikhs are covered by Hindu family law, while Muslims have their own, as do other smaller minorities (Diwan 1978).

[4] Weber's project in *The Religion of India* was to demonstrate how the irrationalities of religions made it impossible for capitalism to have originated there. Although he conceded that capitalism was well established by 1921 when his research was published, the logic of his intellectual project meant that he was uncurious about the impact of coexisting religions on it (1962, p. 325).

132

tics and the construction of the Indian nation has been well established,[5] simple facts about the economy, such as the contribution of the minorities to GDP, are unknown. The effects of religious belief and adherence on the process of wealth creation in India has been so strikingly ignored that one might be forgiven for thinking it unimportant.

In this chapter an attempt is made to show the ways in which India's religious pluralism may give structure to the economy. We start by summarising part of the heavily politicised debate surrounding Hinduism and development. Though the objective is to contribute to an understanding of how India works rather than of how Indianists work, the latter helps explain why the question has been so neglected. These debates also lead to interpretations of the question that enable us to use the meagre literature to begin providing an answer.

Religion and the modern Indian economy

We will focus here on religion as the institutional arrangements and modes of living to which sacred status has been given by a complex of beliefs and values.[6] The latter give legitimacy to the models of behaviour shaping social life.[7] We need to begin with India's hegemonic religion, despite the fact that this is the subject of Chapter 7, because ideas about the relationship of Hinduism to the economy have been influential in shaping social and legal institutions that also affect other religious groups in independent India.

Hinduism and development

Hinduism was one of several religions covered by Gunnar Myrdal in his *Asian Drama* – each associated, as he saw it, with different Asian nations.[8] Following Nehru, he saw religion in general and 'Hinduism' in particular as 'a tremendous force for social inertia' (1968, p. 103). Nehru, Myrdal and the elite of the postwar modernising sociologists took Weber's thesis that the foundations of modern capitalism lay in Protestantism and, by contrast, explored the ways in which the ideas of Hinduism were responsible for India's economic backwardness.[9] Myrdal's argument about

[5] See Ali (1992); Corbridge and Harriss (2000, pp. 173–99); Hansen (1996); Hansen and Jaffrelot (1998) for reviews of the history of this relationship.
[6] Paraphrased from Myrdal (1968, p. 103).
[7] Massenzio 2000, p. 26.
[8] Myrdal (1968, vol. 1, pp. 78–80, 103–8), with extensive footnotes; see also Houtant and Le Mercinier (1980).
[9] And in so doing they are condemned by David Gellner for having committed the most vulgar of the misinterpretations of Weber (Gellner 1982).

Hinduism as a 'force for social inertia', and an obstacle to economic development, is incompletely developed in *Asian Drama*, but Hinduism is seen there as based uniquely on principles of inequality, different degrees of purity and exclusion. The implications of these principles for the economy are that stratification is tolerated, with consequent severe limits to free competition and economic mobility.[10]

The idea that Hindu values were obstacles to development had already been questioned in studies of Indian industry by scholars like Milton Singer and Morris D. Morris. Although this work began to be published well before the completion of *Asian Drama*, Myrdal ignored it.[11] Singer, in particular, concluded that industrial leaders borrowed selectively from Western industrial culture as well as from Hinduism. This enabled them not only to maintain a distinctive Hindu culture, but also to define Hinduism, rather than secularity, as the cultural basis of Indian (capitalist) modernity.[12]

Instead, Myrdal saw religion as being 'part and parcel of a whole complex of belief and valuation, modes of living and working and their institutions' whose 'higher forms' (the religious values of the intelligentsia, which he considered compatible with modernisation[13]) could not be isolated from the 'ballast of irrational beliefs – the superstitions of the majority responsible in part for their poverty'.[14] While Singer's ethnography showed Hinduism being used as a force for change, Myrdal saw in it 'inhibitors and obstacles', 'forces of inertia and irrationality', all needing 'reform'.[15]

We might mark this simply as a minor intellectual stand-off, were it not for the fact that the way in which the need for 'reform' had already been

---

[10] Myrdal 1968, p. 104.

[11] Singer 1961; Morris 1967. If this Hindu social order is also *divisive*, then the widespread co-ordination of movements of social and economic reform also faces obstacles. Recourse to 'Hindu values' helps to explain not only the formidable difficulties faced until very recently by challenges to the social order by the exploited lower castes, but also the fact that the political assertion of low-caste people is not yet a co-ordinated class project for labour, or that the class project for labour is actually asserted in low-caste politics that does not privilege production relations (see Ilaiah (1996) for the first interpretation and Gooptu (2001) for the second).

[12] Singer (1972) discussed in J. Harriss (forthcoming). Singer found that religion was permitting a plurality of norms, one for private life and another for work. In the latter sphere he found an abbreviated and relaxed religiosity where the religious foundations for ethical conduct were of active use to industrialists.

[13] But see Desai's scathing evaluation of higher Hinduism's limited 'capacity to absorb the best elements of other religions', of Congress's transformation of higher Hinduism into an ideology of modernisation, of the Nehru–Gandhi leadership's use of Hindu religion and culture to spread 'secular' ethics, and of the acquiescence in this of the Communist Parties and all but a tiny minority of the intelligentsia (1984, pp. 26–8).

[14] Myrdal 1968, pp. 104–5.

[15] A statement found by John Harriss in Singer's unpublished notes (Singer Papers, Regenstein Library, University of Chicago, Box 99). See J. Harriss (forthcoming); see also Myrdal (1968, pp. 104 and 109).

conceptualised was to have profound consequences for Indian development. The domain in which obstructive religious ideas prevailed was to be reduced through the way the economy was managed. 'Business', 'the State' and 'planned development' were expected to change society, dissolve distortions to the economy and push religion back into the 'private sphere'. Further, the number of casualties caused by the 'blind energy of capitalism' was to be deliberately limited by the state provision of social welfare. So both the State and the market were expected to encourage the replacement of the obscurantist beliefs held by the mass of people by a unified rationalism. '[T]he real thing … is the economic factor. If we lay stress on this and divert public attention to it, we shall find automatically that religious differences recede into the background and a common bond unites different groups' (Nehru quoted in Madan 1987).[16]

In this future – in which state-led capitalism defeats a hostile religion, reversing the direction of causality between religious ideas and capitalist behaviour proposed by Weber – both Nehru and Myrdal betray the influence of Marx's famous description of religion as being the 'heart of a heartless world', and the 'opium of the people'[17]: what would be understood now as an analgesic. In easing the pain caused by capitalist production, this opiate was very useful to the bourgeoisie. Working people, therefore, would be the first to understand and expose the role played by religion in masking the alienation of labour. They would reject the conditions requiring the comfort of religion, emancipate themselves from them and relegate religion to 'private life'.[18]

But in India, at any rate, this has not happened. Neither the State, business, nor the working class relegates religion to the private sphere. As late as the 1960s, Myrdal noted that 'practically no-one is attacking religion'.[19] Economists have subsequently ignored his invitation to research the changing relationships between secularisation and the development

---

[16] And quoted again by Ali (1992, p. 42).

[17] Marx, 'Toward the Critique of Hegel's Philosophy of Right' in (ed.) Coletti (1975, p. 244).

[18] Marx did not expect religion to be rooted out of 'private life' – see Kovel (1995). A Weberian correlate of Myrdal's argument, which seems to have been arbitrarily ignored by him despite its being consistent with his case – the enduring beliefs in reincarnation and compensation, with their unique ultimate objective of renunciation – also has implications for the economy. These have been described by Munshi (1988). Social and economic mobility then would depend on the obedient acceptance of the relativistic social order (Weber 1962, pp. 162–3; and see the quotations in Munshi 1988, pp. 7–9). This would shape the recruitment and discipline of labour (Munshi 1988, p. 15). But the principle of obedience, whether to capital or to religious duty, is in sharp tension with that of indifference to worldly life. As a peculiarly Indian principle that might dominate initiative and industry, it has therefore invited severe criticism (Munshi 1988, pp. 18–21).

[19] Least of all the Communist Parties (Myrdal 1968, pp. 107–8).

of the economy;[20] they have also shied away from analysing the material 'conditions making religion indispensable'.[21] And they have shied even further away from analysing the material conditions that *reproduce* religious plurality.

Secularism, the State and capital

One of the reasons why 'no-one is attacking religion' – while the practitioners of certain religions are being attacked by those of others – and why in India religions remain indispensable is the way religions are treated in the constitution. If Singer could go so far as to speculate about 'religion as a force for change', it is more certain that change is a force for religions. Their role in the economy is most certainly mediated by politics; in particular, the politics of secularism. Paradoxically, it is because of – not despite – the secularist ambitions of the Constitution that distributive politics are organised in part *around* religions. In India, secularism is a state policy of equal public respect for all religions, rather than the state promotion of a public culture opposed to or sceptical of religion.[22] According to many observers, in the early years of independence the Indian State did not attach sufficient priority to controlling communal tendencies, or encourage – let alone enforce – atheism, partly because of 'inhibitions in the planners' (rooted in their complicity or sheer cowardice) and partly because they, like Nehru, expected an inevitable 'decline of the hold of religion on the minds of people'.[23] Hansen concludes 'secularism became in the post-colonial mass-democracy a privileged signifier of equal accommodation and competitive patronage of social groups and cultural communities through state and party' (1996, p. 607). At any rate it is a fact that the fragile constitutional principles of equal status for all religions, and of state distance from them, were alchemised into a principle of toleration (in which inequality between religions was accepted and in which Hinduism was

---

[20] Myrdal (1968, pp. 107–9) in which there is the prescient conclusion that the tactical policy of the Indian elite to relegate religion to private life 'could bring about a violent reaction that could spell disaster for all the efforts toward modernisation and development'.

[21] Engels, *Ludwig Feuerbach and the End of Classical German Philosophy, Section III: Religion and Ethics* in Feuer (1959, pp. 216–42).

[22] The word 'secular' was introduced into the Constitution in the 42nd Amendment. In Articles 14 to 17 the equality of minorities before the law is affirmed. In Articles 25 and 26 the right to freedom of religion – and in Articles 29 and 30 those to the conservation of language to education and freedom of education – are guaranteed. Of this kind of secularism Aijaz Ahmad says: ' It is best to treat it as a certain kind of multidenominational tolerance and decency' (1996a, p. xi). Much earlier, however, Desai had observed that '(t)he Government has defined secularism in a very pernicious and cunning manner' (1984, p. 18).

[23] Madan (1987, p. 757) quoted in Corbridge and Harriss (2000, p. 197).

held to be the 'only religion which is national and secular'). This in turn has provided the nutrient base for more or less xenophobic political campaigns calling for Indian nationhood to be based on the dominant religion – the precise opposite of the originally intended outcome.[24] The privileged signifier of equal accommodation was actually nothing of the sort – it stimulated unequal responses. Competitive patronage (rent-seeking and rent protection based on religion) has had profound implications for the economy as well as for politics. Indian secularity has produced this perverse political outcome as the result of the operation of the very institutions designed to eliminate the influence of 'irrational restrictions' on both capital and labour.

Two propositions in Weber's later writings on the foundations of capitalism help to make sense of this paradox. First, along with private property, free labour and the weakening of 'irrational restrictions' on the economy,[25] he argued two other elements as being particularly important: a rational accounting procedure and a rational, regulative law (under which the scope and limits of 'economic avarice' are defined), together with a public administration to implement it.[26] These were important both in themselves and for the impact they would have on 'irrational restrictions'.

In India, we have already seen that while an extensive body of universalistic laws, rationalist in spirit, has been created to regulate the economy, its implementation is far from being universalistic and its rationale is heavily contested.[27] Equality of citizenship is also actively contested – notably by propertied, high-status, men (as we saw in Chapter 5).[28] Regulation on the ground is shaped by local interests. We saw in Chapters 2 and 3 how important the patriarchal intermediate classes are in the day-to-day regulation of the economy and the next chapter tells the story of the evolution of their caste-corporatist collective institutions.[29] So it is reasonable to ask whether, and if so how, religions may shape regulative practice in the same way that caste does in some parts of India.

What is more, a large body of customary and of personal law, not usually considered to have a bearing on the economy, is organised on religious

---

[24] Desai 1984, p. 25; Gardezi 2000.
[25] In these, as Randall Collins (1992) observes in his review of the field of economic sociology, late Weber converged with Marx.
[26] Weber 1923.
[27] An examination of the extensive amendments of fundamental economic laws, such as the Companies Act, the Industrial Disputes Act and the Essential Commodities Act, shows that they have been made increasingly less formally coherent and rational over time. See Mooij (1998) on the Essential Commodities Act and Banaji and Mody (2001) on the Companies Act.
[28] Chatterjee 1997, p. 244.
[29] McCartney and Harriss-White 2000; Basile and Harriss-White 2000.

lines. This law affects the ways in which resources acquired by inheritance, marriage alliances and family partition are concentrated, divided and gendered. It affects the rights and powers of individuals to allocate resources between uses and between people. Religious law, in effect, shapes the terms of economic participation of the business family.[30] Hinduism also affects the way cattle function as an economic asset and as a force of production.[31] In general, religiously based law and custom violate the principle of the State's neutral distance from all religions.

That Hindu personal law has been more modified than has Muslim personal law over the years since India's independence flouts the secularist principle of equal respect for all religions. There is also a massive regulative void in this pluralist body of personal law in the rights of women belonging to classes with no property. However, as with laws of economic regulation so with personal law, there is a large slippage between the laws pertaining to ownership on the one hand and the day-to-day management rights of members of the propertied classes on the other. In practice, there is thought to be far less diversity in personal law than is allowed for in its letters. 'The burden of regulating control [in the occupation of niches in the structures of economic power] shifts [and] seems to fall to persuasion and perhaps to raw coercion' is Dwyer's significant conclusion (1987, p. 525). It is reasonable to ask what is the role of religion in the forms of authority on which this 'raw coercion' is based.

Weber's second fertile idea, in his later writings, is that, paradoxically, a 'big religion' may be the institutional solvent of the obstacles to development posed by numerous smaller ones and Hinduism is by any account a very big religion. Weber does not suggest that a big religion is either necessary or sufficient as a solvent. It may be necessary to break down the ritual barriers to citizenship and participation that exist between localised religiously based groups, and may encourage a more unified system of authority; but it may be insufficient because, in the

---

[30] Diwan 1978, pp. 633–53. Personal law, the oldest part of the composite Indian legal system, is composed of Hindu and Muslim law. Both claim divine status but the Hindu law has been amended so many times that its claim to divinity is unsustainable! Each has schools: those of Hindu personal law being regional (Dayabhaga in Bengal and Mitakshara elsewhere) and those of Muslims varying according to sect. The rules of inheritance of Sikhs, Jains and Buddhists are as in Hindu law (the Hindu Succession Act of 1956), while those of Christians and Parsis derive from the 1925 Succession Act. In addition, there are *caste- and sect-specific* regional variations in certain kinds of personal law (Diwan and Diwan 1991; Dorin et al. 2000, p. 11). Sunni Memons, for instance, have retained in law their Hindu inheritance practices (Pierre Lachaier 2001, personal communication).

[31] Desai 1984, pp. 28–9. The holiness of the cow has been reflected in the widespread distribution of its ownership, the social organisation of butchery, the disposal of carcasses and meat marketing, and the social profile of demand for livestock products and meat. On reasons for the overstocking and poor quality of cattle, see Moore (1974). The cow is an extreme example of the sacred status of certain commodities. See Chapter 8 on the quiddity of commodities.

absence of other predisposing factors, a big religion may hinder the 'spirit of capitalism'. In the case of Hinduism, Weber thought this hindrance worked through 'the seal set on particularistic groups'.[32] He had *castes* in mind, with what he saw as their overriding of any particular ethic and their inhibiting impact on the mobility of capital and labour.[33] In fact, neither caste nor its impact on capital and labour has prevented capitalism from being developed in India. Nor has religious plurality. So what is the impact of India's 'big religion' on the way the religions of the 'minorities' affect economic life?

To sum up the argument so far, the Indian economy has failed to drive religions out of the public domain because – at the least – the Indian *State* treats religions in a way that is flawed in both its formal and its practical rationality. Its approaches to secularism and to regulation, instead of desacralising the economy, impair its capacity to do this. And if it had implemented universal regulative law, the State could still not have prevented religious competition because, by its own definition of secularism (equal treatment of all religions and of state independence from them) such competition would have been beyond its reach. So religions continue to compete in the economy if only because they have been made one of the informal bases for the distribution of rents. The impact of religious plurality on the economy through its regulative and distributive politics is thus inescapably an important issue, crying out for research. It is not only that religions exist for reasons other than the economic, and that the economic and political *superstructures* make religions indispensable. We must also ask what role production conditions play in *reproducing* religions; and try to disentangle that question from the related question of what role religions play in production.

These are some of the general issues that we hope this brief review of India's minority religions will help to clarify. Given the current state of knowledge one must begin by trying to situate the minority religions in the actually existing Indian economy. From this review, I try to extract some working hypotheses and tentative conclusions about the persistent influence of India's various religions on the process of capital accumulation.

The religious minorities in India's economy

Given their size and economic importance, we should clearly begin with the religious identities of the scheduled castes and tribes, which, it is necessary to re-emphasise, are by no means to be assumed to be incorporated

[32] Collins 1992, p. 93.
[33] On the debate over the reification of caste under colonialism, see Corbridge and Harriss (2000, p. 176); especially footnote 4.

into Hinduism.[34] To explain how the religious identities of scheduled castes and tribes (SC/ST) are deployed in accumulation would be an enormous task, for they are highly heterogeneous. Any explanation will be specific to time and place, and it will involve distinguishing ethnicity from caste as well as from religion. This task is therefore being put aside for another occasion (and quite possibly another scholarly life). But there is a reason beside the sheer enormity of the task for setting it aside. While this book is primarily concerned with accumulation on the part of the large, lower level fractions of the Indian capitalist and intermediate classes that dominate the economy of small towns and villages in which 88 per cent of the population live and work,[35] the vast majority of the people in the SCs and STs are found in the exploited workforce of small and marginal peasants and labourers, and they constitute its largest component. They are also those most politically disenfranchised. When they sometimes convert to Islam, Buddhism or Christianity, they may be using religion to escape extreme social stigma, economic oppression and marginalisation.[36] Despite this structural oppression, they are certainly not 'socially excluded', indeed they are now poised for mass mobilisation. They make up major parts of the Indian mainstream in relation to which the privileged and secure elites are 'the excluded'.

The religious ideas and forms of social organisation that have informed the dispossession of labour from the means of production – the religious justifications for the creation of a labour force free only to sell itself, a process that is as fundamental to capitalism as is the productive investment of surplus – are very obscure.[37] They need to be ascertained and added to the outlined map of caste and the labour force that is provided in Chapter 2.[38] All this is a task for the future.

In what follows here, we examine the economic positioning of some of the minorities: Muslims, Christians, Sikhs and Jains.[39] In this, we follow the approach of Hugh Seton-Watson, of whom A.J.P. Taylor, reviewing a book by Seton-Watson that covered the entire Third World, is reputed to have observed that he resembled the curator of a museum who insists on showing you every room. "'Do we really have to know about Madagas-

---

[34] See footnote 3 and Ilaiah (1996).

[35] McCartney and Harriss-White 2000.

[36] See Ilaiah (1996) for an introduction.

[37] For Weber, 'pariah people' were trading off low ritual status under Hinduism against the monopoly over the work opportunities it created (1962, pp. 16–18). Otherwise this issue seems to be ignored.

[38] See Harriss-White and Gooptu (2000).

[39] For the story of Parsis, see Chopra (1998); Guha (1984); Luhrmann (1994 and 1996). Their *panchayat* system of social security is unique and their strong philanthropy mitigates not only their own inequality but also that of other people's. For Buddhism, see Gellner (2001).

Table 6.1 *Economic power by religion and community, 1995–96*

Religion/Caste	Business houses	Group rank	Turnover Rs crores	Rank
Marwari (H/J)	19	1	51 399	1
Punjabi (H)	7–8	2	18 161	3
Gujarati (H)	5–6	3	16 915	4
Parsi	3	4	35 463	2
Chettiar (H)	2	5	6 367	5
Brahmin (H)	2–3	6	6 172	6
Sindhi (H)	2	7	4 523	7
Christian (Syrian)	1	8	2 011	9
Nair (H)	1	8	2 148	8
Raju (H)	1	8	1 341	10
Muslim	1	8	1 287	11
Others	3	–	5 106	–
Total	47–50		150 893	

H = Hindu; J = Jain
Source: data in *Business Today*, August–September 1997 in Dorin et al. 2000, p. 25

car?", you ask; but "Yes", says Mr Seton-Watson, "you must".' Each of these religions is included because it illustrates aspects of religious plurality and its economic significance.

Table 6.1 sets the scene for this exploration. Here, it can be seen that although the religious minorities amount to 17 per cent of the Indian population,[40] non-Parsi, non-Jain minorities controlled but 2 per cent of the assets of the top 50 business houses in 1996. Counting *in* the minority members of the Hindu religious family they may have controlled as much as 40 per cent.[41] Appendix 3 tabulates the results of an extensive search through the existing literature and summarises the economic positioning of the religious minorities: their geographical locations and networks; their internal religious and economic differentiation; their relative wealth – investments, remittances, inheritance practices – and religious teachings relevant to accumulation; their occupational stratification, labour relations and gender differentiation; their redistributive practices, relations with the State; and their experience of political/economic conflict. The section that follows draws on this catalogue selectively, elaborating some of its more interesting findings and introducing a number of local case studies to illustrate their significance.

[40] Parsis are a minute proportion of the population – some 56 000 – but rank second in India in terms of their economic power with a fifth of the assets of the top corporates.
[41] The difficulty in making this calculation stems from the fact that some Marwaris are Jains and some Hindus.

Muslims

India has more Muslims than any other nation except for Indonesia and Pakistan – 102 million in 1991, making up 12.6 per cent of the population and having a growth rate of 32 per cent in the decade of the 1980s, higher than that of both the Hindu majority (which grew by 25 per cent) and the Christian minority (21.5 per cent).[42] Their uneven dispersal affects the many roles they play in the economy (see Map 6.1). Half of India's Muslims are compacted into the northern 'Hindi heartland' and West Bengal. There are smaller concentrations in peninsular India, on the Kerala coast and by the border with Pakistan. While most Muslims live in rural areas, they are nonetheless twice as urbanised as their population share would suggest.[43] We have noted that 'difference' has been codified in laws grounded in religion, that electoral democracy evolved to cater separately for electorates defined in terms of their religions, and that the history of modern India has been punctuated by eruptions of violence between Hindus and Muslims. But Muslims are not covered by India's laws of positive discrimination. While Hindu nationalists have depicted an Islamic 'community' as both threatening and indulged, if there is a problem of Muslims in the Indian economy it is one of economic backwardness and under-performance, rather than one of superior economic power. In the late 1980s (using the most recent data), Muslims were found to be half again as likely as Hindus to be below the poverty line.[44] In fact, there exists a literature stressing Muslim backwardness which both results from, and reinforces, the construction of religion as a base for economic competition.[45]

It follows from this that although Muslims are disproportionately urban, they are also under-represented in India's capitalist elite. Out of 1365 member companies constituting the Indian Merchants' Chamber of Bombay in the 1980s, some 4 per cent were owned by Muslims, and in 1988 no Muslim-owned company featured in the top 100 corporates, though some do now. Of the 2832 industrial units listed for monitoring in the 1990s by the Centre for Monitoring the Indian Economy, only four

[42] Govt. of India 1999, pp. 194–5.
[43] Calculated from data in Ahmad (1993). There is great variation between cities. While Murshidabad and Malappuram have over 2 million Muslims (respectively 61 and 67 per cent of the total population) and Hyderabad has over 1 million (39 per cent), Lucknow is 20 per cent Muslim, Calcutta 18 per cent, Bombay 17 per cent, Aligarh 15 per cent, Delhi 9 per cent and Madurai but 5 per cent (*Muslim India* 1997, vol. 172, p. 150).
[44] Fifty-three per cent of Muslims were under the expenditure poverty line of Rs 160 per capita per month, contrasted with 36 per cent Hindus, according to NSSO data quoted in Subramaniam (2001, p. 11).
[45] See, for example, Ahmad (1973, 1975); Ali (1992); Ahmad (1993); Khalidi (1995).

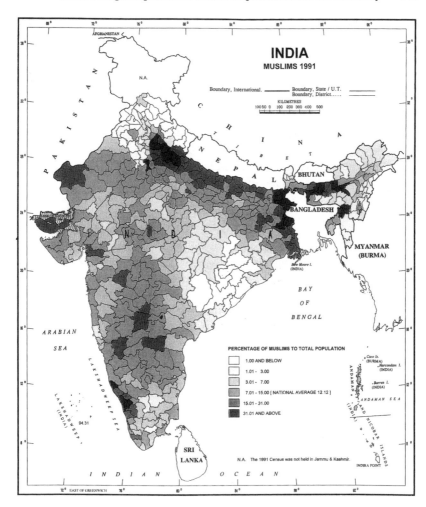

Map 6.1 The distribution of Muslims in India
Source: Indian Census 1991

(0.0014 per cent) were owned by Muslims. Despite the entry of new entrepreneurs, including Muslim women, and despite the fact that Muslims head some of the most successful and dynamic IT corporates, these are still the exceptions that prove the rule. One survey found just over 1 per cent of corporate executives were Muslim.[46] If Muslims are not in the vanguard of business accumulation, they are also under-represented

---

[46] Goyal 1990, pp. 535–44.

in the Indian state apparatus; for example, in the Indian Administrative Service (3 per cent), the Police (2.8 per cent), the Railways (2.65 per cent), in the nationalised banks (2 per cent) and in Parliament (5 to 8 per cent).[47] While there are no data for Muslim representation in education, the Muslim illiteracy rate is 15 per cent higher than that for Hindus (including SC/STs), and the proportion of Hindus who get secondary education is three times that of Muslims.[48]

At the same time, the population of Muslims is highly differentiated in complex ways, according to sect, to internal caste-like stratification, to *biradari* (industrial/occupational guilds) and region.[49] 'Muslims are not a homogenous group but a conglomerate of many communities' (Ali 1992, p. 34). Upon this cultural and religious differentiation, their equally complex economic differentiation has to be mapped. The first element in this differentiation is the Muslim peasantry, most heavily concentrated in Jammu and Kashmir, and the Ganges Valley belt along the southern border with Nepal. While this peasantry is itself internally differentiated by landholding, operational scale and labour process, two features stand out. First, the mass of Muslim cultivators are small peasants in regions of poor irrigation that have lagged in the adoption of new agricultural technology – and in agrarian structures where strong elements of extra-economic compulsion persist.[50] Second, throughout India, while the proportion of rural Muslims engaged in agricultural labour (24 per cent) is close to that of rural Hindus (28 per cent), the proportion self-employed in agriculture is significantly smaller (36 per cent for Muslims, 44 per cent for Hindus). Muslims have a higher incidence of landlessness (35 per cent opposed to 28 per cent), and the proportion of rural Muslims in non-

[47] Respectively Wright (1981, p. 43); Khalidi (1995, pp. 69–75, and see particularly pp. 77–88 on the armed forces (where, though there are no data, Muslims are known to be grossly under-represented)); Ali (1992, p. 44); Ahmad 1993, pp. 40–1; Haider (2001, p. 32)). There is vigorous debate over the causes of this under-representation: poor levels of education versus self-reinforcing communalist discrimination – and over its historical drift.

[48] Subramaniam 2001.

[49] The principal sects are Shias and Sunnis, although there are quite distinct smaller communities such as the *ismaili boras* and *khojas*, and the *memons* along the western littoral. The greatest internal divisions are between the Ashrafi, Persian elite and the *ajlaf*, descendants of native converts. The main upper caste-like groups throughout India are *sheikh*, *saiyyad*, *khan* and *pathan*, while *qureshi*, *ansari*, *idrisi*, *mahaldar*, *raien* and *momin* are considered as of lower status. Among the *biradaris* (or guilds) are *halwais* (sweetmakers), *idrisis* (tailors), *gaddi* (milkmen), *qureshis* or *qassabs* (butchers), *ansaris* (clothmakers), *julahas* (weavers), *zari* (embroiderers), *bidi* (makers, metal workers and locksmiths) (I. Ahmad 1973; Ahmad, 1993; Mann 1992; Mondal 1997). Muslim history is conventionally viewed from the north as a product of forced conquest, whereas Islam actually had a much longer history in south India and spread through persuasion, trade and intermarriage (Ali 1992).

[50] Ahmad 1975, pp. 241–3; Khalidi 1995, pp. 54–9.

agricultural wage work, artisanal craft production and what is still known as 'menial work' (services and petty trade, much of which involves high levels of skill but low levels of pay) is also greater – 36 per cent contrasted with 28 per cent.[51]

On the one hand, the occupational distribution of rural Muslims in contemporary India shows a distinctive 'path dependence' from the Mughal era of courtly patronage and exploitation. On the other hand, their social separation from Hindus and their freedom from Hindus' distinctive social obligations may have encouraged innovative activity. An observation from a south Indian village where Muslims were a small minority still seems pertinent several decades after it was written, for it is often quoted: 'the fact that Muslims seem to have remained on the fringe of the society has made them more versatile ... [while it would never do for a Hindu] peasant to squat on the floor of his shop and offer goods to passers-by, who might be of lower caste or even untouchable ... a Muslim can do this ... [I]f a peasant opened a shop ... he could never make money like a Muslim shopkeeper because a peasant was expected to be charitable and therefore obliged to sell goods on credit, a Muslim need not do this'.[52] Hindu people of 'peasant' castes have, of course, opened shops in very large numbers, and Muslim traders now sell on credit and charge interest.

Another element in the economic differentiation of Muslims is the downward mobility resulting from the migration to Pakistan of professionals and the *ashrafi* elite, and from the political degeneration of Islamic feudalism after Independence. In the wake of the state-enforced *zamindari* abolition in UP and Hyderabad, the absentee landowning aristocracy and their retainers lost their role and, often, their livelihoods, dragging with them the urban and rural artisans whose livelihoods had depended on courtly tastes and demand. Only a small and educated minority of the landed elite remained near the seats of power and obtained employment and new status, often retaining control over their land through renting and letting.[53]

The case of Siliguri

These elements may be seen at work in Siliguri, a rapidly growing town of some 200 000 inhabitants, distributing consumption goods to the plantation region of West Bengal. While the territory of the future town

[51] National Sample Survey, 43rd Round, 1987–88, Table 27r p. 56.

[52] Epstein (1964, p. 33) quoted in Ahmad (1975, p. 243) and in Khalidi (1995, p. 56).

[53] As in the case of the Kidwai lineage of east-central Uttar Pradesh (Ahmad 1975, pp. 235–41; Bhatty 1973, pp. 97–8).

had been owned entirely by powerful Muslim families, 'due to miscalculation, uneconomic habits and family litigation, these Muslim personalities lost their land, capital, power and position' (Mondal 1997, p. 53) and at Partition they were forced to East Bengal. As Siliguri expanded, some 10 000 Muslims migrated there, establishing themselves mainly in slums alongside low-caste Hindus in a 'microcosm of Muslim society and culture' (Mondal 1997). Muslim men work as traders, skilled artisans, recyclers and providers of petty services. Old links between *biradari* (guild) and occupation are dissolving; endogamous groups have become less rigid. All the same, tailoring, cotton-carding, fish-mongering, goat-butchery, greengrocery and book-binding are still carried out by Muslims in occupational groups. While alliances now blur the social boundaries of the *ashrafi* elite and *ajlaf* [54] subordinates, new socioeconomic categories with new economic meanings are being formed. These distinguish the *amir* (the educated, rich few) from the *gharib* (the poor majority). Despite this internal economic and cultural differentiation, Muslims in Siliguri are generally described as being poor, socially separate, passive supporters of the ruling CPI(M) and marginalised by their religion and its impact on their education. Siliguri's Muslims, especially their girls, are relatively poorly educated. Muslim children are educated in separate religious schools (*madrassas*) and in *Urdu* rather than Bengali, the local language. [55]

Another major element in the economic positioning of Muslims is their tendency to occupy niches historically shunned by Hindus for reasons of ritual pollution: butchers may be either untouchables, or Muslims – *qassabs*. Muslim control of tanning, glue, soap, hides and leather (and rubber and plastic), shoe and leather goods production (and now their export) has developed from their important role in butchery. Small-town restaurants ('military hotels') have developed, based on Muslim culinary specialities that include meat, as much as from Hindu rules of commensality, which long prevented all but the ritually purest from running even vegetarian-eating places.

The case of south Indian leather

The case of the leather industry in south India shows how a series of factors have transformed the way it had been stratified by religion, though it is still controlled by Muslims. At the macro level, state policy has required the export of hides to be replaced by semi-finished and finished leather products. At the micro level, the diffusion from upper to lower castes of the practice of demanding dowries has changed Hindu social

[54] See footnote 49.
[55] Mondal 1997.

attitudes to work involving ritually polluting substances, as people come under severe social compulsion to supply dowries. The production of leather goods is being vertically integrated, and the labour process is being transformed from one using casual workforces, confined to Muslim or SC labourers working on-site, to one that includes the subcontracting of stitching and other processes to poor, forward-caste child and female workers. They work at some distance from the tanneries, in the seclusion of their homes and in an atmosphere of 'shame' and of patriarchal compulsion. The worldwide rise in demand for Indian leather products and the entrepreneurial responses to this by Muslim tanners have led to the rapid accumulation of considerable capital and to new portfolios of Muslim investment in agribusiness and property (see Chapter 8). Already in the 1970s, the acquisition of the trappings of high status by Muslims in the leather industry had 'begun to distort the traditional system of social stratification and rank order'(Ahmad 1975, pp. 246–7).

But the transformation of cattle into commodities is not the only route to accumulation that ritually polluting niches in the economy have opened up for Muslims. The Hindu fear of 'outcasting' by overseas travel on the one hand, and the ritual importance for Muslims of the pilgrimage to Mecca on the other, gave Muslims an early incentive to develop the travel industry. The predominance of Muslims in *bidi* (country cigarette) production (where Muslims comprise 80 per cent of the workforce, though they own none of the dominant brands) is explained by both the caste Hindu's avoidance of pollution and by the fact that smoking was introduced into India by Muslims.[56] Muslims also cite 'Hindu ritual pollution' as the reason for their control of the recycling of physically polluting waste and scrap: bone, paper, card, metal, glass and plastics. In many regions, Muslims dominate plumbing, masonry and metal products, hardware, locks and even mechanical and electrical repairs, which are thought to trace back to the conversion to Islam of low-caste Hindu *lohar* blacksmiths.[57] And there have been strong economic incentives for other low-caste or untouchable Hindu castes to convert to Islam – and a significant number have.[58]

Yet another element that has given Muslims a distinctive role in the economy is the revival and expansion of industries whose workforces require highly skilled craftsmen. Craft skills are reproduced in the families of artisans that survived the decline in the 1950s and 1960s of the princely patronage that had given them life. These families responded

[56] Ironic when one of the ways in which Hindus may sometimes assert their identity in the presence of non-smoking Sikhs is by smoking (Pritam Singh, personal communication, 2001)

[57] Mondal 1997, chapter 5.

[58] Khalidi 1995, pp. 25 and 73; Wright 1981, pp. 38 and 41.

to the transformation of services and goods for a few patrons into the supply of commodities for national and international demand. Yet many of the craft-based industries have remained strikingly localised. In Uttar Pradesh, for example, Muslim artisans produce brassware in Morada-bad; pottery in Khurja; glassware in Ferozabad; carpets in Bhadodi and Mirzapur; carpentry and woodwork in Sharanapur; hand-printed textiles in Farrakhabad; cotton and silk embroidery in Varanasi, perfume-manu-facturing (to which the development of *unani* medicines is related) in Lucknow, Kanauj and Jaunpur; and handloom cloth in Mau. In Bihar, large numbers of Muslims are silk and cotton handloom weavers. Mus-lim workers dominate the *bidri* ware[59] and carpet industries in Andhra Pradesh, and silkworm-rearing and toy industries in Karnataka. In Jaipur, Rajasthan, some of the stone-cutters and marble workers are Muslim (though tribal women and children are also used in quarrying), and Gujarat's block- and screen-printing industry employs *chippas*, a Muslim group. Some of these craft-based industries have evolved into a full-blown local Muslim capitalism. The examples most often quoted are Moradabad brassware, which has profited from demand from the Middle East, and cloth and clothing manufacture and trade, which have devel-oped from the skills of Muslim tailors (*darzis*) and weavers (*julahas*).

It is quite common however for the surplus in these industries to be appropriated from the Muslim workers by Hindu and Jain immigrant trading castes, which proceed to reinvest it elsewhere. They routinely supply production and consumption credit and raw materials, and sometimes have been found to provide food as an advance against pay. They arrange sales, state licences, development permits and finance, and organise technical change.[60] Given that in sectors where Muslims provide the uneducated but skilled labour force, the traders are not nec-essarily Muslim; it has often been concluded that the 'Indian Muslim [has a] dislike for trade and commerce' (Ahmad 1993, p. 41). Khalidi commented that 'the generality of Muslims in Hindustan and the Dec-can kept away from trade and commerce, at least up until independence' (1995, p. 68) and Wright that they have been 'devoid of a middle class of businessmen' since then (1981, p. 37).[61] Yet Muhammed himself was a merchant. At the start, Islam flourished in an urban and commercial

---

[59] Ornamental metal work of a pewter–copper alloy inlaid with silver.
[60] Khalidi 1995, pp. 70–3; Cadène 1998a, p. 116.
[61] That migrant small businessmen from India could establish large-scale industries in Paki-stan has not passed unnoticed (Papanek 1967) and has been used to fuel rival arguments: one holds that Muslim capital was drained from India in that process, the other that the lack of accumulation by Indian Muslims is the result of communal discrimination by a State operating in the interest of Hindu business castes (Wright 1981; Ali 1992).

culture.[62] In fact there are many regions in India, especially but not exclusively on the west coast, where Muslims have long been assimilated into the merchant class, both as immigrants and as local converts.

Small-town Muslim commerce

Mattison Mines' study of Muslim merchants in Pallavaram in northern Tamil Nadu is one of the few accounts we have of the impact of the social organisation of any minority religion on economic practice. Published in 1972, it showed that while high-caste Hindus spurned commerce there, the conduct of business by Muslims was regarded as a *sunnath,* a custom of the Prophet's and therefore as 'an occupation conveying religious merit'.

The fact that these merchants were Muslim could not be separated from their being in a type of bazaar trade that was not regulated by the State. Nor could it be distinguished from the fact that it belonged to a particular place. The significance for accumulation of being Muslim was therefore ambiguous. The influence of Islam was expressed in a variety of ways, including a pronounced preference for the employment of Muslim wage labour by Muslim merchants – a spreading of opportunities for livelihood most easily achieved in the bazaar economy. Further, the universalist cosmopolitanism of Islam meant that there were trusted contacts at long distance, including overseas, ready to develop trade networks.[63] At the time of Mines' fieldwork, however, these 'bazaar' merchants had not expanded into national trade networks or industries – whether 'small scale' (as the Muslim leather industry nearby was classified) or corporate. This was attributed by Mines to the constraints of 'embeddedness' in the personalised and informalised bazaar economy. In the bazaar, while credit was available through established links of trust and mutual dependence, its scale was too small and too short-term for investment in industry. In the bazaar too, practical experience was valued above the technical education needed to manage industry. A family- or kin-based workforce was still valued above cosmopolitan contractual relations.[64]

---

[62] A careful study of the doctrines of Islam has failed to find any serious obstacle to capitalist activity. The practice of *riba* condemned in the Koran is not 'interest' but the doubling of principal and interest if the debtor cannot pay when due. The prohibition of usury has always had 'little practical effect', and is understood by scholars as a response to particular circumstances and not as intended to hold for all time (see Rodinson 1987, pp. 73–6). In the rare conditions when Muslims do not take interest it is due to a warping of doctrine. Social institutions owing their origins to misunderstandings of sacred scripture can be found in other religions, notably Christianity.

[63] Mines 1972, pp. 93–8.

[64] Mines 1972, pp. 109 and 112–18.

In the absence of other systematic evidence on the reach of Muslim business, Wright's analysis of advertisements over a run of 14 years in *Radiance*, an English-language, Islamic fundamentalist, weekly magazine, is summarised in Table 6.2. From this information, it seems that both upwardly mobile *ajlaf* and downwardly mobile and adaptable *ashrafi* capitalists formed a largely metropolitan body of Muslim accumulators. But Wright concluded: '(t)he trouble is that as the traditional functional division of labour between religious communities as well as sects and *jatis* breaks down ... competition can and does erupt into politicised violence' (1981, p. 43). This violence has since intensified.

The economic bases of communal violence

Despite the lack of evidence that Muslim capitalists constitute an economic threat at the national level, contemporary communal violence can have an economic base.[65] A Parsi police commissioner is credited by the *Organiser*, the newspaper of the RSS, with the following conclusions:

A riot does not occur in a sleepy little village of UP where all suffer equally, nor in a tribal village of Madhya Pradesh where all live safely in their poverty. It occurs in Moradabad where the metal workers have built up a good industry ... or Aligarh where lock-makers have made good ... or in Bhiwandi where power-loom rivalries are poisonous. It occurs in ... Ahmedabad and Hyderabad and Jamshedpur where there are jobs to get, contracts to secure, houses and shops to capture, and it occurs in Agra and Ferozebad and in all other towns where economic rivalries are serious and have to be covered up with the cloak of communalism.[66]

A list of sites of communal violence compiled by Khalidi (1995, p. 22) shows – contrary to the general impression that south Indian Muslims are better assimilated and/or protected than in the north – that urban and metropolitan sites are targeted throughout India. Riots and pogroms are rarest and most infrequent where Muslims are the smallest proportion of the population. Their incidence is reported not to be affected by the degree of working-class organisation across religious boundaries. One case study of the informalisation of the textiles industry in Kanpur, however, finds that while an older generation of workers clings to union politics as a defence against informalisation, a younger generation of 'flexible', casualised labour is forced for advancement into relations of clientelage for patrons eager to use them to foment

[65] This is not to say that communal violence never erupts for purely religious, political or cultural reasons (see Engineer 1984a, p. 2).

[66] *Organiser* (28 September 1980, p. 14) quoting K.F. Rustomji, 'Communal Violence' in *Opinion* (16 September 1980) and quoted in Wright (1981, p. 43).

Table 6.2 *Distribution of Muslim advertisers by product*

	Number	Chief locations	No.	Category of origin (where known)
A Low-caste occupations				
Hides, leather, shoes	107	Madras	39	butchers (*qassabs*)
		UP	19	
Hardware, metals	74	Bombay	23	Khoja sect
		Calcutta	16	blacksmiths
		Delhi	9	(*lohars* or *karkhanedars*)
		Hyderabad	8	
		Aligarh	6	
		Vijayawada	5	
		Moradabad	1	
Cloth and clothing	73	Madras	22	tailors (*darzis*)
		Bombay	11	weavers (*julahas* or
		Calcutta	9	*momins*)
		Gorakhpur	4	dyers (*rangrez*)
		Ahmedabad	2	
Cigarettes (*bidis*)	43	Tamil Nadu	25	
		Andhra P.	18	
Transportation, electrics, machinery	41	Vijayawada	8	pilgrims (*hajis*)
		Delhi	7	smiths (*lohars*)
Rubber, plastics	33	Calcutta	21	
Hotels, restaurants, food	27	Calcutta	9	cooks (*bhatiyaras*)
		Delhi	8	bakers (*nanbais*) confectioners (*halwais*) grocers (*kunjras*)
10 Glass, optician; watches	19	Delhi	8	bangle-makers (*manihars*)
Perfume, incense	18	Mau, Kanauj	16	oil presser (*telis*)
B High-caste occupations	50	Bombay	8	perfumer (*gandhis*)
Patent medicine, pharmacy	32	Calcutta	7	doctor (*unanihakims*)
Publishing, books, journals	39	Delhi	16	savants (*ulema*)
		Calcutta	5	

Source: Wright 1981, pp. 39–43

communal violence.[67] They are most likely in urban sites where Muslims have visibly accumulated or benefited from remittances, where Hindu social and physical space is being asserted or reclaimed, and where the State's regulatory and repressive capacities are weak or have been captured by a religious group. Although the triggers are usually cultural and religious ('trifling incidents'), although a connection needs

[67] Deponte 2000.

making between a cultural symbol and specific local circumstances, and although the violence that erupts may be to persons, it rarely fails to involve property as well, including business assets.[68] Material explanations focus on the local economic interests, which stand to profit from the physical removal of competition. They are often one and the same as the political interests that gain from the mass-mobilising effect of events that distract attention from conflicts within parties or factions, or between castes, classes or genders.[69]

Christians

The second-largest minority considered here comprised only 2.3 per cent of the Indian population in 1991, though numbering a substantial 20 million. While a third of Goans are Christian, and while Christians form the majority in almost all the small States of the north-east, most Christians are to be found in Kerala, where they account for 20 per cent of total population, and in a belt in Tamil Nadu, where they account for 6 per cent. In half the States of India, Christians number fewer than 1 per cent and are mostly marginal peasants and agricultural labourers. The history and geography of conversion has resulted in distinct and separate groupings and denominations, polarised at their extremes between Syrian Christians in Kerala on the one hand, who trace themselves back to *brahmins* converted by the apostle Thomas (who arrived in India in 52 AD)[70] and *Dalit* and tribal Christians on the other, who converted in mass movements from the last part of the nineteenth century onwards.

Syrian Christians have developed as a 'Jati among other Jatis' (Webster 1992, p. 34). They are said to live in relative social exclusivity to this day, perhaps because of – rather than despite – their having multiplied into no less than 15 denominations, and a long history of accommodation with imperialism by some of them. Joining British capital as workers, supervisors and agents, they differentiated into money-dealing, industrial capital and commercial capitalism. From here, they moved on to establish credit institutions and modern banking on the one hand, and the rubber and tea plantations, the development of vertically integrated agribusinesses (and the joint stock form of corporate ownership) on the other. Syrian

---

[68] Desai 1984, pp. 22–3; Engineer 1984b, pp. 36–41. During the Coimbatore riots of 1997, while police destroyed the assets of Muslim pavement sellers, paid riot-makers simultaneously wrecked Muslim cloth shops (People's Union for Civil Liberties 1998).

[69] Professional agitators, organisers, looters and arsonists have for decades been hired for this purpose (Engineer 1984a, p. 2, 1984b; Khalidi 1995, pp. 20–7 and 50–1; Ali 1992 p. 42). Riots have been broken down into their elements and these have been commodified.

[70] Although Government of India (1999, pp. 198–9) and Chopra (1998, p. 245) both trace them to migrants accompanying Thomas.

Christians are now well represented in the State and in corporate sector management. But using tightly knit credit, Syrian Christians have also invaded low-status sectors. In Kerala and elsewhere they dominate mechanised fishing, chains of beauty parlours and dry-cleaning.

The Christian churches (particularly the Roman Catholic Church under the Portuguese) also accumulated significant capital assets and are now major employers in their own right. Tapping foreign aid and state subsidies too, churches run by high-caste Catholics have invested in educational and medical infrastructure, commercial property, farms and factories. Their surplus is ploughed back and also invested in India's capital markets. Church institutions cannot possibly employ all the low-caste and *dalit* Catholics who need work.[71]

Protestant Christianity, condemning the systems of power expressed both by caste and by the subordination of women, was more successful at eliminating caste within Christian society in north India than it was in the south where it met with opposition from Syrian and Catholic Christians, as well as Hindus. Whether Indian Protestantism has been more successful in its fight against caste than it has against the subordination of women is not known. Certainly, educated Protestant women are a significant minority in the professions.[72]

When *dalit*s converted to Christianity, they were no longer eligible for state support under the system of educational and job reservations for scheduled and other low ('backward') castes. Their livelihoods now depended on education and on wide regional networks of Christian contacts. So a minority of educated Christians 'became teachers, clerks, nurses, hospital attendants, railways and postal employees, drivers, conductors, mechanics and policemen. Some have become doctors, professors, advocates, writers, singers, printers and engineers and a few have become higher level government officials' (Wiebe 1988, p. 192).

---

[71] Kurian 1986.

[72] From 1870–1930 large numbers of low-caste and tribal people converted to Christianity, Webster argues, to escape poverty and demeaning status, and at their behest rather than that of missionaries. Bengal, Orissa, Bihar and Madhya Pradesh witnessed movements among tribals; elsewhere, the specific *jatis* and the proportion of converts varied greatly. The mass movements had a greater impact on the Church – imprinting it with a *dalit* stamp – than on *dalit* converts, many of whom faced economic boycotts and physical abuse (Webster 1992, pp. 41–65). Rural *dalit* Christians could improve their public health environment, and had access to education and medical facilities. But they had limited economic mobility and, grouped with elite Christians who did not share *dalit* interests, they gained nothing by way of representation under the Constitution; and they have continued to be excluded from reserved seats and deprived of protective discrimination, even when these were extended to Sikh *dalits* in 1950 and neo-Buddhist *dalits* in 1990 (Mosse 1994; Shiri 1997; Webster 1992, pp. 126–8 and 190; Wiebe 1988, pp. 182–93).

Their descendants form an urban, propertied, educated, salaried and professional elite, some of whom have interests in rural land. The great majority, however, remain rural wage workers and 'in the highly competitive struggle for upward mobility they face prejudices both as *dalits* and as Christians' (Webster 1992, p. 10).

Caste, Christianity and economic change

David Mosse's study of a village in southern Tamil Nadu where a large *harijan* (outcaste) population is divided between Hindus and Christians, and further between Catholic and Protestant, shows that all the *harijan* castes have been struggling to reduce the relations of subordination in which they are locked – through patronage, dependence on tenancy and many kinds of service provision.[73] Yet, in an elaborate process of status mobility (involving 'downward displacement, role bifurcations and trade-offs between status and resources'), Christianity has helped people to reduce their economic relations of dependence (as in the case of Protestant *harijan paraiyan* caste) but also to achieve specific indicators of higher status (for example, the Catholic *harijan pallar* caste). People at the very bottom of the system of *harijan* caste rankings provide services reciprocally or on a 'market' basis with personalised transactions. Elsewhere, contracts are reworked in the idioms of higher status. Instead of work on order, there is negotiation with honorific presentations, cash payment and the development of new contexts in which services can be provided and received. Demeaning tasks and forms of payment are transferred to women or avoided through migration. Markets for credit and labour have been created and the principle that Christian *harijan pallars* can have rights to private landownership has been established. Mosse finds that 'religion makes no difference to (the) inter caste relations' of hierarchy and rank being replicated and challenged by *harijans*.[74] Each episode of assertion has been organised at the level of the individual economic service performed. The history of emancipation for cattle scavengers is different from that for the operators of irrigation sluices; the history of Catholic and Hindu *pallar* labour, bonded to high-caste agricultural employers, is different from that of Catholic and Hindu *chakkiliyan* labour bonded to *pallar* employers. The struggle for the transformation of the 'idiom' of service has a different history from the history

---

[73] Mosse (1994) uses the word *harijan* as this is the word used by the people he studied, but he reminds us that all words for untouchable imply specific discourses on identity. Ben Rogaly comments that this is true even for 'former untouchable' (2001, personal communication).

[74] Mosse 1994, p. 82.

of the struggle over the use of village space, but there is a common thread in the liberating effects of adherence to a Christian church.

However, not all change has been emancipating. Now that Christian missions have been abandoned and their independent patronage has vanished, Protestant *paraiyans* have been forced back into servile roles.[75] Shiri, studying rural Protestant *dalit*s in south India, confirms that they are now suffering from deteriorating debt, poverty and illiteracy, as the churches and their services disintegrate.[76]

Some Christians, particularly tribal Christians, are the object of growing communal violence, while others, particularly certain Syrian Christians, have seen their churches approved as '*Swadeshi*' by the RSS.[77] In the year 2000, press reports appeared regularly of the desecration of religious property, of the Sangh Parivar's[78] accusations of 'forced conversion', of word-of-mouth hate campaigns, cases of threats, harassment and even murders of priests, nuns and missionaries. Towards the end of the year, it was proposed to reform Christian divorce laws in order to eliminate their gender bias. The chief sites of aggression against Christians are Orissa, Gujarat, Tamil Nadu and the 'potentially Christian States' of the north-east. It is widely held that this persecution has no economic base. But to the extent that churches attempt to protect tribal and *dalit* Christians from exploitation by Hindu money-lenders and traders, and some actively challenge oppression, religion may be the idiom of reprisal.[79]

Sikhs

The Sikh minority is not much smaller than the Christian – 16.3 million in 1991 (1.92 per cent of the total population). Forming a large majority in Punjab, one-fifth lives in neighbouring States where Sikhs form about 7 per cent of the population, while the diaspora pervades India and reaches out to the United Kingdom, the United States and Canada. Like

---

[75] Mosse 1994.

[76] Shiri 1997, pp. 115–34 and 242.

[77] 'Swadeshi' is a term appropriated by Hindu nationalists. It means 'self-provisioning' with reference to the production and consumption of Indian-made goods. In this case the elite, right-wing Rashtriya Swayamsevak Sangh, which has done much to develop the ideology of Hindutva – 'Hindu-ness' – confers Indian 'authenticity' upon certain Syrian Christian Churches.

[78] The Sangh Parivar is the family of (right-wing, Hindu nationalist) organisations.

[79] See reports in Communalism Watch and Governance Monitor: http://www.saccer.org; for example, 'Attacks on Minorities', 6 December 2000, from which the data reported here were obtained. Monthly reports of attacks on people and property also reveal the emergence of a new social movement of poor Christians consisting of a set of organisations with economic agendas.

Christians and Muslims, despite their egalitarian religious ideals, Sikhs are segmented into sects, which are loosely associated with different sectors of the economy. Some 20 per cent of Sikhs are scheduled caste *mazhabis*, mostly poor agricultural producers and labourers with economic interests at variance with Sikh *jats*. The dominant *jat* landowning caste forms two-thirds of the Sikh population. With assured irrigation and with relatively large, consolidated holdings, Sikh *jats* were famously at the forefront of adoption of the seed-fertiliser technology introduced in the mid-1960s.[80] By 1981, on 1.6 per cent of India's land area, with a canal irrigation system built under colonial rule and on holdings consolidated at the time of the devastating movements of population at Partition, Punjab was producing 73 per cent of the wheat procured for public distribution by the State and 48 per cent of all procured rice.[81] Yet, although Punjab still has the highest level of aggregate rural wealth and consumption expenditure in India, the returns to Punjabi agriculture have been notably unequal, reflecting the relatively advanced capitalist production that achieved these results.[82] In the 1980s, estimates of rural poverty varied between 18 and 33 per cent.[83]

However, 'what strikes most about Punjab is the way production and exchange are almost neatly compartmentalised on religious and caste lines. The peasants are Sikhs (*jats*), merchants are Hindus (*khatris, aroras* and *baniyas*). Sikhs cultivate, organise agricultural production. Hindus trade. Peasants live in villages, merchants live in towns' (Singh 1999, p. 191). The religious alignment of the economy is set against a background of unbalanced sectoral development and political turbulence.[84] While 70 per cent of rural households are Sikh, 85 per cent of urban households are Hindu. The segmentation of the Sikh *merchant* castes – they do exist, notwithstanding Singh's valid generalisation quoted above – is so great that not only trade but also industry is dominated by Hindu

[80] Govt. of India 1999, pp. 202–3; Chopra 1998, pp. 190–1; Wallace 1986, pp. 365–6; Singh 1993 and 1997.

[81] Wallace 1986, p. 367. This concentration is now less marked. The relative roles of remittances and local accumulation in the creation of agrarian wealth have been disputed (see Helweg 1987, p. 151).

[82] See for critical evaluation Byres (1981); Bhalla (1999).

[83] Wallace 1986, p. 369; Singh 1999, pp. 103–9. Sikh merchant castes include *pothohari* refugees from West Pakistan who captured markets for cloth in Indian Punjab, Delhi and north-west India and produce cycles, motor parts and radio parts. *Ramgharias* have also developed from being artisan converts – *tarkhan* (carpenters) and *lohar* (blacksmiths) – to occupy substantial accumulation niches in contracting and engineering in the Punjab.

[84] Sikh revivalism has taken two distinct forms: one egalitarian and humanistic, against Sikh casteism, and the depravities associated with increasing consumption; the other sectarian and communal, in reaction to threats to Sikh identity (Singh 1987).

Table 6.3 *Religion and caste of the owners of the top 10 corporate companies in Punjab*

Name of company**	Religious affiliation of Chairman	Sub-caste of the chairman	Caste group
Ranbaxy, Mohali	Sikh	—	Arora
JCT, Hoshiarpur	Hindu	Thapar	Khatri
Hero Cycles, Ludhiana	Hindu	Munjal	Arora
Mahavir Spinning, Ludhiana	Hindu	Oswal	Baniya
Jagatjit, Kapurthala	Hindu	Jaiswal	Baniya
Oswal Agro, Ludhiana	Hindu	Oswal	Baniya
Vardhman, Ludhiana	Hindu	Oswal	Baniya
JCT, Mohali	Hindu	Thapar	Khatri
Malwa Cotton, Ludhiana	Hindu	Oswal	Baniya
JCT Fibres, Hoshiarpur	Hindu	Thapar	Khatri

**The companies have been arranged in the descending order according to sales in the year 1994.
Source: Centre for Monitoring the Indian Economy, 1995, in Singh 1999, p. 153

capital (see Tables 6.3 and 6.4).[85] Agricultural trade is largely in the control of *baniyas* whose accumulation strategy focuses on agro-industry, notably the processing of wheat, rice and oilseeds. Trade in manufactured goods is dominated by *khatri* and *arora* castes. Disrupted at Partition, this trade is now strongly networked into metro-capital unrelated to agriculture and outside Punjab. Despite high levels of both rural and urban consumption, and its top rank in agriculture, industry in Punjab is relatively under-developed, ranking only tenth among states in India. It has a distinctive structure of small-scale industry, limited to eight kinds of activity in cotton-processing and metal-working.[86] This industry derives more from princely patronage prior to Partition, and to the immigration of Hindu *arora* traders, than to the locally generated agricultural surplus. Even the expansion of *ramgharia* artisanal engineering is more

[85] Telford 1992, p. 980. Arvinder Singh presents data from surveys by the Centre for Monitoring the Indian Economy for the 10 largest corporates in Punjab in 1994, showing that only one is Sikh-controlled and that only 9 per cent of board members are Sikh (Singh 1999, pp. 152–3).

[86] Wallace (1986, pp. 371–2): in the 1980s these were woollen textiles and hosiery, cotton-ginning and processing, cotton textiles, sewing machines and parts, steel re-rolling, cycles and cycle parts, agricultural implements, machine tools and sports goods. By the mid-1990s the largest corporates were in textiles, liquor, pharmaceuticals, cycles and TVs. On the all-India scale, industrial firms are numerous, oriented towards trading, with low fixed capital and high working capital components and high levels of debt and gross output per unit of fixed capital. In 1996 only 15 per cent of trading firms were controlled by SCs. These were small firms, largely rurally located, with poor endowments of working capital and barriers to credit (Singh 1999, pp. 144–69).

Table 6.4 *Religious and caste composition of the board of directors of the top 10 corporate companies in Punjab (number)*

Name of Company	Total strength of the Board of Directors	Religion of members			Members of the Board belonging to same sub-caste as of chairman (inc chairman)	Khatris (Hindu)	Aroras (Hindu)	Baniyas	Others
		Sikhs	Hindus	Others					
Ranbaxy, Mohali	9	2	7	–	1	3	–	–	6
JCT, Hoshiarpur	9	1	8	–	3	5	1	–	3
Hero Cycles, Ludhiana	9	–	8	1	7	–	7	–	2
Mahavir Spg, Ludhiana	9	1	7	1	1	2	1	1	5
Jagatjit, Kapurthala	9	2	6	–	3	1	1	3	3
Oswal Agro, Ludhiana	9	–	6	–	1	1	–	2	3
Vardhman, Ludhiana	9	–	8	1	2	–	–	4	5
JCT, Mohali	9	1	8	–	2	3	–	1	5
Malwa Cotton, Ludhiana	9	–	9	–	4	1	–	6	2
JCT Fibres, Hoshiarpur	3	–	3	–	2	2	–	–	1
Total	84	7	70	3	26	18	10	17	35

Source: Centre for Monitoring the Indian Economy 1995, in Singh 1999, p. 154

oriented towards trade in spare parts, and repairs to agricultural machinery, than to machine production. One explanation for this social and economic alignment attributes it to the central State's shyness to invest in a region bordering Pakistan. But Sikh reluctance or inability to invest in sectors dominated by Hindus is also suggested as being equally important – and the reluctance or inability of Hindu trading castes to invest in productive industrial capital may play a part as well.[87]

Whether caused by a lack of push or a lack of pull, the small-scale nature of Punjab's industry structures the demand for non-agricultural labour, which then tends to be supplied by unskilled migrants from Bihar. It repels educated Sikhs, whose unemployment rates are high. At best, they seek work elsewhere, exploiting the mercantile networks of their co-religionists abroad.[88]

Religious plurality and class formation

Religion plays a complicated role in shaping accumulation inside Punjab, even if the State's surpluses feed accumulation elsewhere in India. The structural differentiation of agriculture has been thwarted by continual, politically resented state subsidies and concessions to the Sikh religious minority, which controls a strategic national resource: food grains. Moreover, the communal stratification of production and trade in Punjab defines class formation. While the agricultural sector produces a commercialised surplus, exchange relations in Punjab – to the extent that they are stratified by religion and not open to entry – are not 'pure capitalist'; and where the spheres of production and trade or circulation are both in contention over the surplus, religious alignments are accentuated. The reinforcement of exclusive religious alignments may then serve to carve a local moral space to protect and legitimate access to the surplus. In this instance, Singh (1999) sees communal conflict as a symptom of a transition to an industrialised, *pluralist,* society.[89]

Jains

Jains number 3.3 million, but their economic significance is much greater than their share in the population (0.4 per cent).[90] While their epicentre

---

[87] See, respectively, Wallace (1986, p. 372) and Singh (1999).
[88] Sikhs have been well represented in the State. Another sector, the army, historically important for Sikh employment, has seen the numbers of Sikhs greatly reduced since the secessionist movements of the 1980s (Helweg 1987, p. 151).
[89] Singh 1999, pp. 174–99.
[90] Govt of India 1999, pp. 200–1; Laidlaw 1995, pp. 84 and 92.

is in north-west India (the desert area of Rajasthan once known as Marwar), they are distributed parsimoniously in urban and 'rurban' settlements throughout the subcontinent. With a religious philosophy of non-violence,[91] adherence to truth and the renunciation of worldly passion, and with a claim to be caste-free and ritually egalitarian, Jains are commonly found to be relatively wealthy local merchants, moneylenders and pawnbrokers, and are divided in a complex way into two main sects, and then into further subsects, *jatis* and family lineages defined by locality and occupation.[92] Jainism drew its first support from traders: 'it was because of their adherence to *ahimsa* (non-violence), that they never took to farming or agriculture and turned instead to commerce, trading and banking' (Chopra 1998, p. 167) – and to revenue collection and the keeping of village records under Mughal rulers. As Laidlaw writes (1995, p. 87): 'The social homogeneity of the lay Jain community in subsequent millennia has sometimes been exaggerated, but the extent to which Shvetambar Jainism especially has been a religion of the commercial elite is by any standards remarkable'.

The Jain mercantile diaspora developed under the Mughals and was consolidated under the British. Many of the Jain, *baniya* caste businessmen who laid the foundations of Indian manufacturing industry, began as clerks, brokers and agents in the 'great firms' of the nineteenth century, which dealt in opium-trading, banking, insurance, the wholesaling of gold and the export of wool.

Religion, accumulative and reproductive practices

The question whether Jain capital is organised in a distinctively Jain way with implications for accumulation has generated a rich but inconclusive body of research. It has been argued, first, that Jains are culturally distinct in business and, second, that Jains are organised more effectively than others. On the first point, Laidlaw's insights into a Jain community working in the gem trade in Jaipur show that it is as tightly bound economically as the Tamil Muslim community described by Mines, but in a socially non-binding way. 'Jain communities, because they are not closed

---

[91] In its most distilled form, this requires avoiding the violence done by agriculture to plants; that done by pastoralism to animals; and that done by industry to animals, plants and people. For this reason there are also said to be few Jain medical practitioners.

[92] The two sects are *shvetambaras* (white-clad) and *digambaras* (sky-clad) (Laidlaw 1995, p. 116; Chopra 1998, pp. 166–7). See Jones and Howard (1991) for a study of Jain trader–money-lenders in Rajasthan, where they sell goods on credit to Hindu villagers but act as pawnbokers and money-lenders primarily to *bhil* tribal people. Digambara Jains are in agriculture in southern Maharashtra and northern Karnataka (Pierre Lachaier 2001, personal communication).

or bonded groups, are best seen as the medium and outcome of social clustering around corporate religious property. Families tend to drift out of the community if their membership is not sustained and renewed through some combination of religious observance, economic participation, kinship and marriage links, residential proximity and day-to-day interaction' (Laidlaw 1995, p. 349).[93]

As to whether Jains are organised more effectively, their marriages and alliances are a crucial basis of their capital accumulation. Jain identity structures Jain accumulation. Laidlaw quotes Fox on the Tezibazaar *baniyas*: these are '"business families" not "family businesses"'.[94] A family's 'credit' in business:

... is its stock in the broadest sense, which includes social position, its reputation and the moral and religious as well as the business conduct of all its members ... When a family contracts a good marriage, its credit increases ... (t)he potential impact on business confidence of particular potential alliances are explicit factors for consideration ... because business practice depends ... so much on trust, moral conduct and financial standing ... This means that a family's credit lies not only in the hands of the men who are actually engaged in business, but in those of its women too. When sons succeed automatically to their father's position in the family firm, the future of the business enterprise is, quite literally, in the women's hands. Thus the distinctive religious division of labour in wealthy Jain families – with men making generous donations and women undertaking periodic extended fasts – has an economic dimension (Laidlaw 1995, pp. 355–6).

So Jain religion affects economic activity through the private sphere and its gender division of religious practice and piety.

On the other hand, accumulation quite obviously transcends the bounds of caste and religion.[95] When Ellis studied urban *baniyas* in Rajasthan, half of whom are Jains and half Vaishnava Hindus, he found that Jain merchants themselves identified three areas of difference: the spatial arrangement of the business site, their accounting procedure, and the importance of public and community service.[96] But on close inspection, Ellis found that in none of these respects do Jain merchants actually differ from their Vaishnava counterparts.[97] Further, for both groups of merchants the patrilineage and its economic endeavours are synonymous.

---

[93] He goes on to describe the annual auctioning of silver 'visions' during the festival of *Mahavir janam* through which resources are raised to maintain centripetal institutions such as temples and meeting halls, and the religious and public functions housed in them. Leading families compete for the honour of supporting these institutions (Laidlaw 1995, pp. 349–50).

[94] Fox 1969, p. 143; Laidlaw 1995, pp. 354–5.

[95] Carrithers and Humphrey 1991, p. 8.

[96] Ellis (1991, p. 101); corroborated by Laidlaw (1995, pp. 364 and 374).

[97] Scholars of Jain and Vaishnava *baniya* history such as Gillion (1968), Timberg (1978) and Munshi (1988) have also made the same point.

Business is a religious duty and a source of merit. Business failure is regarded by both religious groups as signifying sin or lack of religious merit. Lack of religious merit may be protected against by religious deeds. Thus, religious deeds are 'priced' in relation to assets, liabilities and commercial risks. 'Credit and merit are cumulative, self-fulfilling and with concrete effects upon survivability, especially where competition is oligopolistic – which is the typical situation of a small market town' (Ellis 1991, pp. 104–5). Ellis was driven to conclude that 'Jains are not culturally distinct as businessmen, nor do they form a separate economic interest group' (Ellis 1991, p. 106).

Religious plurality and small-scale accumulation in south India

The tendency of capitalism has been to do away with different manners, customs, pretty local and national contrasts and to set up in their stead the dead level of the cosmopolitan town (Sombart 1951, p. 274).

The final case study is of Arni, a town like Siliguri but half its size. As we have seen in earlier chapters, it is an administrative centre and the territory of a police station with a complement of developmental state activity and infrastructure. Arni's economic base is in retailing, agro-industrial production and trade, transport, the workshop production of silk cloth, the crafting of gold, and the finance for all this and the rural economy. Unlike the other cases we have cited, in Arni we can see the religious minorities at work together in 'the dead level of the cosmopolitan town'. Together with the SCs they constitute 35 per cent of the population, but without them, a mere 10 per cent, of whom Muslims make up more than half. While Arni's Muslims comprise a great range of ranks and status, Arni's Hindu majority are for the most part relatively low caste, but the richest business families include higher caste immigrants from other regions of India. Family businesses make up 85 per cent of commercial and productive enterprises, under half of which have a wage labour force. The way in which the religions are niched is summarised in Table 6.5. Arni's is a distinctive form of pluralist development. Though minorities are not scattered randomly through the economy, each minority has a wide range of both niches and incomes. While some commodities are the preserve of distinct minorities, only sanitary work and recycling are exclusively so. Religious plurality does not lead to the suppression of competition, either between firms or in the labour market.[98] As shown in

---

[98] Though competition is suppressed by caste-corporatist trade associations, see Basile and Harriss-White (2000).

Chapter 5, the gender division of labour in family business cannot be disentangled from the gendered practices of religious observance. Both affect business reputations. There is no evidence that in Arni the relation between private and public spheres differs according to religions, and this goes for the kinds of business family there are, the type of businesses they undertake and the way private religious merit is linked to public economic reputation. To take just one obvious example, women in the local Hindu business elite are as secluded as their Muslim counterparts.

But differences in authority derived from religion do affect the economy. They work through the tainting of new occupations that can be 'genealogically' related (through the deepening of commodification) to ones that were of ritual significance in the agrarian economy. Lorry ownership, for example, requires relatively large capital, by the standards of this small town. But the status of transport, derived from bullock-carting, is regarded as relatively low, so transport is mainly undertaken by *vanniar gounders*, an upwardly mobile agricultural caste. Religious authority therefore works through the sacred qualities of things. For Hindus, rice is a purer thing than garlic and it also has no protective covering by the time it is retailed, so, although SC labourers may turn paddy on the drying yard with their feet, no SC traders handle milled rice in the main marketplaces. SCs do retail garlic. Unlike Hinduism, Islam declares no divine sanction against the recycling of waste, so, from the recycling of scrap metal from the local rice mills, Muslims have developed an increasingly complex – and now an international – trade network for recycling plastic, card and paper, glass and a range of metals: activities they freely admit are tainted for Hindus by their association with the low Hindu caste status of scavengers and waste-pickers. 'That's no concern to us,' some say, 'there is good money to be made'. Religious groups sometimes also form moral units within which distribution occurs; Jains, for instance, react with solidarity and money to co-religionists' meeting with accidents, sickness, alcoholism, depression and death.

In Arni, there is nothing that distinguishes those members of religious minorities who are most successful at accumulation from successful local capitalists in general. Muslims and Jains are prominent as political representatives in business associations, in philanthropical organisations (in education, housing, town development, commodity associations, the running of mosques or temples and their properties), but Hindu businessmen express their power in exactly the same ways. Differences in the way economic exchanges take place within and across religious boundaries are not marked enough for businessmen ever to have talked about them to me when I was working there. In fact, in the mid-1990s, elite businessmen – both Hindu and Muslim – denied that religion made a

Table 6.5 *Minorities and SCs in Arni, 1997*

Minorities	Estimated % population	% Income distribution Rs/hh/yr				% College Education	% without Home	Economic niches
		< Rs 24k	25–36	37–60	>Rs61k			
Jains	2	12	70	10	8	5	–	North Indian Jains: pawnbroking, goldsmithing, weaving; South Indian Jains: ag. wholesale, finance
Muslims	5	60	20	15	5	5	20	hardware, cloth, sweets, betel, butchering, recycling, platform trade
Catholics	2	75	10	10	5	2	20	mechanics, fitters, fish trading
Protestants	1	30	10	60	–	20	(Huts) 75	Some professionals, labouring
SCs	25	90	6	3	1	3	(Huts) 94	Labouring, rickshaw pulling, roadside-food-trade, scavenging, sanitary work

Source: leaders of minorities, interviewed in 1997

difference to transactions. The religious groups intermix at the public rituals of marriage. There seems to be no difference due to religion in the labour process. Where the workforce is too large to be organised by kinship, the degree of 'cosmopolitanism' of their workforces cannot be explained in terms of the employer's religion.

Nevertheless, religious plurality does regulate the economy of Arni in subtle ways. Although to a lesser degree than in other parts of India, the upper caste Hindus and Jains own most of the physical fabric of the town, and residential areas are structured by religion. This is not because religious patterns coincide with underlying segregating forces of wealth (poverty) and education. SCs and Christians do not differ materially from Jains in their access to college education. Except for Jains and Protestants, a majority of every religious group had annual household incomes under Rs 24 000 in 1997.[99] So people of all religions are quite poor, and each religion has a wide income distribution with only a tiny minority of materially secure families. Nevertheless, they do occupy urban space differently. Some Muslim businesses – cloth, sweets and hardware – are scattered through the commercial heart of town, but others, more exclusively Muslim – notably slaughter houses and recycling – are segregated together, well within town but on the edge of the central commercial hub. SC people live in wards separate from people of other castes. Their traders face open hostility to their occupation of physical roadside space for the smallest kind of trade in fruit and vegetables. Yet they are allowed into the 'secular' territory of the state-run Municipal Market where they mingle with both low-caste and Muslim traders of fish and meat, and with the few higher caste women, widowed or abandoned by their husbands, who have been forced into trade. The local State *can* be used to gain entry to markets that are structured to exclude SC people.[100]

Religious groups do sometimes form distinct units for finance. Whereas Muslim businessmen borrow from private commercial banks, Jains have banks for the exclusive use of Jains. They also have privileged access to state-regulated banks. SCs are rarely given any kind of access to such banks, and compensate by developing their own small but exclusive chit funds: rotating credit associations.

As we saw generally in the introduction to this chapter, so in Arni, religious plurality finds much of its expression in the economy through the interventions and neglects of the State. While the State gives relatively secure employment to uneducated SC sanitary workers, and to some

[99] Rs 24 000 was double the State's poverty line at the time.
[100] Dasgupta (1992) in her study of informal trade in Calcutta finds much the same. In addition, she finds 'unions' or trade associations negotiating access to loans from state banks for those excluded from commerce by 'ethnicity'.

educated SC teachers and members of the police and armed forces,[101] Catholics, Protestants and Muslims have to face open competition. If they benefit at all from state concessions (as one small Catholic trader did, for example, with help for start-up capital), it is the result of clientelism rather than formal state policy. While political parties are increasingly aligned by caste, and their funding is increasingly based on caste and religion, the failure of local political patrons to capture state resources needed to create the infrastructure needed by a town of Arni's size has created a political vacuum. It is significant that this has been filled by local Muslim magnates. Muslim subscriptions and loans have backed the creation of a Teachers' Training College, managed by an extended kin group, registered as a Trust. It suffered from a lack of legitimation, *not* on the part of local Hindu society (from which it recruits eager students from up to 40 kilometres away), but on the part of the State because the official rules of accreditation, based on standards indifferent to religion, had not been fully complied with at the time of our last fieldwork.

Last but not least in this list of forms of social regulation based on religion, the 'big religion' is important for the commodity markets in which Arni's minorities must accumulate their capital. We have argued elsewhere that it provides the overarching ideology consistent with corporatist forms of economic regulation, the more so the smaller the relative size of the minorities.[102] 'We live on and off the Hindus and must continue to be friends' and 'There is no communalism here. We in Arni are secularist' said Muslim traders in Arni, in 1994. 'Being secularist' effectively means taking the regulative institutional practices of Hinduism.

Conclusion

The plurality of religions in India is clearly the result of waves of conquest, of trade, of the evolution of religions in reaction to the 'wild jungle growth'[103] of Hinduism, and finally of the particular concept of secularism adopted by the Indian State. While religious ideas deal with experiences that far transcend economic life, there is nonetheless a relationship between the plurality of religions and the economy, contrary to what the economic literature might lead one to suppose. The economy would not take the form it does were it not for the social organisation of religions, even though the effects are very mixed and the influence of religion varies greatly according to context.

[101] This employment pattern is due in some small part to the policy of reserved places (see Chapter 7).
[102] Basile and Harriss-White 2000.
[103] Panikkar 1955, p. 327.

Yet there has been virtually no research into the implications for economic activity linked to the fact that a plurality of religions exists. How far the way India's different religions promote or block accumulation has not been systematically studied. Nor has the way a plurality of religious authorities is used to discipline, divide and distract labour; nor whether, and if so how, religions supply justifications for economic processes that strip workers of property, or prevent them from acquiring it. Nor is enough known about the relations between the thousands of 'particularistic groups' – sects and sub-castes – and the economy. Why scholars should have disregarded something so evident in daily social life is also not well understood. The reasons probably include the challenge religion poses both to formalist neo-classical economics and to the division of labour in anthropology. The study of religion is seldom conducted on a comparative basis,[104] and the disciplines of sociology and anthropology have been defined in ways that have tended to marginalise or exclude the findings of research that has been carried out into specific religions; while the level at which we can usefully discuss religious plurality is rarely matched by enough ethnographic evidence.[105] For all these reasons our understanding of these relationships remains very limited.[106]

Nevertheless, we must return to the questions raised at the end of the introduction to this chapter, even if the answers we suggest are tentative. I asked:

1   Why religion has not dissolved as a force in the economy – why it has not been banished to private life?
2   How far are the roles that religion, and the plurality of religions, play in the process of accumulation efficient?
3   How far do the conditions of production in India accentuate or even *require*, as much as hinder, a plurality of religions – not religions as 'essence' or as the 'soul of soulless conditions', but religions as socially constituted?

In what follows, we bring the case material to bear on these questions.

---

[104] See Gellner (2001), however, for comparative essays on Hinduism and Buddhism in Nepal and Japan, though Gellner does not address the questions occupying us here of their roles in the contemporary economy.

[105] It is beyond the scope of this project to discover whether any interest, and if so what, stands to gain from this lack in scholarly knowledge.

[106] The new project at the Ecole Francaise de l'Extrème Orient (EFEO), Pondicherry, on 'Interpénétration des Idéaux Religieux et Mercantiles: Representations and Conceptualisations de la Prosperité chez les Marchands et les Industriels Indiens', seems likely to remedy some of this ignorance.

Why religion has not dissolved as a force in the Indian economy.

Religion as an opiate

Myrdal maintained that, 'it is completely contrary to scientific principles to follow the easy approach of explaining the peculiarities in attitudes, institutions and modes of living and working by reference to broad concepts of Hinduism, Buddhism or Islam'. They were, he thought, 'a function of poverty and low levels of living'; religion was simply the 'emotional container of this way of life'.[107] By this reasoning, continued poverty is then enough to explain the continuation of its emotional container.

State encouragement

This is far from adequate even as a materialist explanation of the persistence of religion. Religion also persists because the State has perversely encouraged it. India's religions are sustained by the State's distinctive secularism. With one big religion and several minorities, and with a State that is formally indifferent to religions, yet which is in fact unequally engaged with them, religious-political identities are assumed by religions and their constituent communities. Nothing much stops relations between religious groups from being competitive, especially where economic resources and rents are concerned. Political relationships between 'particularistic groups' vary from equal respect, to tolerance of inequality, religious nationalism and attempts at religious domination. Consequently, while the great bulk of state policy is framed in a language entirely indifferent to religion, its implementation is never indifferent. Even when not asserting itself through positive discrimination, policy will always etch itself out differentially across the religions – according to the specific context.

The collective preconditions for competition

The State's deficient regulation of markets also leaves religions to perform some of the roles that markets need. What are the non-rivalrous, collective requirements of capital? In the sphere of production, rent needs to be preserved and protected; access to finance and productive capital needs rationing; new entrants need to be excluded from markets and competition limited or even suppressed. Information relevant to judgments about transactions needs to circulate; rent-creating network-transactions must be generated and defended; collective representation is organised and distinctive forms of ownership and control of property are

---

[107] Myrdal 1968, p. 112.

legitimated. All these tasks can be, and often are, performed for capital by religions as forms of social organisation, which also supply essential moral elements. Norms of fairness can be enforced on co-religionists and may be manipulated collectively against others.[108]

Authority in market exchange

We have noted the impact of divinely inspired personal and family law on property and firms. More generally, the moral authority that informs economic behaviour is itself non-economic, being supernatural in origin and binding on co-religionists. Of the Jain religion, for instance, it has been said no aspect of life is neglected. How to work, how to earn, how to live in a family, what and how to eat and wear all follow a clearcut code of ethics.[109] Thanks to the coherence of religious authority and the continuity between family and business, the distinctions conventionally made between private and public need re-examination.[110] Religion also governs gender divisions in work and in social reproduction. The gender division of labour and the subordination of women are culturally justified by religious doctrine.[111] Wherever the links between home and work have been researched, the domestic sphere is usually an important key to the distribution of material resources, working through the use of kinship in work and in the control of women. Both in turn cannot be separated from religious observance.[112] Business reputation is also based in part on a family's reputation for piety. Information about reputation is as basic to market exchange as information about prices, supply and demand. Significant cultural and material resources are devoted to the creation and defence of reputation; the

---

[108] This is *not* to argue that the collective preconditions to competition cannot straddle groups defined by religion or by *jati*, sect or *biradari*. Nor is it to assert that limited territories of accountability *cannot* be found in nations with a unified religious culture. It is *not* to argue that the proliferation of castes and sects does not have a history to some extent independent of the economy. It is *not* to argue that muted competition and the protection of rents cannot result from other forces, most notably state regulation.

[109] Sharing this ethic with co-religionists strengthens religious merit (Jain 2001).

[110] The accepted divisions of social institutions and space into productive and reproductive, public and private, foreground and background, even business and religion, and their dichotomous gendering (private as female and public as male) all need questioning.

[111] Divine authority has two aspects, only one of which is handled in this chapter. This is divine sanction for particular behaviour; for example, the subordination of women. The other is the power of religious authorities – bishops, mullahs, priests, god-men, and so on – which is exercised through control of ideas, education, social behaviour – and property.

[112] Even here, caste splits and unites people of different religion in quite specific ways. While Jain and Vaishnavite *marwaris* intermarry, as do Sikh and Hindu *khatris*, Christian and Hindu *nadars* do not intermarry, even though they act as one economic group (Pierre Lachaier 2001, personal communication).

latter structures contacts, credit, investment, the partition of property and the transfers of resources across the generations. Further, female education (on the value of which the religions differ) affects accumulation, not only through its impact on reputation, but also through the capacity of women to socialise their children to markets. The customs of each religion also provide the motive for, and significantly structure, demand for goods and services, particularly for food. The sites and seasons of festivals are as important to the pulse of the economy as are the agricultural seasons.

Security

Religions also compensate in practical ways for the costs of market engagement, reducing risk and providing security; though they do so to varying degrees. Forms of collective insurance based on religious affiliation may compensate for risk and accident; claimants are restricted; sometimes preference may be given to co-religionists in labour recruitment. Moreover, when accountability is defined through religion, wider social obligations may be avoided. The 'trader's dilemma' – how to accumulate while minimising social obligations – is solved.[113]

Religions' role in class formation

The last major reason why religions have not dissolved as a force in the economy is because they slow down class formation and are one of many institutions dividing the working class. In so doing, they protect rates of accumulation.

To sum up: the expectation that capitalist development would replace social regulation by religion with regulation by the State was not well founded. Religions did not need to organise 'resistance'; they simply were able to supply the non-state, non-class institutions and functions needed by emerging capitalist markets, and as a result they have been strengthened, not dissolved.

How far is the role played by India's plurality of religions in the contemporary economy conducive to efficiency?

Functional efficiency

Social institutions and organisations owing their origins to religious authority may persist because they routinise activity. Minorities are

[113] Evers 1994, pp. 4–10.

therefore assumed by some scholars to be efficient for an economy.[114] They are units of information. Their collective reputation reduces the transaction costs of contracts with outsiders and endows members with implicit collateral for credit. Trust replaces costlier forms of contractual enforcement. Inside such a group, a modern 'calculative' trust, which is based on competence and specialised knowledge, may even start to coexist with a trust based on shared identity.[115] The group is a cost-effective institution for the transmission of skills. Networked, repeated transactions are not only exclusive, they also minimise the costs and risks of contract-formation by means of adversarial bargaining. Modelling the minority in this way reveals a purely economic rationality, though the point about a minority is that it is never a purely economic institution. Neither its origin nor its persistence is to be pre-supposed functional for efficiency. Besides, there is no de-institutionalised alternative with which efficiency can be compared.

Tessellation

However, as the division of labour deepens and new commodities and services proliferate, sub-castes and sects also multiply. The descriptive core of this chapter shows that this process of fission is replicated through all the religions in India.[116] The Indian economy has become obstinately *tessellated*.[117] Even new commodities can be imbued with the sacred status of the products they displace or refine. In the tessellation of the economy, religion is objectified in sets of occupational groups with contested status rankings. Ranking is stigmatic. Trade and business, however, are stigmatised, if at all, only by a tiny minority of the small proportion of the highest status groups in the population. For most of the population, trade is ranked high in status and hard to penetrate, accumulation is powerfully protected.

Competition and conflict

Religious alignments may be used as tools in economic competition. Across the borders of such groups may come the discrimination that

---

[114] This theorisation stems from a critique of the 'under-socialisation' of modern economics and its 'over-socialised' dependence upon notions of generalised morality (Svedberg and Granovetter 1992, pp. 6–19).

[115] See, for example, Dasgupta (1992, pp. 251–2 and 295); de Glopper (1972, pp. 319–20); INFRAS (1993).

[116] Of course, the creation of plurality *within* religions is never simply determined by the economy.

[117] Satish Saberwal, following Marx, refers to it as India's social 'cellularity' (1996, pp. 39 and 65; in Corbridge and Harriss 2000, pp. 36–7).

confines minorities to certain 'callings'[118] and the competitive relations that stimulate the system within. Transactions between people of different religions are still (if much less than in the past) conducted according to different sets of rules, which may be significantly more exploitative and costly than those governing internal transactions.

Competition between religious groups may flare into communal conflict, especially where three conditions are satisfied: if religious minorities are relatively large, economic relations with Hindus have become adversarial and the State has allowed religiously aligned inequalities to be perpetuated or deepened. Before bigotry is accepted as being behind each riot, we need to be sure that communal violence is not economic competition by other means.[119] Communal violence may be seen as one of the labour pains of a pluralist industrial society. Yet at the same time, it reduces the nation's competitive advantage through its adverse effect on investment, production and trade.

How far do the conditions of production in India accentuate or even require religion and/or the plurality of religions?

Increased religiosity

In the first place, it is a fact that liberalisation has been accompanied by a *heightened* religiosity. At the wealthiest heights of India's economy we find a 'resurgence' in Hindu religiosity. John Harriss's recent re-survey of south Indian, high-caste 'industrial leaders' who had been studied in the 1960s by Singer found three remarkable developments: an upsurge of belief in god-men and miracles, a notable selective reworking of Vedantic scripture to assert the superiority of Hinduism, and ostentatious investment in the restoration of temples.[120] It is worth asking about the conditions that have

---

[118] Philip 1984, pp. 38–9; Sombart 1951, pp. 238–48.

[119] Communal conflict is not a unique type of violence in India, for violence has been structured along enemy lines of castes, between sects and even between denominations. Desai (1984) gives examples of conflict between Sikh sects and inter-caste rivalry. But religion is *not* scaled-up caste. While the way religions work scaled down at the micro level is very similar to that of caste, the macro politics of religion is different from the macro politics of caste, the former working indirectly though religious competition, the latter directly through positive discrimination.

[120] J. Harriss, forthcoming. Neo-Vedantic scripture consists of a package of the Upanishads, the Gita and the Brahma Sutra. Harriss cannot be sure of the scale of this resurgence because he is unable to distinguish what he suspects is the impact on Singer's emphasis on the early industrial leaders' practice of selective reworking of the essentials of Hinduism into a code of ethics, from a rationalist attitude to religion. The latter was still being influenced in the 1960s by Nehru's project of modernisation. Harriss also suspects that Singer was influenced in his interpretation of this 'selective re-working' by the fundamentalist intellectual project of his colleague, Raghavan.

led to these beliefs and practices, and Harriss's ethnographic material is suggestive. Belief in god-men seems to cater for a craving for security and peace. The much discussed 'crisis' of the family business, when large business families are being forced to employ professional managers, was the condition alluded to by these business leaders.[121] By the same token, miracles reconcile acts of accumulative success with spiritual health. The neo-Vedantic concepts of 'work as worship' and 'the performance of business without attachment' mean that its rewards can be accepted as of divine origin[122] and so divinely legitimated. The superiority of Hinduism is easily elided with Hindu nationalism at a time when India's position in the global economy reveals its weakness as a production site for world markets and its low level of integration into global financial circuits.[123] Gilding the roofs of temples, while it puts gold out of circulation, is a practice that reinforces the status of – and strengthens – the people worshipping in them (some of whom manage the temple property), at a time when family ties are alleged to be weakening. The 'designer'-religiosity of the upper echelons of India's capitalist class seems to be justifying accumulation *ex post*. It seems to provide incentives for accumulation *ex ante* and it requires accumulation for such behaviour to be possible.

The economic role of the big religion

Could such religiosity be a response to the stresses and difficulties of adaptation to more competitive, rationalised and global markets? *Hindutva* itself might be seen as an attempt to impose the norms of the 'big religion' on the nation's economy as a means of rationalising it for global competition. Sombart's 'cosmopolitan towns' – in India – are never dead level. If many religions coexist, there must be potentially many public ethics,[124] presenting a serious problem for a complex economy in a global arena. The public sphere must then be regulated by one (or a combination) of four means: by the modern State, by the ethic of a victor, by a

---

[121] The casualisation of the labour force, or the replacement of labour relations, which have been legitimated by loyalty, by new forms of discipline, are not spontaneously mentioned as disquieting.

[122] A paradoxical relation of a spiritual exchange that is denied to have transactional elements.

[123] 'India has not yet succeeded in seducing one major international corporation into using India as a global production platform' (P.S. Jha 2001, personal communication). He reasons that this is due to fears about the security of investment. These are due in turn to investors' experience of extortion by politicians and administrators. We have shown here that competition between particularistic groups and factions, a competition that is related to the social organisation of religion, plays a role in creating this insecurity.

[124] This creates conditions for the development of a low-trust society every bit as much as for that of the tolerant one that is conventionally depicted (discussed critically in Hansen 1996).

'lowest common moral denominator', or by an ethical consensus or amalgam resulting from a struggle between religions.[125] In the absence of conquest, and if the State fails to impose a consistent regulative order, if it does not require – or is unable to get – markets to provide the revenue resources for generalised security against risk, accident and poverty, or if the legitimacy of its inconsistent and unequal communal practice is not respected, then the task falls to the other two ethical bases for regulation.

The religions of India may have a large 'lowest common moral denominator', but the degree of ethical consensus will depend on the numerical and economic strength of the religions in question – in the context of a given market or a marketplace. *Hindutva* might then be read as an attempt not only to create and defend as large a space as possible for Hindu accumulation, but also to impose a more uniform ethical space on a tessellated economy.[126] That in turn would require control over the commodities and services of minorities, particularly those with religious centres of gravity outside territorial India. In the case of the towns of Arni, for the most part social disciplining by the big religion is not openly coercive. If at all, it is implicitly coercive, working through threat. The imposition of Hindu norms *also* requires control over the 'wild jungle growth' of Hinduism itself. This may help to explain the selective nature – and the political urgency – of the religiosity that we know as 'Hindu fundamentalism', and which the BJP now calls 'true secularism'.[127]

A case can be made, then, for seeing religion as not merely useful but even necessary to India's economy. At the same time, in some parts of India and for sectors of the economy, class divisions are eroding the economic cohesion of religious groups. The case studies presented here reveal marked economic differentiation and segmentation, uneven access and exploitation *within* most of them. Alignments of occupation and caste/religion have also become blurred. The wage labour force is increas-

---

[125] The Yogasutra – 35 rules – of Acharya Hemachandra illuminate this point. Rule 5 advises Jains to adopt the common practices of the place in which they reside if they do not contradict Jain principles. Rule 6 asks Jains to refrain from criticism of higher authorities. Rule 22 requires Jains to act in accordance with the place and time (Jain 2001). If religions were randomly and individually distributed, then the social costs of finding a common moral space for capital, of negotiation or consensus, and imposing an ethic or enforcing state regulation would be much higher than when religions collectively occupy social, economic and physical niches.

[126] If this is *re*working and *re*invention, it is a long and gradual process grounded in the failure of the State from the 1960s onwards and the assault on organised labour that began in the early 1970s. It has been abetted by the private interest theories of States in the new political economy – and the flows of foreign aid that these theories have influenced. The rise of *Hindutva* is thoroughly 'over-determined', by a range of historical explanations, and does not need the fault line of the 1991 reforms to explain it.

[127] Hansen 1996, p. 608.

ingly cosmopolitan. Labour migrates to work for (verbal) contracts that are no longer festooned in non-economic obligations. The ownership of land is being opened up first to sale and purchase, and then to purchase by people previously forbidden – by custom, if not by law – to buy it. The production and trade of some old and many new commodities gives opportunities to new entrants from outside the religious groups that used to monopolise them.

Our overview of religious minorities produces the difficult conclusion that their sites and roles in the Indian economy are consistent both with the hypothesis of a gradual uneven dissolution of the structuring role of religion, as well as with its opposite – that religious plurality is not being dissolved and is even being nourished. It is not possible to conclude that religious plurality acts as a block on growth. While the jury is still out on these large questions, liberalisation has already been seen to strengthen the competitive tensions between religions and the speed with which religious alignments can be defended.

7   Caste and corporatist capitalism

This chapter starts out from the conclusions of the previous one. In it, the role of the 'big religion', and especially the role of caste,[1] is explored further. On the one hand, caste is a force for political mobilisation as never before in Indian history. On the other hand, economic liberalisation and modernisation (by which is understood the rational organisation of economy and society) should be dissolving the economic relations based on caste. Contract should replace custom and acquired characteristics should replace ascribed ones, including caste. Many anthropologists, like most economists, believe this,[2] and some go so far as to say it has already happened. According to Andre Béteille, for instance (1997, p. 450), among metropolitan professional people 'caste is no longer an important agent of either placement or social control', and in 1997 a caste association president in south India explained to us that caste is not a factor in the economy. Can the apparent contradiction between the political importance of caste and its weakening importance in the economy be resolved?

To explore this, we need to look more closely at what '*modernisation*' is thought to entail for caste. First, it is supposed to involve an increased dissociation of castes from their hereditary occupations, as barriers to entry to occupations are dissolved and as new goods, professions, services and technologies are diffused.[3] But under these pressures, caste reveals its 'tremendous flexibility' – as Jayaram (1996) calls it. Caste still screens access to employment in the agrarian non-farm economy.[4] Ele-

---

[1] Caste is taken to mean an inherited birth group, distinguished by intermarriage, by rules about food and those with whom food may be eaten, and by ranked (hierarchised) social status (sometimes still associated with ritual dirt or pollution). In parts of metropolitan India there is no doubt that the social rules of caste are breaking down.
[2] Mendelsohn 1993; Panini 1996, pp. 28 and 60; Jayaram 1996; Lal 1988.
[3] It has been contended that caste was created through the bureaucratic categories of the British Raj (Meillassoux 1971; Breman 1997; Jodhka 1998), a view effectively refuted by Bayly (1988, in Fuller 1996), who argues that it was consolidated as an institution in terms of hierarchy and ritual distinction during the nineteenth century.
[4] See Jeffery (2001) for Uttar Pradesh and Jayaraj (2002) for Tamil Nadu.

ments of the caste system are often just rearranged leaving the principles intact. Some caste groups have shifted their ritual positions, for instance, due to the increasing contact of lower castes with the upper caste, 'great Hindu tradition',[5] yet recent literature shows that caste continues to play a major 'continuity' role as a social allocator of occupations, even as the economy diversifies.[6] It is still possible to observe a caste-clustering in the distribution of contemporary occupations, and caste links in the practice of new and old technologies, commodities and services. In northern Tamil Nadu for example, brick-making has evolved from pottery-making, paint-making from sea-shell-crushing, shoe repair from cobbling, dry-cleaning and power laundries from hand-washing, and hairdressing salons and sound services from barbering (because the barbers are also musicians and loud-speakers are now as essential as tools of the trade as are musical instruments). Yet, in the new institutional economics, the persistence of caste as an economic factor is explained by treating caste as simply a network defined by the distribution of skills and resources, and by labour market imperfections affecting the control of individuals over information on economic opportunities. This school of thought makes no reference to the contested evolution of the Indian status hierarchy in which caste is central.[7]

Modernisation also involves the process whereby 'a low caste takes over the customs, ritual, belief, ideology and style of life of a high caste',[8] improving its economic and political position, a process known as '*Sanskritisation*'. Sanskritisation has also proceeded hand in hand with the contested implementation of discrimination in favour of lower castes under the Indian Government's *Reservations* policy.[9] 'Reservations' – that is, positive discrimination – are applied to places in the public sector, the State and higher education. The minimum proportion of posts reserved for SCs varies according to their proportion in the population of each State, the Government of India following the all-India ratio. In fact, the

[5] Karanth 1996, Panini 1996, p. 34.
[6] See Cadène and Holmstrom 1998. The Mandal Commission Report found in 1980 that the upper and middle castes were under 20 per cent of the population but nearly 90 per cent of the Class 1 services in Government. In 1990 Brahmins still occupied over 50 per cent of Class 1 posts in central government (except in the ministries of finance and petroleum). Until well into the 1990s, there were no SC/ST officers among the 40 Secretaries in central government. Upper and middle castes dominate the administration, management and the professions. Industrialists and heads of business houses are overwhelmingly from trading castes (Govt of India 1980; Ray 1992, reported in Panini 1996, pp. 33–5).
[7] See, for example, Panini (1996, p. 39), Béteille (1996) and the economic model of caste for 'economies pathologically different from Arrow-Debreu utopia' created by Akerlof (1984).
[8] Srinivas 1989, p. 56.
[9] On Reservations, see Galanter (1984) and Guhan (2001).

extent to which reservations are enforced is a matter for local States. In Tamil Nadu, where reservations have been most extensive, they have been limited under a Supreme Court judgement made in 1993 to 50 per cent of public-sector posts, down from an earlier 69 per cent. Three categories of castes are eligible: agrarian 'backward' castes (BC) (20 per cent), labouring 'most backward' castes (MBC) (11 per cent), and ex-untouchable 'scheduled' castes (SC) (18 per cent) and scheduled tribes (ST) (1 per cent). The direct impact of reservations is on employment and incomes, but the indirect impact through education is to expand and diffuse capabilities and access to power. This is despite the fact that BC and SC students' free hostel accommodation is segregated by caste (and of course by sex).

Sanskritisation and reservations between them produce a 'dual culture', in which a caste attempts to claim a low or backward status in relation to the State, while claiming and seeking to protect a high status socially and economically.[10] For instance, all the elite *tulluva vellala* sub-caste of the *agamudaiya mudaliars* (a sub-caste prominent in local agribusiness) in the south Indian town of Arni are hypergamous and vegetarian, while the caste is a BC, otherwise an isogamous and meat-eating caste and currently the dominant agricultural caste in the area.[11]

Modernisation also implies a separation between the religious and the social-economic spheres. Béteille calls this separation a '*truncation*' (1996, p. 158) and concludes that the future of caste lies 'not with religion but with politics'. By this he means that distinctions of social status, even if often still expressed in the idiom of caste, are rooted neither in a caste system nor a caste hierarchy,[12] whose intrinsic legitimacy and integrity have long been eroded, but rather in social groups that are increasingly legitimated in economic terms and terms of 'difference'. In practice, however, state regulation and the decades of planned development have strengthened rather than weakened caste as the basis for 'different' economic relationships. Caste membership still affords the trust necessary for informal or illegal dealings, both within the formal sector and between the formal sector and the State. It still provides the networks necessary for contacts, for subcontracting and for labour recruitment within the informal economy. In fact modernisation in the guise of liberalisation makes these caste-based relationships more important because it places a new premium on the advancement of interests. In so doing, it has revealed a deeply segmented social structure in which caste is ulti-

---

[10] Karanth 1996; Radhakrishnan 1996.

[11] Hypergamy means marrying into a family of equal or higher status; isogamous marriages are those of equal status.

[12] Caste no longer functions as a social system, if it ever did (Armstrong 1997).

mately connected with all the other organisations of civil society that comprehensively regulate economic and social life.[13]

To shed more light on the contradictory effects of market exchange on the role of caste, we need to understand the politics by means of which caste and the economy regulate one another. And to grasp these political processes in sufficient detail, we need to see this at work in concrete examples – drawn once more from the town of Arni in south India.

Small-town economy[14]

The market town of Arni is the central place for more than a hundred villages in northern Tamil Nadu. The volumes of freight flowing through Arni by lorry transport speak of an economic base still dominated in the 1990s by bulky raw materials: rice accounts for 60 per cent of traffic, groundnuts for 20 per cent, provisions for 10 per cent, rice husk (a by-product of milling destined for solvent oil extraction elsewhere) for 4 per cent, and bricks and firewood for 5 per cent. The exceptions are high-value silk and consumer goods, which account for 1 per cent of volume. During the 20 years from 1973 to 1993, the number of businesses identified in our census of businesses in Arni trebled (see Table 7.1). By late 1993 the transformation of its economic base over the previous decade had been nothing short of astonishing. A number of agricultural and 'traditional' artisan activities, such as brass vessels beating, the sewing of leaf plates, cobbling and the repair of leather irrigation equipment (activities feeding into the livestock economy and animal traction), had declined significantly or disappeared altogether. Agricultural inputs firms had stagnated as had agricultural production. But the main activities that had comprised the town's economic base 10 and 20 years earlier had consolidated their position: rice mills had doubled in number, as had food wholesaling firms and durable consumer goods retail units. Urban silk manufacturing units had increased by 50 per cent and surged into the countryside. Deregulation had led to a threefold increase in fuel depots. Increased urban and rural incomes had generated demand for a 30-fold increase in businesses dealing in non-food agricultural products – from textiles through medicines to flowers.

[13] Upadhya 1997; Reiniche 1996; Rutten 1995.
[14] Our empirical material is of two types: a series of three field enquiries into the organisation of local urban capital, labour, commodities and politics by means of business histories obtained from random 6 per cent samples of commercial enterprises in 1973–74, 1982–84 and 1993–94 (Harriss 1991b); and a systematic set of histories of almost all the groups and associations with which the business economy of a small town is linked and in which it is embedded: market and political institutions, civil society organisations and associations, gathered in 1997 (Basile and Harriss-White 1999).

Table 7.1 *Private firms, Arni, 1973–93*

	1973	1983	1993
Rice mills	23	46	86
Rice wholesale	17	45	56
Rice retail	22	30	17
Groundnut mills	5	3	–
Groundnut wholesalers	16	5	–
Groundnut oil retailers	10	10	–
Other foods – factory	9	7	1
– workshops	150	262	210
– wholesalers	9	22	–
– retailers	271	273	1108
Non-food agricultural	4	4	116
– workshops	1	3	44
– wholesalers	60	114	87
– retailers	13	28	32
Silk factories	62	243	345
Handloom weavers			1141
Other goods			
– factory	–	1	41
– workshops	53	77	112
– wholesalers	25	31	–
– retailers	52	86	144
Durables – retailers	20	37	76
Fuel and Energy	12	18	59
Transport	16	38	63
Transport Repair and Service	68	98	131
Other Repair and Services	191	321	623
Financial Services	87	121	152
TOTAL	1196	1923	3503
			(4763)

Notes
i) Bracketed 1993 total includes 1141 handloom weavers not well censussed previously, 72 educational and training establishments and 47 government offices.
ii) As the urban economy changes its structure so the classification requires changing. Within-group diversity has vastly increased over the last decade.
iii) Services includes professional services as well as traditional handicraft services.
iv) Food retailing includes petty food stalls and tea stalls.
Source: Original field mapping, 1973, 1982, 1993 (data for 1973 and 1982 is from B. Harrisss, 1991)

New commodities are of two types, those new to everyone (IT, cable TV), and those new to low-caste rural people previously denied access to them on grounds relating to caste status and poverty (for example, silk clothing). The town's space is also being configured in novel ways, to such an extent that the place is now an institutional melting-pot for the surrounding rural region. New businesses attest not only to the metropolitanisation of the local economy and culture but also to its rapid globalisation. New telecommunications technologies have appeared: satellite and cable TV (and ways to poach it), and new telecommunications rental markets have spread throughout the urban area, along with courier services, xerox and video libraries (some lending 'blue' videos). Although high technology is extremely vulnerable given the initial absence of supporting services for repair, insurance, and so on, new technology does allow elite firms to scale up their reach and complexity. Long-distance trade now extends from point to point throughout the entire national territory. Silk and rice firms have become specialised in particular kinds of product. Arni rice, for instance, is a niched 'brand' of lightly parboiled fine rice. The wholesale role of the town has increased relative to its retail role. Retailing has started to leap-frog into local villages.

The new technologies, however, destroy existing sectors and their labour forces. Cable TV threatens the patronage of cinemas. Global brands of cool drinks turn the local manufacturers of '*kalar*' ('colour': local aerated drinks) into retail trading agents. Offset printing destroys local presses; autorickshaws put cycle rickshaw pullers out of business. Lorries combine with the electrification of fields to destroy demand for cattle in traction and water-lifting, and to put bullock hirers out of work. Mechanical stone-crushers oust manual stone-breakers and saws do the same in timber yards. Calculators displace billing clerks. The mechanisation of jewellery threatens the prosperity of the relatively prosperous goldsmiths' quarter.

The town can now give up to 20 000 'doses' of cinema per day. New finance companies and chit funds (many of them not registered and run with 'black' money), new insurance and share-dealing services, new specialised commercial agencies for corporate products, and a big expansion in the architectural, accountancy and real estate professions all attest to the emergence of sizeable elite markets. Tuition centres, typing and computing institutes, and students' hostels indicate new patterns of skill acquisition and freedom for young people – although the town was extremely under-developed with respect to education until 1999, when a polytechnic and an arts college were established. Auto sales and rentals, tourist cars and van businesses have responded to local piety, curiosity and incomes (for tourism is inextricably linked with pilgrimages and shrine-hopping). Prominent expansions of hotels, bakeries and sweets stalls and booths indicate new patterns of 'commensality'. All these developments have added to the institutional complexity of the town. But while – in terms of numbers of enterprises – the town appears the model of a growth centre, the prevalence and distribution of black finance capital suggests a substantial element of accumulation that is locked up in uses that do not expand physical production. Field research indicates that the output from trade and the income from finance may equal or exceed that from productive industry in Arni.

Arni has the remnants of an occupation-based caste system in which endogamous castes can be seen as organised in loose hierarchies and where several alternative and overlapping hierarchies coexist (see Figure 7.1). Several different principles structure these hierarchies:

1 the *vedic* orders – in which outcastes are ranked lowest and considered separate by many, and in which *kshatriyas* (consisting of warriors) and *vaisyas* (traders) are either self-styled as such, or have migrated from elsewhere (for there were none locally); the caste population is dominated by *sudras* (farmers) and a vestige of *brahmins* (priests);
2 *diet* (vegetarian; meat eaters (in turn non-beef and beef eaters));
3 *religion* (Hindus, Jains, Christians and Muslims, each with endogamous subdivisions and dietary markers);
4 *region of 'origin'/ language* (that further subdivide Jains and Muslims);
5 the *political categories* ('backward', 'scheduled' – explained on p. 178). The latter are what we shall use here.

The control of business by members of 'forward castes' (FCs) is stable in absolute terms; the apparent decline in their share of total businesses masks the massive increase in concentration of their capital. BCs have gained ground as owners, while MBCs and SCs make up around 80 per cent of the casual labour force. Although in the great majority of firms, unskilled workers come from a mix of castes, 10 to 15 per cent of firms still only employ labour of their owners' castes and a majority take skilled labour from their owners' castes or castes ranked close to them. Counting-in family firms, about half the businesses are still single-caste. Low-tech, physically dirty and (still, for some) ritually polluting work, without which the minimal public health infrastructure could not be provided (sanitation, drains, solid waste and disposal of the dead) and the economy could not function, is the safest preserve of SCs.

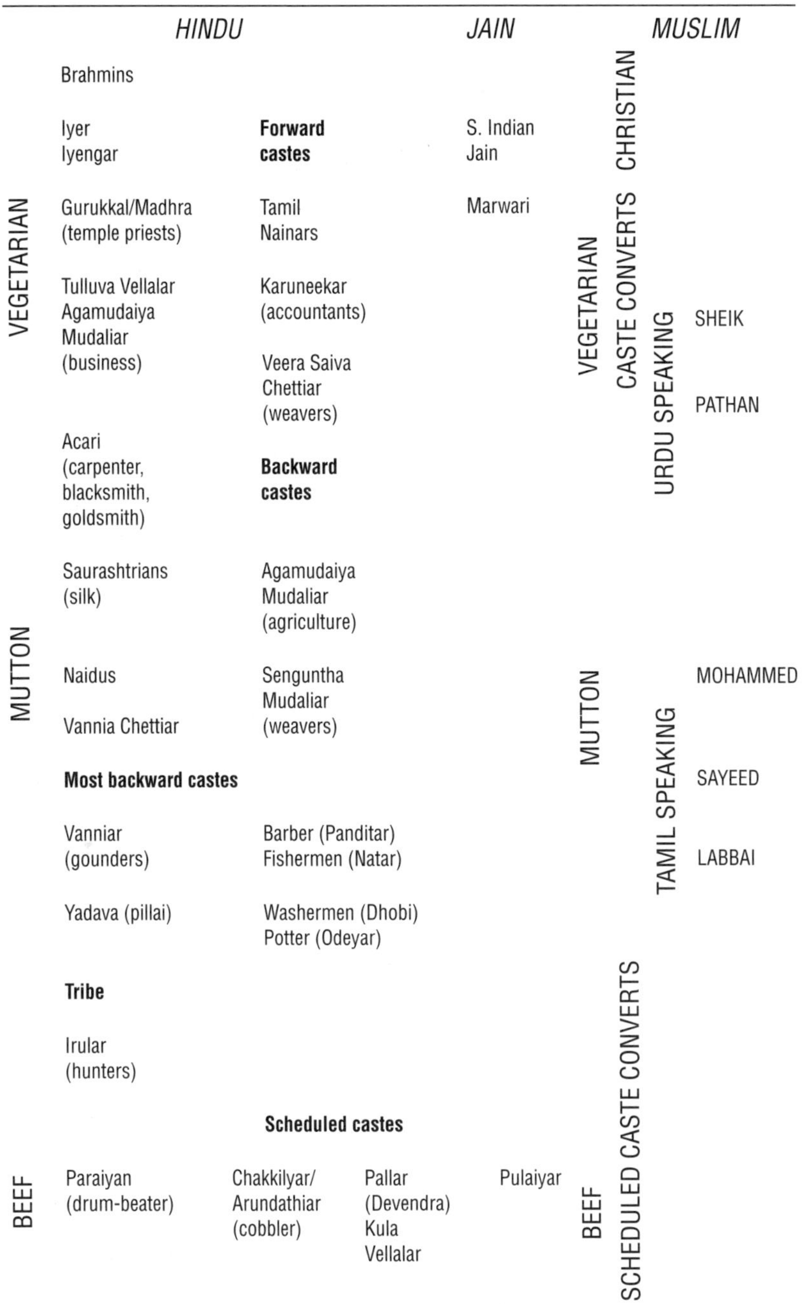

Figure 7.1 — A perception of caste: Arni area

	HINDU		JAIN	MUSLIM

VEGETARIAN

Brahmins

Iyer   **Forward**   S. Indian
Iyengar   **castes**   Jain

Gurukkal/Madhra   Tamil   Marwari
(temple priests)   Nainars

Tulluva Vellalar   Karuneekar
Agamudaiya   (accountants)
Mudaliar
(business)   Veera Saiva
    Chettiar
    (weavers)
Acari
(carpenter,   **Backward**
blacksmith,   **castes**
goldsmith)

MUTTON

Saurashtrians   Agamudaiya
(silk)   Mudaliar
    (agriculture)

Naidus   Senguntha
    Mudaliar
Vannia Chettiar   (weavers)

Most backward castes

Vanniar   Barber (Panditar)
(gounders)   Fishermen (Natar)

Yadava (pillai)   Washermen (Dhobi)
    Potter (Odeyar)

Tribe

Irular
(hunters)

Scheduled castes

BEEF

Paraiyan   Chakkilyar/   Pallar   Pulaiyar
(drum-beater)   Arundathiar   (Devendra)
    (cobbler)   Kula
    Vellalar

Right-hand columns (MUSLIM):

CHRISTIAN / CASTE CONVERTS

VEGETARIAN — URDU SPEAKING: SHEIK, PATHAN

MUTTON — TAMIL SPEAKING: MOHAMMED, SAYEED, LABBAI

BEEF — SCHEDULED CASTE CONVERTS

Figure 7.1   A perception of caste: Arni area

The collective politics of markets

Of late, this urban economy has been being organised into a large number of institutions of collective action (66 in all by 1997), covering most aspects of social and economic life, and regulating it at the levels of the male individual, the household and overlapping groups. The first to be created in the early part of the century were public-service and public-sector unions, together with associations for some of the politically militant but numerically small service castes. Over half have appeared since 1980 and 35 per cent were created in the 1990s. These new organisations are based on new principles: new political parties; town-level, cross-caste organisations; trade associations for new goods and services; organisations for SCs, and a handful for women. Many associations have a cross-class nature in which upper- and lower-class men participate irrespective of their class position. This is most obvious in the caste-cum-occupational associations but it also holds for others, particularly welfare and charitable organisations. Most crucially, the interests of culture and religion come to be organised increasingly through *caste associations*. Some are of very long standing, set up originally to broker marriage alliances and to be a social focus for territorially scattered castes.[15]

Over time, such organisations come not only to serve cultural aims but also political and business ones; indeed, the latter come to dominate. Trade associations proper are often quite recent in origin, defined very precisely by commodity or activity and composed of scaled-up, 'economised' caste associations.[16] While their representative role may wax and wane, lie dormant or react to threats, the economic role of these associations has evolved to become much more elaborate and permanent. Indeed, the urban economy cannot now operate without these hybrid socioeconomic institutions (see Table 7.2). Those controlling the local commanding heights (jewels, gold, rice, wholesale food, silk, lorries, buses and cinemas) operate independently of the State, setting wages, determining the division of tasks and contractual forms, fixing other aspects of the contract (the length of the working day and week, the extent and frequency of days of rest, the terms of employment of women and children) and managing labour disputes. They also fix rates in

[15] Mines (1984) provides an exemplary political history of the collective organisation of 'left-hand' trading *kaikkoolar* castes – unconnected with the land-based, 'right-hand' system of agrarian castes – in which the basis of association has been reworked four times in the twentieth century – from *nadu* (region) through caste association and co-operative to trade association.

[16] The accounts of Mines (1984), Cadène (1998a) and Chari (2000) of associations that regulate trade suggest these are far from either new or unique. What is remarkable is their sudden recent expansion.

Table 7.2 *Economic activity of organised local 'Big business'*

Sector	Date of organisation	Self-regulation				Interaction with state							Philanthropy	
		Info	Physical security	Prices	Contracts	Prices subsidies	Infrastructure	↓State trading	↑Tax	anti-harassment	Organised clientelism	Polit funds	Philanthropy	Piety
a)														
Jewels/Gold	1960	✓	✓		✓				✓	✓				
Rice Mills	1960		✓	✓	✓				✓				✓	✓
Wholesale Food	1963				✓	✓	✓	✓	✓		✓	✓	✓	
Silk Mfg	1989			✓	✓				✓	✓	✓		✓	
Buses	1989			✓					✓	✓	✓		✓	
Cinema	1991			✓					✓	✓		✓		✓
b)														
Chamber of Commerce	1989					✓	✓		✓					
Small Industries Assocn.							✓							

		Linkages	Infrastructure	Resource transfers		
				Health	Education	Livelihoods
Lions	1971	business/international		✓	✓	✓
Lionesses	1977	wives/international		✓		✓
Rotary	1985	professional/public sector/international		✓	✓	✓
Welfare Development Committee	1989	local ginger group	✓ ✓			
Town Welfare Society	1992	professionals, linked to Lions		✓	✓	
Inner Wheel	1995	Rotarian wives/international		✓		✓
Consumer Protection Society		(state) business			✓	

derived markets (raw materials, porterage, sweeping and where possible money and credit, even to the extent of controlling licensing and accreditation); they carve exclusive territories and spatial monopolies, calibrate weight and measures, set rules of dress and behaviour, determine the limits on *over*capacity (on overcrowding in cinemas, on the overloading of buses and lorries); they fix the norms of delay on payments, and the scales of bribes and the limits of acceptance for fines. Last but not least, in the case of gold and rice, they organise the collective physical security and public hygiene without which market exchange and transfers of property rights cannot take place. This regulative agenda still leaves *wide* institutional spaces for the particularistic forms of economic disorder described in Chapter 3, also for patronage and other forms of control (particularly over labour at the level of the individual firm). Aspects of all this regulation are exclusionary and collusive, but it does bring a certain parametric order to market exchange. As one caste association's president said: 'It helps to prevent unruliness'. As with the other aspects of (non-)competition described in Chapters 3 and 6, it also reduces competition and stabilises rates of return.

There is a strong ideological aspect to these groups. Alongside its economic agenda and the economic claims it makes on the State, practically every caste association aims to improve its own welfare and caste solidarity, reproducing within the caste a weak copy of the distributional rules that formerly operated *between* castes in this region (and still can be found vestigially in local villages).[17] The *saurashtrians*, for instance, a BC in the silk trade, make sure all their members have access to a livelihood (for example, providing sewing machines to ensure entry into tailoring). They organise business loans, and help towards the cost of education and sickness for poor caste members. *Vanniars*, an upwardly mobile MBC, systematically support the expenses of the major life events of their poor members. Trade-cum-corporate-caste associations, representing the interests of a stratum of capital that is small to medium by national standards, but which counts as big business locally, also aim to improve – or rather to be *seen* to improve – the welfare of the town itself, through small acts of redistributive charity. Of course, these are also open to interpretation as being a means of legitimating accumulation.

These attempts at internal caste regulation and economic governance are supported by a widespread ideology that conceals class interests under the veil of the wider interest of 'town unity', which is held to extend not only across castes but also across religions. Of some significance here – as we saw in the previous chaper – is the role of Muslim businessmen

---

[17] For instance, the payment of washerfolk annually in kind (rice) at a customary rate.

not only as Muslims (internally segmented by 'caste' but externally 'secularist'),[18] but also as businessmen, as representatives of the town (holding offices in certain trade associations and the chamber of commerce) and as collective investors in the non-religious educational infrastructure, which has been so egregiously neglected by the State, despite years of attempts to obtain it.

In this town so far, then, castes show few signs of the erosion in their economic roles that Panini and others see as the outcome of liberalisation. Instead, caste is being selectively reworked. In this reworking caste is far from being a 'thing of shreds and patches',[19] but it also cannot simply be explained in the universalistic terms of the new institutional economics either. Caste is being reworked to mean quite different things in the local economy according to the economic position of the castes concerned. Let us elaborate.

Scheduled castes account for 15 per cent of the population of the town. Although in 1997 two-thirds were living at or under the State's poverty line of Rs 12 000 annual income per household, a high internal degree of economic diversity and inequality among the members of these castes coexists with severe occupational rigidities. While the biggest single category of work is 'sanitary' (the cleaning of excrement from latrines and drains, and the recycling of solid waste), other rigid categories are butchery, leatherwork and cobbling, and their 'upgrades': the dirty, heavy work of construction; the handling of hot steamed or soggy parboiled paddy; work on the grain-drying yards under the relentless sun where rice is protected from ritual contamination by its husk; and fruit and vegetables trading where skins and the necessity to transform the commodity during food preparation protect the purchaser. For SC people, education is a springboard to (reserved) clerical posts in the State (often moonlighting onwards to trades requiring education (insurance agents)), to the army, teaching (private tutoring) and the police. There are a handful of medical doctors and one lawyer. Nineteen per cent of public-sector jobs are reserved for SCs and STs. At one and the same time, SCs are disunited (drum-players and cobblers having mutual contempt for each other, for instance), but also reputed to be close-knit within their castes. Trade is transforming endogamous sub-castes into single economic interests based upon commodities with certain physical properties (for example, skins, physical dirt and the necessity for further physical transformation). Market entry is above all a physical and geographical

---

[18] Local Muslims are not so defensive that they invent their differentiation from Hindus by denying the existence of caste within their ranks, as has been described by Fuller (1996, p. 24).

[19] Fuller 1996, (quoting Dumont) pp. 1 and 3.

process. SC associations are preoccupied with the defence of territories, with legal recognition and physical security.[20] They also organise rotating credit and insurance schemes in order to compensate for their lack of access to the state banks (effectively barred to SC/STs) and for open discrimination by the private sector. For SCs, caste still constitutes a hierarchy in which higher castes are prevented from entering lower caste and SC occupations, and *vice versa*.[21] It is not that relative status and ranking is a matter of private evaluation while the public idiom is that of difference.[22] It is that caste cannot even be used to identify the ocupational organisations struggling for income and status. A secular and economic label and form of organisation is necessary as a weapon to help SC traders to retaliate against their contemptuous treatment and harassment in public places.[23] It is also the case that an egalitarian and caste-denying public discourse is selectively imposed upon SCs by higher castes.

MBCs are 35 per cent of the population. Although there are five such castes, one – *vanniars* – constitutes 85 per cent of the MBCs. Entitled to an 11 per cent reservation of state jobs, most live only slightly above the poverty line. Those who have made the kind of technological upgrading described at the start of this chapter are exceptions that prove the rule. Most work as labourers, at best at the low end of repairs and engineering, and as marketplace porters. Most services provided by *vanniars* use primitive technologies and labour-intensive processes and, despite the need for basic engineering skill, are associated with poverty. The elite *vanniars* run lorries and their caste-cum-trade association regulates and organises the collective bribery needed for distribution to checkpost guards and the police, through which overloading and low standards of maintenance are tolerated.

By contrast, among *BCs*, caste is more a matter of difference and of economic competition. Such castes are increasingly internally differentiated in economic terms. BCs are a third of the population of the town and consist of nine castes, five being in-migrants. The most numerous caste, *agamudaiya mudaliars*, is the dominant agricultural caste. It is also

---

[20] The occupation of space is often illegal, so official harassment is not necessarily first and foremost caste discrimination. When associations and informal groupings engage in collective precautionary behaviour against future contingencies (pleasing officials with gifts), they are more likely to be responding to their own illegality than attempting to recruit champions against discrimination.

[21] An ongoing battle to enable SCs to enter silk-weaving has lately been won in the town, though numbers gaining access to the informal training are still small. SC status is still a formidable barrier to weaving in villages.

[22] As Fuller comments on Mayer (1996, p. 13).

[23] This is effectively a calling of bluffs in an elaborate public/political game with the Constitution at which actor and audience cynically connive while behaving differently in the 'privacy' of their workshop or office.

the most economically differentiated. Their relative wealth notwithstanding, BCs are entitled to 20 per cent of reserved places in state employment. Here we see the 'dual culture' at work: on the one hand, social
practices signifying a rise in status, and on the other, pressure on the
State to lower the official status of these *mudaliars* for the express purposes
of getting positive discrimination. The economic summits of the town are
small but sheer pinnacles, composed of a blend of castes and strikingly specific kinds of capitals: Jains control *acaris* who control gold; *saurashtrians*
and *veera saiva chettiars* control silk, *chettiars* and *naidus* control rice-milling. Their self-regulative activity has already been discussed. These castes
mobilise in the new political and economic arenas, at regional and national
levels. One of them even allows a women's caste association. Several organise collective bribery and negotiate to evade taxes.

At the top, among the remaining 12 per cent of the population who
belong to the *FCs*, caste ceases to have a role to play in formal economic
regulation, though it certainly does not cease to have a role in economic
and social life (still being of fundamental importance in resource transfers grounded in kinship alliances, for instance (see Chapter 5)). Those
brahmins who are not in transit from the social heat of the villages to the
lustre of the much grander arena that services national and international
capital in India's metropolises, practise locally as lawyers, accountants,
medical doctors, teachers, architects, and so on. The political organisation of FCs takes a different form, with direct links of kinship to office-
holders in the local Municipality, the State Legislative Assembly and the
national Lok Sabha. Their caste organisations not only defend territory
from competition by BCs, they also collude with the State over reforms
to the implementation of policy that threatens their businesses (such as
the collection of commercial taxes)[24] and they routinely patronise all the
political parties by funding them.

So there is a distinctive interplay between the economy and caste associations (and the occupational associations that have evolved from caste
associations), which reveals the *flexibility* of caste – the distancing of caste
from religion, but the adding of economic regulative functions both to
the institution of caste *per se*, and to the formal caste associations. The
very fact that the economic and political roles of caste can be distinguished in their 'dual culture' shows that there remains a loose hierarchy
in which the social solvent of market exchange operates least vigorously
at the bottom, where social disadvantage is most entrenched. If castes are
transformed, secularised and politicised institutions, as André Béteille

---

[24] When BC tax collectors in reserved posts meet FC commercial lobbies, their inferior
social status weakens their relative power.

concludes, they are ineluctably vital as regulators of the economy. Paraphrasing Béteille, their future lies not with religion but with the political economy (Béteille 1996, p. 159).

The relationship between caste and the economy is also consistent with *corporatism*. Corporatism is a form of control over the economic relations between labour, capital and the State, which is regulated by interest groups – and quite compatible with authoritarian politics. The role of the State in a corporatist economy can vary; a distinction is made between State and societal corporatism.[25] In the first form the State plays a 'directive' role and dominates its relationship with interest groups, and their relationships with each other. In the second form, associations are relatively independent from the State. They work through a politics in which the causes of labour are seized by capital and devalued.[26] The State is no neutral arbiter, but actively synthesises corporatist ideals and values that serve to promote the interests of capital.[27] Gramsci, who considered this kind of economic corporatism in Italy, concluded that it fused civil and political society in a novel way. The role played by the State included elements that are normally those of civil society. 'One could say that the state = political society + civil society, which means hegemony armed with coercion' (Gramsci 1971, p. 263).

At the least, the corporatist ideological and institutional framework that we find to be derived not so much from the State as from caste is entirely consistent with Arni's production relations; at most it actively shapes them. Its distinctive features leave their mark on class relations, on the local territorial organisation of the urban economy, on the gendering of regulation and on relations between the urban economy and the State. We will now look more closely at these dimensions of caste-based corporatism in Arni.

Corporatism and class

The town is organised according to the needs of local 'big' capital. Although there are business associations representing capital, and trade unions and workers' *sangams* representing labour, the two rarely confront each other in disputes. Few firms have unionised labour forces, while the

---

[25] Reviewed in White (1996).
[26] Schmitter 1974; Cawson 1985; O'Sullivan 1988.
[27] Corporatist organisations were one of the two economic means by which political fascism was reinforced in Italy. The corporatist economy rested in turn on a tripod: the Fascist Party, trade unions and guilds. Guilds were the main instrument by which to delegitimate class stuggle, though the means were different from the case considered here. Workers were forced into governance of the economy. Guilds also ratified a hierarchical system of social relations by which the economy was controlled.

line between capital and labour is heavily blurred by the 35 per cent of family firms with no wage labour, which are the urban commercial equivalent of the peasant household.

We have seen that local 'big' capital is divided, both according to the commodities it produces or trades in and by corporatised caste. These divisions do not weaken it, however, and are better seen as the way a numerically small class maximises its tactical advantages. A given firm can join in collective lobbying or bribery to shape the course of state regulation through its trade association; its head can network with the local bureaucracy through institutions of philanthropy; and through organisations of town unity, the firm can help to lever telecommunications and other infrastructure. The ubiquitous attempts at collective regulation and control over the markets in which these firms do business (via the State where necessary) are cases in point. The means of labour control include not only wages but also other ways of increasing absolute surplus value (such as hours of work (lengthening), entitlement to rest (none) and resistance to the formation of unions (stiff)). Through this control, capital is able to transform labour productivity extensively (by increasing effort), rather than intensively (by increasing the output of a unit of labour), and this without a rise in mass consumption at all commensurate with that of the profit component of the distributive share. In so doing, capital frequently flouts the laws regulating and protecting labour. At the same time, the process of accumulation is suffused with petty crime and with fraud, particularly with respect to every aspect of taxation (see Chapters 3 and 4).

Labour is weak and not coherently organised. In certain unions the interests of capital are presented as those of labour (self-employed master weavers, for instance, are members of the textiles workers' *sangam*). Other labour unions are even organised by employers, and some are subsequently managed by a small set of big bosses (for instance, skilled labour associations in the silk sector, one of whose mottos is 'unity, discipline, remuneration'). The agendas of large caste associations, by focusing on the State, will distract labour within the caste from confronting capital within the caste.[28] Large fractions of the labour force in the economic base of the town (in rice and transport) are deliberately casualised by employers. Yet this labour toils on contracts with idioms of clientelage. The paramountcy of the patron–client relationship even prevents 'horizontal' organisation of the 'clients' as employees. Wages can then be negotiated *between employers* and imposed on workers across the firms in a given sector. 'Our wages are feudal and do not obey market

[28] It is also a widespread practice in India to have separate labour unions for SC workers.

laws', said a rice mill worker. Extreme deprivation in the labouring class is relieved not only by a skimpy welfare state for those under the poverty line, but also by the redistributive activity (however minimalist) of caste associations.[29] Income fluctuations may be smoothed out by caste-specific insurance and rotating credit schemes operated by and for caste members. Trade unions independent of caste or political parties are almost non-existent.

So it is not surprising that there is very little evidence of organised protest about working conditions, in spite of the fact that, as the major business associations reported in the late 1990s, the town was close to full employment. It is the State, not labour unions, which by law ensures that labour standards are enforced.[30] The town itself is not construed by its elite as being segmented into conflicting interests, despite the fact that this is easily shown. Rather, it is presented as a unified entity, backed up by corporate-urban organisations acting as a unified body, composed of parts among which there is no conflict, or only 'sporadic conflict' (which is how the tense and competitive relations between *vanniars* and SCs are described). A SC worker explained, 'This is a peaceful place where there is harmony between the castes' and, we might add, within the castes, too. Yet, while a modern proverb declares 'Caste is the strongest trade union', even among low-caste workers caste is not used as a basis on which to organise 'labour' as opposed to 'capital'. In certain castes, occupations with a long history of caste-identification are vigorously defended for a mixture of purposes (such as social identity, insurance, trust and economic reputation, job security and credit), but not because they are seen as the way to express the interest of a *class*. The commodity labels under which many people operate signal the relative status of the traders and the commodities traded. But they carry no necessary implications for class position, because these labels (tailors, goldsmiths, autorickshaw drivers) are used by workers as well as owners. Caste has become an instrument to regulate economic participation, as well as to position people in a ranking of status, and the opposition between classes is suppressed.

Of course caste-based business associations are not always active and the collective wage agreements of employers are not always enforced. But there is a structural asymmetry between capital and labour as far as class

---

[29] When the demands of caste are reformulated through the caste association and the market economy, the 'traders' dilemma' (the dilemma of maximising investible surplus while maximising social status, the latter which depends on more or less generous redistribution) is solved by an unintended outcome of the Constitution, since its state-led project can always be invoked to repudiate excessive demands.

[30] The State – in the guise of Factories Acts inspectors, health and sanitary inspectors – can however be subverted corruptly by bosses.

consciousness is concerned. The capitalist class has a strong identity, reinforced by an ideology about the duties of the local elites in promoting urban welfare. By contrast, labour has a very weak perception of its class identity due to the absence of political representation and due to the pervasive presence of caste.

Corporatism and the locality

There are two aspects of locality that shape the organisation of the local urban economy. First, in the tidal wave of commercial capitalist expansion in the 1960s, the town started to organise itself as a social unit that cut across caste divisions and, to a lesser extent, across class and gender divisions, to make claims on the State for resources for infrastructure and welfare. Over time, this role of corporate claimant has involved confronting the State, as well as trying to work collusively with it (the hostile campaign to get redress for the backward state of the town's telecommunications infrastructure being an example of confrontation). Then, second, the majority of local civil-society organisations are components of hierarchical federations with their apexes in state or national capital cities. This has two contradictory consequences. On the one hand, such local organisations are networked into higher level contacts, with skill and resources. On the other, branches in Arni may be manipulated by their headquarters' leadership for struggles in political arenas elsewhere.

Gender

While just under half the workforce is female, only a small handful of businesses are managed by women, and practically no business is owned by women. Corporate associational life is intensely male. Some educated women (extremely few of whom are SC and even fewer BC) find employment in clerical jobs in local government, in medicine or teaching. They have a toehold in other professions. It is very rare to find a woman lawyer or member of the police force. Those with other skills (such as computing) work in organised-sector firms outside the locality. The educated wives of the local business elite operate on the outer margins of Arni's collective life, their role being to buttress and reinforce the ideological legitimation of the business elite through philanthropy. Women are but tiny minorities in a few caste and trade associations, and, where they form an important minority (as in tailoring), their interests are managed by men, just as the interests of labour are frequently managed by capital. We have seen in Chapters 2 and 5 how women are deliberately casualised and attempts to organise them are crushed. Urban civil society therefore tends towards the reinforcement of patriarchy in the market economy. And it is the local State that has provided opportunities for the relative empowerment of women, through education and employment – though women are still conspicuous by their absence higher up in the administration.

Corporatism and the State

The State works at a range of scales in a given place. It consists of the Municipality, local departments of the State, and the central government and branches of State and national parastatal corporations. As well as performing central place service roles (in health, education, agricultural extension and inputs) and revenue-raising functions, the State in the town of Arni is empowered to organise, promote, mediate, protect, regulate and redistribute economic resources. It does this through the provision and maintenance of infrastructure, including electricity and solid waste recycling, the nationalised banking system, the courts, the police and fire services, vigilance forces and inspectorates, the administration of the Municipal (retail) Market, the Regulated Agricultural Wholesale Market, local branches of state trading and warehousing corporations, and the network of marketing co-operatives. The State also administers a mass of subsidies and 'social sector' schemes, notable among which is the Public Distribution System for essential commodities, run through Fair Price Shops, the Noon Meal Scheme, for schools and crèches (but also reaching old-age pensioners), and the social safety net (with pensions for old age, widowhood, disability and grants for maternity in theory for those who can prove poverty and a lack of family support). Last but not least, the State is bound to provide opportunity for BCs and SCs through job reservations and free schooling, together with free health care for the poor.[31]

In so doing the State redistributes economic power between the genders, shapes the fortunes of castes, creates and regulates classes, and formalises 'locality'. If it ever was a secular institution, it is definitely being *de*secularised in the current era. Chapter 4 outlines how its effectiveness is being shaped by the private social status of its officials.[32] The relatively low social (caste) status of tax collectors is said to shape the structure of municipal revenue, since they can be bullied and their demands evaded by local business elites. As a result, the total budget of the Municipality is roughly equal to the gross output of a single elite firm. Chronic underfunding then explains the poor quality of the physical infrastructure – roads, lighting, drains, and so on – on which the current efflorescence of

---

[31] Mooij 1999; B. Harriss 1991b; Guhan 1994.
[32] Sengupta 1998; Banik 1999.

market exchange depends. At the same time, the local State is riddled with incompetence, arbitrariness and oppressive practices. While private status limits capacity, private interest and private discretionary power tempt officials to corruption.

More quantitatively important than corruption is fraud, in which the returns from the estimated half of the economy that is black are shared between individual politicians and the local business elite. But the State has little purchase over the trade and caste associations. At the very most, state officials connive selectively with caste-cum-trade associations to reduce taxes and to standardise the informal costs of obtaining licences; officials and politicians receive and distribute the collective bribes and annual gifts presented by certain of the town's business associations.

Yet it is this State, and the sectors of the economy that are its bailiwick, to which political appeal is made through the caste and trade associations. Caste associations in Arni work to get the State to do seven main things:

1 set prices and subsidies to combat the 'unruliness' of market exchange; some claims are highly self-interested (for example, *saurashtrians*' campaigns for subsidised loans) while *vanniar* caste politics uses a paternalistic discourse pleading on behalf of other castes;
2 regulate networks and space (particularly caste-cum-trade associations dealing with transport and haulage);
3 intervene directly in commerce (trading in raw materials or finished products, regulating access, terms and conditions of finance and loans);
4 collude with capital to control labour;
5 collect – or fail to collect (or reduce obligations to provide) taxes;
6 build and maintain infrastructure (not only physical but also financial and social infrastructure); and
7 manage caste reservations and employment.

As long as the State is embroiled in these struggles (and from our evidence its role has been intensifying – rather than declining – over the first decade of liberalisation) the tension between political inclusion and economic exclusion will persist. Yet, the control and exploitation of labour falls well short of alienating it politically. The State is too important as a focus and a resource for the economic aspirations of upwardly mobile castes to be significantly compressed or downsized.[33] So the terms of political inclusion will continue to cause tension.

[33] Its interests are already illegally compressed. In 1999, in Tamil Nadu, a State with a long history of struggle against discrimination, an evaluation of reservations found no lack of qualified SC candidates, but instead evidence of under-reporting, manipulation and non–co-operation (*Frontline*, 26 November 1999, p. 97). See also Jeffrey (2001) for the high entry barriers to reserved places in Uttar Pradesh.

The State's performance is heavily influenced by the balance of force between it and the castes involved. The private status of officials, which is highly context-specific, will affect this balance. 'Elite' MBCs and BCs lobby the State for communications and financial infrastructure; they collectively bribe state officials so as to defraud the State and are required to bribe them to gain allocations of all kinds. *Vanniars* and other MBC organisations lobby the State for preferments involving grants, subsidies and allocations. For SCs the State is crucial to economic mobility, through reservations in education and public-sector employment, through developmental infrastructure, transfer payments, and the regulation of public space, especially that of the market*place*. At the same time, SCs face harassment and oppression by the State (sometimes, too, by SC employees of the State). The State therefore shapes the accumulation possibilities, as well as the exploitation and oppression of the lowest castes. Low-caste distributional politics is deviously threatened by the neo-liberal project of the Washington consensus. The local politics of discrimination and reservation meets the global politics of fiscal deficits and debt repayment in an embrace that both fans and crushes the economic aspirations of precisely those groups least able to accumulate.

An increasingly restive political society with new, and newly assertive parties, packed with organisations representing lower castes (some of which are internally democratic), does not necessarily mean that civil society is democratising. Instead, even as electoral democracy is being transformed by parties based on caste[34] and by caste-based factions within parties, a caste-based politics other than electoral party politics is emerging at the local level. It combines a politics of market regulation with attempts to seize the economic resources of the State. Party political alignment and caste are not congruent and may compete as principles for securing votes. The town is at a stage in its political development when an increasingly caste-based electoral politics contests power through extortion; investment in the purchase of votes has to yield returns afterwards, and it does so through corrupt intermediation, collusion in fraud and non-compliance and control over the creation and protection of rents.[35] Caste-cum-trade associations are key to these returns.

Conclusion

So the prediction of many economists and anthropologists with which we began this chapter – that with liberalisation, markets would disembed

---

[34] For example in Tamil Nadu, the PMK representing *Vanniars*, and the Indian Republican Party and Dalit Panthers representing SCs. For the caste parties in UP, their mediation of intra-caste disputes and their caste-based patronage behaviour, see Jeffrey, 2001.
[35] Harriss-White (1996b); theorised for Asia by Khan (2000b).

themselves from caste – has not been realised, at least not yet. Market exchange does not always lead to 'contracts' replacing 'custom'; contracts prove compatible with a certain amount of custom. Both are malleable institutions. 'Different activities need different bases for co-operation' concluded Nadvi.[36] Market exchange and competition are impossible without collective action, which (as was shown in Chapter 6) is grounded in caste and in caste-like groups in other religions.[37] Caste, the 'specifically Indian form of civil society',[38] is being reworked as a regulative institution in ways depending on a caste's position in the status ranking. In the elaboration of the 'dual culture' of state-run positive discrimination and market-based economic and social advancement, caste associations have developed another dual role. They both woo the State for concessions and repel the State's own attempts to regulate. Collective action of this type moves between collective advancement on the one hand and the internal mediation of potentially conflicting interests on the other.

Pace Fuller (1996, p. 26), who concluded that caste is increasingly ambiguous, inconsistent and variable as a social fact, the variety of apparently slow and unsystematic ways in which caste is being transformed tend in *one main direction*: to provide support to local capital in its political, cultural and ideological hegemony over local society. The form of economic social regulation emerging from the transformation and secularisation of caste is *corporatist*. Corporatism, to recapitulate, is a mode of economic regulation that limits class conflict *inter alia* by involving both capital and labour in managing markets. There are two aspects to corporatism, one institutional and one ideological, which together suffuse production relations in a distinctive way. In this process, caste seems to play a triple role. First, it provides an ideological backcloth (albeit not a monolithic or consistent one), what Béteille (1997, p. 446) calls a 'social morphology',[39] for the corporatist 'project'. Second, it generates (and is consistent with the formalisation of) the institutional structure on the back of which corporatist organisations have evolved. In Arni's fast-expanding urban economy, caste *still* supplies a broadly hierarchical social order.[40] Through caste, the link between ideology and institutions is particularly strong. The ideology itself – simply in *distinguishing* castes – is the source of the institutions. Caste ideology is a social structure of accumulation. Institutions are shaped by caste, not only directly through

---

[36] Nadvi 1999a, p. 144.
[37] Indeed, Cawson argues (1985, p. 7) in his review of corporatist regulation that social bonds developing out of self-interest between 'competitors' are not an aberration from the free market, but define the essence of the exercise of power in the market.
[38] Fuller 1996, p. 26.
[39] Although not in the kind of context we are describing here.
[40] An order entrusted to the State in the Italian case (Mancini et al. 1983).

economised caste associations, but also indirectly through the influence of caste on non-caste regulative institutions. This can be seen, for example, in the use of caste patronage to organise and control labour *within* firms so as to allow employers to co-ordinate their control *between* firms through caste-corporate trade associations. Another illustration is provided by the proliferation of associations structured around 'town unity' and in the branding of the town's main traded products. Third, caste helps to create the conditions for the overlap between economy and society that is necessary to the working of a corporatist form of development.

This is not to argue that the local economy is entirely organised on corporatist lines,[41] or only through caste associations,[42] or that the way the economy is regulated by caste operates solely through caste associations, or that the economy is regulated in this fashion throughout India.[43] But it is to argue that there is no contradiction between caste and corporatist capitalist development.

A form of corporatism sprung from caste has the following implications for development. First, a striking multiplicity of organisations of economic interest are created and controlled or tolerated and permitted by the State. Such institutions do not necessarily contribute to democra-

[41] Labour, in particular, can be organised with formal independence of caste and with an agenda in clear opposition to capital. The problem has been the weakening of labour due to the splitting of the three main parties that organise it (Dravidian, Congress and Communist Parties), which has subsequently yielded space for a caste-based politicisation of labour, and the separate Ambedkar unions for SCs.

[42] Caste drops out as an explanation for the organisation and functioning of markets for high-tech new goods and services (cable TV, keyboard skills, and so on), which rely on informal regulation through networks based on education and locality. These markets are, however, extremely risky and poorly regulated, and are used rarely in their lifetimes by the mass of consumers; and caste is crucial for low-tech new goods and services (for example, lottery tickets, fast food stalls). See Harriss-White (1996c) for details of the state regulation of agricultural markets. For the *non*–caste-based collective action of business associations (though it is further rent asunder by faction, both of a rent- and a subsidy-seeking nature, *and* in conflict with a politics of technocratic representation), see Gorter (1997, pp. 92–3).

[43] In this respect it is likely that there are significant differences between south India and the north, where the politics of caste taxonomies is far less stable and that of livelihoods even more urgent. The role of economic resources in marriage alliances is discussed in Chapter 5. In day-to-day business, traders are prepared to forfeit profits to producers and consumers of the same caste (an expression of solidarity, a means of informal collective advancement and a solution to the traders' dilemma (how to cope socially with an increasing inequality of wealth (Evers and Schrader 1994)). The role of caste-based trading networks is discussed in Chapter 8, and the use of caste-networks to cement links between commercial capital and the bureaucracy in Chapter 4. See also the study of *kamma* entrepreneurs in Andhra Pradesh by Upadhya (1997, pp. 62–7). In describing caste in the economy we are not aligning ourselves with general explanations from new institutional economics (NIE), for the economy is structured to an important extent through an institution with a plurality of logics that operate at a lower level of abstraction than that of NIE.

tisation, not least because these forms of collective organisation of economic life are socially exclusive. Second, over a period of history when the local economy has been transformed by waves of capital formation (first, that of the green revolution in the 1970s and second the new wave of the non-farm economy in the 1990s) the institutions of collective economic interest – business and trade associations – have developed roles that are not confined to issues of representation or of narrow advancement. They now extend to the internal mediation of potentially conflicting economic interests, defusing some of the antagonism between capital and labour.

While the role of caste-corporatist regulation in accumulation is clear enough, their role in development more generally depends on the synergies between social structures of accumulation. While religion still acts in part as an opiate, caste corporatism anaesthetises labour and thereby helps sustain accumulation. In Arni, its developmental impact is quite clearly to sustain backward forms of intermediate capital. But elsewhere, in industrial clusters like Tiruppur some 200 miles south – to which we turn in the next chapter – corporatist regulation has enabled the development of cutting-edge flexible specialisation.

8   Space and synergy

We have to avoid the alternative of speaking either of space, locality and territory or of lineage, descent etc. The question is of losing sight of neither and of specifying more precisely their relation (Dumont 1964, in Lambert 1996, p. 76).

Economic activity is conducted in specific places, and the spatial patterns this activity makes – the sites, the routines, flows and interactions – also condition the results. So space is also one of the social structures of accumulation, although it has never been considered as such.[1]

Here we will ask what is distinctive about the spatial character of the Indian economy, and what effects this has on capital accumulation. Examples will be drawn mainly (though not exclusively) from the south, focusing on Tamil Nadu, because this State has a rich literature that exemplifies the points I wish to raise.[2] While nowhere is typical of 'all-India', the south Indian material helps us understand the ways in which social and spatial relations of accumulation manifest themselves unevenly throughout the subcontinent.

Given that some 88 per cent of India's population live in settlements of under 200 000 (see Table 1.1 and Figure 1.1), and that the concentration of capital in local towns is so vast, compared with rural areas, it is India's smaller towns and their regions that are the key arenas for the

---

[1] As with caste, class and State, so with space, definitions range widely, in this case from a static flat surface or extent, through an 'envelope' in which the meaning of identity, nation, boundary can be contested or stabilised, to 'chaotic depthlessness'. Massey, who discusses these definitions (1994, pp. 5 and 25), observes that different concepts of space provide different bases for politics. There have been lively debates between economic geographers and economists: first, concerning the assumptions about the economy, space and time on the basis of which spatial distributions may be modelled and predicted; second, about the uniqueness and path dependence of spatially distributed phenomena; and third, about the degree to which generalisations can be made about the interactions in space of the great variety of social institutions in which the economy is embedded.

[2] It is possible to use evidence quite selectively however to support many kinds of case: Lipton's theory of urban bias *Why Poor People Stay Poor* (1977), Mellor's *New Economics of Growth* (1976) and Bates' exposition of new political economy *Markets and States in Tropical Africa* (1981) have been imaginative and very influential examples.

study of accumulation. Yet India is poorly urbanised, and its rate of urbanisation is actually slowing down,[3] some regions being almost completely stagnant. The 'Bimaru belt'[4] of poverty particularly stands out for its lack of urban growth. The real poles of population growth are the biggest metropolitan cities, but they still account for under 12 per cent of India's population.

From an analysis of the distribution of towns, the first distinctive feature of India's spatial structure of accumulation emerges. Urbanisation is highly uneven.[5] Some regions are highly urbanised, others not. Tamil Nadu stands out as well urbanised; this has been so for a long time.[6] A relatively high proportion of the total population is urban and the towns are well dispersed. According to Rukmani this is due to three factors:

1   the even regional spread of irrigation infrastructure (canals, wells and tanks), giving rise to mixes of wet and dry crops based on water availability and management, and generating a significant marketed surplus;
2   the relative absence of large-scale industry, which means that industry has a workshop- and home-based character throughout the region; and
3   the decentralised and dispersed physical infrastructure (roads, railways and marketplaces).[7]

While some economic activity – retailing, agricultural wholesaling and processing, goldsmithing and pawnbroking, for instance – is common to settlements throughout India, a remarkable feature of these dispersed market towns is the degree to which their economic bases are specialised. Taking Tamil Nadu again, for instance, the Palar Valley specialises in leather, Cheyyar in mats, Arni and Kancheepuram in silk, Vellore and Salem in construction, Tiruchengode in drilling equipment and lorry bodies, Salem and Bhavani in textiles, Tiruchirapalli in gems, Coimbatore in textiles and

---

[3] The reasons are not well understood (Chapman and Pathak 1997). It is possible that this is a spurious result of the form in which Census data are presented: the urban population may be under-enumerated, or growth is suburbanised and disguised in official records. Alternatively, rural–urban migration may have slowed, and the birth rate of new towns declined.

[4] Bimaru is a sober pun. It means 'ailing' or sick in Hindi, and its use as an acronym covers Bihar, Madhya Pradesh, Rajasthan and Uttar Pradesh. This part of India is also the 'Bermuda Triangle' for excess female child mortality. In the case of urbanisation, the belt needs shifting a notch eastwards. The stagnant region is eastern Uttar Pradesh, Madhya Pradesh, Bihar but also West Bengal and Orissa.

[5] Chapman and Pathak 1997. The north-west, the south and the environs of Mumbai are better and more evenly urbanised. Towns litter the west and east coasts, but throughout much of the Deccan plateau and in the hinterland of Calcutta they are conspicuous by their absence.

[6] Baker 1984.

[7] Rukmani (1996); see also Baru (2000, pp. 208–14).

Table 8.1 *Demographic and economic characteristics of towns in Saurashtra*

Towns	Population in Lakhs and decadal growth (%) 1991	Sex ratio 1991	Proportion of population in slum (%)	Main commodity base of the town
Rajkot	6.54 (47)	923	13.50	Diesel engines, machine tools, auto parts
Bhavnagar	4.05 (31)	926	11.30	Plastic rope, vehicle spares, chemicals
Jamnagar	3.88 (20)	919	7.10	Building hardware, brass parts
Junagadh	1.67 (39)	949	6.60	Edible oil, mangoes, tin containers
Porbandar	1.60 (20)	955	9.90	Building stone, soda ash, cement
Morbi	1.20 (64)	934	6.30	Wall clocks, tiles, pottery
Surendranagar	1.16 (27)	928	28.20	Lathes, textile machinery, aluminium/brass utensils
Wadhavan	0.50 (29)	931	–	Fire fighting equipment, thermometer
Veraval	0.97 (14)	958	–	Rayon yarn, fish, fish powder, onion
Jetpur	0.95 (51)	924	15.00	Cotton sarees, printed cloth, thread
Gondal	0.81 (22)	935	12.40	Groundnut oil
Dhoraji	0.79 (2)	987	20.00	Groundnut oil, oil cakes, cattle feed
Amreli	0.69 (19)	940	12.40	Groundnut oil, silk cloth, tiles
Savarkundla	0.66 (28)	943	–	Weighing machines, material made from iron sheets, plastic rope, wooden toys
Botad	0.65 (29)	936	–	Cotton bales, oil engines, agricultural equipment
Mahuva	0.64 (14)	877	–	Groundnut oil
Dhangadhra	0.58 (13)	877	–	Soda ash, cotton bales, oil engines
Upleta	0.52 (–6)	983	27.00	Groundnut oil, *Khandesari*, detergent powder
Keshod	0.50 (57)	915	–	Crockery, groundnut, plastic goods

Source: Kashyup and Guha 1997, p. 91 (Table 13 (excerpted))

engineering, Tiruppur in knitted cotton, Sivakasi in matches, Palladam in chewing tobacco, Annur in cooking oil, Kangeyam in cattle, and so on ... This list is far from comprehensive. Table 8.1 provides another example from north-west India and Map 8.1 shows (in black circles) that regional variations in the tendency to specialise are draped quite exactly over regional variations in growth. In a word, development in India is characterised by *clusters*.

Clusters: building blocks for modern capitalism?

A cluster can be defined as having the following characteristics: reasonably stable spatial boundaries, one or more prevailing industries, a population of relatively small firms that interact through networks and a culturally rooted population.[8] Clusters show great variety, and have been seen as both 'good' and 'bad' for development.[9]

They are said to be good for development on the grounds that in the face of the competitive squalls of liberalisation and globalisation, small and medium-sized firms are vulnerable unless they huddle together in space; are cemented together by information, trust and mutuality; and are able to produce things flexibly through networks of contacts and control. Such small firms can take advantage of entrepreneurship and appropriate technology, have speedy access to inputs and services, are geographically dispersed, produce cheap consumer goods, and reward and motivate a skilled and adaptable workforce. Solidarity, reinforced by ties of kin, caste and neighbourhood, generates competitive efficiency. A firm with access to information and derived markets enjoys external economies that reduce production costs and give it a competitive advantage. A set of firms, just by being a set, can achieve 'passive collective efficiency', while joint action through trade associations generates 'active

---

[8] Beccatini 1979, p. 38.
[9] A number of typologies have been offered. Holmstrom distinguishes (1) subcontracting to large firms; (2) flexible specialisation with services provided by business associations or public bodies; (3) geographical dispersal; and (4) decentralisation within a large firm (1997, pp. 49–53). Another influential typology is of: (1) long-established manufacturing towns characterised by mono-production, high degrees of labour segmentation and low levels of technology; (2) spatially unstructured industrial development on urban peripheries; (3) spatial concentrations of firms specialised in a given sector within a single town or spread across contiguous towns; (4) growing industrial towns using new technology and integrated into national and international markets (Benei and Kennedy 1997; Nadvi 1992). They differ in a key respect from clusters growing in Africa, which have been provoked by the destruction of parastatal corporations and other formal sector production under structural adjustment programs in an unplanned process termed 'informalisation' (Baker and Pedersen 1992). In Africa 'flexible specialisation' means something different: a reliance on family networks and hierarchical patron–client relations that may often be exploitative but may guarantee survival in times of crisis (Pedersen 1998).

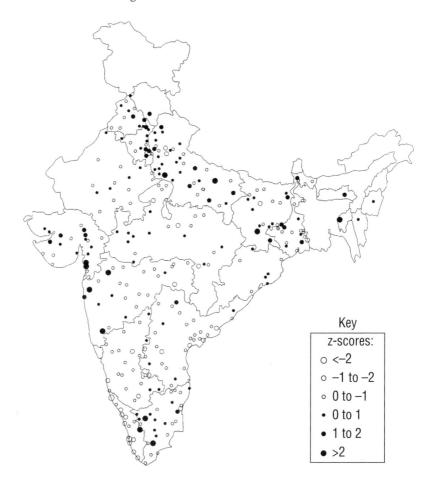

Map 8.1 Variations in degree of urban employment specialisation
Note: Data are from the 1991 census. Black dots denote specialisation, dot size
denotes degree of specialisation. Dots are standardised 2-scores with a mean of
0 and standard deviation of 1
Source: Chapman and Pathak 1997.

collective efficiency'.[10] Passive and active efficiencies combine in a synergistic cluster to form an 'industrial district'.

In this model of synergy the State does not play an active developmental role. Clusters are supposed to have achieved their existing levels
of development without direct state support. Government policy has
either avoided the urban marketing and industrial sector, or had negli-

[10] Schmitz and Nadvi 1999; Holmstrom 1998a.

gible impact on it, and whatever effects macroeconomic policy had on it were unintended.

But as geographers have long noted, the synergy of clusters can also have negative developmental effects. Operationally small units of operation may conceal concentrations of ownership, and be largely a cost- and welfare-minimising response to factory legislation. Clusters may be symptoms of unequal exchange and economic dependency, as in the case of the 'subsistence engineer', described by John Harriss. A large engineering firm closed its machine shop and got workers to take the machines home, busting the CITU union in the process and reducing the costs of machined parts; what looked like a synergistic cluster was really a disaggregated company.[11] Unproductive and illegal activity can also be clustered where the activity can be concealed (typically sited in residential quarters to avoid law enforcement – or state harassment). And we have already seen that clusters of firms often have highly exploitative labour relations (particularly with female casual labour). They may resist innovation and grow through making workers work longer, rather than increasing labour productivity. They can thrive on various forms of primary or primitive accumulation in a nexus of corruption and fraud (especially tax evasion), since the local business elite is often much stronger than the local State. And as we saw in Chapter 7, the regulation of business and the containment of social conflict may be achieved by forms of societal corporatism (guilds, trade associations, caste associations and town welfare sangams), if anything more reminiscent of the economic project of fascist Italy than of that of the 'Third Italy'.[12] Table 8.2 shows the clusters of services and industries centred on Arni; it suggests that there are many reasons for clusters and that several types may coexist in a single settlement.

In the most recent literature on industrial districts and clusters in India and developing countries, however, the positive effects of synergy tend to be stressed. Clusters are seen as typical of the most modern form of local response to globalised industrialisation: the 'Emilia-Romagna' view of 'post-industrial' capitalism (after the region of Italy that abounds in decentralised, flexibly specialised, high-technology workshop industries).[13] Here, 'clusters' belong to a bundle of concepts, including 'industrial districts',

[11] J. Harriss 1982.

[12] The Third Italy is that part of the Italian economy based on industrial districts.

[13] Holmstrom 1998b; Cadène and Holmstrom 1998; Schmitz and Nadvi 1999. Also see forward to the discussion of the relationship between industrial clusters and agriculture (pp. 214–18). There are, of course, other models of post-industrial capitalism, notably of the disintegration of the kind of clusters being described here, to be replaced with new 'regions' integrated through cyberspace, consisting of cores of information, communications, producer services, telecommunications, transport, tourism and leisure (Lasch and Urry 1994/9).

Table 8.2 *Clusters in Arni town*

---

1 goldsmithing money-lending and pawnbroking: Shroff bazaar
(reasons: extreme process-specialisation, specialised castes, site is early C20 centre of town)
2 paddy wholesale and brokerage
(reasons: information economies, new communications technology, relinquishing of financial power to rice millers, concentrated in the centre of the town in 1970s but spun to the periphery and vertically integrated with rice mills by mid-1990s)
3 consumer goods
(reasons: the town centre – zone of maximum consumer traffic)
4 fertiliser, gunny, rope and hardware shops
(reasons: geographical inertia – originally located beside paddy wholesalers)
5 scrap metal, paper and plastics recycling
(reasons: association of religious/caste and occupations – rapid growth in last 10 years near Suriyakulam (tank) in a Muslim ward located close to the housing colony for Municipal scavengers)
6 silk-weaving
(reasons: process-specialised, niched caste, concentration of ownership and credit, three specialised wards of town)
7 cinemas
(reasons: mass purchasing power, though land-intensive, cinemas occupy prime sites of consumer traffic in the centre of town)
8 rice mills
(reasons: land-intensive, inertia, south-east and north-eastern peripheries and residues in the centre of town e.g. near old bus stand and behind former paddy mundy (wholesale market)).

'flexible specialisation', 'networks' and 'collective efficiency' (defined in Holmstrom 1998b), which offer an upbeat characterisation of one response to the crisis of Fordism. Khalid Naðvi, for instance, sets out the following relations of economic synergy between firms, expressed in geographical proximity, sectoral specialisation and social networks, which he sees as leading to 'collective efficiency':

1   ease of information exchange: both general information available to all within the cluster, and particular information restricted to those groups within the cluster linked by more extensive production networking and interactive relations. We would want to add that agglomeration economies of both general and particular information also reduce search costs for customers;

2   personalised exchange that lowers transaction costs: the difference between actually existing transaction costs and those of depersonalised contracts is an 'external economy';

3   subcontracting arrangements within the cluster, leading to process specialisation;

4 the separability of components, to minimise any efficiency losses due to site; and

5 an evolutionary, time-bound process of incremental technological innovation through multiple levels of user-producer interaction.[14]

And we might also add some social or public-sector advantages:

6 infrastructural economies for public provisioning; and

7 reductions in the administrative costs of regulation.

Philippe Cadène, evaluating the distinctiveness of industrial clusters in India, argues as follows:[15] clustered development is a common, rather than an exceptional, form of economic development. In clusters, production is based on an unusually fine and longstanding division of tasks. Low technology is usual (Bangalore's 'silicon plateau' is an exception).[16] Graduation from low to high technology is rare (although on the increase as 'globalisation' leads to the replacement of export markets for low-quality goods by domestic markets for high-quality products demanded by the elite). Production and distribution are based on mutual acquaintance. Both managerial and labour skills result from the 'artisanal tradition' (that is, the artisan castes: smiths of many kinds). Lastly, in India's clusters the highest returns accrue to trade, not production.

In this way, Cadène argues, a national 'system of systems' or markets is coming into being. It is selective (being most active in finance, transport, chemicals, engineering and machine tools), socially differentiating and highly exclusive in both social and regional terms. Nonetheless, Cadène sees India's clusters as evidence of 'the emergence in India of a developmental model corresponding to that of industrial clusters as they have been described in other countries' (1998b, p. 394); that is, the distinctive 'Emilia-Romagna' form of development.

Five distinctive features of Indian clusters

The 'Emilia-Romagna syndrome' (whose origins we will discuss in a little more detail below, in a comparison with India's clusters) may be present here and there in India, but it would be a mistake to conclude, from the

---

[14] Nadvi 1992, p. 16.
[15] Cadène 1998a, pp. 139–69. The question of the appropriate national experiences with which to compare the Indian case is not addressed in this literature. (But see Hart (1996) on Taiwan and South Africa; Cecchi (1997) on Italy; Nadvi (1999a and b on Pakistan)). The Special Issue of *World Development*, Sep 1999 on *Industrial Clusters in Developing Countries* (in Schmitz and Nadvi 1999) does not problematise national character, but it does problematise success and failure.
[16] This region is the source of inspiration for Holmstrom's new map of Indian industrial society (1999).

research done largely on places like Bangalore and Tiruppur, which are exceptional in this respect, that most Indian clusters have such developmentally positive potential. A small minority of Indian clusters do form that kind of 'industrial district'. But if clustered development is examined more generally, our attention is forcibly directed to five distinctive features of clusters, when considered as the characteristic spatial structures of accumulation of India: the *quiddity* of commodities, the *viscosity* of capital, the *internal relations of labour control*, the *peculiarities of competition and accumulation*, and the *social acceptance of vast negative externalities*.

Quiddity

Quiddity is an archaic word meaning 'the essence or particularity of a thing', and can be replaced as soon as a better one-word label is found. In India most commodities are far from being 'emptied of meaning and affective charge', let alone of 'material content' as the commodities typical of post-modernity are said to be (Lasch and Urry 1994/9, pp. 12 and 15), [17] so that choosing an archaic word for them in this context makes a useful point. Quiddity has two broad dimensions. One refers to the physical characteristics of particular commodities, and the way they determine the economic and social, and also spatial characteristics of their production and trade. The other refers to the socially given meanings of particular commodities. Items of food, for instance, contain inherent moral qualities; the social thermodynamic concepts of 'hot' and 'cold' run through all foodstuffs and related commodities, and affect the status and esteem of those who transact them. [18] Physical quiddity will affect production and trade in it in predictable ways (for example, with a perishable commodity unseasonal trade will depend on technologies of preservation or close proximity to final consumption markets). But quiddity is often a mix of the physical and the social, so that things determine markets in unpredictable ways. Take land – both a good and a bad example, since the meaning of land is almost universal. In India, land, whether urban or rural, [19] has intense 'quiddity' as both capital stock and a factor of production, and as the territorial component of governance and a

[17] Nor is there a distinct division of cultural space into one (public) in which a given commodity (say milk) has a material meaning and another (private) where it is consumed in a ritualistic way as in East Africa (Tim Kelsall 1999, personal communication).

[18] 'While heat is vital for life, reproduction and strength, in isolation it is potentially perilous and has to be counteracted through cooling substances' (Simpson 2001, p. 3). In Mandvi, Gujarat, cool products are dominated by Jain and Hindu merchants, while hot, non-vegetarian foods are restricted to the Muslim areas of the town (Simpson 2001, p. 3).

[19] On markets for urban land in India, see Auclair (1998).

powerful basis for status. As a result, the market in land has enduring characteristics: the stickiness in the outright transfer of ownership rights; the ubiquity of brokers;[20] and the proliferation of rental, mortgage and interlocked contracts, such that the very concept of a 'contract' might be better interpreted as part of a process of blurring of the concept of 'ownership'. Alternatively, take TV programmes: their quiddity lies in their being regarded as public goods, in their need for novelty, in their dependence on expensive labour inputs, in the unpredictability of the synergies needed for success and their susceptibilities to certain kinds of market failure. The consequences are a tendency towards monopoly, and a lack of fit with competitive capitalist production relations.[21] A common aspect of the physical quiddity of many of the commodities produced in Indian clusters is the technical separability of components of production. The manufacturing of T-shirts and Y-fronts, for example, can be divided into several technical stages, each carried out by a number of separate firms.

The 'viscosity' of capital

Outside the metropolitan and increasingly globalised concentrations of 'apex' capital, the private generation of start-up capital in Indian clusters is extremely localised and it is very hard to break the established patterns through which it is accomplished. With the exception of *baniya* and *marwari* traders, there are serious barriers (of caste, region of origin and language) that prevent owners of capital migrating elsewhere. Different forms of capital – money, labour, the means of production and commodities – will have different degrees of 'viscosity' and make characteristic patterns; money being, paradoxically, the most viscous, and commodities being the most fluid.[22] This viscosity of capital is enough alone to make each cluster unique.[23] It also sets limits to success: path dependence (or inertia) results from it alone. Local systems are dominated by brokers who link the cluster to wider markets and dispose of its products in the regional, national and global economies, and who may also organise and finance production. The two available 'solvents' of this viscosity – this immobilisation of capital – are capital belonging to the numerically small, though economically powerful, migrant merchant castes (see pp. 227–9), and the movement of money by the nationalised banks, though their typical effect is to draw rural deposits to the metropolitan

---

[20] Given that it is rare that land is not seen prior to purchase, the market is also distinctively face-to-face.

[21] Leys 2001.

[22] Lasch and Urry 1994/9.

[23] Kattuman 1998; Neelakanthan 1995; Tewari 1998.

centres. Otherwise, to dilute viscosity calls for exceptional entrepreneurial energy and independence of the kind Schumpeter thought capitalism depended on, but which is so far rare in small-town India.

The internal relations of labour control

Institutional controls over labour are a key element making accumulation possible. As we saw in Chapter 2, labour is organised in a hierarchy of contractual arrangements rather than in textbook markets. The family character of production, the intense segmentation of the labour process, the social divisions in the workplace, the impermanence of the labour process under subcontracting and outright unemployment all militate against the integration of labour markets. They also undermine the political consciousness of labour. This type of labour process is also a means by which the laws protecting labour can be evaded. Crucial to the capacity of firms to keep labour weak are: vertical subcontracting, bilateral collaboration (in consortia) and multilateral collaboration (through trade associations). Such arrangements are often described as egalitarian.[24] However, Pamela Cawthorne's study of the effects of contracting-out on the labour process in the cotton knitwear industry in Tiruppur, Tamil Nadu, shows how networks between firms (subcontracting) and within firms (internal contracting) work to the advantage of the subcontractors or internal contractors.[25] This so-called 'job-working' allows larger firms to accumulate capital by 'vertically *dis*integrating' the production process. In this way the firm evades labour supervision costs and minimises capital investment. Simultaneously, it retains control of the finished product and retains the capacity for flexible production under conditions of variable demand by offloading the risk on to the job-workers. Cawthorne terms this splitting of firms in order to control labour, 'amoebic capitalism'. In Tiruppur in the early 1990s there were about 850 firms using this system. The varied contractual relations she describes can also be seen as an efficiency response, averting risk and reducing transaction costs. But it would be a mistake to assume that the existence of such contracts entails transaction costs efficiency.[26] The process that generates this 'amoebic capitalism' is one of the forms of 'informalisation'. It is proliferating not, as in Africa, because of the destruction of state enterprises, but as a result of private firms' efforts to reduce costs of production. (Women shoulder most of the burden of this informalisation, both in the workplace and at home, but there are signifi-

---

[24] For example, see Nadvi (1999a, p. 144).
[25] Cawthorne 1992.
[26] Cawthorne 1996. See also, J. Harriss 1982.

cant regional differences in this respect. In 1991 female participation in the labour force of medium-sized towns in south India was 40 per cent, but in north-west India it was only 5 per cent.)[27]

Peculiarities of competition and accumulation

Firms attempt to *avoid* competition in distinctive ways, as we saw in Chapters 3, 6 and 7. One of these is by combinations and permutations of activity that are diverse, complex and with strong tendencies towards uniqueness. Such uniqueness is a primitive form of branding, inviting loyalty and repeated transactions, while the entire cluster in which such a firm operates, and the networks to which it is linked, possess a plastic resistance to shocks of all sorts, whether environmental, political or economic.

Networks operate on at least three levels. One is where specialisation in production within clusters is organised through networks based on kinship, caste, and neighbourhood or locality. As we noted in Chapter 5, families and kinship shape both the internal structure of firms and the repeated vertical and horizontal contractual arrangements between them, and this sets the limits to competition. Individual and collective reputations are policed, collective entry barriers are erected and transaction costs are regulated on a *local* basis. These arrangements blunt competition, although there are also some countervailing forces at work in a locality, such as espionage and the poaching of clients, which may offset this. At the regional level, clusters are integrated through networks. Even at the national and international levels there are networks in the diasporas – emigrants from the local clusters and networks – who organise trade and seek to reduce competition there, too.

At every level there are intermediaries and brokers. With small amounts of capital these men organise the information and contacts necessary for process-specialised production and for trade. With larger amounts of capital they finance it, too. By these means they also link local clusters or systems of clusters, the gaps between networks being barriers to accumulation every bit as important as the much more famous gap between agriculture and industry.

The reason why intermediaries are so important is that exchange through networks is *not* pure market exchange.[28] Networking cuts the full costs of market exchange by being co-ordinated, reciprocal, interdependent and based upon *trust*. Trust means that many major transaction costs

---

[27] Kashyup and Guha 1997, p. 89.
[28] See Davis (1992) and Harriss-White (1995b) for critical reviews of definitions of market exchange.

can be dispensed with. Trust can also dispense with the need for a public reputation, which has its own costs to create and maintain.[29] Relational, repeated contracts,[30] the commonest forms of exchange in networks, taking years to develop, reproduce the networks and the class relations they embody. Abstracted from this context a single contract tells us little about its real meaning.

Repeated contracts may be an efficient response to incompletely developed markets for information and insurance, reducing transaction costs, hindering delinquency, smoothing price fluctuations and reducing uncertainty, and they may also be responses to the 'trader's dilemma', where the drive to accumulate conflicts with social obligations to redistribute. These obligations may be resolved or avoided by restricting trade to groups which are outsiders, exempt from duties to redistribute; by investing in the accumulation of social rather than economic status; and by restricting activity to a petty scale. (The textbook solution – that is, the depersonalisation of economic relationships – is going to be a slow process, and unlikely to be completed anywhere soon.) [31]

Repeated contracts may also be expressions of the power and social control of the buyer (or financier) and of the seller's lack of power. They may also be a source of capital for the seller (or borrower). They may result from 'choice', but only in the sense that the alternative for the weaker partner will be wage labour; to be locked into 'relational' trade may be the most free that a firm with very few assets can be. But when access to money, information, storage, processing and transport is attached by credit to a trading-patron, and spiked with additional non-contractual obligations, a small firm in a network has very little capacity to accumulate. Displays of power are common in these relational contracts, in the form of uncompensated delays in payment. This is easiest for corporate capital, which can demand instant or even advance payment while delaying its own payments and not compensating for this delay, thereby stymieing accumulation by the firms that supply advances. Networks of transactions are also cemented by interlocked contracts involving money advances and goods in return. Great webs of repeated contracts can spread into the hinterlands of clusters with loans at interest rates that increase as one moves outwards. The terms and conditions of the contracts of these 'credit webs' vary a great deal and levels of development cannot be read off from the contracts *per se*. Ben Crow and Firdoz Murshid, for example, contrast a backward region in

---

[29] Power can also be used to exclude, to create dependency and circumscribe the independence required for competition.

[30] These contracts are given to the firm dealt with regularly, not an unknown firm offering a lower price or apparently better value.

[31] Evers and Schrader 1994.

Bangladesh where 70 per cent of contracts reflected the existence of 'tied' trade, regulated by physical coercion or its threat, with an advanced region where only 8 per cent of contracts took this form.[32] They believe that in the latter case it is not technical change and commercialisation that have dissolved tied relationships, it is rather that the two regions differ with respect to their structural parameters of agrarian accumulation. Lastly, these – mostly verbal – contracts are laden with 'intangibles', with mutual non-contractual obligations. For example, the money lender or commodity purchaser may be obliged to lend small quantities of money for urgent need, to distribute 'perks', to give advice and act as a loyal social and political intermediary. The commodity seller or money borrower may be obliged to sell all their product or raw materials to the lender, to deposit cash, and to be loyal. These typically asymmetrical mutual obligations can be construed as incentives, as forms of oppression, as relationships that guard against the uncertainties of future outcomes, or as all these things.

The toleration of negative externalities

Nowhere is the imperative of predatory and primitive accumulation more visible than in the physical degradation of the public environment in the small towns where Indian accumulation occurs. Outside a few dozen cities and towns, the State implements environmental law with extreme reluctance and selectivity, because the power structures of 'clustered' urban life thwart it. The variety and severity of the pollution that is tolerated in India has a social impact not only on the immediate labour force (through occupational diseases, and so on), but also much more widely, increasing the costs of reproduction for the poor, particularly for poor women. Further, its impact is felt much more widely than just in the administrative territories of towns, adding costs to other sectors of the economy.[33] At its extreme, as when the quantity and quality of drinking water are threatened, it will limit the development of clusters. Responses are typically evasive – firms move activities to satellite locations out of town rather than accept the costs involved in reducing environmental damage.

Explaining India's clusters

These five characteristics, exhibited by most of India's 'clusters', are not *prima facie* conducive to development in the way imagined by the 'Emilia-Romagna' interpretation. To get a sense of how rooted the characteristics

[32] Crow and Murshid 1994; see also Crow 2001.
[33] Baud and Schenk 1994; Beall 1997; Kennedy 1999.

are, however, we need to know more about what has produced India's 'clusters'. The literature and field experience suggest three main determinants: the agrarian structure of the hinterlands of clusters, castes (particularly the merchant castes) and the influence of the local State.[34] In effect, clusters appear as 'secondary' structures of accumulation – the effects of other, arguably primary, structures. We will try to assess the respective impact of each.

The agrarian structure of the region around a cluster

The size and spacing, the economic character and the growth of clusters have been understood by some writers as expressing the history of the agriculture of their hinterlands. In Table 8.3, the agrarian structures of three kinds of region are related to the character of their towns. The idea is that the extent of 'agriculturalisation', the differentiation of the peasantry, and the character of agriculture's capitalist transformation all strongly influence the supply of labour, capital and commodities, and the control of that supply. They also strongly influence the social character of demand and the nature of the home market.[35]

While the case of sharecropping tenancy will be discussed in detail later (pp. 221–2), we can use Tamil Nadu to illustrate two of the three models of the agrarian origins of clusters set out in Table 8.3. First, on the twentieth-century land frontiers around Coimbatore, where the land was colonised in substantial estates, with a migrant landless labour force to hand, the rural agricultural sector has developed alongside a precocious industrialisation.[36] Based originally on local cotton, but rapidly

[34] Following Kaviraj, we are using the idea of determination not being as actions that must inevitably follow, but in terms of ranges of action most likely to happen given x. These ranges will depend on the kind of structure under consideration; in particular, whether it is *explicit* (in which case sanctions and incentives can be directly traced to outcomes (as might be the case in a political party, or the set of official procedures through which a policy utterance is translated into allocations of resources, or the activity of a caste association)), or whether the structure is *abstract* and *fundamental* (as in the case of class which evolves at a glacial pace and often through other structures). The sad contradiction is that '(t)he cost of being fundamental is to have only indirect results' (Kaviraj 1988, pp. 165–6). Determination is further masked by volatile contingent circumstances. This means that acts of interpretation are required and these are likely to be contested.

[35] That forms of distribution can be read off deterministically from forms of production has been disputed both theoretically and using evidence of the degree of institutional autonomy of markets, or of reverse determination (of production by the sphere of circulation). This is an empirical issue. Empirical work has also shown that the agrarian transition to capitalism is quite capable of generating many more kinds of non-agricultural linkages than the Prussian and American roads theorised by Marx (or the version of the American Road theorised by Mellor (1976) as 'Growth Linkages from Agriculture'); see also Baru 2000, pp. 208–14.

[36] Baker 1984.

Table 8.3 *Agrarian base of urbanisation*

Agrarian structure	Product	Mechanism of surplus extraction	Supply of 'wage goods' (food, clothing, etc.)	Demand for 'wage goods'	Size/spacing of towns	Functions
1 Tenancy landlords + tenants/ sharecroppers	grain/food	rent and interest	dominated by landlords	low-mass poverty	small, sparse, stagnant	admin. security, political; (poor have access to periodic mkts; elite have access to metropolis)
2 Capitalist owners + labourers	(non) food/ agro-industrial products	surplus value (migrant labour)	imported	high and polarised	large, dense, growing	admin. etc.: process-specialised industrial clusters
3 Peasant	food	surplus product; interest (super-exploitation of female labour)	local imported	medium ? polarised	small, dense suburbanising	admin. etc. specialised (niche) agro-processing; mass retail; entrepôt

drawing its raw material from the entire span of southern India, local agro-industry spawned related engineering sectors and locked itself into horizontally and vertically integrated sets of process-specific firms, drawing its labour (sometimes seasonally, sometimes part-time) from agriculture. Large industrial districts are proliferating rather than small market towns. The region has a net deficit in rice, and its food security depends on substantial imports from other regions and Indian states.

By contrast, in the northern Coromandel Plain, historically a region of *ryotwari* (small peasant landholder) cultivation with a lower degree of inequality and a marketed surplus, which is largely controlled by a mass of direct small producers, there has long existed a dense network of small agricultural market towns with both specialised and common clusters.[37] The silk handloom-weaving clusters have a nation-wide reach in both raw materials and finished products, owing their existence on the one hand to castes of merchants and weavers that migrated there in the past for aristocratic patronage, and on the other to pauperised agrarian petty-producers who have entered weaving. The latter exploit their own domestic and child labour resources in work contracted out from merchants and master weavers. A range of weaving technologies coexist and the new rural labour reserve means that primitive technologies become cost-effective. The industry is characterised by technological retrogression. The work is hazardous and unregulated by the State. Here, agriculture has subsidised the weavers, and a new class of petty agricultural producers has been formed whose chief occupation is industrial labour.[38]

The influence of the agrarian structure on clusters is vividly seen wherever the returns to *commercial* capital are persistently the highest, generating *trade-based clusters* that grow with the local marketed surplus and the development of entrepôt functions. Merchants' capital then shows an awkward persistence, resisting subordination to industrial capital and often sprouting very vigorous tendrils of industrial capital itself. Some of the clusters in the hinterland of Coimbatore in south India are good illustra-

---

[37] The relation between agrarian structure and urbanisation has a long history here. Under colonial rule, agricultural commercialisation without technical or social transformation generated insecurity and intensified poverty. Episodic factors (diseases, famines, violent shocks to markets) led to waves of migration and swollen streams of cheap factory labour. This urbanisation was transient since the very factors causing entitlement failures would limit the markets for urban and industrial goods. After Independence, the State has been responsible for policies that have somewhat mitigated the impact of episodic factors and underlie a more sustained trajectory of industrial growth. More recently, however, towns have become saturated, because of the failure to develop mass markets. Growth may also have spilled over into suburbs where it is well disguised in official records (Baker 1984; Rukmani 1996; Chapman and Pathak 1997).

[38] See Jayaraj 2002; Nagaraj et al. 1996. Hart (1996) generalises the effects of cheap labour, rents and pre-emptive development as 'urban push', distinguishing them from those of agricultural growth linkages ('rural pull').

tions. There, powerful traders in raw cotton, groundnuts and tobacco have gone into the manufacturing of textiles, cooking oil and cigars. Trade may dominate industrial production in such clusters, characterised by firms with risk-minimising, sprawling portfolios, trading through long-distance networks, and operating with low fixed capital and cost structures dominated by raw materials. Merchants' capital may then develop markets for new *'incentive goods'* (for example, fridges, bikes and scooters, home theatres (video players) and mechanical wet grinders of spices). These may spur the capitalist transformation of agriculture by means of credit for their purchase (as has certainly been the case in parts of Punjab).[39]

In other situations, accumulation through commerce, heavily stratified by caste or religion, may compete with accumulation in agriculture and industry. Development will then proceed through a struggle between these sectors (and the State) over shares of productive capital. But agriculture does not necessarily generate the resources for industrialisation. There are instances where industrial capital or remittances have led the transformation of agriculture (for example, many instances where army veterans had remitted money while on active service in order to buy land that they farm with productivity-enhancing technology in their retirement; and the cases described in Chapter 5 in which the business elite buys land and invests in new crops (fruit, vegetables and perennial tree crops), new technologies (spray irrigation), new labour processes (skilled professional management, contract labour, and so on) and new markets (contracts with corporate agribusiness)).[40] In some clusters industry has developed on the basis of the savings and investments of artisans (for example, clusters based on rope, mats and matches), from state-subsidised capital and from industry's own productively reinvested surplus. Where agro-commercial capital takes concentrated and specialised forms, and where it is segmented by commodity or by the type of demand into subsystems that are more or less discrete in terms both of the technologies used and their spatial patterns, then there will be 'clusters within clusters'. These can be seen in the case of chewing tobacco in Palladam, Coimbatore district, a sub-cluster within the local tobacco industry; or rice-husking in the Birbhum district of West Bengal, a sub-cluster within the milling cluster.

An unorthodox relation between industrial clusters and agriculture[41] was first noticed not in India but in Tuscany by Beccatini, who explained

---

[39] A. Singh 1999.

[40] Upadhya 1997; Jayaraj 2002.

[41] The orthodox relation being modelled as driven by industry rather than agriculture, with the agrarian question reduced to the mechanisms whereby agriculture will yield the surplus of labour, capital, food and raw materials necessary for industrialisation (Byres 1974).

the distinctive pattern of industrial development in central and eastern Italy – based on clusters of small firms that were stronger and more flexible than large ones in times of crisis – as being due to a distinctive relationship with a local form of sharecropping (*mezzadria*).[42] It was a mode of organisation of agricultural production in which the sharecroppers (*mezzadri*) monitored farm labour on behalf of the landowner. They organised production, were deeply engaged in a form of commercial exchange that was personalised and characterised by custom and trust, and, last but not least, they had barns that were convertible into workshops at low capital cost, and which could house diverse technological assets. This gave tenant-producers the capability to take the agro-industrial leap, first as workers and subsequently as entrepreneurs. They were able to integrate their new industrial activity with agriculture spatially (locally), in time (part-time, seasonally) and sometimes in the same commodity sector (for example, the Parmesan cluster of Parma, Chianti wine in Gaiole, processed tomatoes in Maremma, and Mozzarella cheese from the buffaloes of Caserta).[43] The agro-industrial clusters in the Coimbatore hinterland based on tobacco, oil and cotton are comparable examples in India, and there are many more.

The location and role of pre-existing merchant castes

The structure and organisation of trading has differed widely between clusters without impeding flows of goods, though it has required considerable flexibility in commercial techniques. Such flexibility (a quite different form of flexible specialisation from that of industrial districts) may amount to the extraction of surplus through a variety of modes, merchants being simultaneously 'businessmen of the epoch of primitive accumulation and modern entrepreneurs' (Levkovsky 1966, p. 234). Industrial production, finance and trade are still dominated by the *vaisya* (merchant) castes (there being no 'industrial castes' above the level of artisans). These are the castes that have found it easiest to make the transition from the indirect control of agriculture – through elaborate systems of pre-harvest finance – to direct investment in industry.[44] We have seen in Chapters 6 and 7 that caste still

---

[42] Beccatini 1979.

[43] However Cecchi (2001) takes care to problematise the notion of an agro-industrial region. The boundaries of agrarian regions are always blurred by commodity flows. Unlike industry, agriculture cannot take advantage of agglomeration economies in order to process-specialise. Competition for land raises rents and threatens agriculture altogether. If agriculture survives, the continuity of agrarian culture collapses due to the different logics to the velocity of turnover in agriculture (slow, affected by nature and seasons) and industry (fast), so that the sole continuity rests in (part-time) labour and sites of residence. On this theme see also Fua (1988) and Paloscia (1991).

[44] Cadène 1998b, pp. 394–9.

defines and stratifies economic sectors. In Punjab, for instance, where the upheavals of Partition transformed merchant castes from being distributed throughout mutually exclusive regions to being concentrated in towns scattered throughout the State and organised across economic sectors, the agricultural wholesale trade is overwhelmingly dominated by *baniyas*, while *khatris* and *aroras* control consumer goods and durables. Trade by scheduled castes (SCs) is on a small scale and restricted to rural areas (A. Singh 1999). The lack of a position in the caste-based moral order for *capitalists* – as opposed to artisans or traders – over most of India has allowed the slow development of small-scale capital formation, but has distinctly discouraged the emergence of 'polyvalent', 'big' capitalists from the lower castes.[45] And the caste-based moral order is, as we have seen, very far from the point of destruction.

The local State

Much of the discussion of the State in the 'Emilia-Romagna' literature on industrial districts is normative – calling for policy to be based on the 'Emilia-Romagna' model – and so is not relevant here.[46] What is relevant is a contradiction that lies unresolved at the centre of this literature's account of the model as applied to India. On the one hand, the role of the local State in clustered development is not confined to research and development, vocational training, marketing, information and infrastructure. It provides the public health environment without which there can be no market exchange, and the equally essential electricity. It shifts capital by means of the nationalised banks, and through taxation it extracts resources and redistributes incentives. We will have more to say about these roles later. On the other hand, outside the 40–50 towns and cities in which big corporate capital is concentrated, the State is generally unsuccessful at regulating private capital. The tax base of towns is extremely limited, confining municipalities to the provision of some housing and water, and the removal of solid waste. All levels of the State (central, state and municipal), as they are manifested in the typically 'clustered' town, are too weak to

---

[45] Gujarat is a notable exception. Here caste rules never prevented entry into business and 'business is ranked high' (Chaudhuri 1975, p. 114; see also Timberg 1978, p. 9).

[46] Schmitz and Nadvi (1999, p. 1511) take the view that the State can substitute for failures of clustering. For information failures (what they term 'cognitive inbreeding'), the State can organise information, marketing, technical knowledge and networking, especially with foreign buyers. In the face of network failure and entry barriers, the State can organise co-operation. Faced with lack of synergy, the State can act sequentially and synergistically. The State can also sort macroeconomic policy so that it is favourable to exports, monitor and fine-tune exchange rates, set protective trade barriers where useful to nurture industries, discourage the export of primary commodities, and aid and abet export contracts.

prevent the evasion by capital of its obligation to contribute its share of the resources needed even for the provision of basic public goods, let alone those required for assisting those labelled 'poor'. The weakness of the local State means it lacks the power to overcome the inertial force of the typical cluster's path dependency.

The developmental implications of India's clustered accumulation structures

We are now in a better position to assess the implications for development of the five distinctive features of India's clustered pattern of urban accumulation – quiddity, capital viscosity, labour control, 'relational' patterns of accumulation and competition, and the acceptance of negative externalities – by considering the roots of each in the three 'primary' structures of accumulation we have just outlined.

The local agrarian structure and 'quiddity'

Many Indian clusters have an agro-industrial base, but the particularities of the raw materials used cannot be inferred mechanically from the nature of local agro-ecological environment – which in any case is in part a social construct, most obviously with respect to irrigation. The role of agrarian structure also changes over time. For sure, food industries grow from local production, but they are also a product of transformation technologies and the kind of capital needed to set them up. The latter are in turn conditioned by the social distribution of the returns to the marketed surplus, the types and scale of differentiated surplus accumulation in agriculture and the modes of extraction of surplus by merchants, as much as by what happens to be the physical output of local agriculture. For that reason, it is common for several processing technologies to coexist, with finely differentiated products, sometimes with limited substitution possibilities and with distinct locations for the final effective demand. In the Palladam tobacco cluster, for instance, pit- and sun-cured chewing tobacco goes to Madras/Chennai, tobacco stems go to periodic marketplaces in Andhra Pradesh via Chittoor, and Jaffna-cured tobacco goes to Quilon and Kottayam in Kerala. The technology of transformation then locks-in local production to a particular commodity (for example, ginning clusters based on hinterlands of cotton, refineries based on sugarcane tracts). A succession of 'asset-specific' technologies, with increasing economies of scale, then drive specialised agro-industrial clusters to develop, and these may grow to be independent of local agriculture and may rely on flows of bulky raw materials from quite far away. To take an extreme example, sea water is conveyed from the southern tip of Tamil Nadu far inland to Jaffna tobacco-curing sheds at Palladam, in south-central Tamil Nadu; the cotton supplied to Coimbatore and Tiruppur, the groundnuts supplied to Annur's oil-pressing cluster, and the hides supplied to the Palar Valley tanneries in northern Tamil Nadu, all come from distant sources. Other examples are Arni's rice-milling (which uses paddy from the length and breadth of the State, with final demand from the regions of origin) and silk-weaving (which uses cocoons from the region around Bangalore and gold thread from Gujarat, to supply saris to the national market), and Ahmedabad's industrial starch industries, which are supplied with millet from southern Tamil Nadu.[47] Such locational autonomy is often reinforced by fixed environmental endowments. Intense and reliable sunshine and water of reliable softness or salinity are critical to the processing of many agricultural products. Most semi-perishable products need to be dried before being stored, and, with the scrambling of agricultural seasons, they are increasingly harvested during monsoons. The old techniques for drying crops under monsoon squalls may have been suited to small batches but become inappropriate with the increasing size of the marketed surplus. The latter needs rapid shipping-out to dry, sunny regions. Hence, some clusters develop that are based on climate.[48]

The local agrarian structure and the relative 'viscosity' of capital

The agrarian origins of many Indian clusters – in agricultural products, or in the artisanal crafts that flourished in villages before their comprehensive agriculturalisation – help explain why for the most part private capital in Indian clusters doesn't easily flow elsewhere. The scenarios of capitalist agriculture and of peasant production in Table 8.3, and discussed earlier on pp. 214–17, show the close relations between types of local accumulation and agro-industrial clusters. Conversely, in cases where capital is not viscous but extracted from agriculture and siphoned out of the region, it may not be invested productively in industry at all. An agrarian scene dominated by pauperised tenants, whose technology is stagnant, and from whom surplus is extracted by a

---

[47] Wholesale markets do not require towns. Where the density of demand for exchange goods is low, the latter may be traded through the system of rural periodic markets (Bohle 1992). The marketed surplus may be extracted directly from farm to factory, mills or warehouse (commonly by rural agents of urban merchants), and bypass towns completely, as is commonplace in the industrialised agriculture of Western Europe and North America.

[48] For instance, the wet season timing of the crucial harvest in Thanjavur has long required the rapid export of paddy inland to the dry sunny climate of Kongunad for storage and processing. The rice-milling clusters are far inland at long distance from the epicentre of paddy production.

coalition of landlords–traders–money-lenders (as in Bhaduri's formal model of semi-feudalism in West Bengal) does not support a dense network of towns.[49] Towns perform security, administrative and political functions, and service the demand of agrarian elites, but very few will have clusters, even ones based on agro-processing. Landlord elites invest surplus in the professions and in finance. Under landlord agriculture, even where 'green revolution' production technology has been adopted (as it has under agrarian tenancy in the Kaveri delta in Tamil Nadu), the circulation of mass goods for the rural population is effected through periodic markets rather than towns, because the rural population is too poor for their demand to support fixed commercial centres. In this productive delta region there are few towns and industrial clusters are remarkable for their absence.[50]

The local agrarian structure and labour control

The division of labour is most fully revealed in the relations between a cluster and its region. In the early phases of industrialisation, relations of production in industry may draw directly on – and in some cases mesh with – those of agriculture. Chari's research on the knitwear cluster of Tiruppur reveals a 'peasant-worker' transition that has much in common with the account Beccatini gives for Tuscany, particularly the continuities of labour control (in Chari's case, between agriculture and knitwear), but with the significant difference of a very rapid scaling-up and absorption of technical innovations in Tiruppur. Owners latched on to the task-specific conventions of local agriculture (for example, the long length and divisions of the working day, the super-exploitation of women and children) and applied them to industry, effectively and competitively exploiting labour. Relations of demonstration or 'example' between owner-workers and wage-workers, with their origins in agricultural practice, prevented trade unions from defending workers against decentralisation, 'the ripping apart of units', or against the imposition of piece rates (both deployed tactically to evade the Factories Acts). Finally, owners' associations regulated piece rates. Only when the need for precision in the timing of consignments for export gave labour a point of leverage did the owners' association concede regular labour agreements with unions. Even so, the agreements are acknowledged in the breach and need not be acknowledged at all where labour (especially female and child labour) is not organised, as is – of course – the case with agriculture.[51]

[49] Bhaduri 1983.
[50] Bohle 1992; Rukmani 1994; Harriss-White 1996a.
[51] Chari 2000, chapter 6.

The agrarian structure and clustered patterns of competition and accumulation

We have already seen that there are many roads to capitalist development at the micro level which reflects the struggle over surplus between land controllers and merchant/moneylenders.[52] Chari's work traces a range of accumulation trajectories involving labour, among which are: (1) from 'peasant'[53] to agricultural trade to a specialised process in knitwear; (2) from labouring peasant to labouring worker, to subcontracting (with capital from savings from wages, gifts from owners, chit funds, dowries (even mother's savings) and land sales) to an independent firm; (3) ditto, with (temporary) capitalisation from moneyed partners or credit from banks (the latter being increasingly important); and (4) key agricultural capitalists eventually developing control over networks of process-specialised firms for the co-ordination necessary to reap synergistic gains from exports. Figure 8.1 shows these accumulation possibilities. Continual technical upgrading has enabled these rurally rooted capitalists successfully to out-compete the *brahmin* elite, an older generation of mercantile firms, the local landlord elite, and a powerful subset of Muslim producers – not to mention the biggest local corporate in textiles – and to seize control of the major trade associations.[54]

The agrarian structure and the toleration of negative environmental externalities

The relation between agriculture and industrial clusters involves many aspects of the environment without which market exchange cannot take

---

[52] The terms of trade are the basic mechanism here, determining the patterns of the migration of capital between sectors of the economy. Despite pan-territorial procurement prices for agricultural commodities, the importance of residual 'open' markets ensures that the actual terms of trade are distinctive to agro-ecological regions, as well as to social classes (B. Harriss 1984a and b). However, the importance of agriculture for industrial or commercial clusters is dynamic – over time the importance of agriculture declines and changes. A cluster may have nothing to do with the land around, except for the disposition of land rents and the conditions of surplus of agrarian labour. An agro-cluster may also owe its origins to aristocratic patronage and subsequent inertia (see the cases of silk in Arni (Nagaraj et al. 1996), and marble in Rajsamand (Cadène 1998a, p. 147))

[53] Actually *gounder* landowners are the dominant caste in the region and Baker (1984) was in no doubt that a substantial fraction were agrarian capitalists; see also Chari (2000).

[54] De Neve (2001), describing the same process and cluster, puts the emphasis elsewhere, finding large numbers of migrants belonging to a variety of regional, caste and class backgrounds – as well as women migrants. He sees their regular and committed hard work, exploited by owners, as the manipulation both of an agrarian idiom but more materially of their own abject dependency. The possibilities for upward mobility of migrant outsiders stem much more from the organisation of the knitwear cluster, particularly from the institutions of job-working and partnerships than they do from what is undoubtedly the 'necessary condition' of hard work. And it is owners (risen from the ranks of workers) rather than current workers who have union cards.

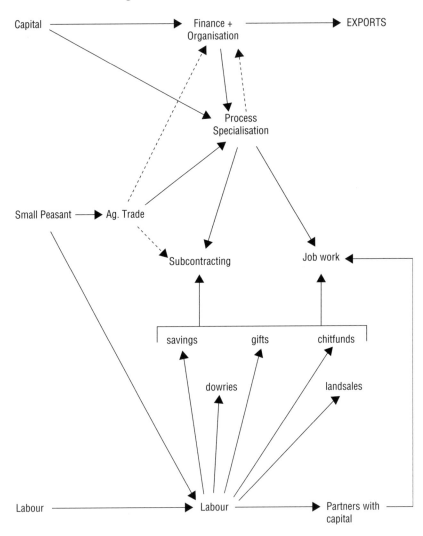

Figure 8.1 Accumulation trajectories: Tiruppur, south India

place, but in which negative externalities can arise. There is space here to consider only one, *water*, which is needed for agriculture, industry and domestic use (drinking, cooking and cleaning). A variety of technologies of supply and extraction coexist, often in close spatial proximity. Here the causal relationship between agrarian structure and clustered development is apt to be reversed over time. At best, competition for water leads to the establishment of satellite settlements. At worst, clustered development can lay waste the immediately adjacent agricultural land, and land rents collapse (see Figure 8.2).

The electrification of agricultural production through the expansion of private well-irrigation has mined water tables irreversibly. It has led to the out-migration of producers who lack the capital or credit to deepen wells, and to the reversion of wet agriculture to dry or water-sparing perennial crops throughout wide tracts of peninsular India. The addition of clustered industrial activity increases the competition for the water table with the following general consequences for water. (The details are taken from a study of the town of Hosur, population 35 000, with a state-planned industrial estate, in the Tamil hinterland of Bangalore, but they are widely relevant.)[55] Water competition results in the seasonal drying of hand pumps and shallow wells, followed by the decline of the water table – by 10 to 30 metres within a decade. It causes crowding-out and pollution (by salination in this case),[56] first of domestic wells and then of agricultural wells. Well-water is substituted by state-organised long-distance piped water supplies, or water transported by tanker. (Such supplies are rationed and paradoxically they add to the reproductive burden of women. In households with access to piped water, women's work burdens should be reduced, but they have to be in attendance throughout the periods of anticipated water supply, or when tanker-borne water is expected.) In addition, lowered water tables provoke the State into installing subsidised deep bores for industry. Last but not least, competition for water leads to an increase in the multiple use and the pollution of surface supplies. These are often the only water sources available for those excluded from rationing. Tanks (open reservoirs) are used for irrigation, toilet, clothes-washing, the cleaning of buses, lorries and agricultural vehicles, and the drinking and cooling of animals. They become dirty, unhealthy places. These kinds of negative externalities imply further social and economic differentiation.

The mercantile castes and quiddity

Quiddity is affected by caste in three ways. First, castes, especially (migrant) merchant castes, have been occupationally specialised. Commodities traded by them have symbolic meanings. Traders in rice, for instance, will not trade in onions and garlic, for the latter would be

---

[55] Leestemaker 1992.

[56] Elsewhere subterranean water has been directly polluted by untreated workshop-industrial effluent; for example, chromium from tanneries in the Palar Valley, cotton and silk-dyeing chemicals in Kancheepuram and Tiruppur (Krishnakumar 1999).

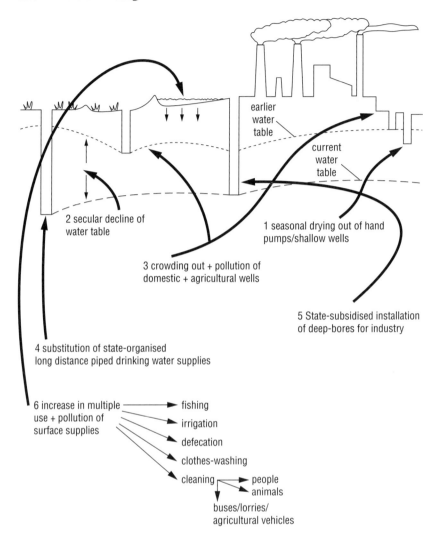

earlier
water
table

current
water
table

2 secular decline of
water table

1 seasonal drying out of hand
pumps/shallow wells

3 crowding out + pollution of
domestic + agricultural wells

5 State-subsidised installation
of deep-bores for industry

4 substitution of state-organised
long distance piped drinking water supplies

6 increase in multiple ──────► fishing
use + pollution of   ──► irrigation
surface supplies
                            defecation

                          clothes-washing

                          cleaning ──► people
                                   ──► animals
                          buses/lorries/
                          agricultural vehicles

Figure 8.2   Rural-urban competition for water

defiling. Mines (1984) depicts the identity and status of the *kaikkoolar* artisan-merchant castes as being strongly bound up with the indispensability of their occupation (weaving and trading in textiles), the second-biggest sector in the Indian economy. The second way caste affects the character of products is through specialisation by sub-caste; in the case of *kaikkoolars* this works through the kind of textile, its style and the type of demand. In the case of the textile trade, different segments of the market are catered for in ways that are now differentiating the caste internally: furnishings in Chennimalai; carpets and rugs in Bhavani; coarse clothing in Salem; silk in Kancheepuram and Arni; *lungis* in North Arcot and Chingelepet; coarse sarees in Tiruchengode; fine sarees in Coimbatore and Madurai; handkerchiefs in Chennai (see Map 8.2) – all with differing rates of return – and specialisation continues.[57] Caste interacts with class and with the process of accumulation in ways that are place-specific. In Tamil Nadu, *nattukottai chettiars* specialise in textiles and engineering; Muslims in leather (in the north); *senguntha mudaliars* in textiles; *nadars* in cotton and jaggery (in the far south); *kamma naidus* in cotton (in the centre); and *brahmins* in corporate industry and commerce (in Chennai). The spatial distribution of castes is both a barrier to entry and the institutional means through which economic growth is localised. Third, the way in which caste is used to structure the labour process is part of the character of an industry, as Chari observes in his study of the highly labour-intensive knitwear cluster. Here the reputation for 'hard work' of the agrarian *vellalar* caste has enabled it to impose a *participant* supervisory control over labour that has led to productivity gains, but also to their developing a near-monopoly.[58]

Mercantile castes and capital viscosity

The regionalisation of caste has been an important factor explaining the local character of capitalist transformation and accumulation. Artisan-merchant castes have long been urban; they have a political and economic arena independent of agrarian castes, based on networks rather than territory; and they have long histories of supra-local organisation; so it is counterintuitive that they do not move their capital over long distances. One would expect the opposite. Yet the capital controlled by merchant castes typically remains deployed over small regions, and linked only where such castes have a supra-local political organisation to connect them. The unusual nature of investments at long distance is due to the localised way in which the collective preconditions for both accumulation and market regulation are organised – which we argued in Chapters 6 and 7 are still often mapped onto caste and religious sect, at least outside metropolitan India.

Marwaris (Jain and Hindu *banias* from Rajasthan) are the exceptions to prove this rule. Their migration from the region of Marwar throughout India – to regions weak in *local* trading castes – began around 1850.

---

[57] Mines 1984, pp. 18–19.
[58] Chari 2000.

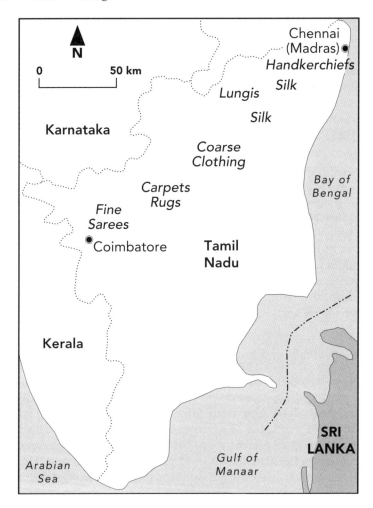

Map 8.2   South India: clusters of *kaikkoolars*

Marwaris migrated in successive currents and in small groups, semi-permanently, cornering trade in a great range of basic commodities, almost all outside their region of origin.[59] In small settlements, *Marwaris* created new sectors – for example, pawnbroking – which were subsequently penetrated by local castes.[60] Where they have graduated from trade to small industry, the labour process has been characterised by putting-out or 'job-work', 'by

[59] Timberg 1978, pp. 86, 93 and 181–228.
[60] Harriss-White 1996a, p. 241.

a combination of capitalist and usurious methods' (Chaudhuri, 1975, p. 117), by the granting of credit on preferential terms to co-religionists and fellow caste members. Yet even this most mobile of caste groups, which provides networks of support for its migrant capital (loan funds and hostels at destinations, joint families at origins) over extremely long distances, operates everywhere only on the scale of the immediate locality.[61]

In general, there are still strong barriers to entry for non-merchant castes, especially if rural–urban (or urban–urban) migration and entry into trade or industrial production are attempted simultaneously. 'The men here do not venture out to other places to start business.' 'People here find closed shops when they try setting up elsewhere.' Where local agrarian or artisan castes have been able to accumulate and invest, one of the most striking features of recent waves of capital formation is the transformation of individuals from agrarian-caste wage workers to small capitalists. This accumulation trajectory involves savings from wage labour, entry into partnerships and the development of job-working firms we described earlier.[62]

The way caste determines capital viscosity has no unambiguous implications for the development of trade. The case of Tiruppur demonstrates that strong trade associations, or caste-cum-trade associations, are able to make profitable arrangements with global capital. But the caste-corporate configuration of other clusters (such as those regulating trade in silk textiles) may be an effective barrier to such collaboration.

The mercantile castes and labour control

In Indian conditions, a shift to the flexible specialisation of the Emilia-Romagna type is generally assumed to be impossible where the castes of merchants/owners are different from those of their workers. This situation is supposed to result only in low-level equilibria based on sweat-shop labour. When both capital and labour come from within the same caste, on the other hand, enthusiasts of the Emilia-Romagna model believe that the balance of power and trust can yield dynamic outcomes.[63] But this is too simple a distinction, and too simple a prediction. The history of the dominant caste may be more useful than the degree of ritual distance between

---

[61] The Weberian thesis that Marwari accumulation is rooted in culture, notably in the congregational nature of Jainism, has been challenged by Timberg who sees two economic institutions as enough to explain their entrepreneurship: (1) resource groups that provided information, accommodation and contacts; and (2) intra-caste credit, radiating from the great firms (Timberg 1978, pp. 32–40, 120 and 175).

[62] Nagaraj et al. 1996; de Neve 2001.

[63] Dupont 1998.

owners and workers for explaining differences in the dynamism and the growth of capital. Two different cases concerning *vellala gounders* – a dominant agricultural caste in Tamul Nadu – are instructive. In Tiruchengode they have invested in lorry-body building and drilling equipment with a labour force of a different caste; in Tiruppur a *vellala* capitalist, making the transition from commercial agriculture to process specialised knitwear, belongs to the same caste as much of his workforce. Both have grown, though the latter more spectacularly. In Tiruchengode, migrant *acari* ('smiths') form the labour force in process-specialised and subcontracted segments of production. About such production, Cadène comments that labour control is a 'reorganisation in an industrial and urban context of links maintained by peasants and cartwrights in the villages' (1998a, p. 153), right down to the performance of rituals celebrating the finished product. Marie-Louise Reiniche, however, studying the same cluster, attaches importance to a *vellalar* culture of 'cunning' work and of 'force', harnessed to caste-specific resource-pooling and to networked access to credit from nationalised banks.[64] Chari also sees effective competition as being due to caste-based cultural conventions about work that are reinterpreted, in industry, into exploitation by mutual engagement and by relational subcontracting. 'The lines between ex-worker, loyal worker, good worker, relative and caste fellow blur in *gounders'* expansive notions of their kin. So do lines of effective control' (Chari 2000, p. 52). The networked form of labour control (which Chari calls a 'peasant' form) enables owners to crush labour militancy and exploit casualised/feminised close-kin employees, just as it enables them to engage in process-specialisation. The simple lack of a difference in caste between labour and capital is clearly not enough to explain dynamism and synergy.

In Pierre Lachaier's study of Sangli in Maharashtra it is possible to discern the impact of caste stratification (among many other things) on the organisation of clusters. The clusters (spices and mechanical engineering) that are controlled by migrant castes are structured through subcontracting and job-working, where risk is transferred to low-caste direct producers. The cluster dominated by 'peasant-warriors' has developed in a more egalitarian way, with state backing through agro-industrial co-operatives. In this territorial concentration of capital, a plurality of accumulation logics is clearly at work.[65]

Even in Peter Knorringa's case study of the famous footwear cluster in Agra (employing 60 000 workers), which the destruction of the mass market in the Soviet Union and its replacement by a national demand for 'premium' products has differentiated into new segments, it is a section

[64] Reiniche 1996.
[65] Lachaier 1997, pp. 105–12.

of second-generation Punjabi trading castes that have accumulated, innovated and co-operated. Those to whom work is subcontracted (*jatavs* and *chamars*), manning the blurred, frontier territory between self-employment and wage work, 'face ever more desperate conditions' (Knorringa 1999, p. 1605).[66] Here, caste tensions between producers and traders and between producers themselves do appear to prevent the shift to flexible specialisation. They keep labour subordinated and poorly paid, casualised and with bad physical working conditions. This case reveals that lack of open conflict is not evidence of 'mutuality' or lack of exploitation in the labour process. It can just as well be evidence of low-cost 'efficiency' based on extremes of labour oppression.

The mercantile castes and competition and accumulation

The freeing-up of the same link between caste and occupation, and the modernisation of some caste-based occupations, have propelled waves of capital formation, spreading out to agricultural castes. Complex, process-specialised production is said to be frequently associated with a high degree of caste complexity. Even though this low-level capital formation may be dispersed among several castes, it cannot escape caste stratification and unequal concentration.[67] Under conditions of caste stratification, trust is not so easy to enforce and co-operation is more difficult. Trade associations, as we saw in Chapter 7, are more often than not reworked caste associations. Few Indian towns have generated the sort of 'active collective efficiency' that gives rise to Emilia-Romagna-style industrial districts, and Schmitz and Nadvi note that 'in the Indian clusters, multilateral co-operation seems to have played little (Agra) or no role (Ludhiana)' (1999, p. 1508). The reason is that the reworked caste associations that are the concrete form of 'multilateral co-operation' in these clusters have altogether different political and economic goals from that of active collective efficiency. They include the control of labour, upward mobility and collective political leverage, among other things.

   In the case studied by Chari, shared caste is still the preferred basis for partnerships, for preferential contracts, for joint access to subsidised credit from nationalised banks and for the capture of the largest trade association. Kinship and caste also play a major (though never an exclusive) role in the shaping of networks, in preferential subcontracting and job-work, as well as in accumulation through partnerships. Partnerships may be a means of accumulation for those with skill but without capital,

---

[66] There are strong parallels with the distributive shares to Muslim owners and SC leather workers in the Palar Valley tanneries in Tamil Nadu (Kennedy 1997, 1999).

[67] Cadène 1998a, pp. 154–64.

but they also fulfil other functions, enabling networks of contacts to fuse, and allowing assets to be concealed from the Revenue Department.[68]

At the extreme, such caste-based arrangements make capital unfungible. Investments do not follow a simple 'logic of comparative profitability'.[69] The migration of capital from rural to urban areas occurs simultaneously with 'contraflows' of capital from urban to rural areas. Urban capital exporters are unable, because of caste differences, to invest in urban sectors that are open to rural migrant capital, and for the same reason rural capital cannot be invested in the rural elements of the non-farm economy.[70]

The implications for efficiency of unfungible local capital aligned with caste depend on the definition of efficiency. Markets that are segmented by caste, and which for this reason prevent the exploitation of economies of scale, cannot be technically efficient in the sense of maximising output from the given inputs of a de-institutionalised production function. Nor can sets of firms in which a great diversity of modes of ownership, labour processes, activity combinations, cost structures and rates of return coexist cheek by jowl, be allocatively efficient in the sense of production taking place at the point where marginal revenue and marginal costs coincide. And allowing for the limitations of such studies, analyses of the price behaviour of the food-system clusters in the north-east and south-east of India do show comparatively poor levels of the kind of integration that is taken to connote competitive efficiency.[71] As regards adaptive efficiency, however – a looser notion of efficiency that refers to the flexibility of the 'norms and institutions' shaping accumulation[72] – the jury is still out. On the one hand, we have seen how caste, like gender, still structures accumulation. The caste-corporatist form of industrial districts makes them dependent on collective action and/or specialised intermediaries to negotiate subcontracting for global capital. On the other hand, caste-based accumulation allows for the entry of same-caste, but small-scale petty commodity producers and traders (even if after entry they are acutely dependent, and even if the barriers to reaching the commanding heights of industrial clusters are high). Meanwhile, business measures are increasingly standardised (weights, volumes and qualities);

[68] Cadène 1998b, p. 395.
[69] Adnan 1985, p. 60.
[70] Harriss-White and Janakarajan 1997. This is the case with flows of investment in rural weaving and urban rice mills in northern Tamil Nadu.
[71] See Palaskas and Harriss-White (1993) for West Bengal and (1996) for Tamil Nadu.
[72] North 1990, pp. 80–2.

telecommunications have released constraints on the quantity and clarity of information; verbal property rights are increasingly clear; labour relations are mostly mediated by cash (the food element in pay to urban wage labour having widely dropped out over the last 15 to 20 years); and credit for production is being slowly wrenched from compulsory repayment in kind to include the freer possibility of cash repayment. Merchant-caste domination has certainly not always limited industrial development.

The role of mercantile castes and the tolerance of negative externalities

Levels of pollution are marked by extreme micro-level inequalities. Caste structures both the creation of pollution and the responses to it. The case of *solid waste* can be used to illustrate this point. Residential and industrial clusters gradually engulf urban open spaces, which can then no longer be used for defecation. Sections of public highways and alleyways in the central business areas become intensively used and the human waste is recycled by pigs and dogs. These places become serious public health hazards. Although the houses of the local elite will have flush latrines, few are connected to septic tanks, so that semi-closed drains hold street waste, untreated sewage plus workshop-industrial effluent.

The physical public domain is thus not recognised as a realm of order or accountability and becomes instead one of dirt and danger. Who copes with it? That such coping is ordered by caste and gender is the stuff of life in India. The honour and status of households is in part expressed in the management of waste. Rubbish marks the boundary between the domestic interior, which is considered the realm of women,[73] and the 'outside', which used to be considered a male realm, though it is now increasingly open to women, too. 'Women invest in their security in their patriarchal households by ensuring clean inside space. However, ensuring clean outside space brings no benefit and falls into the public domain of men' (Beall 1997, p. 228). However, caste males do not handle waste in either realm. In the household this 'service work', considered demeaning, is done by women, though it is the first task to be shed by them, being shifted when possible to paid female domestic waste-workers for 'inside' and male sweepers for 'outside'. Solid waste disposal is done by SC/*dalit* workers employed by local municipalities, who often supplement their

[73] We have noted in Chapters 4 and 5 that 'male' business transactions may take place inside the home, as does the business of government.

relatively low wages with private contracts (and by supplying waste as raw material to recycling firms and waste-pickers).[74]

The response of the State to waste is a case of 'unto everyone that hath shall be given, but from him that hath not shall be taken away, even that which he hath' (Matthew 25: 29). By focusing urban services on wealthy areas the local State reduces the costs of reproduction of local capital and, by depriving working-class areas of waste-disposal services, it adds to theirs. The low status and stigmatisation of sanitary workers invites abuse by officials in the local State (who routinely appropriate their provident funds, delay paying their wages, and so on). This lowers motivation, leads to low-quality work and reinforces incentives for sanitary workers informally to privatise provision – that is, to do it in return for unofficial payments. Privatised informal provision then complements rather than substitutes for state provision. While the residential quarters of the business elite will have both types of provision, those of the poor may have neither.[75]

The state and quiddity

A political consensus exists about commodities essential to India, deemed 'essential commodities' under regulative law (kerosene, food grains and textiles – but there are no less than *60* such commodities altogether)[76] and 'strategic activities' (fertilisers, heavy industry and defence); this consensus legitimates extensive state regulation of them. Other commodities are heavily regulated due to their being of public interest, like liquor, because of its sensitive dual role as both a generous revenue cash cow and a source of public disorder and domestic distress, or like textiles, because of the political sensitivity of the livelihoods dependent on them.[77] The State regulation of essential commodities gives rise to heavily planned and even entirely state-owned industries. These in turn have clustered, often partly 'informalised' networks of

[74] Baud and Schenk 1994.

[75] In Khanpur, sanitary workers have an interest in leaving piles of refuse throughout the town, not only because of the incentives this presents to wealthy households to privatise refuse disposal, but also because the *khatik* sanitary workers have supplementary pig-rearing enterprises, which depend on the waste. The *khatik*'s interests are backed up by those of the *kabadi* caste who recycle waste. Both are able to pressurise the Municipality to maintain extremely low standards of public hygiene (Deponte 2000).

[76] See Mooij 1999.

[77] State regulation may cover the alignment of products with technologies, the terms and conditions of inputs subsidies and output prices, the rules of capitalisation and competition from state-subsidised co-operatives for production and marketing (Mines 1984; Nagaraj et al. 1996).

components suppliers (for example, components for the defence industries) and agents working on contract (for example, food grains).

State *demand* for some commodities and services has also stimulated, reinforced and 'modernised' skills that have later been used in some industrial clusters, especially the skills of the artisanal castes/class of rural blacksmiths and carpenters. The colonial State's demand for infrastructure, repairs to rolling stock, cutlery and fine metal work, for example, enabled castes of smiths to graduate from making agricultural implements to the metal-working that is at the heart of Ludhiana's bicycle, hosiery and textiles machine parts cluster in Punjab.[78] The evidence on religion in Chapter 6, on the other hand, shows that there are still many commodities and services from which state regulation has not succeeded in stripping religious meanings, so that they still cannot be produced by just anyone, anywhere.

The local state and capital viscosity

No general statement can cover all the crucial roles played by the State in shaping the geography of accumulation. As it falls to the nationalised banks to move capital around, typically siphoning deposits from less-developed to more developed agrarian regions, from rural areas to urban ones and from towns to metropolitan capitals,[79] one might expect the State to be a major force making clustered capital less 'viscous'. But the State also encourages development that has opposite effects. The characteristics of clustered development are rippling into the rural hinterlands of the towns as capital moves out in order to evade state surveillance, especially taxation and labour laws (as well as being attracted by lower rents and cheap labour). And there can be no doubt that, despite the Planning Commission's rhetoric of balanced regional development, the State's net redistributive role has been differentiating rather than equalising, so that resources do not flow freely from advanced to less-advanced regions.[80] Even so the State has been instrumental through planning in enabling the national market to form. The viscosity of local capital can be thinned. The local arm of the upper levels of the State so far plays an equivocal role in this respect, rather than the unequivocal and central role that is needed.

---

[78] Tewari 1998, pp. 251–8.
[79] Harriss, B. 1988.
[80] Meher 1999.

The local State and labour control

The effectiveness of the labour laws declines rapidly as one moves outwards from the metropolitan cities. In smaller places the State subsidises small capital by supplying wage goods at prices lower than those of the market through the Public Distribution System (operated by the Food Corporation of India, and the central and state-trading and storage corporations, with the biggest subsidy in all Asia), and Fair Price Shop retail outlets. In a few States this is supplemented by a skeletal social security system for claimants below the poverty line and without family support, which reduces the need for private capital to pay living wages or make social security provision.[81]

The local State and competition

Politicians and officials are strategically placed by their caste networks to jockey for positions controlling taxation, public investments and the police – so as to be able to 'negotiate' with or circumvent the state, to defend private accumulation from regulative threats and actively to advance private accumulation by preferential allocations (or 'seizures of rights' (Khan 1996) or 'rents' (Khan 2000a)). The allocations most important to clusters are clearly land titles (and land-use status, in cases where planning law can be implemented) and rights of access to infrastructure such as roads and electricity.[82]

The 'developmental' State also defines categories of industry eligible for subsidies and protection. These may take many forms. Sites with infrastructure, loans for investment and working capital, and state marketing institutions are those most commonly made available to small-scale industry. The nationalised banks are not allowed to lend on concessional terms for storage or trade. But Pieter Gorter has shown how subsidies and rent-seeking can be meshed together, not only in the kinds of ways modelled by public choice theory (in which venal officials privatise public resources and sell them for bribes), but also within the institutions of collective action in 'civil society', in which there may be antagonistic components.[83] Preferential subsidies may be collectively sought from the bureaucracy, while power is also sought in order to protect helpful and effective individual bureaucrats from predatory forces elsewhere within the State.

---

[81] See Mooij (1999) and Swaminathan (2000) on the PDS; and Guhan (1994) and Harriss-White (1999a) on Social Security. Most of the rest of the raft of promotional social security or anti-poverty policy is rural; see Harriss, Guhan and Cassen (1992).

[82] Cadène 1998b, p. 399; Baviskar 1998.

[83] Gorter 1998, p. 359.

The provision of state-directed credit has helped accelerate the velocity of working capital. In the case of Tiruppur it had to await political decisions on rules allowing for third-party security, receipts as collateral and advanced credit.[84] Even so, regulation frequently has unintended consequences and in this instance, 'front' companies were being created to disguise ownership, and ineligible forms or modes of operation. With so many loopholes, the real intentions of the law-makers must be open to doubt.

The local State and negative externalities

The State's capacity to regulate pollution declines steeply as one moves out of the largest cities, where pollution is anyway most visible. The State may even be more heavily implicated in the creation of negative externalities than in their solution. The case of the apparently unintended outcomes for *water* of the Palar Valley leather cluster is very instructive. A policy to increase domestic value-added by means of the progressive banning of international exports of raw hides (in the 1970s) and of semi-finished leather (after 1988) was reinforced by state credit, state-financed research and export promotion services, and the endorsement of a switch to an upgraded tanning processing technology using chromium and 176 other chemicals. In the course of this transition a complete disregard for anything other than private profit, and the inadequate and negligent enforcement of effluent standards by the Tamil Nadu Pollution Control Board, has led to an estimated 14 000 hectares of agricultural land being contaminated to the point of being unfit for agricultural use; to drinking water being denied to hundreds of thousands of rural people; and to an increase in environmentally caused diseases in the region, especially apparent among the rural poor. While the 600 tanneries have responded to the 1995 Supreme Court Order banning the emission of untreated effluent by building collectively owned treatment plants, the State has yet even to identify a site for the disposal of the toxic sludge treated by these plants, let alone to organise compensation.[85]

In sum

To interpret the famous patchiness and specialisation of economic activity characteristic of India as a trend towards a model of 'industrial districts' is unconvincing. Both the specificity and the synergy of the varied

---

[84] Chari 2000, chapter 6.
[85] Kennedy 1997, 1999; Krishnakumar 1999; Kjellberg and Banik 2000.

pathways to local-level accumulation, and the clustered concentration of non-agrarian capital, still depend to a significant extent on the mediating capacity of the local agrarian structure and the distribution of castes. The State, the only institution that might thin the viscosity of local capital, has operated in the main to thicken it. It has complemented the differentiating logic of market exchange rather than substituted for it.[86]

[86] To substantiate this requires research comparing the costs and benefits of the Public Distribution System, Social Security, all Anti-Poverty Policy, Primary Health and Reservations policies with the costs and benefits of incentives to agriculture and industry, and the benefits of tax evaded. To my knowledge this class and sector analysis has not been done.

9   How India works

The economy analysed in this book is not the entire Indian economy, but the non-corporate one in which 88 per cent of Indians live and work. To analyse how social structures of accumulation govern the economy experienced by the remaining 12 per cent who live in metropolitan India, where corporate capital is concentrated, is another urgently needed task. Of course, the two Indias are one and inseparable. Metropolitan cities teem with informalised labour and firms, and with socially regulated markets. Products of the corporate sector (biscuits, soap, cosmetics and drugs) reach the smallest rural periodic marketplaces. However, the weight of the economy of the rural and small-town workforce and the intermediate classes, that we have described here with evidence drawn for the most part from field economics and economic anthropology, has its own significance for the whole edifice.

In analysing the economy as a set of social structures of accumulation we have departed in three ways from the usual focus of the scholars who developed this concept. First, unlike them, we have used it statically, as a way of imposing an analytically useful order on the immense complexity of the Indian economy, rather than with a view to developing any thesis about its historical evolution through eras or stages. Second, whereas most scholars of social structures of accumulation focus on legal-institutional structures belonging to the State, or established by it, the structures of accumulation we have been concerned with lie predominantly outside the State. While our list of such structures might be extended,[1] it does cover what seem to be the most important of them. What their study shows without shadow of doubt is that in India they influence the operation of legal-institutional, state structures as well as the market. Third, while it is possible to discuss each individual element of the state structures regulating an economy, the non-state social structures of accumu-

---

[1] For instance, the intriguing relations of languages to the Indian economy – as media of economic activity and as markers of regional, political and even class identity – have not been developed here.

lation are not at all easy to isolate. Considering each without the rest runs the risk of making an essentialist caricature of them. Considering all together confuses and conflates different kinds of power and agency. The approach offered here uses examples, works historically and treats each social structure of accumulation both in itself and in relation to others. The result is a set of '*essais*': different kinds of exploration of the social regulation of the Indian economy and of the impact on the economy of forms of power which also operate outside the economy.

So much for the scope and limitations of this project. The questions asked and the answers yielded by the evidence appear to justify a cautious degree of generalisation. In spite of India's regional diversity – and regional geographies of accumulation are also urgently needed[2] – the evidence reviewed here suggests an underlying consistency in the social structures of accumulation nation-wide. Similarly, in spite of the fact that recent years have witnessed dramatic policy changes, and have been seen by many scholars as a period of political flux, with structural fault lines beginning to gape, our evidence suggests more continuity with the past than radical change.

What are the main elements of this continuity and what is their significance? Let us first summarise our main findings about the social structures of accumulation in the India of the 88 per cent and then try to use what we have learned about the recent past to look – however speculatively – into the future.

India's social structures of accumulation

India is very far from having the preconditions for the kind of technical policy agendas that litter textbooks on development, on structural adjustment and liberalisation, and that typically presuppose a single rationality governing the operation of the economy. The evidence we have reviewed makes it clear that economic rationality is only one of several social rationalities at work in the economy. Accumulation is not only organised through labour, capital and the State, but also through gender, religion and caste. All these are mapped on to space.

The vast majority of the Indian *workforce* has no formal contracts with employers, as most workers still do even now in Western economies. The livelihoods of the vast majority come from (casual) wage labour and self-employment – dispersed and fragmented petty production and trade. Only about 3 per cent of the workforce are unionised and even this

[2] For inspiration for such a project, see Raj (1976), Bharadwaj (1995), Thorner (1995) and Baru (2000).

degree of labour organisation has long been under attack from corporate capital. The great majority of workers are hardly regulated by the State for they lack enforceable rights at work and, in most cases, rights to social security. This does not mean that labour is not regulated. It is regulated through the social structures of gender, religion and caste, and of local markets. Labour is also controlled through the supply of infrastructure, in public spaces and in domestic life, as well as at work. The State actively regulates the reproduction of labour (that is, the lives of labouring families outside their work, through their (lack of) housing, water supply, education and their use of space and leisure) perhaps more comprehensively than it regulates their work.

Outside India's metropolitan cities the economy is dominated by the *intermediate classes*, a loose coalition of the small-scale capitalist class, agrarian and local agribusiness elites, and local state officials. They control the supply and the prices of basic wage goods on which labour depends. While they often align themselves politically with corporate capital their interests are different. The intermediate classes directly appropriate the returns to rents of all kinds and are able to control the availability of basic goods. They are able to do this through oligopolistic collusion in markets and through structures of regulation that remain hardly touched by liberalisation.[3] They connive with local officials to secure the protection of rents they create in markets and of the state resources they capture. They seek state subsidies, but more importantly they secure beneficial concessions by influencing policy in its implementation rather than its formulation. Their evasion of tax is the equivalent of a major subsidy to mercantile accumulation while depriving the State of capacity and legitimacy.

So far the intermediate classes have survived the acute threats posed by the expansion of corporate capital and by policies of economic liberalisation. Much of the state-regulative structure, on the sabotage of which they thrive, remains intact. Meanwhile, the process of accumulation has acquired a renewed unruliness. A new wave of accumulation has been occurring among lower agrarian castes and has diffused through rural and small-town India. A sharp struggle over surplus is under way since the rate of agricultural growth has been mediocre, resulting in a considerable amount of disorder in the intermediate classes' relations with consumers, labour and the State. The accumulation of these classes can take 'primitive' forms, but these persist and coexist with advanced

---

[3] See Chapter 4 footnote 50 for the political manipulation of food policy so as to ensure high returns for the producers of marketed surplus, particularly in the north-west of India, and the accumulation of grossly excessive buffer stocks, both of which deliberately coexist with chronic malnutrition in central and eastern States.

forms of capital rather than being superseded by them. This 'primitive accumulation' persists partly because the Indian State leaves a significant space for it. But informal economic regulation and the widespread development of private protection forces for property and persons have now reached the point where they challenge the State's monopoly of coercion, at least where the protection of property is concerned.

The Indian *State* is a large-scale economic actor, providing infrastructure and organising finance, production and trade. However, much of the economy is beyond its direct control, either because its units (small firms) are under the size threshold for regulation, or because the State neglects to regulate it (or is actively prevented from regulating it in the ways discussed above). Just as the informalised markets in which intermediate classes operate create their own institutions to regulate and protect them – their 'informal State' – so the State by its interventions creates many informal markets.

At the same time the State is shaped by non-state social structures of accumulation as much as it shapes them. It is the ambivalent agent of gender empowerment – a more progressive employer than private enterprise, an initiator of development projects to empower women, and an enactor of reforms to expand female representation and political participation. At the same time, by making it very difficult for women to qualify for licences and development credit, the State effectively reinforces male rights to property. It does little to counter a prevailing anti-female bias in education and has not proved able or willing to resist the alarming deterioration in the relative status of girls. It is also a distinctly ambivalent agent of secularisation in the economy. Its constitutional obligation to keep equi-distant from all religions is formally observed, but personal and family laws, divinely authorised under several religions, decisively affect the governance of property. The same policy of religious 'equi-distance' reinforces the tendency for the economy to become an arena for competition between religious groups. Acts of Hindu religious observance have long been incorporated into state office routines and state development expenditure is being channelled through NGOs and trusts that are 'fronts' for religious organisations. Through the policy of job reservations the State is the important yet flawed champion of the social and economic emancipation of oppressed castes and tribes, yet the loan conditions imposed by international lending institutions have called for the State to downsize employment. As a result, competition between castes has been reinforced, and an informal system of job reservations has been developed through patronage practised by all castes. The State seems to have become less and less able to regulate, redistribute or subsidise accumulation at a distance from capital cities. At the local level it is deeply permeated by private status (its effective capacity depending on the mix of social identities of the officials), as well as by private interest (officials using their powers of discretion both to extract rents for themselves and to protect the rents of others). A 'shadow' State is created – a penumbra of people living from intermediation and corruption, with a strong interest in its perpetuation.

With or without further state intervention, *gender relations* seem bound to continue to constitute a pervasively important structure of accumulation in India. The intermediate economy is for the most part a matter of family businesses, which are both the prime sites for the oppressive control of workers (of whom the most oppressed and exploited are women) and also structures of hierarchical authority between men – patriarchy in its oldest sense. As firms grow in size, the demand for male family labour increases, but as fertility declines the number of male agnates decreases. Yet instead of drawing women family members into these firms, local elite women tend to be deprived of productive work. Increasingly, and even in regions of India where the kinship system used not to involve dowry, marriage alliances between business families require large transfers in consumer durables as well as gold, and these are vested in the groom's family instead of remaining the property of the bride. A number of consequences for both the efficiency of the economy and the welfare of women follow. To keep strong family control over young male property owners, they are often educated only to the level compatible with living at home. The edge of competitive innovation and technical change is thereby blunted and rates of accumulation are kept high.

The rapidly deteriorating and low life chances for females in the families of business elites must be accounted for by a culture of male supremacy. For though gender bias can be explained by low relative female status arising from lack of earned income, the costs of dowry and the demand for male family labour in firms, these business families are relatively wealthy and not bound by material constraints.

Religions – and India has a notable plurality of them – supply collective identities that in turn provide indispensable preconditions for capital accumulation. In India religious affiliation can be found to govern the creation and protection of rent, the acquisition of skills and contacts, the rationing of finance, the establishment and defence of collective reputation, the circulation of information, the norms that regulate the inheritance and management of property, and those that prescribe the subordination of women. In addition, religious groups are often found regulating and distributing livelihoods, providing insurance and last-resort social security. The distinction between the private and the public sphere is blurred and forms of non-economic and divine authority may still be found to govern economic behaviour.

The most potent and visible of these forms is *caste*. In south India (which we think does not differ much from most other regions in this respect) case studies show that the local economy is increasingly organised in corporatist forms based directly or indirectly on caste. Although occupations, types of commodity, party politics, religion, philanthropy and redistributive obligations all play a part in the way the local economy is organised and regulated, by far the most significant structures are caste-cum-trade associations. While some are intermittent and called into life only when the trade is threatened, many are playing an increasing role in regulation: in the definition of proper contracts, the settlement of disputes, collective insurance, collective representation to the State, the creation of rents and the way they are shared with state officials and politicians, the control of labour and the control of prices. Reinforcing caste, patriarchy and the rhetoric of town unity, caste ideology works to support the economic interests of the intermediate classes.[4]

All these determinant structures of accumulation are mapped on to distinctive patterns of economic *space*. Capital is accumulated in towns and cities, yet India is weakly urbanised and its urbanisation displays a distinctive pattern of economic clusters. Their character varies according to local structures of property ownership and agrarian accumulation, and according to the varying roles played in each cluster by merchant castes and the State. The spatial distributions of these three social structures of accumulation strongly influence the kinds of commodities produced in a given area. They keep accumulation highly localised, shape the way labour is controlled, limit competition and perpetuate the toleration of vast negative environmental externalities.

Real structural adjustment

In the understanding of international development agencies, structural adjustment and liberalisation consist of rafts of policies to remove distortions caused by protection and by domestic subsidies, in effect to adjust the domestic price structure to that of the world market and so to let the structure of production reorganise itself. The results of planned development and those produced by market forces differ, as the politically determined locations of steel plants and heavy industry in India clearly show. It follows that liberalisation ought to generate spatial dislocations by replacing non-market allocations by those of markets. Indeed, this is pre-

---

[4] And in exactly the manner Gramsci (1971) thought to be the essence of civil society.

dicted, unintentionally, by the advocates of liberalisation, who maintain that liberalisation is capable of *reversing* regional differentiation, which has been in part the unintended consequence of the Indian Finance and Planning Commission's bureaucratic controls over production, investment and trade. If markets respond with allocative efficiency to relative factor scarcities, if regions with lower capital–labour ratios have a higher marginal productivity of capital and therefore offer higher rates of return to capital, then regional disparities ought to be reversed by deregulation and replaced by regional convergence. However, what this book suggests is that the reverse is what is likely to occur: an accentuation not only of regional disparities but also of disparities within regions.[5]

The adjustment of structures of prices and production is also accompanied by adjustments in social structures of accumulation, and in ideas and practices of accountability. We have seen that if Indian capitalism is a *social solvent*, it works sluggishly (to say the least) at the local level that has been our focus. In fact if anything the reverse seems true: because capital accumulation relies on social structures of accumulation, the effect of liberalisation is not to abolish or transform those in which markets are embedded, but to encourage them to rework themselves as economic institutions and to persist. In the era of liberalisation and globalisation, the structural adjustment that is taking place is not only the replacement of state-planned development, and 'custom', by market and contract. It is also the intensification of the tensions between markets and the 'non-market' institutions without which markets cannot operate. *Gender* relations are the most resistant to change, and operate to advantage men quite disproportionately to women in the class that accumulates; there is no reason to see liberalisation as transforming for them. *Caste* and *religion* are much more flexible, but are emerging as structures that may generate exclusive, networked forms of accumulation and corporatist forms of economic regulation, and that tend to operate to control labour to the advantage of capital. It is a separate point that liberalisation has been quite strikingly associated with an upsurge in religiosity, rather than the reverse. In fact, Hindutva may be seen as an attempt to carve a moral space for Hindu accumulation at the expense of other religions.

The *state* structures aimed at promoting livelihoods for, and the upward mobility of, lower castes are completely at loggerheads with the aims of liberalisation, but their abolition is not an option. Meanwhile, the State is so riddled with fraud and corruption that an enormous shadow has built up around it which depends on the state and feeds off it. Long

---

[5] For the case, see Bhagwati (1993); for data on regional inequality, see Mohan and Thottan (1992) and Meher (1999).

ago Myrdal (1968, p. 66) called this a 'soft' State; if anything it has become softer – Weber's 'steel cage' has rusted – while the social structures around it have hardened. It looks less, rather than more, like the instrument of market rationality that the advocates of liberalisation envisage. State capacity has become increasingly dependent on the private social identities of the personnel who happen to occupy positions in the local State. Reforms using the formal legal infrastructure face three contradictions. First, while development requires the rule of law, in India law is often unimportant – since much of the economy is not regulated by law and since locally influential and respectable people appear frequently to be convinced that they are entitled to be above the law.[6] Law is at best compromised by a mass of unintended and unforeseen consequences; at worst it is a mere base for extortion, formally counterproductive but informally very productive – for legislators and bureaucrats. Second, any attempt to 'downsize' or even shed inappropriate laws means a capitulation to those already breaking them, which delegitimises the State. Third, attempts to shed laws that are inappropriate because they are impossible to implement result in looser laws that are easily abused.[7] And what is true for the law is likely to be true more widely for the institutions that implement the law.

The *intermediate classes* remain potent players. The capacity to accumulate has now spread from castes and classes that have hitherto resisted paying tax to lower agrarian castes, which have never before been required to pay them – at least not directly. A new wave of small capital, based on primary accumulation, is reinforcing and expanding the informal and black economy, intensifying the casualisation of labour and transferring the risks of unstable livelihoods to the workforce. The informal economy accounts for two-thirds of GDP; at least half of the informal economy is 'black'. Finally, accumulation is increasingly specialised and *spatially* clustered and is driving regional as well as social differentiation.

'Policy' is then best understood as the outcome of the way political resources have been deployed in the struggles for rents that take place at all stages – discursive, procedural and allocative – of the so-called 'policy-making process'. Liberalisation will not destroy these rents but will intensify the struggle for them.

The other kind of unorthodox structural adjustment, and one long preceding that of the World Bank and the IMF, is that caused by under-funding the State. The leaching of taxable resources to the rapidly expanding

---

[6] Of course, this practice is by no means confined to India; see Joly (2001) on this phenomenon in France.

[7] McBarnet and Whelan 1991.

black economy deprives the State of resources. The State responds by protecting salaries at the expense of equipment and investment. Unavoidable freezes on recruitment play havoc with lines of reporting accountability, with enforcement capacity, the time taken to achieve objectives, and the quality of goods and services. Low-quality provision encourages informal private or black alternatives. The loss of legitimacy resulting from this kind of structural adjustment is self-reinforcing.

Students of development are often invited to evaluate whether what exists is 'inefficient'. Such an exercise implies that some alternative set of social structures of accumulation is imaginable with which those that actually exist might be compared. Nothing in the relationships and trends we can currently observe seems to suggest that this is at all possible. India's social structures of accumulation are deeply entrenched.

The relations between the formal State, the formal economy, the 'shadow' State and the informal economy are the outcomes of political struggles. Unless and until there is a strong public mandate for tax compliance and against corruption – both of which are essential first steps towards accountability, and have been invoked as 'solutions' for decades[8] – the prospects for the intermediate classes still look good. Fraud and tax evasion are part and parcel of Indian capitalism. For non-compliance to be so widespread, people's moral world – their units of accountability – must be immediate or restricted. The bulk of the economy is beyond the direct control of the State, and the State's convection system of taxation and distribution takes place shorn of civic egalitarianism. Countering this literally anti-social economy calls for the emergence of a more robust and active culture of collective accountability in which the legitimacy of the State would also need to be renegotiated. If a point of leverage for change exists at all, it lies in mechanisms that might make capital more accountable to the State, and the State to other parts of civil society. These are urgent questions that are *prior* to exercises of technical choice, prior to the listing and evaluation of policy options and sequences that are the stock-in-trade of development policy. These questions are at a considerable distance from the World Bank's adoption of, at best, a narrowly electoral and formal concept of democracy, together with the abstract and unreal conceptions of economy and polity that currently prevail in mainstream economics and in much of the other social sciences. Development policy needs rethinking as that set of political and institutional forces required to prevail against the *obstacles* to a democratically determined accountability.

[8] See Myrdal (1973), for instance.

10   Postscript: proto-fascist politics and the economy

My book could easily have ended at this point, but over the period it has been written, variations on the term 'fascist' have been used in the media and by scholars in order to describe not only the increasingly active and violent communalist movements of the Sangh Parivar but also the regime ruling India at the turn of the millennium. Fascism is a kind of politics distinguished by ideology, although it draws on no single or coherent philosophy. Full-blooded fascist States have been ones espousing authoritarianism, militarism, a majoritarian kind of nationalism, racism, statolatry, elitism and the ruthless suppression of labour. Out of crises, they have developed institutions that contrive to unify apparently antagonistic class interests in the name of 'the nation'. Analysts of fascist States have emphasised the primacy of politics. They also point to the considerable variety of political and ideological forms this politics has taken. Yet, while they also argue that there is no model economic base,[1] comparative historical studies of the economies of fascist States in Europe and Latin America have shown there to be economic conditions and institutions that are necessary to give fascism state power – even if they are not by themselves sufficient for fascism to develop.[2] Although it takes me outside the original project, outside the Indian economy and outside my conclusions, my last task needs to be to ask how the proto-fascist tendencies in India's politics and culture relate to the larger part of India's economic base, which is socially rather than state-regulated.[3] It seems that there are two ways to go about answering this question. They involve applying the book's findings about social structures of accumulation to examine India, with respect first to the common elements of fascist political ideology and

---

[1] See the discussion on the fascist movements in Carsten (1967) and the comparison of European and Latin American economies under fascism in Loucks and Hoot (1948, pp. 627–720).

[2] Loucks and Hoot 1948.

[3] This is a different task from that of characterising Indian fascism. The latter task is one with which the research in this book does not qualify me to engage.

second to theories of its class origins. While Aijaz Ahmad's warning that '(i)t is dangerous to seek parallels or apply ideas of another context' is well heeded, the fasces themselves were emblems from another context, that of ancient Rome. If we are to build a more precise understanding of the relations between the intermediate economy and Indian fascist politics, it is useful to reflect on the 'resonances' of the experiences of fascist States.[4] This preliminary exercise points to a compelling activist research agenda in political economy.

Key elements of fascism

None of the elements of fascism lined up in this section are *inventions* of fascism, but fascist states have tended to practise all of these elements.

Authoritarianism

A fascist regime has to walk the tightrope between the creation of a radical project that has a popular endorsement and the consolidation of an authority that is anti-democratic. It can do this by making it impossible for labour to exist as a political force outside a single party welded to a militaristic State. Wars can expel soldiers into peacetime militias when the economy does not absorb their labour. Preparation for war helps to create employment. 'Aggressive war is the only logical conclusion.' [5]

Although military spending has increased very markedly (and there are dangerously aggressive relations between India and Pakistan), although the development agenda has been seriously encroached on by a security agenda,[6] and although labour is comprehensively socially controlled, the evidence does not yet permit the conclusion that India has a politically dominant military-industrial complex. It is also moving in the opposite direction from domination by a single consolidated party – at least at the level of formal politics. The multiple forms of non-state authority through which labour is controlled are also ways labour gains identity and contests its own control. They are the very opposite of a unified and consolidated social project. They currently deprive labour of rights rather than offering rights to labour as a *quid pro quo* for compliance. Without mass participation in politics, labour cannot be mobilised for (or incorporated in a non-military way into) the fascist project.

---

[4] Ahmad 1996b, p. 226.
[5] Loucks and Hoot 1948, p. 715.
[6] Dreze 2000.

Nationalism, racism and xenophobia

A fascist regime is able to construe, through a selective reading of history and myth, a nation with a unique integrity – be it racial or religious – and with a glorious past. 'Others' are defined who are then persecuted.

It is certain that the education system is being used to construct such a myth. The curriculum is being reformed to this effect, particularly in history, and scholarly material is censored, institutions of educational governance are being packed with proto-fascist sympathisers, formal curbs are attempted to be placed on intellectual exchanges with foreigners, and the state-owned media encouraged to support this project of myth-making. Religious minorities, particularly Muslims and Christians, are being persecuted as never before, the output of critical scholars is being censored and their public engagement thwarted, and radical and revolutionary politics are suppressed with renewed ruthlessness. The emancipating agendas of new social movements are also being appropriated for the purpose of myth fortification, particularly in the fields of women's roles and rights, and of the environment.

However, a myth based on the slogan 'Hindi, Hindu, Hindustan' privileging male, upper caste, Vaishnavite north Indians excludes more than it includes. Communalism *per se* is not fascism and communalism can be manipulated for a variety of ends, including contradictory ones.[7] India's is a society able to expose and contest such activity, of late notably through the Supreme Court, the National Commission on Human Rights, the activist media and many incidents of resistance, even though such freedom has not prevented the escalation of communal violence. The privatisation and international ownership of some of the media does contradictory things for the process of myth-making. It presents the myths, it also presents symbols and images that intensify aspirations and shape them to corporate requirements, it dilutes political content and acts as a distraction. But the Indian media and the scholarly academy retain the capacity to be a sharp and independent critical tool.

By virtue of this essential and xenophobic nationalism, and because the purity of fascist States is threatened at their boundaries, the economic base of fascist regimes has been nationalist and protectionist. In extreme circumstances it has been geared towards self-sufficiency.

India's project of economic nationalism, *Swadeshi*, exists as a concept, but it has never been convincingly theorised in economic terms and it is not a coherent practical project of either intermediate or corporate capital.[8] The corporate sector even lacks unity over basic issues such as

---

[7] For example, simultaneously to advance the interests of Hindu business and finance capital; yet also to limit them within the confines of *Swadeshi* (see Appendix 1).

[8] Hansen 1997, 1998. The rather different RSS concept of 'modernisation without westernisation' has also not been clearly developed.

corporate governance.[9] While finance capital is still strongly nationally regulated – and organised labour is still a major stumbling block to the dismantling and privatisation of state financial institutions – the Indian economy is being slowly integrated into the global economy. Without doubt, it is becoming less, not more, self-sufficient.

Statolatry

Fascist States have actively regulated production, trade, infrastructure and the mass standard of living. Unemployment is reduced, as is the real wage, by the heavy control of private property and state direction of the capitalist economy. In fascist States the tension between the protection and promotion of private property, and the socialisation of property in the mass national interest, is managed through state corporatist regulation.

The Indian State, while still controlling certain leading sectors, is unable directly to regulate the larger part of the economy. Such is the segmentation of labour markets that unemployment is rising, but so too is the real wage.

There are two views on the seeds of fascism that are both relevant to India. One is that it emerges from a weak State that has been unable to contain the contradictions of capitalist accumulation.[10] The other is it is not the State that is weak, it is rather that big business is unable to assert its interests through the State, and it has to find novel ways of altering the State to co-opt other social and economic interests.[11]

On the first view, the Indian State has been shown to be weak, except, importantly, with respect to certain public-sector industries together with the means of repression – although even there it faces challenges to its capacity to protect property. It is quite unable to force private business of all sorts to serve the national interest, to make capital auxiliary to politics. Rather, the State is under siege from corporate interests at the centre, but it seems to be surviving a marital crisis with the intermediate classes elsewhere. The dispersed nature of intermediate capital (particularly of its control of key sectors such as the food grains economy) and the decentralised accommodations it makes with the State make intermediate capital a serious obstacle to the expansion of corporate capital. It is true that the State has not well contained the contradictions of capitalist

---

[9] Banaji and Mody 2001.

[10] In Germany, the major contradictions were a rapid build-up of capital, combined with a failure to integrate the economy, and between state-regulated monopoly capital and non-monopoly capital that acted as an obstacle. In Italy, the major contradiction concerned the interests of industrial capital in the north and landlord rule in the *mezzogiorno* (Laclau 1977/1982).

[11] Laclau 1982.

accumulation. Non-state social structures do this. The State is on track to be weakened further, not potentiated to take a comprehensive regulative role. On the second view, all forms of capital have long asserted themselves through forms of regulative politics involving the placing of leverage on the State at the point of *action*. But Indian 'monopoly capital' will not be able to assert a general hegemony unless and until it can incorporate or subjugate the intermediate classes.

Where should the search begin for novel ways in which antagonistic class forces might be incorporated? In Chapters 6 and 7 we saw that India's informal economy – in which nearly 70 per cent of total income is generated – has a distinctive structure of accumulation tessellated by corporatist regulative organisations that owe their origins to the idioms of caste and of groups based on religion. These limit the mobility of capital, but also permit the lowering of transaction costs and define social relations policed by trust and non-economic authority. In so doing they define economic 'others' who may be exploitable by primitive means. They are also means to control and pacify labour. However, while corporatist regulation may be a necessary condition for fascism, it is not a sufficient one. The Indian State is not an active shaper of these organisations, but instead a passive condoner, complicit by default rather than by design. Although some of these organisations manage collective bribery, by and large these organisations have not put pressure on the State by means of party political funding. Where individual local capitalists fund party politics, which is uncommon, this funding tends to be opportunistic, defensive and across the political board.[12] Corporatist regulation is distinctive and on a rapid expansion path, but it is not novel. It is also far from being a means of regulating private property in which all individual, class and corporate interests could be subordinated to that of the nation.

Ideology and leadership

A fascist State develops a unifying ideology to which the other social ties locating the individual can be subordinated. It does this through the instrument of a charismatic leader, capable of rousing violence against political enemies and of co-opting elites in the administration and army.

Although attempts are being made to develop a unifying Hindu ideology and to co-opt elites by means of this ideology, and although there certainly are a number of local charismatic leaders fully able to rouse violence,[13] there is no single, towering all-Indian Leader. The ideology of Hindutva is actively contested, both in party politics, where other organ-

[12] Harriss-White 1993.
[13] Deshpande 2001.

ising principles such as region and caste have become significant, in market-driven politics at the micro level (where sectoral, regional and factional interests of local capital prevail) and last but not least in the politics of militant organisations.

So, using an analytical approach that admittedly violates the totalising conceptions of fascism by separating them into components, it is indeed concluded that the political groundwork for a fascist State is being actively initiated by fascist movements. However, these manifestations of Indian fascism are not yet well supported by predisposing conditions or institutions in the larger part of the Indian economy that is socially regulated.

The class origins of fascism

Another way to evaluate the prospects of fascist currents in India is to compare class formation with the class origins of fascism elsewhere. From the perspective of the intermediate economy, I will summarise and comment on two attempts to theorise the fascist solution – through ideology and politics – to the problem of unifying antagonistic class forces in order to strengthen the nation.

First, for Poulantsas who theorised European fascism,[14] fascism emerged from conditions of deadlock between dominant class fractions unable to impose leadership through parliamentary democracy or 'their own methods of organisation'. Then a *crisis* was necessary for totalitarian monopoly capital to assert itself, for classes and class-based parties to shatter their links, and for labour to be decisively defeated both in politics and in the economy.

Nothing like this is happening yet in India. Monopoly capital is unable to assert itself directly through a political party openly representing its own interests. With exceptions, most parties have not been class-based. The most profound recent change to big business is that its accommodations with the State, which had previously been made as informal concessions over several decades of apparent political hostility, are now made freely and at long last at the level of discourse. Although the organised working class is seeing a protracted erosion of its rights, and although the informalisation of the economy transforms the arena of labour struggles from the formal politics of unions to the informal politics of social institutions, the vast bulk of the labour force has never been organised enough to be defeated. Indeed, it is still at its strongest where it confronts corporate capital. As for crises, on the one hand Indian development has been continually assailed by them. On the other hand the liquidity crisis of

[14] Poulantsas 1980.

1991 did not affect the real economy; and India weathered the east Asian financial crisis. At the time of writing it has seen no crisis remotely like the Depression, even if the National Democratic Alliance has been at such tremendous pains to depict India as a strong global economic player that it fails to disguise the fact that it is weak, with well under 1 per cent of world trade.

Under fascism, all classes except for 'profiteers, financial gangsters, rapacious capitalists and reactionary landowners'[15] are incorporated. Non-polar, intermediate or 'lower middle' classes, the petty bourgeoisie, artisans, tradesmen and lower grade government employees need to be recruited, because such classes never actively seize power themselves in a period when fascism is being consolidated. For Poulantsas, who fully recognised their numerical and territorial significance even in the European cases, their economic power was in any case not as significant as were the ideologies sustaining them. Yet, he had difficulty separating out a distinctive petit bourgeois ideology. In the end he isolated a 'sub ensemble' dissociated from big business, but believing in upward mobility and relying on the State as its mechanism. These were the elements contributing to the 'lowest common denominator': the ideology capable of unifying the forces in contention under capitalism.

In India, this loose coalition of non-polar classes expresses itself through a distinctive politics of markets (described in Chapter 3), and has significant control over large areas of the economy. Although dominant ideological elements in their regulative activity are derived from caste (and also privilege capital over labour), these classes operate opportunistically with respect to the polar classes.[16] Intermediate classes have conflicts of interest with both polar classes and have yet to be subsumed in a stable way under big business. The unifying idea of *Swadeshi* has increasingly less economic content and clout. Furthermore, significant fractions of this class coalition operate in the black economy and are currently subsumed within the State, if at all, through the nexus of corruption that underpins fraud. Such fractions are precisely those defined by Carsten as economic *enemies* under fascism. So, on two counts, the absence of a lowest common denominator, and the large size and far from marginal nature of the kind of groups which were enemies of fascism in European cases, India's intermediate classes are not likely to be easily incorporable into a fascist state project.

A second theory of the class origins of fascism is that of Laclau,[17] for whom Poulantsas' equation of classes with ideologies is misleadingly

---

[15] Carsten 1967, p. 320.
[16] There is detailed case material in B. Harriss (1981) and Harriss-White (1993; 1996a).
[17] Laclau 1977/1982.

mechanical. The challenge is then to explain how fascist ideology captures the imaginations of workers and intermediate classes sufficiently for them to bury their own sectional economic interests of class or patronage. Laclau suggests that this process works through the 'levels' at which ideology is borne. These 'levels' are what we call social structures of accumulation. For him, *family, kinship* and *politics* are the crucial institutions capable of being transformed ideologically to make a single coherent power bloc.

In contemporary India, we need to search urgently to see whether and how patriarchy and kinship, caste and religion, faction, patronage and clientelage, and new collective institutions of mediation and regulation show signs of developing a cross-class coherence. We saw signs of this in the increasing propensity to cull girl children, though there are still strong class, caste and regional variations in this type of violence. Then, despite the profoundly divisive stigmas of caste in many regions of India, some corporatist regulative institutions have proved themselves capable of recruiting labour and then controlling it through these organisations. However, in no case *to date* where these trade associations or 'business trades unions' have been studied have links of any sort been reported between them and India's fascist organisations. We also detected cross-class mobilisation in the new and rapidly proliferating institutions of town unity, but to date they are of *town* not national unity, and their main functions are currently representative and redistributive, not regulative. Lastly, while the actions of groups in civil society such as the Shiv Sena and the RSS may be backed politically by parties espousing Hindutva and by the local State, for the most part the politics of NGOs and new social movements, as with those of parties of caste and region, remain separate and divisive rather than coherent and unifying.

So the provisional conclusion we made from a disaggregated approach to the study of fascist States can be carried through to this brief analysis of class and social structures of accumulation. In India's intermediate economy there is no sign yet of a big unifying project for capital of the sort necessary to a fascist State. Nonetheless, the seedlings of fascist institutions, ones with distinctively Indian characteristics, can definitely be found sprouting in the economy, as well as in politics. There are therefore solid reasons to keep a very close watch on the evolving relationships between the intermediate economy, its informal institutions of corporatist economic regulation, the national (and global) corporate sectors, the black economy and its politics, the State, and India's other social structures of accumulation.

Appendix 1
Liberalisation and Hindu fundamentalism

The BJP has gained power despite antagonism between its political agenda and the economic interests of its support base. The concentration of BJP support among groups constituting the old intermediate classes has been difficult to avoid noticing: 'Small industrialists and businessmen, traders and employees in the lower ranks of the professions and civil service, i.e. the petty bourgeoisie' (Bose 1997, p. 1118). It is certainly not everywhere (Hansen 1998) and not completely, but it is quite systematically spreading through India's territory.[1] *Hindutva* is the Hindu nationalists' philosophy of politics; it 'is a unifying principle which alone can preserve the unity and integrity of our nation. It is a collective endeavour to protect and re-energise the soul of India, to take us into the next millennium as a strong and prosperous nation.'[2] *Hindutva* has been one of the two ideological responses of this fraction of capital to a pincer movement. One arm of the pincer takes the form of a globalised secularism that has been intensified by liberalisation and new waves of capital in the economy. The other arm is the result of 'the upward thrust of the hitherto underprivileged' in the political domain (Aloysius 1994, p. 1451). *Hindutva* can then be seen as an ideological cover behind which the classes of the era of the intermediate regime are *buckling* under the strains imposed by a globalising capitalist economic structure. *Swadeshi* is the other ideological response.[3] *Swadeshi* is a loosely connected set of ideas espousing economic nationalism with varying degrees of autarchy, of calls to preserve agriculture and small-scale industry and of self-restraint in consumption, all in the service of a higher, Hindu humanist goal. Globalisation (on which the BJP has not taken a stable position) has been encouraged for (and until the deregulation of General Insurance in late 1999 it has been confined to) consumer dura-

---

[1] There is a deconstruction of support for 1995 in Gujarat: for the BJP among the business class it is 56 per cent (Congress 22 per cent) and among upper castes 67 per cent (Congress 20 per cent) (Balagopal 1993, p. 790).

[2] BJP 1996, 'For A Strong and Prosperous India: Election Manifesto 1996', p. 6, in Hansen and Jaffrelot (1998, p. 2).

[3] *Swadeshi* is more a matter of national pride than of economic interest. It originated at the start of the century as a symbolic rejection of British goods, has developed as broadly supportive of national capital and has been absorbed by the BJP from its partners as one of its two contradictory economic strategies. The other is globalisation. *Swadeshi* and globalisation are mutually contradictory economic strategies, but *Swadeshi* is nothing if not discursively flexible, able to be scaled at the level of nation, State, village or even caste and linguistic groups (Hansen 1998, pp. 291–314).

bles and technologies of service to national capital. Coherence in economic policy has not been high on the Hindu fundamentalist agenda, for first it must consolidate the ideology to which the economy must be subservient. 'The individual and society are one and indivisible ... The complete identification of the individual with society is itself a state of complete development for the individual. The individual is the medium and means of the completeness of society.'[4] 'Swadeshi is not a businessman's ideology. It is a view of a political party ... we are not a Chamber of Commerce. Businessmen do not have an ideology', some need imported technology, some need economic protection (Jay Dubashi, Convenor of the Economic Policy Cell, when interviewed by Thomas Blom Hansen, 1996).[5]

At the start of the twenty-first century, it is not at all obvious that the BJP and its coalition wish to prosecute the project of *Swadeshi*. The economic agenda clearly favours liberalisation as the BJP develops the image of a modernising party representing national business interests. All the while, if it is to be electable, the BJP has to look outside the sectors with interests in liberalisation, or *Swadeshi*, to a mass base. This search generates its own contradictions, notable among which are Forward Castes representing backward castes and interests gained from globalisation needing *Swadeshi* as a bait for voters.

---

[4] Deenadayal Upadhyaya (1965) in *Integral Humanism*, influential on the Jana Sangh party, quoted by Hansen (1998, p. 294). In this concise statement some of the key attributes of fundamentalism (seen by Elmer Altvater in his treatise on *The Future of the Market* as a reaction to be found all over the world to alienation and the socialisation deficits of market rationality) are clearly evident: anti-individualism, anti-universalism (while claiming universal validity) and anti-rationality (of a form 'postulating solidarity regardless of nationality') (Altvater 1993, pp. 44–6; see also Amin 2002).

[5] Hansen 1998, p. 305, footnote 33.

Appendix 2
Relations between the developmental State and the intermediate classes[1]

In a study of development discourse, Sudipta Kaviraj argued that policy is transformed in implementation 'beyond all recognition' (1988, p. 2440). This does not mean we cannot recognise patterns in the means and mechanisms by which those denoted as victims in the 'grand discourse' of development have become material beneficiaries and *vice versa*. The process of transformation in implementation is partly generated within the State. It operates at three levels. Within the central State, although the developmental bureaucracy is more shielded from political pressure, there is interdepartmental or ministerial competition over goals and resources. There, the multiplicity of levels of decision-making can check, distort or ignore the implementation of policy. State bureaucracies are more vulnerable to politicisation and state administrations may add to the entropy in policy implementation by 'horizontal' turf wars between departments. Geographical, political and socioeconomic distance also creates entropy (Landy 1998; Banik 1999).

In this appendix we note the transformations that are due to the interaction between the State and society. Unless these transformations are unravelled and exposed, there is no non-Utopian basis upon which to develop reforms. We list them from the perspective of state procedure (1 to 5) and progress to implementation by the State (6 to 14) and then to types of seizure, sabotage and other responses (14 to 19). We have 20 twenty kinds of pattern (of different analytical 'status'), but no doubt there are more.

Procedure

1   Exemption from state control: this is a 'negative' but carefully worked relation: non-policy is policy. It results from associative politics – a civil society that is neither very civil nor very social – and from lobbying at the political

[1] This evidence is drawn from Bharathan 1981; Clay et al. 1988; Copestake 1992; Dasgupta 1992; Dreze and Sharma 1998; Erb and Harriss-White 2002; Galanter 1984; Guhan 1992; Guhan and Paul 1997; Harriss, B. 1984a, 1987, 1991a and 1993; Harriss, J. 1986 and 1989; Harriss-White 1996a; Herring 1983 and 1999; Kumar and Stewart 1992; Rao and Gulati 1994; Roy 1996; Sen 1997; Wanmali and Ramasamy 1994; Weiner 1991.

source. For example, the quite high gross output thresholds for commercial taxes, rural assets (which are not controlled at all), rural land (which is badly controlled) and agricultural income tax (not levied).

2 'Technically' low-quality law (for example, the land reform laws that have enabled landowning elites to consolidate substantial holdings, evict tenants and release miserably little land to the State for redistribution).

3 Non-mandatory law: the laws guaranteeing reservations for the lowest castes – and for disabled people – in government employment and in public-sector undertakings and the articles encouraging universal education are the most important of these, but most economic rights are of this sort. They are not guaranteed or enforceable under the constitution, though public interest litigation has gingered the higher judiciary into an active developmental role directing government. Non-mandatory law is the most powerful implement by which most of the Indian workforce is 'socially excluded'.

4 Overt neglect (on the one hand, India's reservations, child and bonded labour and social security provisions – where the constituency is too weak to enforce claims to what the State has declared itself obliged to provide; on the other hand, the regulation of rural market sites – where the State is too weak to enforce its own provision): existing economic power is reinforced by such open neglect.

5 The segmentation of regulative law and procedure: differentials in the legal and management frameworks that prevent state institutions from competing with the private sector as mandated. (These are well exemplified by regulations of investment, technology and trading practices in the co-operative sector versus the private sector in agricultural markets, where co-operatives suffer competitive disadvantages in all but a few, well-known cases.)

The first two mechanisms enable landed interests to accumulate rural assets and to enter and dominate commerce, from which position they exercise through money-lending an indirect control over agricultural production, which is efficient in terms of transaction costs. In enabling the capture and perpetuation of social and economic advantages, non-mandatory and neglected law positively penalises the poor. The non-level agro-commercial playing field allows private trade to score the goals. The State in action aggravates inequality in the very society it is rhetorically committed to rendering more equal.

Implementation

6 Incapacitating budgetary under-provision (especially on materials subheads): there are many such instances: the employment-creating Food for Work Programme; drinking water schemes; the Public Works Department; the National Rural Employment Programme; and regulated markets (staff and enforcement), education and health. These are the most conspicuous. Cases of urban land-use planning and rural infrastructure show not only that such under-funding makes a mockery of implementation as planned, it also reveals the weakness of the State's developmental project, and results in civil

society responding informally (often in the form of collective action battened on to such schemes) in ways that may be socially divisive, exclusive, differentiating and/or physically threatening.

7   Delayed finance: the relationship between the Reserve Bank of India and the Cotton Corporation and Food Corporation amounts to domination of the latter by the former in such a way that private merchants buy cheaper and sell dearer than would be the case without delayed finance.

8   Lack of commensuration between technique and competence: administrative 'co-ordination' problems. These are classically exposed in the literature on targeting policy and practice – examples are the Integrated Rural Development Programme, the National Rural Employment Programme and the Public Distribution System.

The relative over-development of technique in the formation of state policy agendas and the relative under-development of competence in implementation intensify the incentives for the absorption of elements of the State into the informal economy.

Types of seizure and capture

The mechanisms and politics of subversive access to the State's 'political settlement' include the opportunistic funding of political parties, aggressive lobbying, the infiltration of state institutions and the formation of coalitions and tactical alliances between agents of the State, market and institutions of civil society:

9   The deployment of official discretion, not necessarily corruptly, at widely differing scales and significances: take, for example, the 'miscellaneous' category of priority sector credit planning, in which the actual lending achievements of local banks invariably exceed the targets that they are required to meet ('miscellaneous' opening the possibility of lending for trade); reservation quotas, discretion in the implementation of which means that non-scheduled castes take the place of scheduled castes, men take the place of women, non-disabled of disabled, and so on; the disadvantaged access of those eligible to entitlements (for example, in the case of Tamil Nadu's Noon Meals Scheme, one of the developmental goals is inter-dining but scheduled caste children have been discriminated against in feeding).

10   Nepotism: Integrated Rural Development Programme (IRDP) targets have been found to depend on party political allegiances. The proliferating Lions and Rotary Clubs are places where officials mingle with businesspeople; new economic relations of caste and kinship are developing, in which trading castes (which one generation ago avoided government) now routinely and deliberately lodge kin in the bureaucracy (and in which kinship and caste groups rework their identities as business associations – see Chapter 7).

11   Fraud and crime: fraud by officials – depriving the State of resources (for example, the under-valuation of stamp duties on transfers of property, the profits from which are shared), the theft of state resources by non-state personnel (for example, 'leakages' of food grains from the Public Distribution

System), and defrauding the State (for example, the ubiquitous evasion of taxes and duties, and the non-recovery of loans). There is an entirely separate issue of the criminality of laws as they stand, in relation to the developmental goals of social justice or the ambitions of the Indian Constitution.

12 The commercialisation of politics: 'politics has now been perfected into a well organised profession or business where the investment brings forth manifold and profitable returns'.[2]

13 The commercialisation and (party) politicisation of the bureaucracy: of the entry, postings and velocity of transfer; the commercialisation of audit, enforcement, the means of redress, and of the institutions of transparency and accountability. Concealment and secrecy are handmaidens to the profitable abuse of administrative power.

14 Open capitulation in implementation; for example, price policy, especially that for wheat; food and fertiliser subsidies, which have failed to be reduced under liberalisation; industrial estates for small-scale industries, which have been colonised by medium and large-scale enterprises; and anti-poverty policies, which are captured by the non-poor or the least poor of the poor. The BJP's refusal to capitulate to transport owners over their strike against diesel prices (in October 1999) is an exception to prove the rule.

15 Co-option by local commercial elites of policies and practices specifically intended to undermine their power; for example, the management of co-operatives intended to compete with or replace private trade by private traders themselves, the domination by traders of access to National Warehousing Corporation facilities intended for small farmers, and access to finance generally (to finance corporations, to the Co-operative Development Corporation; land development banks; the Consumer Council packed with business nominees; and so on).

16 Pre-emptive informalisation; for example, in response to state regulation such as the trade unions law, the Factories Acts, licences and industrial controls, and land reform law, where the structure and behaviour of regulated sectors develop so as to avoid regulation, or even the threat of regulation. Industrial labour forces are deliberately casualised, muster rolls are falsified, factory scale is deliberately miniaturised, and production processes are deliberately dispersed while actually being centrally controlled.

17 Unreported commercial crime: chicanery with weights and measures, counterfeiting of brands and labels, contractual delinquency, oppressive and illegal labour relations.

18 Coercion; for example, privileged access (using private mafias or the conspicuous possession of firearms as a means of intimidation) to police and courts to defend illegal interests (traders/bus owners/money-lenders), forced informal deductions by politicians from officials' salaries to finance private and public projects, and politicians holding informal extra-legal courts in the interests of their financial backers.

[2] Ganesan 1997, p. 34. We wonder about the self-fulfilling role of rational choice theory which has been taught as the hegemonic theory of the State to a generation of aspiring administrators and politicians.

19 Corruption: a critical issue in the last decade of the twentieth century under policies designed to eliminate it. According to Transparency International, India ranks with China and Indonesia as the most corrupt nations in the world.[3] No longer can the poorly salaried official be usefully seen as the prime mover of corrupt transactions; resources in the black economy are as necessary to a corrupt transaction as a privatised public resource (Khan 1996; Harriss-White 1996d). Nor is corruption confined to the grand scale. Certainly, the investigative press has unearthed huge scandals at the top. In the Centre: the Bofors arms scandal; the HDW submarine scam; the securities, sugar, urea, housing, petrol pumps, railways and telecom scams; the Jharkand Mukti Morcha; and the Havala money-laundering scams. In the States: the fodder scam of Bihar; the ENRON electricity scam of Maharashtra; and the cloth and school uniforms, colour TV sets, transport spare parts, steel doors, slippers, crematorium, furniture purchase and coal import scams of Tamil Nadu (Guhan and Paul 1997; Visvanathan and Sethi 1998).

Order in contracts, in market exchange and in rights over property is pervasively informalised. Regulative law works when it coincides with self-regulation. The informal economic relations through which state capitulation is expressed are at the heart of the State and meshed with it. They are sometimes part of the cost structures of the formal economy and not (only) a separate 'economy within the economy'. They shape state activity and force the State into formal and informal concessionary pay-offs.

Paul and Shah assert that corruption in public-service delivery – what they term 'retail corruption' – does not attract public attention (1997, p. 144), even though it clearly involves widespread public practice and connivance. In a five-city study, in which we may expect underestimated admissions, one in four people in Chennai and one in eight in Bangalore were found to pay bribes when dealing with the administration, telecom or electricity. Among urban slum dwellers the frequency of bribing is universally very much greater than in the population as a whole (Paul and Shah 1997, pp. 151–3). The episodic nature of retail corruption may explain public apathy about its reform. However, no evidence has been marshalled to show that retail corruption is not now politicised, or that the fear of a present or future reprisal explains the apparent public 'apathy', the lack of which is a necessary condition for anti-corruption reform.

When the workforce is unconvinced about its rights – and when it experiences corruption as a means of access, or bribes being balanced (no doubt asymmetrically) by political hand-outs before elections – the State's legitimacy is called into question. The trade in bribes is concentrated and unequal, and its outcomes are differentiating. Corruption has long been decentralised and its centre of gravity seems to have shifted from being State-driven to being driven

[3] This means that over two-fifths of the world's population, competing in economies the size of Belgium (India) and California (China), face the most extensive corruption worldwide.

by powerful elements in local society. Decentralised corrupt relations are also rapidly being politicised in the India of the 1990s: officials are agents rather than principals. When politics is informalised and reduced to a risky investment requiring rapid returns, it is open to question whether politicians are principals or whether instead it is the 'clients' belonging to the intermediate classes in civil society who hold the balance of power as principals in corrupt transactions. Certainly, the mass public interest, to which the State should be accountable, is not the principal. In prevalent multi-agent, corrupt transactions (involving the politician, official, carrier, trader and protector), the roles of principal and agent become loaded with the non-contractual obligations more familiarly associated with clientelage. The roles of patron and agent also rotate. Over time, power accretes to those members of a multi-agent transaction who hold the micro-monopoly of force.

Appendix 3 *Roles of religious minorities in the Indian economy*
Compiled by Pauline von Hellermann

	Muslims	Christians	Sikhs	Jains	Parsis
Population in 1991	101.59 million	19.64 million	16.25 million	3.33 million	56 000
% of Indian population	12.12%.	2.34%.	1.94%.	0.4%	
Regional concentration	Throughout India, but highest concentrations in Lakshadweep (94.31%), Assam (28.34%), West Bengal (23.61%), Kerala (23.32%), Uttar Pradesh (17.33%), Bihar (14.80%) and Karnataka (11.63%).	Mostly north-east: Nagaland (87.46%), Mizoram (85.73%), Meghalaya (64.57%) and Manipur (34.11%). Also Goa (29.85%), Andaman and Nicobar Islands (23.94%), Kerala (19.31%) and Arunachal Pradesh (10.29%). Between 2.85 and 7.22% in Pondicherry, Tamil Nadu, Assam, Sikkim and Darman & Diu.	Highest concentration in the Punjab (62.95%). Also Chandigarh (20.29%), Haryana (5.81%) and Delhi (4.83%). Except for Himachal Pradesh (1.00%) and Rajasthan (1.47%), less than 1% in the rest of India.	Mainly in the west. Highest percentage in Rajasthan (1.27%), Maharashtra (1.22%), Gujarat (1.18%) and Delhi (1.00%). In the remaining States less than average of 0.4%.	No statistics available, but concentrated in Bombay.
Sects	Main sects are the Sunni and Shia, but also Ahmadiyya, Sufi, Dawoodi Bohra and Sulaimani Bohra.	Syrian, Catholics, Protestants (many more internal divisions).		Shvetambaras (white-clad) and Digambaras (sky-clad)	

Groups/ stratification	Supposed to be egalitarian, but historical division between Ashrafi (elite, of Persian origin) and Ajlaf (native converts). But many other, 'caste-like' groupings, or *biradaris*.	Supposed to be egalitarian, but great caste/class divisions. Syrian C equiv. of high caste. Some higher caste converts, but majority are of scheduled caste or tribal origin. Great inequalities within the church.	Supposed to be egalitarian, but in fact segmented communities: Namdhari, Pothokar, Ramgarhia and *jats*. Divisions between each 'caste'; however, not as great as among Hindus.	Supposed to be egalitarian, but divided into castes. However, in rituals all treated equally.	Supposed to be egalitarian. Few internal divisions as a very small community.
Income relative to total population	Mixed; some high and middle income; some relatively poor.	High income among Syrian C in Kerala, some high and middle income in other parts, many poor *dalits*.	Relatively high, few poor.	Relatively high, a few poor.	High, but less so than in the past.
Landownership	Some, but relatively less than Hindus.	Some Syrian C in Kerala are big landowners, otherwise very little.	Sikh *jats* own most land in the Punjab, but negligible amounts in other parts of India.	Some land owned in Rajasthan, and in the south.	
Agriculture	Small peasants, agricultural labourers.	Big farms and plantations owned by Syrian C, otherwise mostly agricultural labourers.	Dominate agriculture in the Punjab, but not in agriculture elsewhere.	Some Jains in the south are farmers.	

Appendix 3 *continued*

	Muslims	Christians	Sikhs	Jains	Parsis
Petty production, craft and services	Butchers, greengrocers, tailors, sweet vendors, locksmiths, pharmacists, shoe- and sandal-makers, leather workers, *bidi* workers. Brassware (Moradabad), pottery (Khurja), carpets (Bhadodi and Mirzapur), woodwork (Sharanapur), hand-printed textiles (Farrakhabad), *zari* and silk embroidery (Varanasi), *kargha* and handloom cloth (Mau). Silk and handloom weavers (Bihar). Bhiwandi, Maharashtra's power looms are owned predominantly by the Muslims. *Bidri* ware, woollen carpet industry (Andhra Pradesh), *bidri* ware, silk-rearing and	No specific information. Rural *dalit* Christians perform 'menial' tasks and agricultural labour.	In transport (taxi drivers, bus drivers, etc.). Small-scale traders, mechanics, engineers, etc.	Owner/managers in the gem industry in Jaipur, some shop owners in rural Rajasthan.	

Trade	toy industry (Karnataka), gem and marble-cutting (Rajasthan), and textile crafts involving block and screen printing (Gujarat). Also car mechanics.	Regional variations. Big trading communities on the west coast and in the bazaar economy of Tamil Nadu towns. Fewer in trade in other areas.	Some Syrian C large traders, other coastal caste Christians are in trade, but few *dalit* Christians.	Not involved in the Punjab, but have entered trade; e.g. as motor part dealers and textile dealers in other areas of India.	Almost exclusively involved in trade, banking, money-lending. Jains almost synonymous with Banias.	
Industry		A number of the small-scale businesses have expanded into larger enterprises (leather, beauty products, restaurant chains, car industry, etc.). However, no Muslim promoters in 100 biggest firms index before 1990s.	Syrian Christians since colonial times.	Some Ramgarhias are industrial entrepreneurs.	Leading figures in industry, and big business, especially the Marwaris, many of whom are Jains.	Leading industrialists (e.g. Tata, Godrej)

Appendix 3 *continued*

	Muslims	Christians	Sikhs	Jains	Parsis
Government	Under-represented in government jobs, including army and police.	In colonial times, greater access to government jobs. Still likely that more than 2% of Civil Service Christian (but no official statistics available).	Yes, but no data.	Yes, but no data.	Yes, but no data.
Professionals	Relatively less since Partition, but still many journalists, academics, etc.	Yes, though no systematic data.	Especially in science, but also other fields.	Yes, but no details.	Yes, but no details. Eminent Parsi lawyers, scientists, doctors, government, university teachers.
Credit facilities/ banking	Muslim banks; credit available almost exclusively from other Muslims.	Banking and credit organisations set up very early by Syrian Christians; easy access to capital. Also set up in many villages by churches and missionaries for *dalits*, but no information on the extent these still exist today, or on their effectiveness.	Sikh banks plus credit networks, almost exclusively within Sikh community.	Jains lend money to other communities, but do not borrow from others. Well established as bankers and money-lenders.	Big in banking and money business.

Investment	Mostly in family business, little investment in land, and, until recently, in education.	Syrians invest in a variety of areas: education, land, industry and banking. No information on whether this is exclusively within the Christian economic world – expected not to be.	Little or no investment in Punjab industry by Sikh Jats, far more likely to reinvest in agriculture or in businesses in other parts of India; also in education.	Reinvestment in business, but also in education, and, one could say, in reputation, with large contributions at religious festivals: most probably within Jain community.	
Labour	Strong preference for self-employment or family businesses. Prefer to employ close relatives, or at any rate Muslims. Under-represented in formal private sector. But employed in *bidi* and gem-cutting industry, with Hindu or Jain managers.	Also family businesses, but less pronounced than for Hindus or Muslims. Religion seems not to play an important role for Christians (neither Syrian C nor *dalits*), in structuring labour relations.	There seems to be a preference to work for and with Sikhs. However, clearly also enter the 'formal' labour force (army, police force, etc.).	Family businesses dominate, or 'business families'. But some exceptions.	
Charity organisations/ redistribution	*Waqfs* and others.	Missionary hospitals, schools, charity organisations.	Pothoharis, for example, have organisations like the Sikh Educational Conference and the Arya Samaj, which have created social awareness.	Jains are very active in Jain temples and other organisations, and donate great sums of money to these. They also do community service.	Renowned philanthropists. Panchayats are a social security system for the community.

	Muslims	Christians	Sikhs	Jains	Parsis
Networks	Islam is a unifying agent for Muslims all over India, although not applicable to the same degree. Strong networks exist.	Church organises events, etc., and provides contact with other Christians, though less so between high and scheduled castes.	Sikh networks all over India.	Very tight though segmented networks between communities all over India.	Important networks.
Mobility	Quite great.	Syrian C and other high-caste Christians very mobile, those of *dalit* origins are now found in cities, but rural *dalit* Christians least mobile.	Great mobility; ever since Guru Nanak's journeys.	Great mobility for traders.	Mobile.
Income from abroad	Remittances from Gulf and elsewhere.	Mainly through churches.	From diaspora in the UK, US, Canada and East Africa.	From diaspora in the UK, US, Canada and East Africa.	From diaspora.
Attitude to wealth	Perhaps more concerned with redistribution than other 'minority' religions (*waqfs*, tithe, inheritance laws, etc.) But no stricture against wealth *per se*.	A certain ambivalence. Wealth-creation not shunned.	Culture of hard work; it is certainly considered good to amass wealth.	Ambivalent, it seems. Asceticism encourages reinvestment in business.	Not ascetic; it is good to amass wealth, but great emphasis on righteousness.

Inheritance laws	Muslim law. Distribution between large number of relatives, less to women than to men.	Succession Act of 1925; patrilineal heredity; dowry system; single heir possible.	Succession Act of 1956 (Hindu Law)	Succession Act of 1956 (Hindu Law)	Succession Act of 1925, with variations.
Gender	Women not equal to men, less educated, less in employment than other women, but starting to change in cities.	Well-educated women to be found working in formal sector and modern occupations.	Supposedly equal. In practice women are better educated than national average for women, and found working in professions.	Highly educated, and inherit property. Not involved in family business directly, but indirectly very important and influential. Women priests and gurus.	Modern *parsi* women very well educated and independent.
Accumulation	Accumulation is said to be prevented by inheritance laws and egalitarianism. There are, however, very rich Muslims.				
Communalism	Long history of conflict since Partition with Hindu aggression against Muslims. Muslims are improving their relative economic status. Muslim property always destroyed in riots, so very likely to have an economic basis.	*Dalit* Christians have a long history of harassment and persecution. It is only recently that Christians in general, including priests and missionaries, have been the victims of widespread communalist attacks: these not primarily due to economic competition.		Relations relatively peaceful until the 1980s, then very intense movement from 1983–84, based on a politics of secession and autonomy. Recent lowering of tension.	

References

Abrams, P. 1988, 'Notes on the Difficulty of Studying the State', *Journal of Historical Sociology* 1, 1: 58–89.

Ades, A. and di Tella, R. 1996, 'The Causes and Consequences of Corruption: A Review of Recent Empirical Contributions', pp. 6–11, in (eds) Harriss-White and White.

Adnan, S. 1985, 'Classical and Contemporary Approaches to Agrarian Capitalism', *Economic and Political Weekly XX*, 30, Review of Political Economy, pp. 53–64.

Adnan, S. 1997, 'Class, Caste and *Shamaj* Relations among the Peasantry in Bangladesh: Mechanisms of Stability and Change in the Daripalla Villages, 1975–86', pp. 277–310, in (eds) Breman et al.

Agarwal, B. 1994, *A Field of One's Own: Gender and Land Rights in India*, Cambridge University Press, Cambridge.

Agnihotri, S. 1997, *Sex Ratio Imbalances in India – A Disaggregated Analysis*, PhD thesis, School of Development Studies, University of East Anglia.

Agnihotri, S. B. 2000, *Sex Ratio Patterns in the Indian Population: A Fresh Exploration*, Sage, New Delhi, London.

Ahluwalia, I. J. 1992, *Productivity and Growth in Indian Manufacturing*, Oxford University Press, New Delhi.

Ahmad, A. 1993, *Indian Muslims. Issues in Social & Economic Development*, Khama Publishers, New Delhi.

Ahmad, A. 1996a, *Lineages of the Present: Political Essays*, Tulika, New Delhi.

Ahmad, A. 1996b, 'Fascism and National Culture: Reading Gramsci in the Days of Hindutva', pp. 221–66, in Ahmad, A.

Ahmad, I. (ed.) 1973/78, *Caste and Social Stratification among the Muslims in India*, Manohar Book Service, New Delhi.

Ahmad, I. 1975, 'Economic and Social Change', in Imam (ed.).

Ahmed, E., Dreze, J., Hill, J. and Sen, A. 1991, *Social Security in Developing Countries*, Clarendon, Oxford.

Ahmed, S. 1999, 'Occupational Segregation and Caste-based Discrimination in India', pp. 67–92 in (ed.) Shah.

Akerlof, G. A. 1984, 'The Economics of Caste and of the Rat Race and other Woeful Tales', pp. 23–44 in *An Economic Theorist's Book of Tales: Essays that Entertain the Consequences of New Assumptions in Economic Theory*, Cambridge University Press, Cambridge.

Albeda, R. and Tilly, C. 1994, 'Towards a Broader Vision: Race, Gender and Labor Market Segmentation in the Social Structures of Accumulation Framework', pp. 212–31, in Kotz, McDonough and Reich (eds).

Ali, A. 1992, 'The Quest for Cultural Identity and Material Advancement: Parallels and Contrasts in Muslim Minority Experience in Secular India and Buddhist Sri Lanka', *Journal Institute of Muslim Minority Affairs*, 13, 1, January 1992, pp. 33–57.

Aloysius, G. 1994, 'Trajectory of Hindutva', *Economic and Political Weekly*, 11 June: 1451.

Altvater, E. 1993, *The Future of the Market: An Essay on the Regulation of Money and Nature after the Collapse of 'Actually Existing Socialism'*, Verso, London.

Amin, S. 2002, 'Economic Globalisation and Political Universalism: Convergence or Divergence?', Wolfson College Lecture in series: *Globalisation and Insecurity*, Wolfson College, Oxford, in (ed.) Harriss-White, 2002d.

Armstrong, N. 1997, 'From Patron to Politician: Pursuing Power in Modern India', Institute of Social and Cultural Anthropology, Oxford.

Arrow, K. (ed.) 1988, *The Balance between Industry and Agriculture in Economic Development: Volume 1: Basic Issues*, International Economics Association, Macmillan, Basingstoke.

Athreya, V. 1999, *Frontline*, 20 November, p. 109, <www.frontlineonnet.com/>.

Athreya, V. 2001, 'Census 2001: Some Progress, Some Concern', *Frontline*, 26 April.

Athreya, V., Djurfeldt, G. and Lindberg, S. 1990, *Barriers Broken: Production Relations and Agrarian Change in Tamil Nadu*, Sage, New Delhi.

Auclair, C. 1998, *Ville à Vendre: Voie Libérale and Privatisation du Secteur de l'Habitat à Chennai (Inde)*, Publications du Département de Sciences Sociales 4, Institute Francais du Pondicherry, Pondicherry.

Bagchi, A. 1994, 'India's Tax Reform: A Progress Report', *Economic and Political Weekly*, 22 October.

Baker, C. 1984, *An Indian Rural Economy, 1880–1955: The Tamilnad Countryside*, Oxford University Press, New Delhi.

Baker, J. and Pedersen, P. O. (eds) 1992, 'The Rural–Urban Interface in Africa, Expansion and Adaptation', *Seminar Proceedings no. 27*, Nordiska Afrikainstitut, Uppsala.

Balagopal, K. 1992, 'Economic Liberalism and Decline of Democracy: Case of Andhra Pradesh', *Economic and Political Weekly*, 12 September:1959.

Balagopal, K. 1993, 'Why Did December 6th, 1992, Happen?', *Economic and Political Weekly*, 24 April: 790.

Banaji, J. 1999, 'Metamorphoses of Agrarian Capitalism', *Economic and Political Weekly*, vol. XXXIV, 2 October, pp. 2850–8.

Banaji, J. 2000, 'Workers Rights in a New Economic Order', Queen Elizabeth House Working Paper number 55, <www.qeh.ox.ac.uk>.

Banaji, J. and Hensman, R. 1990a, *Beyond Multinationalism: Management Policy and Bargaining Relations in International Companies*, Sage, New Delhi.

Banaji, J. and Hensman, R. 1990b, 'Outline of an Industrial Relations Theory of Industrial Conflict', *Economic and Political Weekly*, vol. XXV, no. 34, 25 August, pp. 135–6.

Banaji, J. and Hensman, R. 1998, 'A Short History of the Employees Unions in Bombay, 1947–1991', paper presented to the First Annual Conference of the Association of Indian Labour Historians, 16–18 March, New Delhi.

Banaji, J. and Mody, G. 2001, 'Corporate Governance and the Indian Private Sector', Queen Elizabeth House Working Paper QEHWPS73, <http://www2.qeh.ox.ac.uk/research/qehwp-list2.html>. Oxford.

Banik, D. 1999, *The Transfer Raj: Indian Civil Servants on the Move*, Centre for Development and the Environment, Oslo; also 2001 in *European Journal of Development Research*, 13, 1.

Bardhan, K. 1993, 'Gender and Class: The Structure of the Difference', in A. Clark (ed.).

Bardhan, P. 1984, *The Political Economy of Development in India*, Oxford University Press, New Delhi.

Bardhan, P. 1988, 'Dominant Proprietary Classes and India's Democracy', in Kohli (ed.).

Bardhan, P. 1989, 'The Third Dominant Class', *Economic and Political Weekly*, 21 January.

Bardhan, P. 1992, 'A Political Economy Perspective on Development', in Jalan (ed.), pp. 321 and 323.

Bardhan, P. 1997, 'Method in the Madness? A Political Economy Analysis of the Ethnic Conflicts in Less Developed Countries', *World Development* 25, 9: 1381–98.

Bardhan, P. 1998, *The Political Economy of Development in India: Expanded Edition with an Epilogue on the Political Economy of Reform in India*, Oxford University Press, New Delhi.

Baru, S. 2000, 'Economic Policy and the Development of Capitalism in India: The Role of Regional Capitalists and Political Parties', pp. 207–29 in (eds) Frankel et al.

Basile, E. and Harriss-White, B. 1999, 'The Politics of Accumulation in Small Town India', *Bulletin of the Institute of Development Studies*, 30, 4: 31–9.

Basile, E. and Harriss-White, B. 2000, 'Corporative Capitalism: Civil Society and the Politics of Accumulation in Small Town India', QEH Working Paper QEHWPS38, <http://www2.qeh.ox.ac.uk/research/qehwp-list2.html>. Oxford.

Basu, K. 1991, 'Markets, Power and Social Norms', in *Economic Graffiti*, Oxford University Press, Bombay.

Bates, R. 1981, *Markets and States in Tropical Africa*, University of California Press, Berkeley.

Bates, R. (ed.) 1989, *Towards a Political Economy of Development A Rational Choice Perspective*, University of California Press, Berkeley.

Baud, I. S. A. 1983, 'Women's Labour in the Indian Textile Industry: The Influence of Technology and Organisation on the Gender Division of Labor', *IRIS Report 23*, Development Research Institute, Tilburg University, The Netherlands.

Baud, I. and de Bruijne, G. (eds) 1992, *Gender, Small Scale Industry and Development Policy*, Intermediate Technology Publications, London.

Baud, I. and Schenk, H. 1994, *Solid Waste Management: Modes, Assessments, Appraisals and Linkages in Bangalore*, Manohar, New Delhi.

Baviskar, A. 1998, 'Towards a Sociology of Delhi', *Economic and Political Weekly*, 33, 49, 5–11 December: 3101–2.

Bayly, C. 1988, *Indian Society and the Making of the British Empire*, Cambridge University Press, Cambridge.

Beall, J. 1997, 'Households, Livelihoods and the Urban Environment: Sociological Perspectives on Solid Waste Management in Pakistan', PhD thesis, London School of Economics.

Beccatini, G. 1979, 'Dal "Settore" Industriale al "Distretto" Industriale: Alcune Considerazioni sull'Unità di Indagine dell'Economia Industriale', *Rivista di Economia e Politica Industriale*, 1: 35–48.

Benei, V. and Kennedy, L. (eds) 1997, *Industrial Decentralisation and Urban Development. Pondy Papers in Social Science, 23*, French Institute, Pondicherry.

Benewick, R., Blecher, M. and Cook, S. (eds) 1999, 'Politics in Development: Essays in Honour of Gordon White', special issue, *Bulletin of the Institute of Development Studies* 30: 4.

Benjamin, S. and Bengani, N. M. 1998, 'The Civic Politics of Industrial Districts in Delhi', pp. 376–92, in (eds) P. Cadène and M. Holmstrom.

Béteille, A. 1996, 'Caste in Contemporary India', in (ed.) Fuller.

Béteille, A. 1997, 'The Family and the Reproduction of Inequality', in (ed.) Uberoi, pp. 435–51.

Bhaduri, A. 1983, *The Economics of Backward Agriculture*, Academic Press, New York.

Bhagwati, J. 1993, *India in Transition: Freeing the Economy*, Clarendon, Oxford.

Bhalla, S. 1976, 'New Relations of Production in Haryana Agriculture', *Economic and Political Weekly*, 1, 13, 27 March.

Bhalla, S. 1999, 'Liberalization, Rural Labour Markets and the Mobilization of Farm Workers: The Haryana Story in an All-India Context', *Journal of Peasant Studies*, 26, 2/3: 30.

Bharadwaj, K. 1985, 'A View of Commercialization in Indian Agriculture and the Development of Capitalism', *Journal of Peasant Studies*, 12, 1: 7–25.

Bharadwaj, K. 1995, 'Regional Differentiation in India', in (ed.) Satyamurthy.

Bharathan, K. 1981, 'Development through Industrialisation: Analysis and Case Study of Backward Area Development', *MIDS Working paper no. 24*, Madras Institute of Development Studies.

Bhatia, D. P. 1996, *National Accounting; Concepts and Estimates*, Khanna Pub, New Delhi.

Bhattacharyya, S. 2000, *Class Differentiation and Agricultural Credit: A Study of West Bengal*, Concept, New Delhi.

Bhatty, Z. 1973, 'Status and Power in a Muslim Dominated Village of Uttar Pradesh', pp. 96–115, in (ed.) I. Ahmad.

Bhowmik, S. 1998, 'The Labour Movement in India: Present Problems and Future Perspectives', *The Indian Journal of Social Work*, 59, 1: 147–66.

Binswanger, H. and Rosenzweig, M. (eds) 1984, *Contractual Arrangements, Employment and Wages in Rural Labour Markets in Asia*, Yale University Press, New Haven.

Bohle, H.-G. 1992, 'Real Markets and Food Security with Evidence from Fish Marketing in South India', in (ed.) Cammann.

Bose, S. 1997, 'Hindu Nationalism and the Crisis of the Indian State: A theoretical Perspective', pp. 104–64, in (eds) Bose and Jalal.

Bose, S. and Jalal, A. (eds) 1997, *Nationalism, Democracy and Development: State and Politics in Development*, Oxford University Press, Delhi.

Boserup, E. 1987, *Women's Role in Economic Development*, Gower, Brookfield Vt.

Bourdieu, P. 1984, *Distinction; A Social Critique of the Judgement of Taste*, Harvard University Press, Cambridge (Mass.).

Brass, T. 1993, 'Some Observations on Unfree Labour, Capitalist Restructuring and Deproletarianisation', in (eds) Brass et al.

Brass, T., van der Linden, M. and Lucassen, J. (eds) 1993, *Free and Unfree Labour*, International Institute for Social History, Amsterdam.

Braudel, F. 1982, *Civilisation and Capitalism, 15th to 18th Century: Vol. II, The Wheels of Commerce*, Fontana, London.

Breman, J. 1976, 'A Dualistic Labour System? A Critique of the Informal Sector Concept', *Economic and Political Weekly*, 27 November, 4 and 11 December.

Breman, J. 1996, *Footloose Labour: Working in India's Informal Economy*, Cambridge University Press, Cambridge.

Breman, J. 1997, 'The Village in Focus', pp. 15–76, in (eds) Breman, Kloos and Saith.

Breman, J. 1999, 'The Study of Industrial Labour in Post-colonial India – The Informal Sector: A Concluding Review', pp. 407–32, in (eds) Parry et al.

Breman, J., Kloos, P. and Saith, A. (eds) 1997, *The Village in Asia Revisited*, Oxford University Press, New Delhi.

Bromley, R. (ed.) 1985, *Planning for Small Enterprises in Third World Cities*, Pergamon, Oxford.

Buiter, W. H. and Patel, U. R. 1993, 'Budgetary Aspects of Stabilisation and Structural Adjustment in India', *Working paper 9506*, Dept of Applied Economics, University of Cambridge.

Byres, T. J. 1974, 'Land Reform, Industrialisation and the Marketed Surplus', in Lehmann (ed.).

Byres, T. J. 1981, 'The New Technology, Class Formation and Class Action in the Indian Countryside', *Journal of Peasant Studies*, 8, 4.

Byres, T. J. 1996a, 'State, Class and Development Planning in India', in (ed.) Byres 1996c, p. 67.

Byres, T. J. 1996b, 'Introduction: Development Planning and the Interventionist State versus Liberalisation and the Neo-liberal State: India 1989–1996', in (ed.) Byres 1996c.

Byres, T. J. (ed.) 1996c, *The State, Development Planning and Liberalisation in India*, Oxford University Press, New Delhi.

Byres, T. J. (ed.) 1998, *The Indian Economy: Major Debates Since Independence*, Oxford University Press, Delhi.

Cadène, P. 1991, '"Development in a Backward Area" as a Result of General Development: A Case Study of the Marble Industry in a Tehsil of South Rajasthan', in (eds) Rothermund and Saha.

Cadène, P. 1998a, 'Network Specialists, Industrial Clusters and the Integration of Space in India', pp. 139–68, in (eds) Cadène and Holmstrom.

Cadène, P. 1998b, 'Conclusion: A New Model for Indian Industry', pp. 393–403, in (eds) Cadene and Holmstrom.

Cadène, P. and Holmstrom, M. (eds) 1998, *Decentralised Production in India: Industrial Districts, Flexible Specialisation and Employment*, Sage, New Delhi/London.

Callari, A., Cullenberg, S. and Biewener, C. (eds) 1995, *Marxism in the Postmodern Age: Confronting the New World Order*, Guilford Press, New York.

Cammann, L. (ed.) 1992, *Traditional Marketing Systems*, DSE, Munich.

Carrithers, M. and Humphrey, C. (eds) 1991, *The Assembly of Listeners. Jains in Society*, Cambridge University Press, Cambridge.

Carsten, F. L. 1967, *The Rise of Fascism*, University of California Press, Berkeley.

Cassen, R. and Joshi, V. (eds) 1995, *India: the Future of Economic Reform*, Oxford University Press, New Delhi.

Casson, M. 1990, 'Enterprise and Competitiveness: A Systems View of International Business', pp. 105–24 in *The Economics of Trust*, Clarendon, Oxford.

Cawson, A. (ed.) 1985, *Organised Interests and the State: Studies in Meso-Corporatism*, Sage, London.

Cawson, A. 1985, 'Varieties of Corporatism: The Importance of the Meso-level of Interest Intermediation', in (ed.) Cawson.

Cawthorne, P. 1992, 'The Labour Process under Amoebic Capitalism: A Case Study of the Garments Industry in a South Indian Town', in (eds) Baud and de Bruijne.

Cecchi, C. 2001, 'Rural Development and Local Systems: The Genesis of the Local System Concept' (Dept of Public Economics, La Sapienza, Rome); chapter of 'Rural Development and Local Systems: The Case of Maremma Rural District', PhD thesis, Dept of City and Regional Planning, University of Wales, Cardiff.

Central Statistical Organisation, Dept of Statistics 1999, *National Accounts Statistics*, Ministry of Planning and Programme Implementation, New Delhi.

Centre for Monitoring the Indian Economy 1994, *Basic Statistics Relating to the Indian Economy*, CMIE, Mumbai.

Centre for Monitoring the Indian Economy 1995, *Five Hundred Private Corporate Giants*, CMIE, Mumbai.

Centre for Monitoring the Indian Economy 1997, *Profile of States*, CMIE, Mumbai.

Chakraborty, P. 1997, 'Tax Reductions and their Revenue Implications – How Valid is the Laffer Curve?', *Economic and Political Weekly*, 26 April.

Chambers, R. and Wickremanayake, B. 1977, 'Agricultural Extension: Myth, Reality and Challenge', pp. 155–67, in Farmer (ed.) 1977.

Chandavarkar, R. 1998, *Imperial Power and Personal Politics: Class Resistance and the State in India, c.1850–1951*, Cambridge University Press, Cambridge.

Chandok, H. L. 1990, *India Database, the Economy*, LM Books, New Delhi.

Chandrasekhar, C. P. 1996, 'Explaining Post-reform Industrial Growth', *Economic and Political Weekly*, Special Number, September.

Chandrasekhar, C.P. 1997, 'The Economic Consequences of the Abolition of Child Labour: An Indian Case Study', *Journal of Peasant Studies*, 24, 3: 137–79.

Chandrasekhar, C. P. and Ghosh, J. 1993, 'Economic Discipline and External Vulnerability: A Comment on Fiscal and Adjustment Strategies', *Economic and Political Weekly*, 10 April: 667.

Chandrasekhar, C. P. and Patnaik, P. 1995, 'Indian Economy under Structural Adjustment', *Economic and Political Weekly*, 25 November: 3066.

Chapman, G. P. and Pathak, P. 1997, 'Indian Urbanisation and the Characteristics of Large Indian Cities Revealed in the 1991 Census', *Espace, Populations, Sociétés*, 2, 3, pp. 193–210.

Chari, S. 2000, 'The Agrarian Question Comes to Town: The Making of the Knitwear Industry in Tiruppur, South India', PhD Thesis, Department of Geography, University of California at Berkeley.

Chatterjee, P. 1997, *A Possible World: Essays in Political Criticism*, Oxford University Press, Delhi.

Chattopadhyay, B. 1965, 'Marx and India's Crisis', in (ed.) Joshi.

Chaudhuri, A. 1975, *Private Economic Power in India: A Study in Genesis and Concentration*, Peoples' Publishing House, New Delhi.

Chaudhuri, B. and Sevoz, J.-F. 1997, 'A Theoretical Framework for Studying the Dynamics of Urban and Industrial Growth', pp. 57–61, in (eds) Benei and Kennedy.

Chhibber, A. 1996, 'The State in a Changing World: Ideas from the forthcoming "World Development Report"', *Transition*, 7, 9–10: 14–16.

Chinnappa, B. N. 1977, 'Adoption of the New Technology in North Arcot District', Chapter 8, in (ed.) Farmer.

Chopra, P. N. (ed.) 1998, *Religions and Communities of India*, Vision Books, New Delhi.

Chowdhury, R. 1998, 'Women's Movements in India', *Visiting South Asian Scholarship Programme Report*, Queen Elizabeth House, Oxford.

Chunkath, S. R. and Athreya V. B. 1997, 'Female Infanticide in Tamil Nadu: Some Evidence', *Economic and Political Weekly*, 26 April.

Clark, A. 1983, 'Limitations on Female Life Chances in Rural Central Gujarat India', *Economic and Social History Review* 20, 1: 1–25.

Clark, A. (ed.) 1993, *Gender and Political Economy: Explorations of South Asian Systems*, Oxford University Press, New Delhi.

Clay, E. J., Harriss, B., Benson, C. and Gillespie, S. 1988, *Food Strategy in India*, Overseas Development Institute, London.

Colatei, D. and Harriss-White, B. 2002a, 'Social Stratification and Rural Households', Chapters 2 and 5, in Harriss-White, Janakarajan et al.

Colatei, D. and Harriss-White, B. 2002b, 'Rural Credit', chapters 2–5, in Harriss-White, Janakarajan et al.

Coletti, L. (ed.) 1975, *Karl Marx – Early Writings*, Penguin and New Left Books, London.

Collins, R. 1992, 'Weber's Last Theory of Capitalism: A Systematisation', pp. 85–110, in (eds) Granovetter and Svedberg.

Copestake, J. 1992, 'The Integrated Rural Development Programme: Performance During the Sixth Plan, Policy Responses and Proposals for Reform',
pp. 209–230, in (eds) Harriss, Guhan and Cassen.

Corbridge, S. and Harriss, J. 2000, *Reinventing India*, Polity, London.

Cox, A. and O'Sullivan, N. (eds) 1988, *The Corporate State: Corporatism and the
State Tradition in Western Europe*, Edward Elgar, Aldershot.

Crow, B. 2001, *Markets, Class and Rural Change in Bangladesh*, Palgrave, London.

Crow, B. and Murshid, F. 1994, 'The Finance of Foodgrains Markets in Bangladesh', *World Development* 22, 7: 1011–30.

da Corta, L. and Venkateshwarlu, D. 1999, 'Unfree Relations and the Feminiza-
tion of Agricultural Labour in Andhra Pradesh, 1970–95', *Journal of Peasant Studies*, 26, 2/3: 71–139.

Dandekar, V. M. and Rath, N. 1971, *Poverty in India*. Indian School of Political
Economy, Poona.

Dandekar, V. M. 1993, 'A Complacent Budget', *Economic and Political Weekly*,
10 April.

Das, A. 1994, *India Invented: A Nation in the Making*, Manohar, New Delhi.

Das, S. 1998, *Civil Service Reform and Structural Adjustment*, Oxford University
Press, New Delhi.

Das, S. 2001, *Public Office, Private Interest: Bureaucracy and Corruption in India*,
Oxford University Press, New Delhi.

Dasgupta, M. and Bhat, P. N. 1995, 'Intensified Gender Bias in India: A Consequence of Fertility Decline', *Working Paper no. 2*, Centre for Population
and Development Studies, Harvard University, Cambridge, Mass.

Dasgupta, N. 1992, *Petty Trading in the Third World*, Avebury, London.

Dass, J. R. 1988, *Economic Thought of the Sikh Gurus*, National Book Organisation, New Delhi.

Davala, S. (ed.) 1992, *Employment and Unionization in Indian Industry*, Friedrich
Ebert Stiftung, New Delhi.

Davis, J. 1992, *Exchange*, Oxford University Press for the Open University,
Buckingham.

de Alcantara, C. 1992 *Real Markets: Social and Political Issues of Food Policy
Reform*, Cass, London.

de Glopper, D. 1972, 'Doing Business in Lukang', pp. 297–326, in (ed.) Wilmott.

de Neve, G. 1999, 'Asking For and Giving *Baki*: Neo-bondage, or the Interplay
of Bondage and Resistance in the Tamil Nadu Power-loom Industry',
pp. 379–406, in (eds) Parry, Breman and Kapadia.

de Neve, G. 2001, 'Modern Migrants: Commitment and Mobility Among
Urban Migrants in Tirupur, South India', School of Asian and African
Studies, University of Sussex.

Deponte, G. 2000, 'Desindustrialisation, Précarisation du Travail et Transformation des Réseaux Politiques Urbains: Le Cas de la Ville de Kanpur
(UP)'. Paper to symposium 'La Ville en Asie du Sud: Quelles Spécifi-
cités?', Paris, Centre d'Etudes de l'Inde et de l'Asie du Sud.

Desai, A. R. 1984, 'Caste and Communal Violence in the Post-Partition Indian
Union', pp. 10–32, in (ed.) Engineer.

Desai, K. 1999, 'Secondary Labour Market in India – A Case Study of Workers in Small Scale Industrial Units in Gujarat', pp. 13–28, in (ed.) Shah.

Deshpande, C. 2001, 'Empowering Women of the Hindu Right: A Case Study of Shiv Sena's Mahila Aghadi', MPhil. Dissertation, Queen Elizabeth House, Oxford University.

Deshpande, S. 1999, 'Gender-based Discrimination in Segmented Labour Markets in India', pp. 118–29, in (ed.) Shah.

Dhagamwar, V. 1992, 'The Disadvantaged and the Law', pp. 433–48, in (eds) Harriss, Guhan and Cassen.

Diwan, P. 1978, 'Family Law', pp. 632–56, in (ed.) Minattur.

Diwan, Pa. and Diwan, Pe. 1991, *Family Law (Hindus, Muslims, Christians, Parsis and Jews)*, Allahabad Law Agency, Law Publishers, Allahabad.

Dore, R. 1992, 'Goodwill and the Spirit of Market Capitalism', pp. 159–80, in (eds) M. Granovetter and R. Svedberg.

Dorin, B., Flamant, N., Lachaier, P. and Vaugier-Chatterjee, A. 2000, *Le Patronat en Inde: Contours Sociologique des Acteurs et des Pratiques*, Centre de Sciences Humaines, New Delhi.

Dreze, J. 2000, 'Militarism, Development and Democracy', *Economic and Political Weekly*, 35, 14, 1 April, pp. 1171–83.

Dreze, J. and Sen, A. K. (eds) 1990, *The Political Economy of Hunger*, Clarendon, Oxford.

Dreze, J. and Sharma, N. 1998, 'Rural Credit in Palanpur', in (eds) Lanjouw and Stern.

Dreze, J. and Sharma, N. 1998, 'Palanpur: Population, Society, Economy', pp. 66–76, in (eds) Lanjouw and Stern.

Dubey, S. 1992, 'The Middle Class', pp. 137–64, in (eds) Gordon and Oldenburg.

Dumont, L. 1964, *Homo Hierarchicus: The Caste System and its Implications*, University of Chicago Press, Chicago.

Dupont, V. 1998, 'Industrial Clustering and Flexibility in the Textile Printing Industry of Jetpur', pp. 308–30, in (eds) Cadène and Holmstrom.

Dwyer, D. H. 1987, 'Gender, Law and Property Control', pp. 517–27, in (eds) Ghai et al.

Dwyer, D. and Bruce, J. (eds) 1988, *A House Divided: Women's Income in the Third World*, Stanford University Press, Stanford.

Ellis, C.C.M. 1991, 'The Jain Merchant Castes of Rajasthan: Some Aspects of the Management of Social Identity in a Market Town', pp. 75–107, in (eds) Carrithers and Humphrey.

Ellis, F. 1993, *Peasant Economics: Farm Households and Agrarian Development*, Cambridge University Press, Cambridge.

Ellis, F. 2000, *Rural Livelihoods and Diversity in Developing Countries*, Oxford University Press, Oxford.

Engelshoven, M. 1999, 'Diamonds and Patels: A Report on the Diamond Industry of Surat', pp. 353–78, in (eds) Parry et al.

Engineer, A. A. (ed.) 1984a, *Communal Riots in Post-independence India*, Sangam/Orient Longman, Hyderabad.

Engineer, A. A. 1984b, 'The Causes of Communal Riots in the Post-Partition Period in India', pp. 33–41, in (ed.) Engineer.

Epstein, T. S. 1964, *Economic Development and Social Change in South India*, Manchester University Press, Manchester.

Erb, S. and Harriss-White, B. 2002, *Outcast from Social Welfare: Adult Incapacity and Disability in Rural South India*, Books for Change, Bangalore.

Evans, P. 1995, *Embedded Autonomy: States and Industrial Transformation*, New Jersey, Princeton University Press, Princeton.

Evers, H.-D. 1994, 'The Traders' Dilemma: A Theory of the Social Transformation of Markets and Society', pp. 1–10, in (eds) Evers and Schrader.

Evers, H.-D. and Schrader, H. (eds) 1994, *The Moral Economy of Trade: Ethnicity and Developing Markets*, Routledge, London.

Farmer, B. H. (ed.) 1977, *Green Revolution?*, Macmillan, London.

Fay, B. 1985, *Critical Social Science*, Polity, London.

Feuer, L. S. (ed.) 1959, *Marx and Engels: Basic Writings on Politics and Philosophy*, Anchor, New York.

Fine, B. 2000, *Social Capital versus Social Theory: Political Economy and Social Science at the Turn of the Millennium*, Routledge, London.

Foster, A. and Rosensweig, M. 1999, *Missing Women, the Marriage Market and Economic Growth*, University of Pennsylvania (draft).

Fox, R. 1969, *From Zamindar to Ballot Box: Community Change in a North Indian Market Town*, Cornell University Press, Ithaca.

Frankel, F., Hasan, Z., Bhargava, R. and Arora, B. (eds) 2000, *Transforming India: Social and Political Dynamics of Democracy*, Oxford University Press, New Delhi.

Frankel F. R. and Rao, M. S. A. (eds) 1990, *Dominance and State Power in Modern India – II*, Oxford University Press, New Delhi.

Fua, G. 1988, 'Small-scale Industry in Rural Areas: The Italian Experience', in Arrow (ed.).

Fukuyama, F. 1995, *Trust: The Social Virtues and the Creation of Prosperity*, Penguin, London.

Fuller, C. 1996, 'Introduction: Caste Today', in (ed.) Fuller.

Fuller, C. (ed.) 1996, *Caste Today*, Oxford University Press, New Delhi.

Fuller, C. and Benei, V. (eds) 2001, *The Everyday State in India*, Social Science Press, New Delhi.

Galanter, M. 1984, *Competing Equalities: Law and Backward Classes in India*, Oxford University Press, New Delhi.

Galanter, M. 1997, *Law and Society in Modern India*, Oxford University Press, New Delhi.

Ganesan, K. 1997, 'Corruption in the Political Process: A Case for Electoral Reform', pp. 29–59, in (eds) Guhan and Paul.

Gardezi, H. N. 2000, 'Islamist and Hindutva Politics: Identities, Outlook and Objectives', paper to the joint session of The Pakistan Council of Social Sciences and Islamabad Social Science Forum, Dec; and Communalism Watch and Governance Monitor; Dec. 28th 2000, <www.saccer.org>.

Gellner, D. 1982, 'Max Weber, Capitalism and the Religion of India', *Sociology*, 16, 4, pp. 526–543.

Gellner, D. 2001, *The Anthropology of Buddhism and Hinduism: Weberian Themes*, Oxford University Press, New Delhi.

George, S. (ed.) 1998, *Female Infanticide, Search Bulletin*, vol. XIII, no. 3.

George, S., Abel, R. and Miller, B. 1992, 'Female Infanticide in Rural South Asia', *Economic and Political Weekly*, 30 May.

Ghai, Y., Luckham, R. and Snyder, F. (eds) 1987, *The Political Economy of Law*, Oxford University Press, Delhi.

Ghose, A. 1999, 'Current Issues of Employment Policy in India', *Economic and Political Weekly*, vol. XXXIV, no. 36, 4 September, pp. 2592–2608.

Ghosh, J. 1997, 'State Intervention in the Macroeconomy', in (ed.) Patnaik.

Ghosh, J. 1998, 'Liberalisation Debates', in (ed.) Byres.

Ghosh, J. 1999, 'Macro-economic Trends and Female Employment', pp. 318–50, in (eds) Papola and Sharma.

Giddens, A. 1990, *The Consequences of Modernity*, Polity Press, Cambridge.

Gillespie, S. and McNeill, G. 1992, *Food, Health and Survival in India and Developing Countries*, Oxford University Press, Delhi.

Gillion, K. L. 1968, *Ahmedabad: A Study in Indian Urban History*, University of California Press, Berkeley.

Goodman, R., White, G. and Kwon, H.-J. 1998, *The East Asian Welfare Model: Welfare Orientalism and the State*, Routledge, London.

Gooptu, N. 2001, *The Urban Poor and the Politics of Class, Community and Nation: Uttar Pradesh between the Two World Wars*, Cambridge University Press, Cambridge.

Gordon, D., Edwards, R. and Reich, M. 1982, *Segmented Work, Divided Workers*, Cambridge University Press.

Gordon, L. and Oldenburg, P. (eds) 1992, *India Briefing 1992*, Westview, Boulder.

Gorter, P. 1997, 'The Social and Political Aspirations of a new Stratum of Industrialists: Local Politics on a Large Industrial Estate in West India', pp. 81–114, in (eds) Rutten and Upadhya.

Gorter, P. 1998, 'Representation or Racket? Political Networks in an Industrial Estate in West India', pp. 359–75, in (eds) Cadène and Holmstrom.

Goulet, D. 1977, *The Uncertain Promise: Value Conflicts in Technology Transfer*, IDOC, North America, New York.

Government of India 1961, *Third Five Year Plan: 1961–66*, Planning Commission, New Delhi.

Government of India 1980, *Report of the Backward Classes Commission*, New Delhi.

Government of India 1983, *Economic Administrative Reforms Commission Reports on Tax Administration, 1981–83*, Ministry of Finance, New Delhi.

Government of India 1985, *Aspects of the Black Economy in India*, Government of India, New Delhi.

Government of India 1997, *Indian Public Finance Statistics*, Dept of Economic Affairs, Ministry of Finance, New Delhi.

Government of India 1999, *1991 Census Atlas*, Government of India, Census Commission, New Delhi.

Goyal, S. 1990, 'Social Background of Indian Corporate Executives', pp. 535–44, in (eds) Frankel and Rao.

Gramsci, A. 1971, *Prison Notebooks*, International Publishers, New York.

Granovetter, M. 1985, 'Economic Action and Social Structure: The Problem of Embeddedness', *American Journal of Sociology*, 91, 3: 481–510.

Granovetter, M. and Svedberg, R. (eds) 1992, *The Sociology of Economic Life*, Westview, Boulder.

Greenhalgh, S. 1994, 'De-Orientalising the Chinese Family Firm', *American Ethnologist* 21, 4: 746–75.

Griffiths, J. 1979, 'Is Law Important?', *New York University Law Review*, 54: 339–75.

Guha, A. 1984, 'More about the Parsi Seths – Their Roots, Entrepreneurship and Comprador Role, 1650–1918', *Economic and Political Weekly*, 19, 3: 117–32.

Guhan, S. 1992, 'Social Security in India: Looking One Step Ahead', pp. 282–300, in Harriss, Guhan and Cassen.

Guhan, S. 1994, 'Social Security Options for Developing Countries', *International Labour Review*, 133, 1: 35–53.

Guhan, S. 1995, 'Centre and States in the Reform Process', in (eds) Cassen and Joshi.

Guhan, S. 1997, 'Introduction', pp. 9–28, in (eds) Guhan and Paul.

Guhan, S. 2001, 'Comprehending Equalities', pp. 209–26, in (ed.) Subramanian.

Guhan, S. and Nagaraj, K. 1995, 'Adjustment, Employment and Equity in India', *Employment Programme Paper*, no. 4, International Labour Office, Geneva.

Guhan, S. and Paul, S. (eds) 1997, *Corruption in India: Agenda for Action*, Vision, New Delhi.

Gupta, A. 1993, 'Blurred Boundaries: The Discourse of Corruption, the Culture of Politics and the Imagined State', *American Ethnologist*, pp. 375–401.

Gupta, D. B. (ed.) 1997, *Special Issue on the Informal Sector*, Margin 30, 1, National Council for Applied Economic Research, New Delhi.

Haddad, L., Hoddinott, J. and Alderman, H. (eds) 1997, *Intrahousehold Resource Allocation in Developing Countries: Models, Methods and Policies*, Johns Hopkins, Baltimore.

Haider, B. K. 2001, *Communal Harmony: A Multi-pronged Approach*, VSAF Report, Queen Elizabeth House, Oxford.

Hale, A. (ed.) 1999, *Trade Myths and Gender Reality: Trade Liberalisation and Women's Lives*, Global Publications Foundation, Uppsala.

Hansen, T. B. 1996, 'Globalisation and Nationalist Imaginations: Hindutva's Promise of Equality Through Difference', *Economic and Political Weekly*, 9 March.

Hansen, T. B. 1997, 'Governance and myths of state in Mumbai', Paper to the Workshop on the Anthropology of the Indian State, London School of Economics, and pp. 31–67 in (eds) Fuller and Benei, 2001.

Hansen, T. B. 1998, 'The Ethics of Hindutva and the Spirit of Capitalism in India', pp. 291–314, in (eds) Hansen and Jaffrelot.

Hansen, T. B. 1999, *The Saffron Wave: Democracy and Hindu Nationalism in Modern India*, Princeton University Press, Princeton.

Hansen, T. B. and Jaffrelot, C. (eds) 1998, *The BJP and the Compulsions of Politics in India*, Oxford University Press, New Delhi.

Harriss, B. 1981, *Transitional Trade and Rural Development*, Vikas, New Delhi.

Harriss, B. 1984a, *State and Market*, Concept, New Delhi.

Harriss, B. 1984b, *Exchange Relations and Poverty in Dryland Agriculture*, Concept, New Delhi.

Harriss, B. 1985, *Agricultural Change and The Mercantile State: A Study of Public Policy in Tamil Nadu*, Cre-A Publications, Madras.

Harriss, B. 1987, *Differential Female Mortality and Health Care in South Asia*, Centre for the Study of Relief Administration, New Delhi.

Harriss, B. 1988, 'Government Revenue and Expenditure in an Agrarian District of South India', *Journal of Public Administration and Development*, 8, 4: 437–57.

Harriss, B. 1990, *The Intrafamily Distribution of Hunger in South Asia*, in (eds) Dreze and Sen, pp. 351–424.

Harriss, B. 1991a, 'The Arni Studies: Change in the Private Sector of a Market Town, 1971–83', in (eds) Hazell and Ramasamy.

Harriss, B. 1991b, *Child Nutrition and Poverty in South India*, Concept, New Delhi.

Harriss, B. 1993, 'Markets, Society and the State: Problems of Marketing under Conditions of Smallholder Agriculture in West Bengal', *Development Policy and Practice, Working paper 26*, Open University, Milton Keynes.

Harriss, B., Guhan, S. and Cassen, R. 1992, *Poverty in India: Research and Policy*, Oxford University Press, New Delhi.

Harriss, B. and Harriss, J. 1984, 'Generative or Parasitic Urbanism? Some Observations from the Recent History of a South Indian Market Town', pp. 82–101, in (eds) Harriss and Moore.

Harriss B. and Kelly C. 1982, 'Food Processing; Policy for Rice and Oil Technology in South Asia', *Bulletin, Institute of Development Studies* 13, 3: 32–44.

Harriss, J. 1980, 'Urban Labour, Urban Poverty and the so-called Informal Sector', *Bulletin of the Madras Institute of Development Studies*, October.

Harriss, J. 1981, *Capitalism and Peasant Farming*, Oxford University Press, New Delhi.

Harriss, J. 1982, 'Character of an Urban Economy: Small Scale Production and Labour Markets in Coimbatore', *Economic and Political Weekly*, XVII, 23, pp. 945–54 and 24, pp. 993–1002.

Harriss, J. 1985, 'Our Socialism and the Subsistence Engineer: The Role of Small Enterprises in the Engineering Industry in Coimbatore, South India', in Bromley (ed.).

Harriss, J. 1989, 'Vulnerable Workers in the Indian Urban Labour Market', in Rodgers (ed.).

Harriss, J. 1999, 'Comparing Political Regimes Across Indian States: A Preliminary Essay', *Economic and Political Weekly*, 34, 48, 27 November, pp. 3367–77.

Harriss, J. 2000, 'How Much Difference Does Politics Make? Regime Differences across Indian States and Rural Poverty Reduction', in (eds) Houtsager, Moore and Putzel.

Harriss, J. 2001a, *Depoliticising Development: The World Bank and Social Capital*, Left Word Books, Mumbai.

Harriss, J. 2001b, 'On the Anthropology of the Indian State', in Fuller and Benei (eds).

Harriss, J. forthcoming, 'The Great Tradition Globalizes: Reflections on Two Studies of "The Industrial Leaders" of Madras', *Modern Asian Studies*.

Harriss, J., Hunter, J. and Lewis, C. (eds) 1995, *The New Institutional Economics and Third World Development*, Routledge, London.

Harriss, J., Kannan, K. P. and Rodgers, G. 1989, 'Urban Labour Market Structure and Job Access in India: A Study of Coimbatore', *Discussion Paper 15*, International Institute for Labour Studies, Geneva.

Harriss, J. and Moore, M. (eds) 1984, *Development and the Rural–Urban Divide*, Cass, London.

Harriss-White, B. 1993, 'The Collective Politics of Foodgrains Markets in South Asia, *IDS Bulletin* 24, no. 3, pp. 54–62.

Harriss-White, B. 1995a, 'Efficiency and Complexity: Distributive Margins and the Profits of Market Enterprises', in (ed.) Scott, pp. 301–24.

Harriss-White, B. 1995b, 'Maps and Landscapes of Grain Markets in South Asia', in (eds) Harriss, Hunter and Lewis.

Harriss-White, B. 1996a, *A Political Economy of Agricultural Markets in South India: Masters of the Countryside*, Sage, New Delhi.

Harriss-White, B. 1996b, 'Free Market Romanticism in an Era of Deregulation', *Oxford Development Studies* 24, 1: 27–45.

Harriss-White, B. 1996c, 'Order, Order ... Agro-commercial Micro-structures and the State – The Experience of Regulation', in (eds) Subrahmanyam and Stein.

Harriss-White, B. 1996d, 'Liberalisation and Corruption: Resolving the Paradox', pp. 31–40, in (eds) Harriss-White and White.

Harriss-White, B. 1996e, 'Primary Accumulation, Corruption and Development', *Review of Development and Change* 1, 1: 85–101.

Harriss-White, B. 1998a, *Agricultural Markets from Theory to Practice: Field Methods and Field Experience in Developing Countries*, Macmillan, London.

Harriss-White, B. 1998b, 'Female and Male Marketing Systems: Analytical and Policy Issues for West Africa and India', pp. 171–89, in (eds) Jackson and Pearson.

Harriss-White, B. 1999a, 'State, Market, Collective and Household in India's Social Sector', pp. 303–28, in Harriss-White and Subramanian.

Harriss-White, B. 1999b, 'Gender-Cleansing: The Paradox of Development and Deteriorating Female Life Chances in Tamil Nadu', in (ed.) Sunder Rajan.

Harriss-White, B. 2002a, 'Infrastructure, Markets and Agricultural Performance', Chapter 2.2, in Harriss-White, Janakarajan et al.

Harriss-White, B. 2002b, 'Socially Inclusive Social Security: Social Assistance in the Villages', Chapter 3.6, in Harriss-White, Janakarajan et al.

Harriss-White, B. 2002c, 'Policy for Agricultural Development and Social Welfare', Chapters 1.2, in Harriss-White, Janakarajan et al.

Harriss-White, B. (ed.) 2002d, *Globalisation and Insecurity: Economic, Political and Physical Challenges*, Palgrave, London.

Harriss-White, B. 2002e, 'Rural Development in a Poor State', Chapter 4.1, in Harriss-White, Janakarajan et al.

Harriss-White, B. and Gooptu, N. 2000, 'Mapping India's World of Unorganised Labour', pp 89–118, in (eds) Panitch and Leys.

Harriss-White, B. and Janakarajan, S. 1996, 'Rural Infrastructure, Urban Civic Services and the Micro-politics of Governance', paper to the workshop on Adjustment and Development: Agrarian Change, Markets and Social Welfare in South India, Madras Institute of Development Studies, Madras, March.

Harriss-White, B. and Janakarajan, S. 1997, 'From Green Revolution to Rural Industrial Revolution in South India', *Economic and Political Weekly*, XXXII, 25: 1469–77.

Harriss-White, B. and Janakarajan, S. et al. 2002, *Reforms and Rural Development*. <www.livelihoodoptions.info>

Harriss-White, B. and Subramanian, S. (eds) 1999, *Illfare in India: Essays on India's Social Sector in Honour of S. Guhan*, Oxford University Press, New Delhi.

Harriss-White, B. and White, G. (eds) 1996, *Liberalisation and the New Corruption*, Special Issue, *Bulletin, Institute of Development Studies* 27, 2.

Harriss-White, B. and White, G. 1996, 'Corruption, Liberalisation and Democracy', pp.1–5, in (eds) Harriss-White and White.

Hart, G. 1996, 'The Agrarian Question and Industrial Dispersal in South Africa: Agro-Industrial Linkages through Asian Lenses', *Journal of Peasant Studies*, 23, pp. 2–3.

Hazell, P. and Ramasamy, C. 1991, *The Green Revolution Reconsidered*, Johns Hopkins, Baltimore.

Heins, J. J. F., Meijer E. N. and Kuipers, K. W. 1992, *Factories and Families: A Study of a Growth Pole*, Manohar, New Delhi.

Helweg, A. W. 1987, 'India's Sikhs: Problems and Prospects', *Journal of Contemporary Asia*, 17: 2.

Hensman, R. 1999, 'How to Support the Rights of Women Workers in the Context of Trade Liberalisation in India', pp. 71–88, in (ed.) Hale.

Hensman, R. 2000, 'Organizing Against the Odds: Women in India's Informal Sector', pp. 249–59, in (eds) Panitch and Leys.

Herring, R. 1983, *Land to the Tiller: the Political Economy of Agrarian reform in S. Asia*, Yale University Press, New Haven.

Herring, R. 1999, 'Embedded Particularism: India's Failed Developmental State', in (ed.)Woo-Cumings.

Heyer, J. 1992, 'The Role of Dowries and Daughters' Marriages in the Accumulation and Distribution of Capital in a South Indian Community', *Journal of International Development*, 4, 4.

Heyer, J. 2000, 'The Changing Position of Agricultural Labour in Villages in Rural Coimbatore, Tamil Nadu, between 1981/2 and 1996', Queen Elizabeth House Working Paper QEHWPS57, Oxford. <www2.qeh.ox.ac.uk>

Hodgson, G. 1988, *Economics and Institutions*, Polity Press, London.

Holmstrom, M. 1997, 'Which Kind of Decentralisation Do You Want and Why?', pp. 49–55, in (eds) Benei and Kennedy.

Holmstrom, M. 1998a, 'Bangalore as an Industrial District: Flexible Specialisation in a Labour Surplus Economy', pp. 169–229, in (eds) Cadène and Holmstrom.

Holmstrom, M. 1998b, 'Industrial Districts and Flexible Specialisation – The Outlook for Smaller Firms in India', pp. 7–24, in (eds) Cadène and Holmstrom.

Holmstrom, M. 1999, 'A New Map of Indian Industrial Society: The Cartographer all at Sea', *Oxford Development Studies*, 27, 2: 165–86.

Houtant, F. and Le Mercinier, G. 1980, *The Great Asiatic Religions and Their Social Functions*.

Houtsager, P., Moore, M. and Putzel, J. (eds) 2000, *Politics and Policy*, Routledge, London.

Ilaiah, K. 1996, *Why I am Not a Hindu: A Shudra Critique of Hindutva Philosophy, Culture and Political Economy*, Samya, Calcutta.

ILO 1992, *World Labour Report*, International Labour Office, Geneva.

ILO 1999, *Decent Work*, International Labour Office, Geneva.

Imam, Z. (ed.) 1975, *Muslims in India*, Orient Longman, New Delhi.

INFRAS 1993, *Rural–Urban Interlinkages: A Case Study Based on the Nepalese*, Swiss Development Agency, Zurich.

Iyer, R. 1999, 'Labour Market Segmentation and Women's Employment and Earning Differentials in India', pp. 130–51, in (ed.) Shah.

Jackson, C. 1999, 'Men's Work, Masculinities and Gender Divisions of Labour', *Journal of Development Studies*, 36, 1, pp. 89–108.

Jackson, C. and Pearson, R. (eds) 1998, *Feminist Visions of Development: Gender Analysis and Policy*, Routledge, London.

Jacob, P. 1997, 'On Strengthening the Indicators of the Informal Sector's Contribution to the National Economy', pp. 89–94, in *Margin* (NCAER), Special Issue on the Informal Sector, 30.1.

Jagganathan, V. 1987, *Informal Markets in Developing Countries*, Sage, New York.

Jain, P. 2001, 'Balancing the Seer and the Doer', *The Hindu*, April 6, <www.indiaserver.com/thehindu/2001/04/06/stories/130613h.htm>.

Jain, S. 2001, 'The Jains', *The Hindustan Times*, July, p. 11.

Jalal, A. and Bose, S. 1999, *Modern South Asia: History, Culture, Political Economy*, Oxford University Press, New Delhi.

Jalan, B. 1991, *India's Economic Crisis: The Way Ahead*, Oxford University Press, New Delhi.

Jalan, B. 1992, *The Indian Economy: Problems and Prospects*, Oxford University Press, New Delhi.

Janakarajan, S. 1993, 'Triadic Exchange Relations: An Illustration from South India', *Bulletin, Institute of Development Studies*, 24, 3, pp. 75–82.

Janakarajan, S. 1997, 'Village Resurveys: Issues and Results', pp. 413–425, in (eds) Breman, Kloos and Saith.

Jayaraj, D. 2002, 'Social Institutions and the Structural Transformation of the Non Farm Economy', Chapter 1.6, in Harriss-White, Janakarajan et al.

Jayaraj, D. and Subramanian, S. 1999, 'Poverty and Discrimination: Measurement and Evidence from Rural India', pp. 196–226, in (eds) Harriss-White and Subramanian.

Jayaram, N. 1996, 'Caste and Hinduism: Changing Protean Relationship', in (ed.) Srinivas.

Jeffery, P. and Bose, A. (eds) 1998, *Appropriating Gender*, Routledge, New York.

Jeffery, P. and Jeffery, R. 1998, 'Gender, Community and the Local State in Bijnor, India' in (eds) Jeffery and Bose.

Jeffrey, C. 1998, 'Soft States, Hard Bargains: Money, Class and Power in Northwest India', paper to the 15th European Conference on Modern Asian Studies, Prague.

Jeffrey, C. 1999, *Reproducing Difference: The Accumulation Strategies of Rich Jat Farmers in Meerut District, Western UP*, PhD Dissertation, University of Cambridge.

Jeffrey, C. 2001, '"A Fist is Stronger than Five Fingers": Caste and Dominance in Rural N. India', *Trans. Inst. British Geog.* (New Series), 26: 217–36.

Jenkins, R. and Goetz, A.-M. 1999, 'Constraints on Civil Society's Capacity to Curb Corruption', pp. 50–9, in (eds) R. Benewick et al.

Jha, P.K. 1997, *Agricultural Labour in India*, Vikas, New Delhi.

Jha, P.S. 1980, *The Political Economy of Stagnation*, Oxford University Press, Delhi.

Jhabvala, R. and Subrahmanya, R.K.A. (eds) 2000, *The Unorganised Sector: Work Security and Social Protection*, Sage, New Delhi.

Jodhka S. S. 1998, 'From "Book View" to "Field View": Social Anthropological Constructions of the Indian Village', *Oxford Development Studies* 26, 3: 311–32.

Joly, E. 2001, *Notre Affaire à Tous*, Les Arènes, Paris.

Jones, J. and Howard, M. 1991, 'Jain Shopkeepers and Moneylenders: Rural Informal Credit Networks in South Rajasthan', in (eds) Carrithers and Humphrey.

Jones, T. 1988, *Corporate Killing: Bhopals Will Happen*, Free Association, London.

Joshi, C. 1992, 'The Formation of Work Culture: Industrial Labour in a North Indian City, 1890s–1940s', *Purusartha*, no. 14, pp. 155–72.

Joshi, P. C. (ed.) 1965, *Homage to Karl Marx*, People's Publishing House, New Delhi.

Joshi, P. C. 1996, *India's Economic Reforms: 1991–2001*, Oxford University Press, New Delhi.

Joshi, V. and Little, I. M. 1994, *India: Macroeconomics and Political Economy: 1964–91*, Oxford University Press, New Delhi.

Justino, A. 2001, *Social Security and Political Conflict in Developing Countries with Special Reference to the South Indian State of Kerala*, PhD Thesis, School of Oriental and African Studies, London University.

Kagami, M. and Tsuji, M. (eds) 2000, *Privatization, Deregulation and Economic Efficiency*, Edward Elgar, Cheltenham.

Kalecki, M. 1972, *Essays on the Economic Growth of the Socialist and the Mixed Economy*, Unwin, London.

Kanbur, R. and Haddad, L. 1994, 'Are Better-off Households More Unequal or Less Unequal?' *Oxford Economic Papers 46*, pp. 445–58.

Kannabiran, K. and Kannabiran, K. 1991, 'Caste and Gender: Understanding Dynamics of Power and Violence', *Economic and Political Weekly*, 14 September.

Kapadia, K. 1994, '"Bonded by Blood": Matrilineal Kin in Tamil Kinship', *Economic and Political Weekly*, 9 April, pp. 855–61.

Kapadia, K. 1995a, 'The Profitability of Bonded Labour: The Gem Cutting Industry in Rural South India', *Journal of Peasant Studies*, 22, 3: 446–83.

Kapadia, K. 1995b, *Siva and her Sisters: Gender, Caste and Class in Rural South India*, Westview, Boulder.

Kapadia, K. 1999, 'A Study of Gender and Caste Transformations in India in Relation to Translocal Modernities and the Question of Social Exclusion', World Bank, Washington.

Kapadia, K. and Lerche, J. 1999, 'Introduction', *Journal of Peasant Studies*, 26, 2/3: 1–9.

Kaplinsky, R. 1999, 'Is Globalization All it is Cracked up to be?', *Bulletin of the Institute of Development Studies*, 30, 4: 106–15.

Karanth, G. K. 1996, 'Caste in Contemporary Rural India', in (ed.) Srinivas.

Kashyup, S. and Guha, G. S. 1997, 'Clusters of Small Size Firms across City Sizes in the Saurashtra Region of Gujarat', pp. 87–95, in (eds) Benei and Kennedy.

Kattuman, P. 1998, 'The Role of History in the Transition to an Industrial District: The Case of the Indian Bicycle Industry', pp. 230–50, in (eds) Cadène and Holmstrom.

Kaur, U. J. 1990, *Sikh Religion and Economic Development*, National Book Organisation, New Delhi.

Kaviraj, S. 1988, 'A Critique of the Passive Revolution', *Economic and Political Weekly* Special Number, November, pp. 2429–44.

Kaviraj, S. 1991, 'On State, Society and Discourse in India', pp.72–99, in (ed.) Manor.

Kay, J. 2002, 'Global Business in Search of Security', pp. 173–83, in (ed.) Harriss-White, 2002d.

Keane, J. 1988, 'Introduction', in (ed.) Keane.

Keane, J. (ed.) 1988, *Civil Society and the State*, Verso, London/New York.

Kennedy, L. 1997, 'When are Vertical Links Enabling?', pp. 131–8, in (eds) Benei and Kennedy.

Kennedy, L. 1999, 'Cooperating for Survival: Tannery Pollution and Joint Action in the Palar Valley (India)', *World Development*, 27, 9, pp. 1673–92.

Khalidi, O. 1995, *Indian Muslims Since Independence*, Vikas Publishing House, New Delhi.

Khan, M. 1996, 'A Typology of Corrupt Transactions in Developing Countries', pp. 12–21, in (eds) Harriss-White and White.

Khan, M. 1997, 'Corruption in South Asia: Patterns of Development and Change', Paper to the IDS Conference on Corruption and Development.

Khan, M. 2000a, 'Rents, Efficiency and Growth', pp. 21–69, in (eds) Khan and Jomo.

Khan, M. 2000b, 'Rent-seeking as Process', pp. 70–144, in (eds) Khan and Jomo.

Khan, M. and Jomo, K. S. (eds) 2000a, *Rents, Rent-seeking and Economic Development: Theory and Evidence in Asia*, Cambridge University Press, Cambridge.

Khan, M. and Jomo, K. S. (eds) 2000b, 'Introduction', pp. 1–20, in (eds) Khan and Jomo.

Khandwalla, P. N. 1995, 'The Cult of Vishnu and India's Economic Development', *The Indian Journal of Social Science*, 8, 2, pp. 147–59.

Khilnani, S. 1997, *The Idea of India*, Hamish Hamilton, London.

Kjellberg, F. and Banik, D. 2000, 'The Paradox of Pollution Control: Regulations and Administration in a South Indian State', Department of Political Science, *Research Report No. 2/2000*, University of Oslo.

Knorringa, P. 1998, 'Barriers to Flexible Specialisation in Agra's Footwear Industry', pp. 283–307, in (eds) Cadène and Holmstrom.

Knorringa, P. 1999, 'Agra: An Old Cluster Facing the New Competition', *World Development*, 27, 9, pp. 1587–1604.

Kohli, A. (ed.) 1988, *India's Democracy: An Analysis of Changing State–Society Relations*, Princeton University Press, Princeton.

Kohli, A. 1990, *Democracy and Discontent: India's Growing Crisis of Governability*, Cambridge University Press, Cambridge.

Kotz, D. 1994, 'The Regulation Theory and the Social Structures of Accumulation Approach', pp. 85–98, in (eds) Kotz, McDonough and Reich.

Kotz, D. M., McDonough, M. T. and Reich, M. (eds) 1994, *Social Structures of Accumulation: The Political Economy of Growth and Crisis*, Cambridge University Press.

Kovel, J. 1995, 'Marxism and Spirituality', pp. 42–50, in (eds) Callari, Cullenberg and Biewener.

Krishnakumar, A. 1999, 'Along the Polluted Palar', *Frontline*, 16, 20, 8 October, pp. 111–15.

Krishnaraj, M. and Deshmukh, S. 1993, *Gender in Economics*, Ajanta, Bombay.

Krueger, A. O. 1974, 'The Political Economy of the Rent-seeking Society', *American Economic Review*, 64: 3.

Krugman, P. 1998, 'What's New about the New Economic Geography?', *Oxford Review of Economic Policy*, 40, pp. 959–67.

Kumar, A. 1995, 'Reinterpreting Retreat of the State in a Second Best Environment', *Economic and Political Weekly*, 6 May.

Kumar, A. 1999, *The Black Economy in India*, Penguin, New Delhi.

Kumar, G. and Stewart, F. 1992, 'Tackling Malnutrition: What can Targeted Nutritional Interventions Achieve?', pp. 229–58, in (eds) Harriss, Guhan and Cassen.

Kumar, S. and Das, K. 1997, 'Regulation Theory, Flexible Specialisation, Social Embeddedness', pp. 95–100, in (eds) Benei and Kennedy.

Kundu, A. 1999, 'Trends and Patterns of Female Employment', pp. 52–71, in (eds) Papola and Sharma.

Kurian, M. V. 1986, *The Caste–Class Formations. A Case Study of Kerala*, B. R. Publishing Corporation, New Delhi.

Lachaier, P. 1997, 'A Case Study of Networks in the Towns of Southern Maharashtra', pp. 105–12, in (eds) Benei and Kennedy.

Laclau, E. 1977/1982, *Politics and Ideology in Marxist Theory: Capitalism, Fascism, Populism*, Verso, London.

Laidlaw, J. 1995, *Riches and Renunciation. Religion, Economy, and Society among the Jains*, Clarendon Press, Oxford.

Lal, D. 1988, *The Hindu Equilibrium, Vol. 1: Cultural Stability and Economic Stagnation 1500 BC to 1980*, Clarendon Press, London.

Lambert, H. 1996, 'Caste, Gender and Locality in Rural Rajasthan', pp. 92–124, in (ed.) Fuller.

Landy, F. 1998, 'Deconstructing the Indian Food Policy', paper to the 15th European Conference on Modern Asian Studies, Prague.

Lanjouw, P. and Stern N. (eds) 1998, *Economic Development in Palanpur over Five Decades*, Clarendon Press, Oxford.

Lasch, S. and Urry, J. 1994/99, *Economies of Signs and Space*, Sage, London.

Lau, M. 1996, 'Access to Environmental Justice in Karachi', Contemporary South Asia Seminar Series, Queen Elizabeth House, Oxford.

Leestemaker, J. H. 1992, 'The Struggle for Water: Competition between Industries and Households', pp. 105–16, in (eds) Heins et al.

Lehmann, D. (ed.) 1974, *Agrarian Reform and Agrarian Reformism*, Faber, London.

Lenin, I. 1960/86, *The Development of Capitalism in Russia*, Lawrence and Wishart, London.

Lerche, J. 1995, 'Is Bonded Labour a Bound Category? Reconceptualising Agrarian Conflict in India', *Journal of Peasant Studies*, 22, 3: 484–515.

Lerche, J. 1998, 'Agricultural Labour, the State and Agrarian Transition in Uttar Pradesh', *Economic and Political Weekly*, 33, pp. A29–35.

Lerche, J. 1999, 'Politics of the Poor: Agricultural Labourers and Political Transformations in Uttar Pradesh', *Journal of Peasant Studies*, 26, 2/3: 182–241.

Levkovsky, I. 1966, *Capitalism in India – Basic Trends in its Development*, People's Publishing House, Bombay.

Leys, C. 1996, *The Rise and Fall of Development Theory*, James Currey, London.

Leys, C. 2001, *Market Driven Politics*, Verso, London.

Lipton, M. 1977, *Why Poor People Stay Poor: Urban Bias in Development*, Temple Smith, London.

Loucks, W. and Hoot, J. 1948, *Comparative Economic Systems*, Harper, New York.

Luckham, R. and White, G. (eds) 1996, *Democratisation in the South: The Jagged Wave*, Manchester University Press.

Luhrmann, N. 1979, *Trust and Power*, John Wiley & Sons, Chichester.

Luhrmann, T. M. 1994, 'The Good Parsi: The Postcolonial "Feminisation" of a Colonial Elite', *Man*, 29, 2, pp. 333–57.

Luhrmann, T. M. 1996, *The Good Parsi. The Fate of a Colonial Elite in a Postcolonial Society*, Harvard University Press, Cambridge, Massachusetts.

Madan, T. N. 1987, 'Secularism in its Place', *Journal of Asian Studies*, 46: 4.

Madan, T. N. 1997, 'The Hindu Family and Development', pp. 416–434, in (ed.) Uberoi.

Mahalanobis, P. C. 1955, 'The Approach of Operational Research to Planning in India', *Sankhya: The Indian Journal of Statistics*.

Mancini, O., Perrillo, F. and Zagari, E. (eds) 1983, *La Teoria Economica del Corporativismo*, Two Volumes, ESI, Napoli.

Mani, S. 1991, 'External Liberalisation, Domestic Technology Development and the Need for an Institutional Support in Indian Industry', Centre for Development Studies, *Working Paper*, Trivandrum.

Mani, S. 1994, 'Financing Technology-based Small Firms and Venture Capital Funds: The Indian Experience', *Development Studies Working Papers 78*, Luca d'Agliano Studies Centre/Queen Elizabeth House, Torino and Oxford.

Mani, S. 2000, 'A Survey of Deregulation in Indian Industry', in (eds) Kagami and Tsuji.

Mann, E. A. 1992, *Boundaries and Identities. Muslims, Work and Status in Aligarh*, Sage, New Delhi.

Manor, J. (ed.) 1991, *Rethinking Third World Politics*, Longmans, Harlow.

Manor, J. 1993, *Power, Poverty and Poison: Disaster and Response in an Indian City*, Sage, New Delhi.

Martin, R. 1999, 'The New "Geographical Turn" in Economics: Some Critical Reflections', *Cambridge Journal of Economics*, 23, pp. 65–91.

Marx, K. 1967, *The Communist Manifesto*, Penguin Books, London.

Marx, K. 1976, *Genesis of Capital*, Progress Publishing, Moscow.

Massenzio, M. 2000, 'Réligion et Sortie de la Réligion', *Gradhiva*, 28: 23–32.

Massey, D. 1994, *Space, Place and Gender*, Polity Press, London.

Mathur, K. (ed.) 1996, *Development Policy and Administration: Readings in Indian Government and Politics – 1*, Sage, New Delhi.

Mayer, A. 1996, 'Caste in an Indian Village: Change and Continuity, 1954–1992', pp. 32–63, in (ed.) Fuller.

McBarnet, D. and Whelan, C. 1991, 'The Elusive Spirit of the Law: Formalism and the Struggle for Legal Control', *The Modern Law Review*, 54, 6, pp. 848–73.

McCahery, J., Picciotto, S. and Scott, C. (eds) 1993, *Corporate Control and Accountability: Changing Structures and the Dynamics of Regulation*, Oxford University Press, Oxford.

McCartney, M. and Harriss-White, B. 2000, 'The Intermediate Regime and Intermediate Classes Revisited: A Political Economy of Indian Development from 1980 to Hindutva', Queen Elizabeth House Website, Working Paper number 34, <www2.qeh.ox.ac.uk>.

Meher, R. 1999, 'Inter-state Disparities in Levels of Development and the Implications of Economic Liberalisation on Regional Economies of India', *Review of Development and Change* 4, 2, pp. 198–224.

Meillassoux, C. 1971, *The Development of Indigenous Trade and Markets in West Africa*, Oxford University Press, London.

Mellor, J. 1976, *The New Economics of Growth*, Cornell University Press, Ithaca.

Mencher, J. 1988, 'Women's Work and Poverty: Women's Contribution to Household Maintenance in South India', in (eds) Dwyer and Bruce.

Mendelsohn, O. 1993, 'The Transformation of Power in Rural India', *Modern Asian Studies*, 27, 4, pp. 805–42.

Mendelsohn, O. and Vicziany, M. 1998, *The Untouchables: Subordination, Poverty and the State in Modern India*, Cambridge University Press, Cambridge.

Mies, M. 1986, *Patriarchy and Accumulation on a World Scale: Women in the International Division of Labour*, Zed, London.

Miliband, R. 1983, *Class Power and State Power*, Verso, London.

Minattur, J. (ed.) 1978, *The Indian Legal System*, Oceana, New York.

Mines, M. 1972, *Muslim Merchants: The Economic Behaviour of an Indian Muslim Community*, Shri Ram Centre for Industrial Relations and Human Resources, New Delhi.

Mines, M. 1984, *The Warrior Merchants: Textiles, Trade and Territory in South India*, Cambridge University Press, Cambridge.

Mitra, A. 1977, *The Terms of Trade and Class Relations*, Cass, London.

Mohan, R. and Thottan, P. 1992, 'The Regional Spread of Urbanisation, Industrialisation and Urban Poverty', pp. 76–141, in (eds) Harriss, Guhan and Cassen.

Mollinga, P. 1998, 'On the Waterfront: Water Distribution, Technology and Agrarian Change in a South Indian Canal Irrigation System', Doctoral Thesis, Wageningen Agricultural University.

Mondal, S. R. 1997, *Muslims of Siliguri*, Institute of Objective Studies, Qasi Publishing, New Delhi.

Mooij, J. 1998, 'The Black Box of the State: Studying Interventions in Food Markets', Chapter 4.4 in (ed.) Harriss-White.

Mooij, J. 1999, *Food Politics and Policy in India. The Public Distribution System in South India*, Oxford University Press, New Delhi.

Moore, B. Jr 1966, *Social Origins of Dictatorship and Democracy: Lord and Peasant in the Making of the Modern World*, Penguin, London.

Moore, M. P. 1974, 'Some Secular Aspects of the Sacred Cow', Institute of Development Studies *Discussion Paper number 58*, Institute of Development Studies, Sussex.

Moore, M. P. 1994, 'How Difficult is it to Construct Market Relations? A Comment on Platteau', *Journal of Development Studies*, 30, 4, pp. 818–30.

Moore, M. P. 1999, 'Truth, Trust and Market Transactions: What do we know?', *Journal of Development Studies*, 36, 1, pp. 74–88.

Morris, M. D. 1967, 'Values as an Obstacle to Economic Growth in South Asia: An Historical Survey', *The Journal of Economic History*, vol. 27, pp. 588–607.

Mosse, D. 1994, 'Idioms of Subordination and Styles of Protest Among Christians and Hindu Harijan Castes in Tamil Nadu', *Contributions to Indian Sociology*, 28, 1, pp. 67–106.

Mosse, D. 1997, 'The Symbolic Making of a Common Property Resource: History, Ecology and Locality in a Tank-irrigated Landscape in South India', *Development and Change*, 28, 3: 467–504.

Mukhajan, G., Pai, S. and Jayal, N. G. 1994, 'State and New Liberal Agenda in India', *Economic and Political Weekly*, April, p. 1112.

Mukherjee Reed, A. (ed.) 2000, *Corporate Capitalism in Contemporary South Asia*, Special Issue, *Contemporary South India*, vol. 9, no. 2.

Mukherjee Reed, A. and Kundu, A. 2000, 'Corporate Capitalism: Realities and Interpretations', pp. 127–40, in (ed.) Mukherjee Reed.

Munshi, S. 1988, 'Max Weber on India: An Introductory Critique', *Contributions to Indian Sociology*, 22, pp. 126–34.

Myrdal, G. 1968, *Asian Drama. An Inquiry into the Poverty of Nations*, Penguin Books, Clinton, Massachusetts.

Myrdal, G. 1973, *Against the Stream: Critical Essays on Economics*, Vintage, New York.

Nadvi, K. 1992, 'Industrial Clusters in Less Developed Countries: Review of Experience and Research Agenda', *Institute of Development Studies Discussion Paper*, Institute of Development Studies, Sussex.

Nadvi, K. 1996, 'Small Firms in Industrial Districts in Pakistan', PhD thesis, University of Sussex, Brighton.

Nadvi, K. 1999a, 'Shifting Ties, Social Networks in the Surgical Instrument Cluster of Sialkot', *Development and Change*, 30, 1, pp. 143–77.

Nadvi, K. 1999b, 'Collective Efficiency and Collective Failure: The response of the Sialkot Surgical Instrument Cluster to Global Quality Pressures', *World Development* 27, 9, pp. 1105–26.

Nagaraj, K. 1985, 'Marketing Structure for Paddy and Arecanut in South Kanara: A Comparison of Markets in a Backward District', in (eds) Raj et al.

Nagaraj, K. 1986, 'Infant Mortality in Tamil Nadu', *Bulletin: Madras Development Seminar Series*, 16, 1, pp. 27–69.

Nagaraj, K. 1999, 'Labour Market Characteristics and Employment Generation Programmes in India', pp. 77–80, in (eds) Harriss-White and Subramanian.

Nagaraj, K., Janakarajan, S., Jayaraj, D. and Harriss-White, B. 1996, 'Sociological Aspects of Silk Weaving in Arni and its Environs', paper to the Workshop on Adjustment and Development, Madras Institute of Development Studies, Chennai.

Nagaraj, R. 1994, 'Employment and Wages in Manufacturing Industries: Trends, Hypotheses and Evidence', *Economic and Political Weekly*, 22 January.

Namboodiripad, E. M. S. 1973, 'On Intermediate Regimes', *Economic and Political Weekly*, 1 December.

Narayanan, H. 1997, 'The Plot Thickens: Rhetoric and Reality in the Context of the Urban Land (Ceiling and Registration) Act 1976 and its Application to Mumbai', paper to the Seminar on Work and Workers in Mumbai, Mumbai.

National Sample Survey Organisation, 1989, *43rd Round, 1987–88*, NSSO, New Delhi.

Neelakanthan S. 1995, 'Aspects of the Development of Karur', Madras Institute of Development Studies, mimeo.

Nillesen, P. 1999, 'The Survival of the Girl Child', MSc. Thesis in Economics for Development, University of Oxford.

Nillesen, P. and Harriss-White, B. 2002, 'Life Chances: Development and Female Disadvantage', Chapter 3.2, in Harriss-White, Janakarajan et al.

Noorani, A. G. 1997a, 'Commissions of Inquiry', pp. 21–250, in (eds) Guhan and Paul.

Noorani, A. G. 1997b, 'The Right to Information', pp. 114–43, in (eds) Guhan and Paul.

North, D. C. 1990, *Institutions, Institutional Change and Economics*, Cambridge University Press, Cambridge.

Offer, A. 1996, 'Between the Gift and the Market: The Economy of Regard', *Oxford Papers in Economic and Social History no. 3*, Nuffield College, Oxford.

Oldenburg, P. (ed.) 1993, *India Briefing 1993*, Westview Press, Boulder.

Olsen, W. K. 1993, 'Competition and Power in Rural Markets', *Bulletin, Institute of Development Studies*, 24, 3, pp. 83–9.

Olsen, W. K. 1996, *Rural Indian Social Relations*, Oxford University Press, New Delhi.

Olsen, W. K. forthcoming, *The Limits to Conditionality*, Worldview, Oxford.

Olson, M. 1982, *The Rise and Decline of Nations: Economic Growth, Stagflation and Social Rigidities*, Yale University Press, New Haven.

Omvedt, G. 1993, *Reinventing Revolution: New Social Movements and the Socialist Tradition in India*, M. E. Sharpe, New York.

O'Sullivan N. 1988, 'The Political Theory of Neo-corporatism', in (eds) Cox and O'Sullivan.

Pacey, A. and Payne, P. 1984, *Agricultural Development and Nutrition*, Hutchinson, London.

Pakkinar, K. M. 1955, *Asia and Western Dominance*, Allen & Unwin, London.

Palaskas, T. B. and Harriss-White, B. 1993, 'Testing Marketing Integration: New Approaches with Case Material from the West Bengal Food Economy', *Journal of Development Studies*, 30, 1: 1–57.

Palaskas, T. B. and Harriss-White, B. 1996, 'Identification of Market Exogeneity and Market Dominance by Tests Instead of Assumptions: An Application to Indian Material', *Journal of International Development*, 8, 1: 111–23.

Paloscia, R. 1991, 'Agriculture and Diffused Manufacturing in the Terza Italia: A Tuscan Case Study', in (eds) Whatmore et al.

Panini, M. N. 1996 'The Political Economy of Caste', in (ed.) Srinivas.

Panitch, L. and Leys, C. (eds) 2000, Working Classes, Global Realities, *Socialist Register 2001*, Merlin Press, London.

Pannikar, K. M. 1955, *Asia and Western Dominance*, Allen & Unwin, London (cited in Myrdal 1968).

Papanek, G. 1967, *Pakistan's Development: Social Goals and Private Incentives*, Harvard University Press, Cambridge, Mass.

Papanek, H. 1990, 'To Each Less Than She Needs: For Each More Than She Can Do – Allocations, Entitlements and Value', in (ed.) Tinker.

Papola, T. S. and Sharma, S. (eds) 1999, *Gender and Employment in India*, Vikas, New Delhi.

Parry, J., Breman, J. and Kapadia, K. (eds) 1999, *The Worlds of Indian Industrial Labour*, Sage, New Delhi.

Patnaik, P. 1994, 'Macro-economic Policy in Times of Globalisation', *Economic and Political Weekly*, 16 April.

Patnaik, P. 1996, 'Critical Reflections on Some Aspects of Structural Change in the Indian Economy', in (ed.) Byres.

Patnaik, P. (ed.) 1997, *Macroeconomics*, Oxford University Press, New Delhi.

Paul, S. and Shah, M. 1997, 'Corruption in Public Service Delivery', pp. 144–65, in (eds) Guhan and Paul.

Pedersen, J. D. 2000, 'Explaining Economic Liberalisation in India: State–Society Perspectives', *World Development*, 28, 2, pp. 265–82.

Pedersen, P. O. 1998, *Small African Towns – Between Rural Networks and Urban Hierarchies*, Avebury, London.

People's Union for Civil Liberties 1998, 'Communal Violence in Coimbatore between November 29th and December 1st 1997', *Frontline*, 15, 5, 20 March, pp. 115–19.

Philip, D. C. 1984, *Cross-cultural Trade in World History*, Cambridge University Press, Cambridge.

Pisani, E. and Zaba, B. 2000, 'Son Preference, Sex Selection and the Marriage Market', cited in Agnihotri (2000), p. 373.

Platteau, J.-P. 1993, 'The Free Market is not Readily Transferable: Reflections on the Links between Market, Social Relations and Moral Norms', *Journal of Development Studies*, 30, 3, pp. 533–77.

Platteau, J.-P. 1994, 'Behind the Market Stage where Real Societies Exist: The Role of Private and Public Order Institutions', *Journal of Development Studies* 36,3, 30, 4, pp. 753–817.

Polanyi, K. 1957/1985, 'The Economy as Instituted Process', in Polanyi, K. et al. (eds).

Polanyi, K., Arensburg, C. and Pearson, H. (eds) 1957, *Trade and Markets in the Early Empires: Economies in History and Theory*, Free Press, Glencoe (reprinted in 1985).

Poulantsas, N. 1980, *State, Power, Socialism*, Verso, London.

Pradhan, B. K. and Saluja, M. R. 1997, 'Estimating the National Product in India: Explaining the Unorganised Sector; A Review of Methodology', Special Issue on *The Informal Sector*, *Margin* (NCAER, New Delhi), 30, 1, pp. 45–62.

Putnam, R. D. 1993, *Making Democracy Work: Civic Traditions in Modern Italy*, Princeton University Press, Princeton.

Radhakrishnan, P. 1996, 'Mandal Commission Report: A Sociological Critique', in (ed.) Srinivas.

Raj, K. N. 1973, 'The Politics and Economics of Intermediate Regimes', *Economic and Political Weekly*, 7 July.

Raj, K. N. 1976, 'Growth and Stagnation in Indian Industrial Development', *Economic and Political Weekly*, XI, numbers 5–7, Annual Number, pp. 223–36.

Raj, K. N., Bhattacharya, N., Guha, S. and Padhi, S. (eds) 1985, *Essays on the Commercialisation of Indian Agriculture*, Oxford University Press, Bombay.

Rajagopal, A. 1994, 'Ram Janmabhoomi: Consumer Identity and Image-based Politics', *Economic and Political Weekly*, 2 July: 1659.

Ramachandran, V. K. 1990, *Wage Labour and Unfreedom in Agriculture: An Indian Case Study*, Clarendon, Oxford.

Ramamurthy, P. 1995, 'The Political Economy of Canal Irrigation in South India', PhD Thesis, Syracuse University.

Ramanujam, A. K. 1990, 'Is There an Indian Way of Thinking?', *The Book Review*, Jan.–Feb., pp. 18–23.

Rao, C. H. H. and Gulati, A. 1994, *Indian Agriculture: Emerging Perspectives and Policy Issues,* Indian Council of Agricultural Research, New Delhi, and International Food Policy Research Institute, Washington.

Razavi, S. 1999, 'Gendered Poverty and Wellbeing: Introduction', Special Issue on *Gendered Poverty and Wellbeing*; *Development and Change*, 30, 3.

Reiniche, M.-L. 1996, 'The Urban Dynamics of Caste: A Case Study from Tamil Nadu', in (ed.) Fuller.

Reserve Bank of India 1999, *Report on Currency and Finance*, 1997–98, Reserve Bank of India, Mumbai.

Roach, J. R. (ed.) 1986, *India 2000: The Next Fifteen Years, The Papers of a Symposium Conducted by the Center for Asian Studies of the University of Texas at Austin as Part of the 1985–86 Festival of India in the United States*, The Riverdale Company.

Robinson, M. and White, G. (eds) 1999 *The Democratic Developmental State*, Oxford University Press, Oxford.

Rodgers, G. 1975, 'Nutritionally-based Wage Determination in the Low-income Labour Market', *Oxford Economic Papers*, New Series 27, pp. 61–81.

Rodgers, G. (ed.) 1989, *Urban Poverty and the Labour Market: Access to Jobs and Incomes in Asian and Latin American Cities*, International Labour Office, Geneva.

Rodgers, G. and Rodgers, J. 2001, 'Semi-feudalism Meets the Market: A Report from Purnia', *Economic and Political Weekly*.

Rodinson, M. 1987, 'Islam and Capitalism', pp. 70–8, in (eds) Ghai et al.

Rogaly, B. 1996, 'Agricultural Growth and the Structure of "Casual" Labour-hiring in Rural West Bengal', *Journal of Peasant Studies*, 23, 4: 141–60.

Rogaly, B., Biswas, J., Cloppard, D., Rafique, A., Rana, K. and Sengupta, A. 2000, 'Seasonal Migration, Welfare Regimes and Adverse Incorporation: A Case Study from East India', paper for the Global Social Policy Regional Workshop, D. D, Koitta, Bangladesh, March, p. 2.

Rothermund, D. and Saha, S. K. (eds) 1991, *Regional Disparities in India. Rural and Industrial Dimensions*, Manohar, New Delhi.

Rowthorn, B. 1977, *Capitalism, Conflict and Inflation*, Lawrence and Wishart, London.

Roy, R. 1996, 'State Failure: Political–Fiscal Implications of the Black Economy', pp. 22–31, in (eds) Harriss-White and White.

Roy, R. 1998, 'Riches amid Sterility: Debates on Indian Fiscal Policy', in (ed.) Byres.

Roy, T. and Basant, R. 1990, 'The Urban Informal Sector: A Critical Review', *Working Paper 27,* Gujurat Institute of Area Planning, Ahmedabad.

Rudolph, L. and Rudolph, S. 1987, *In Pursuit of Lakshmi: The Political Economy of the Indian State*, University of Chicago Press, Chicago.

Rudra, A. 1989, 'Emergence of the Intelligentsia as a Ruling Class in India', *Economic and Political Weekly*, 24, 3, 21 January.

Rudra, A. 1992, *A Political Economy of Indian Agriculture*, K. P. Bagchi, Calcutta.

Rukmani, R. 1994, 'Urbanisation and Socio-economic Change in Tamil Nadu 1901–91', *Economic and Political Weekly*, 17 December, pp. 3263–72.

Rukmani, R. 1996, 'Factors Underlying High Dispersal of Towns in Tamil Nadu', *Review of Development and Change* 1, 1, pp. 133–45.

Rutten, M. 1995, *Farms and Factories: Social Profile of Large Farmers and Rural Industrialists in West India*, Oxford University Press, New Delhi.

Rutten, M. 1997, 'Co-operation and Differentiation: Social History of Iron Founders in Central Java', pp. 173–210, in Rutten and Upadhya (eds).

Rutten, M. and Upadhya, C. (eds) 1997, *Small Business Entrepreneurs in Asia and Europe: Towards a Comparative Perspective*, Sage, New Delhi.

Sachs, J., Varshney, A. and Bajpai, N. 1999, *India in the Era of Reforms*, Oxford University Press, New Delhi.

Saith, A. 2001, 'From Village Artisans to Industrial Clusters: Agendas and Policy Gaps in Indian Rural Industrialisation', *Journal of Agrarian Change*, 1, 1: 81–123.

Saith, R. and Harriss-White, B. 2002, 'Anti-Poverty Policy: Targeting and Screening for Eligibility', chapter 3-1 in Harriss-White, Janakarajan et al.

Sandaresa, J. C. 1991, 'New Small Enterprise Policy: Implications and Prospects', *Economic and Political Weekly*, 19 October.

Sanghera, B. S. 1992, 'A Critique of Williamson's Transactions Costs Economics and of its Relevance to Agricultural Economics', MSc. Thesis, Queen Elizabeth House, Oxford.

Sanghera, B. S. and Harriss-White, B. 1995, 'Themes in Rural Urbanisation', *Discussion Paper 39*, Development Policy and Practice, Open University, Milton Keynes.

Saradamoni, S. (ed.) 1985, *Women, Work and Society*, Indian Statistical Institute, Calcutta.

Satyamurthy, T. V. (ed.) 1995, *Industry and Agriculture in India Since Independence*, Oxford University Press, New Delhi.

Schmitter, P. C. 1974, 'Still the Century of Corporatism?', *Review of Politics*, 36.

Schmitz, H. and Nadvi, K. 1999, 'Clustering and Industrialisation: Introduction', Special Issue on *Industrial Clusters in Developing Countries*, *World Development*, 27, 9, pp. 1503–14.

Scocpol, T. et al. 1990, *Bringing the State Back In*, Harvard University Press, Cambridge.

Scott, G. (ed.) 1995, *Prices, Products and People: Analysing Agricultural Markets in Developing Countries*, Lynne Reinner, Boulder.

Sen, A. 1992, 'Agriculture and Economic Liberalisation: The Indian Outlook', workshop on Meanings of Agriculture, July, School of Oriental and African Studies, University of London, Centre of South Asian Studies.

Sen, A. K. 1990, 'Gender and Co-operative Conflict', in (ed.) Tinker.

Sen, A. K. 1997, 'Economics and the Family', pp. 452–66, in (ed.) Uberoi.

Sengupta, A. 1998, 'Embedded or Stuck? The Study of the Indian State, its Embeddedness in Local Institutions and State Capacity', MPhil thesis in Development Studies, Queen Elizabeth House, Oxford University.

Shah, A. M. (ed.) 1996, *Social Structure and Change Vol. 2*, Sage, New Delhi.

Shah, M. (ed.) 1999, *Labour Market Segmentation in India*, Himalaya, Mumbai.

Shahabuddin, S. 1984, 'Communal Violence – A Challenge to Plurality', pp. 104–17, in Engineer (ed.).

Shakir, S. 1983, *Islam in Indian Politics*, Ajanta Publishers, Delhi.

Shanin, T. 1999, *Informal and Expolary Economy*, Moscow School of Social and Economic Sciences, Moscow.

Shariff, A. 2002, 'Some Thoughts on the Nature and Persistence of Poverty in India'. Paper to seminar on 'Alternative Realities: Different Concepts of Poverty', NCAER, New Delhi.

Shiri, G. 1997, *The Plight of Christian Dalits. A South Indian Case Study*, Asian Trading Corporation, Bangalore.

Shurmer-Smith, P. 2000, *India: Globalization and Change*, Arnold, London.

Silberstein, B. 1997, 'Locality, Time and Process: Their Role in Vertical Integration within the World Market', pp. 145–50, in (eds) Benei and Kennedy.

Silberstein, B. 2000, 'La Ville et le Développement Economique Local et Mondial', paper to the symposium 'La Ville en Asie du Sud: Quelles specificités?', Centre d'Etudes de l'Inde et de l'Asie du Sud, Paris.

Simeon, D. 1999, 'Work and Resistance in the Jharia Coalfield', pp. 43–76, in (eds) Parry, Breman and Kapadia.

Simpson, E. 2001, 'Of Some Import: The Role of Commerce and Religious Intermediaries in Transacting Foreign Things in West India', London School of Economics, <e.l.simpson@lse.ac.uk>.

Singer, M. 1961, 'The Religion of India: The Sociology of Hinduism and Buddhism', *American Anthropologist*, vol. 63, pp. 143–51.

Singer, M. 1972, *When a Great Tradition Modernises: An Anthropological Approach to Indian Civilisation*, Praeger, New York.

Singh, A. 1999, *Industrial Transition in an Agricultural Surplus Region. A Study of Punjab*, Doctoral Thesis, Jawarhalal Nehru University, New Delhi, Centre for Development Studies, Trivandrum (Kerala).

Singh, G. (ed.) 1987, *Punjab Today*, Intellectual Publishing House, New Delhi.

Singh, P. 1987, 'Two Facets of Sikh Revivalism', pp. 167–79, in (ed.) Singh.

Singh, P. 1993, 'Punjab's Economic Development and the Current Crisis', *Seminar*, 40, January.

Singh, P. 1997, *Political Economy of the Punjab: An Insider's Account*, MD Publications Pvt Ltd, New Delhi.

Sinha, A., Sangeeta N. and Siddiqui, K. A. 1999, 'The Impact of Alternative Policies on the Economy with special Reference to the Informal Sector: A Multisectoral Study', National Council for Applied Economic Research, New Delhi.

Smart, A. 1993, 'Gifts, Bribes and *Guanxi*: A Reconsideration of Bourdieu's Social Capital', *Cultural Anthropology*, 8, 3, pp. 388–408.

Sombart, W. 1951, *The Jews and Modern Capitalism*, Free Press, Glencoe, Illinois.

Sridhan, E. 1993, 'Economic Liberalisation and India's Political Economy: Towards a Paradigm Synthesis', *Journal of Commonwealth and Comparative Politics*, November.

Srinivas, M. N. 1966, 'A Sociological Study of Okhla Industrial Estate', in UNESCO.

Srinivas, M. N. 1989, *The Cohesive Role of Sanskritisation and Other Essays*, Oxford University Press, Delhi.

Srinivas, M. N. (ed.) 1996, *Caste: Its Twentieth Century Avatar*, Viking, Delhi.

Sriskandarajah, D. 1997, 'Liberalisation in India: The Case of Carbonated Soft Drinks', MA Thesis, Dept of Economics, University of Sydney.

Srivastava, N. 1999, 'Striving for a Toehold: Women in the Organized Sector', pp. 181–205, in (eds) Papola and Sharma.

Srivastava, R. 1999, 'Rural Labour in Uttar Pradesh: Emerging Features of Subsistence, Contradiction and Resistance', *Journal of Peasant Studies*, 26, 2/3: 263–315.

Stanley, J. 2002, 'A Common Cluster in a Crowded Market: The Gold Ornaments Cluster in Arni, Tamul Nadu, India', M.Phil Thesis, Queen Elizabeth House, Oxford University.

Stein, B. 1998, *A History of India*, Blackwell, London.

Storper, M. 1995, 'The Resurgence of Regional Economies, Ten Years Later: The Region as a Nexus of Untraded Interdependencies', *European Urban and Regional Studies*, 2, 3, pp. 191–221.

Storper, M. 1998, *The Regional World: Territorial Development in a Global Economy*, Guilford, New York.

Streefkerk, H. 1978, *Lichte Intustrie in een kleine Indiase Stad*, Doctoral Dissertation, University of Amsterdam; and *Industrial Transition in Rural India*, Sangam, Hyderabad.

Subrahmaniam, R. 1996, 'Gender Bias in India: The Importance of Household Fixed-Effects', *Oxford Economic Papers* 48, 2, pp. 280–99.

Subrahmanyam, S. and Stein B. (eds) 1996, *Institutions and Economic Change in South Asia*, Oxford University Press, New Delhi.

Subramaniam, G. 2001, 'How the Muslims Figure', *The Hindu*, Friday, 23 February, p. 11.

Subramanian, S. (ed.) 2001, *India's Development Experience: Selected Writings of S. Guhan*, Oxford University Press, New Delhi.

Subramanian, S. and Harriss-White, B. 1999, 'Introduction', pp. 17–47, in (eds) Harriss-White and Subramanian.

Sundari, R. and Thombre, M. 1996, 'Declining Sex Ratio: An Analysis with Specific Reference to Tamil Nadu State', *Indian Economic Journal*, 43, 4: 30–47.

Sunder Rajan, R. 1993, *Real and Imagined Women: Gender, Culture and Post-Colonialism*, Routledge, London.

Sunder Rajan, R. (ed.) 1999, *Signposts: Gender Issues in Post-Independence India*, Kali for Women, New Delhi.

Svedberg, R. and Granovetter, M. 1992, 'Introduction', pp. 1–28, in (eds) Granovetter and Svedberg.

Swaminathan, M. 2000, *Weakening Welfare: The Public Distribution of Food in India*, Leftword Books, New Delhi.

Tamas, G. M. 2000, 'On Post-Fascism', *Boston Review*, 25: 3.

Tanner, C. 1995, 'Class, Caste and Gender in Collective Action: Agricultural Labour Unions in Two Indian Villages', *Journal of Peasant Studies*, 22, 4, pp. 672–98.

Tawney, R. H. 1926, *Religion and the Rise of Capitalism: A Historical Study*, John Murray, London.

Telford, H. 1992, 'The Political Economy of Punjab. Creating Space for Sikh Militancy', *Asian Survey*, 32, 11, pp. 969–87.

Tewari, M. 1998, 'The State and the Shaping of Conditions of Accumulation in Ludhiana's Industrial Regime: An Historical Interpretation', pp. 251–82, in (eds) Cadène and Holmstrom.

Tewari, M. 1999, 'Successful Adjustment in Indian Industry: The case of Ludhiana's Woollen Knitwear Cluster', *World Development*, 27, 9: 1651–72.

Thorner, A. 1982, 'Semi-feudalism or Capitalism? Contemporary Debate on Classes and Modes of Production in India', *Economic and Political Weekly*, 4, 11 and 18 December.

Thorner, D. (ed.) 1995, *Ecological and Agrarian Regions of South Asia circa 1930*, Oxford University Press, Karachi.

Timberg, T. 1978, *The Marwaris: From Traders to Industrialists*, Vikas, New Delhi.

Tinker, I. (ed.) 1990, *Persistent Inequalities*, Oxford University Press, New York.

Toye, J. F. J. 1993, *Dilemmas of Development*, 2nd edition, Cass, London.

Uberoi, P. (ed.) 1997, *Family, Kinship and Marriage in India*, 2nd edition, Oxford University Press, New Delhi.

UNESCO 1966, *Small Industries and Social Change*, UNESCO, New Delhi.

Unni, J. 1999, 'Women Workers in Agriculture: Some recent Trends', pp. 99–121, in (eds) Papola and Sharma.

Upadhya, C. 1997, 'Culture, Class and Entrepreneurs: A Case Study of Coastal Andhra Pradesh', in (eds) Rutten and Upadhya.

Van Wezel Stone, K. 1993, 'Labour Markets, Employment Contracts and Corporate Change', in (eds) McCahery, Picciotto and Scott.

Varma, A, Chauhan, P. and Rehman, M. M. 1997, *Indian Labour: A Select Statistical Profile*, Giri National Labour Institute, Noida.

Varshney, A. 1993, 'Battling a Past, Forging a Future? Ayodhya and Beyond', pp. 9–42, in (ed.) P. Oldenburg.

Varshney, A. 1999, 'Elite and Mass Politics in the Context of Economic Reform', in (eds) Sachs et al.

Veblen, T. B. 1919, *The Theory of the Leisure Class, An Economic Study of Institutions*, Macmillan, New York.

Venkateshwarlu, D. and da Corta, L. 2001, 'Transformations in the Age and Gender of Unfree Workers on Hybrid Cotton Seed Farms in Andhra Pradesh', *Journal of Peasant Studies*, 28, 3:1–36.

Vera Sanso, P. 1995, 'Community, Seclusion and Female Labour Force Participation in Madras, India', *Third World Planning Review*, 17, 2, pp. 155–67.

Vikas, M. 1984, *The Church and Tribal Development. A Profile of Vikas Maitri Regional Seminar 1982*, Vikas Maitri, Ranchi.

Visaria, P. 1999, 'Level and Pattern of Female Employment, 1911–94', pp. 23–51, in (eds) Papola and Sharma.

Visvanath L. S. 1996, 'Female Infanticide and the Position of Women in India', in (ed.) Shah.

Visvanathan, S. and Sethi, H. (eds) 1998, *Foul Play: Chronicles of Corruption, 1947–1997*, Banyan Books/Seminar–Business India, New Delhi.

Wade, R. 1985, 'The Market for Public Office: Why the Indian State is not Better at Development', *World Development* 13, 4, pp. 476–97.

Wade, R. 1988, *Village Republics*, Cambridge University Press, Cambridge.

Wadley, S. 1993, 'Family Composition Strategies in Rural North India', *Social Science and Medicine*, 37, 11, pp. 1367–80.

Walby, S. (ed.) 1990, *Theorising Patriarchy*, Blackwell, Oxford.

Wallace, P. 1986, 'The Sikhs as a "Minority" in a Sikh Majority State in India', *Asian Survey*, 26, 3, pp. 363–77.

Wanmali, S. and Ramasamy, C. (eds) 1994, *Developing Rural Infrastructure: Studies from North Arcot, Tamil Nadu*, Indian Council for Agricultural Research, New Delhi, and IFPRI, Washington.

Weber, M. (trans. F. Knight) 1923, *General Economic History*, Allen & Unwin, London.

Weber, M. (trans. and eds H. H. Gerth and D. Martindale) 1962, *The Religion of India: The Sociology of Hinduism and Buddhism*, The Free Press, Glencoe, Illinois.

Weber, M. (trans. Talcott Parsons) 1965, *The Protestant Ethic and the Spirit of Capitalism*, Allen & Unwin, London.

Weber, M. 1970/1994, *General Economic History*, George Allen & Unwin, London.

Webster, J. 1992, *The Dalit Christians. A History*, ISPCK, Delhi.

Weiner, M. 1986, 'India's Minorities: Who are They? What do They Want?', pp. 99–134, in (ed.) Roach.

Weiner, M. 1991, *The Child and the State in India*, Oxford University Press, New Delhi.

Westwood, S. 2000, '"A Real Romance": Gender, Ethnicity, Trust and Risk in the Indian Diamond Trade', *Ethnic and Racial Studies*, 23, 5, pp. 857–70.

Whatmore, S., Lowe, P. and Marsden, T. (eds) 1991, *Rural Enterprise – Shifting Perspectives on Small Scale Production*, David Fulton, London.

White, G. 1993, 'Towards a Political Analysis of Markets', *Bulletin, Institute of Development Studies*, 24, 3, pp. 4–12.

White, G. 1996, 'Corruption and Market Reform in China', pp. 40–7, in (eds) Harriss-White and White.

White, G. 1996, 'Chinese Trade Unions in the Transitions from Socialism: Towards Corporatism or Civil Society?', *British Journal of Industrial Relations*, 34: 3.

White, G., Howell, J. and Shang Xiaoyuan 1996, *In Search of Civil Society in China*, Clarendon Press, Oxford.

Wiebe, P. D. 1988, *Christians in Andhra Pradesh. The Mennonites of Mahbubnagar*, The Christian Literature Society, Madras.

Wilmott, W. (ed.) 1972, *Economic Organisation in Chinese Society*, Stanford University Press, Stanford.

Wilson, K. 1999, 'Patterns of Accumulation and Struggles of Rural Labour: Some Aspects of Agrarian Change in Central Bihar', *Journal of Peasant Studies*, 26, 2/3: 316–55.

Wolfenson, J. 1999, 'Social Audit Proposal', World Bank, Washington.

Woo-Cumings, M. (ed.) 1999, *The Developmental State*, Cornell University Press, Ithaca, New York.

World Bank 1989, *India: Poverty, Employment and Social Services*, IBRD, Washington.

World Bank 1997, The State in a Changing World, *World Development Report*, IBRD, Washington.

Wright, E. O. 1985, *Classes*, Verso, London.

Wright, T. P. Jr. 1981, 'The New Muslim Businessmen of India: A Prospectus for Research', *Conference Paper at the 7th European Conference on Modern South Asian Studies*, School of Oriental and African Studies, University of London, July 1981.

Yadav, Y. 1996, 'Reconfiguration in Indian Politics – State Assembly Elections', 1993–5', *Economic and Political Weekly*, 13 January.

Yadav, Y. 1999, 'India's Third Electoral System, 1989–99', *Economic and Political Weekly*, vol. XXXIV, no. 37, 11–17 September.

Yadav, Y. 2000, 'Understanding the Second Democratic Upsurge: Trends of Bahujan Participation in Electoral Politics in the 1990s', in (eds) Frankel, Hasan, Bhargava and Arora.

Young, L. C. and Wilkinson, I. F. 1989, 'The Role of Trust and Co-operation in Marketing Channels: A Preliminary Study', *European Journal of Marketing*, 23, pp. 109–22.

Index of names

304

Index of places

Index of subjects

accountability 96, 99, 100, 102, 245, 247
accumulation 4, 6, 17, 43, 46–7, 54, 63, 64,
   69, 72, 88, 90, 106–19, 120, 121, 127,
   128, 139, 140, 141, 147, 150–1, 159, 161,
   163, 167, 170, 171, 173, 182, 186, 191,
   199, 200, 201, 206, 208, 210–13, 220–37,
   240–6, 248, 255
agro-industrial mercantile 18, 88, 147, 213,
   241
   concentration of 43, 57, 223
   gender as 103–31, 240–5, 255
      labour as 17–42
      language as 209, 239
      religion as 132–85, 245, 255
      space as 200–38, 246
      state as 72–102
   state 59, 248–55
      trajectories 109, 156, 157, 160–2,
         223–34, 229, 230–2, 241, 245
   niches for 147, 156, 163, 164, 174, 175
   primitive 68, 69, 70, 113, 206, 213, 218,
      241, 242, 252
   regions of 21, 232, 240
   social structures of (SSA) 14–16, 18, 72,
      175, 179, 239–47
      capital as 43–71, 241, 244, 245,
         251–52
      caste as 176–99, 250, 253, 254, 255
      essentialism in 104
agrarian structure 144, 159, 215, 216, 220–5,
   238 see also agriculture; land
agriculture 18, 19, 22–5, 82, 93, 103, 112,
   116, 127, 144, 156, 157, 160, 181,
   214–18, 221–5, 238
   elites in 154, 155, 156, 165, 215, 221, 222,
      223, 241
   extension in 194
   gender in 28, 116
   green revolution in 22, 48, 55, 144, 156,
      199, 222
   growth linkages from 214–18
   labour force in 22–4, 45, 62, 140, 144,
      152, 215, 218, 223, 229, 230
   mode of production in 43, 214, 217, 218,
      230
   raw materials from 56, 179, 195
   see also capital; feudal elements; labour;
      land; peasants; trade
army 159, 187, 249, 252

banks 49, 92, 93, 112, 116, 118, 131, 144,
   152, 165, 194, 209, 219, 223, 230–1, 235,
   236, 246 see also credit; finance
bourgeoisie see capital; class
bribes 37, 38, 45, 66, 70, 71, 73, 78, 81, 82,
   83, 92, 96, 113, 189, 191, 196, 234, 236,
   252 see also corruption; tax evasion
Buddhism 132, 140, 153, 167, 168
business 2, 98, 106–21, 143, 149, 179, 181,
   182, 193, 217, 219, 229
   associations 190–9, 255
   corporate 40, 43, 53, 56, 142, 152, 217,
      250–1
   cycles 14
   family 19, 103–31, 138, 161, 162, 163,
      173, 182, 191, 243
   local 117, 162, 163, 185, 186, 206, 217,
      234
   reputation 53, 65, 75, 109, 113, 127, 162,
      163, 169, 170, 171, 192, 211, 212,
      227, 243
   see also capital; corporate sector; family;
      firms; trust

capital 73, 79, 111, 120, 130, 139, 146, 147,
   148, 160, 161, 168, 169, 179, 190–5, 197,
   199, 200, 209, 210, 237, 239–47, 250,
   251, 252, 253, 254
   agricultural 43, 48, 55, 61, 98, 126, 127,
      178, 214, 215, 217, 218, 222–3
   commercial 193, 198, 216, 218, 219, 227
   domestic (large scale/corporate/monopoly)
      40, 43, 48, 49, 56, 68, 98, 102, 136,
      142, 152, 159, 163, 212, 219, 235,
      237, 239, 241, 250, 251, 252, 253
   finance 111, 119, 120, 182,
   fixed 157, 217
   foreign 59–60, 68, 101
   global 10, 22, 232
   intermediate 43–71, 102, 116, 121, 140,
      162–6, 179, 186, 197, 199, 216–17,
      235, 253, 255
   merchants' 18, 159, 160–2, 216–17
   petty 18, 45, 64, 69, 90, 97, 100, 110, 112,
      219, 221, 227, 228, 229, 232, 236, 237
   social 15, 109
   spatial organisation of 200–38
   starting 109–10, 199
   viscosity of 208–9, 221–2, 227–9, 235, 238
   working 157, 236

308

Beyond the Legend: Sacagawea. Biography

MARKO D

ISBN:9798863085432

Table of Contents

Acknowledgments

Have you ever pondered the web of human interactions and how they shape history? The story of Sacagawea is not just about her but about the countless unsung heroes who played pivotal roles in her life, shaping her journey from a young Shoshone girl to an American legend.

Firstly, a profound nod to the Shoshone tribe. This indigenous community nurtured Sacagawea, grounding her with invaluable life skills and knowledge about the terrain and nature. Were it not for the Shoshone's upbringing, would Sacagawea have been equipped to guide Lewis and Clark across the vast and unpredictable American frontier? One wonders...

The Hidatsa tribe, into which she was taken and where she later met her husband, Toussaint Charbonneau, played a complex role in Sacagawea's life. While her time there might have been riddled with challenges, the Hidatsa land also became a starting point for the expedition that made her a key figure in American history.

Ah, Lewis and Clark. Who could forget them? They're the explorers in many narratives, and Sacagawea is a footnote. But isn't it marvellous to think that their journey might have looked so different without her? Sacagawea wasn't merely a guide; she was a bridge between cultures, a peacemaker, and often the difference between survival and despair for the Corps of Discovery. While their names headline the expedition, it's crucial to remember the harmonious dance of collaboration between them. How did they communicate, you wonder, across barriers of language and culture?? With patience, gestures, and trust.

Acknowledging Jean Baptiste, Sacagawea's son, is essential. Born amidst the expedition, this young soul encapsulated the fusion of worlds and symbolized hope. How might Sacagawea have felt, carrying her infant through vast landscapes, exposing him to the raw forces of nature and the melting pot of cultures? There's a kind of magic in that, isn't there?

Lastly, the American landscape itself deserves acknowledgement. From the rugged Bitterroots to the sprawling plains, the challenging terrains Sacagawea navigated were as much characters in her story as any human. Can you picture her tracing ancient trails, listening to the whispers of the wind, and translating them into guidance for her team?

Sacagawea's story isn't just history: it's a testament to resilience, collaboration, and the indomitable human spirit. As you delve deeper into her life, spare a thought for those acknowledged here and the many more unsung contributors long forgotten by time. They, too, shaped a narrative that continues to inspire and captivate. What might they have felt, seen, and lived? Dive in and discover...

Beyond the Famous Dollar Coin

Imagine standing at the crossroads of history, with the vast uncharted American wilderness stretching endlessly before you. Please think of the audacity, the courage, the grit it would take to venture into the unknown. Now, consider being a young woman, a mother, and a pivotal guide and interpreter in one of the most iconic expeditions in American history. This is the riveting tale of Sacagawea, a figure whose legacy is woven into the tapestry of our nation's past.

Who was Sacagawea, really? Beneath the layers of legends, beneath the countless tales told and retold, who was this woman who has intrigued generations? To truly understand her, one must journey back to the tumultuous times she lived in an era marked by exploration, territorial conquests, and cultural clashes.

She was more than just a guide for Lewis and Clark. Sacagawea was a beacon, symbolizing hope and collaboration in the harshest environments. A Native American woman, she navigated the rugged terrains and the intricate web of relationships, bridging the gap between indigenous tribes and the expedition team. How did a young woman, often facing insurmountable challenges, rise above her circumstances and etch her name in American history?

Our journey into her life will be more than a chronological recounting of events. We'll explore her emotions, her aspirations, and her fears. We'll walk beside her, feel the weight of the young child on her back, and experience the vastness of the American frontier through her eyes. We'll delve deep, unearthing the intricacies of her relationships with the explorers and her own people. How did she, an indigenous woman, navigate the complexities of a world between two civilizations?

The life of Sacagawea is a testament to the indomitable human spirit, to resilience in the face of adversity, and to the bridges that can be built even in the most challenging circumstances. Through her story, we'll explore broader identity, belonging, and transformation themes.

Ready to embark on this incredible journey? The story of Sacagawea beckons, inviting us to step into a world of adventure, challenges, and the enduring power of human connection...

Chapter 1

Birth in the Lemhi River Valley

Have you ever stood at the edge of a river, feeling the pulse of the water, and wondered about the stories it holds? Our tale begins in the vast stretches of the Lemhi River Valley, nestled amidst the rugged terrain and pristine waters. This isn't just the story of a river but of a life intertwined with its rhythms: the life of Sacagawea.

With its verdant fields and sparkling waters, the Lemhi River Valley was more than a mere backdrop for Sacagawea's birth. It shaped her, moulded her, and whispered ancient tales that would later guide her through the treacherous paths of the American wilderness. How, you ask? Well, let's delve a little deeper.

In around 1788, as the sun painted the valley in hues of gold, Sacagawea entered this world. She wasn't born into royalty or privilege but into the heart of the Lemhi Shoshone tribe. With its deep-seated traditions and profound respect for the land, this community became Sacagawea's first teacher. Imagine the young girl learning the language of the winds, understanding the murmurs of the water, and decoding the patterns in the sky. Exciting.

But life in the valley was not without its challenges. Intertribal conflicts were commonplace, and the ever-looming threat from neighbouring tribes meant that Sacagawea's early years were far from idyllic. Rather than being just playful frolics by the riverbank, her formative years were interspersed with survival, resilience, and adaptability lessons. Doesn't this make you wonder about the mettle of this young girl, born in the heart of nature yet constantly braving the storms that life threw at her?

Sacagawea's birthplace wasn't just a geographical location but a crucible that forged her spirit. The Lemhi River Valley, an amalgamation of serene beauty and raw challenges, mirrored Sacagawea's life in many ways. As she navigated her journey from the valley to the vast expanses of the American frontier, one thing remained unchanged: her indomitable spirit. And where did she inherit this spirit from? One could say it was the gift of the Lemhi River Valley...

In the following chapters, we'll see how this spirit, born and nurtured in the valley, played a pivotal role in shaping American history. Ready to continue the journey? Onward we go!

Shoshone Culture and Traditions

Amidst the vast tapestry of the American frontier, a vibrant thread winds its way, embodying a legacy rich in culture and tradition: the Shoshone. Sacagawea, our central figure, hailed from this very community. So, what's so intriguing about the Shoshone? Let's dive in.

Nestled in the heart of the American West, the Shoshone people thrived. Their lands spanned expansive terrains, from verdant valleys to arid deserts. Now, imagine a child born into this setting, breathing in tales from generations past, and you've glimpsed the early years of Sacagawea.

Life for the Shoshone was a delicate dance between man and nature. Every rustle in the leaves, every shift in the wind carried messages. Can you feel it? The Shoshone did. Their keen connection to the environment wasn't just about survival; it was a profound relationship, fostering respect and symbiosis. The mountains, rivers, and vast plains weren't just geographical features but lifelines, narrating stories and guiding daily routines.

Communal life revolved around tight-knit family units. Within these, stories and traditions passed down, weaving a rich tapestry of oral history. Do you ever think about the tales our ancestors shared around the fire? For the Shoshone, these stories served as guiding lights, shaping their understanding of the world and their place within it.

One of the most riveting facets of Shoshone life was their ceremonies. These weren't just rituals but moments of connection – between the community, the individual, and the universe. Picture this: a sea of dancers, their bodies moving in rhythm, their voices rising in unison, all against the backdrop of the vast American skies. The Shoshone ceremonies were reflections of gratitude, of hope, and of a continuous dialogue with the cosmos.

And, of course, we can only discuss the Shoshone by mentioning their prowess in hunting and gathering. With their keen eyes and agile limbs, the men pursued game like deer and bison. Meanwhile, with wisdom passed down through ages, women would forage, recognizing plants that healed and those that harmed. This knowledge wasn't just useful; it was sacred. For every herb picked, there was a whisper of gratitude; for every animal hunted, a silent prayer of thanks.

Speaking of the Shoshone women, their roles extended beyond foraging. They were the community's backbone, ensuring the transmission of traditions, shaping young minds, and crafting essentials like clothing and tools from nature's offerings.

For Sacagawea, growing up amidst these traditions, the Shoshone way of life wasn't just a cultural backdrop but her foundation. It moulded her perspectives, her instincts, and her resilience. The Shoshone legacy ran deep in her veins, influencing her choices and the paths she tread.

To truly understand Sacagawea, we must first appreciate the Shoshone culture and traditions. It's akin to studying a magnificent painting: to grasp its true essence, one must comprehend the individual strokes that created it. Ready to delve deeper into this captivating tapestry? Let's journey together!

Kidnap by the Hidatsa

There's an inexplicable juncture in everyone's life, a sudden twist of fate that forever alters their path. For young Sacagawea, this life-changing moment was her abduction by the Hidatsa tribe.

Who could imagine a serene day in Shoshone territory would spiral into chaos? The Hidatsa, a tribe distinct from the Shoshone, swooped down, creating a turbulence that would ripple across the years. In the tumult, young Sacagawea found herself separated from her family, trapped in a whirlwind not of her making.

Now, think for a moment: How would most of us react? Grief, rage, despair? Yes, the heart of Sacagawea surely ached. And yet, within her was an indomitable spirit, a resilience that defied her youth.

While with the Hidatsa, Sacagawea's life underwent profound changes. Among them was her union with Toussaint Charbonneau, a French-Canadian trader. To some, this might seem like a mere marriage of convenience. But delve deeper, and you'll uncover layers of interwoven destinies. Sacagawea's union with Charbonneau wasn't just about companionship; it was a bridge to a future neither could have envisioned.

The Hidatsa days, though darkened by the shadow of separation from her native people, weren't entirely bleak for Sacagawea. The tribe had its own rich tapestry of traditions and values. And as days turned into months and months into years, Sacagawea began to understand and assimilate these with her astute observational skills. It wasn't about forgetting her Shoshone roots but enriching her worldview. Can you see her? Amidst the Hidatsa, learning, growing, adapting?

Then there's the critical juncture that this new chapter led her to the Lewis and Clark Expedition. When the famed duo Meriwether Lewis and William Clark, embarked on their expedition, they sought guidance. And who better than Sacagawea, with her intricate knowledge of the terrains and tribes?

Intriguing. Sacagawea might never have been intertwined with this historic journey if not for that fateful day of her abduction. Her initial ordeal, though harrowing, paved the way for her to become an indispensable asset to one of America's most celebrated expeditions. How's that for destiny playing its cards?

In life, some events, though traumatic at the outset, might be the prelude to something monumental. For Sacagawea, the experience with the Hidatsa, while painful, became a stepping stone to her eventual legacy. It's a poignant reminder: In the grand tapestry of life, every thread, no matter how twisted, has its place. And Sacagawea? She wove her threads with grace, resilience, and an unwavering spirit.

Chapter 2

A New Tribe, A New Life

Imagine, for a moment, standing at the threshold of something unfamiliar, unknown. That's where Sacagawea found herself, not once, but multiple times in her life. Born to the Shoshone, she faced a radical shift when she was whisked away and found herself amidst the Hidatsa.

Now, what does one do when placed amidst a completely different tribe? For many, the first instinct might be to recoil, to seek the familiar, the comfortable. But Sacagawea's tale wasn't one of retreating. It was about embracing, learning, and finding her own space within this new milieu.

The Hidatsa, while distinct from the Shoshone, had their own rhythm of life. Their traditions, beliefs, and daily activities created a vibrant tapestry of culture, waiting to be unravelled. And Sacagawea? She didn't just watch from the sidelines. The young woman made herself an integral part of this canvas.

While living with the Hidatsa, she met Toussaint Charbonneau, a French-Canadian trader. Their union was a merging of two souls and a confluence of cultures and experiences. Through him, Sacagawea glimpsed a world beyond the tribes, a world of trade, exploration, and uncharted terrains.

But life has its own way of throwing curveballs. When Sacagawea might have settled into her new life with the Hidatsa, destiny beckoned again. Enter Meriwether Lewis and William Clark. Their famed expedition sought someone who knew the terrains, the tribes, and the languages. And who better than Sacagawea?

Now, one might wonder: How does a young woman, barely in her teens, become an indispensable part of such a significant expedition? It wasn't just about her knowledge. It was her spirit, her resilience, and her ability to adapt. Sacagawea had already shifted from one tribe to another, learned their ways, and carved a niche for herself. So, when the call came to guide Lewis and Clark, she was more than ready. She was primed for it.

Isn't life full of such beautiful paradoxes? The very event – her relocation to the Hidatsa – which might have seemed like an upheaval became the gateway to an adventure that would etch her name in the annals of history. Sacagawea's journey from the Shoshone to the Hidatsa alongside Lewis and Clark is a testament to human resilience and adaptability.

Sacagawea's life was a series of transitions from the familiar terrains of the Shoshone to the bustling life of the Hidatsa and then into the wild yonder with Lewis and Clark. But through it all, she emerged not just as a guide, translator, or symbol. She became an embodiment of strength, courage, and adaptability.

In the end, what can we glean from her story? It's this: Life will often take us to unexpected places, to unfamiliar terrains. But like Sacagawea, with an open heart and a resilient spirit, we too can weave a narrative of triumph amidst change. After all, isn't that what life is all about?

Sacagawea's Marriage to Toussaint Charbonneau

In the tumultuous tapestry of the American frontier, few narratives are as intricately woven as Sacagawea's. And within this tapestry, a thread binds her to Toussaint Charbonneau. Their relationship, born out of adversity, transformed into a partnership that would indelibly mark the pages of history.

What draws two souls together in the vast expanse of the wilderness? For Sacagawea and Charbonneau, the beginnings were anything but idyllic. Sacagawea, a young Shoshone woman, was trapped by the Hidatsa tribe, living miles away from her natal home. Amidst this upheaval, entered Charbonneau, a French-Canadian trapper and trader. The two didn't come together in the typical whirlwind of courtship; their union was born out of their time's societal norms and necessities.

Now, one might ask: What could a seasoned trader see in this young indigenous woman? But Charbonneau recognized something invaluable in Sacagawea. She deeply understood the terrains and languages, vital skills in a world driven by exploration and trade.

Theirs was not a union defined by grand gestures or elaborate declarations. But as their lives interlaced, a partnership emerged. They became a team, each bringing their strengths to the fore. Sacagawea's unparalleled knowledge of the land and its people complimented Charbonneau's experience in the fur trade and his connections with explorers.

But the real test of their partnership was yet to come. Enter Lewis and Clark. With their expedition on the horizon, Sacagawea's role evolved. From being a wife and an expected mother, she became an invaluable asset to the Corps of Discovery. And Charbonneau? He was right beside her, serving as an interpreter and a guide.

In this dynamic, Sacagawea often outshined her husband. Isn't it remarkable how a young woman, once a captive, now navigated the corridors of power, negotiating with tribal chiefs and guiding a team of seasoned explorers? While Charbonneau had moments of uncertainty and hesitation, Sacagawea emerged as a beacon of strength and resilience.

Their journey together was punctuated with challenges, but it was also adorned with moments of triumph. The birth of their son, Jean Baptiste, amidst the expedition stands as a testament to their enduring spirit.

Sacagawea and Charbonneau's relationship was as multifaceted as the terrains they traversed, from their unconventional beginnings to their adventures with Lewis and Clark. In the grand narrative of exploration, their partnership reminds us of the power of collaboration, resilience, and the human spirit. After all, behind every great expedition are stories of individuals, partnerships, and shared dreams. And in the case of Sacagawea and Charbonneau, their shared journey was nothing short of extraordinary.

A Glimpse of the Incoming Americans

In the vast panorama of American history, moments define the trajectory of its people and land. Sacagawea's encounter with the incoming Americans within this expansive tableau stands out as one of those pivotal intersections.

Who were these foreigners, these explorers who seemed to surge into the territories like an incoming tide? They hailed from a young nation, driven by a sense of destiny, a nation known as the United States. Eager eyes looked westward, seeking land, riches, and opportunities, hoping to solidify their emerging identity on a continental scale.

Imagine the scenario: Indigenous communities, each with distinct cultures, languages, and rhythms, coming face-to-face with these outsiders. What ran through the minds of these native inhabitants? Curiosity? Apprehension? Excitement? With her unique perspective, Sacagawea stood at the nexus of this exchange.

The Americans she encountered were not mere wanderers but ambassadors of a burgeoning nation, symbols of a shifting world order. Led by Meriwether Lewis and William Clark, they embarked on what would later be celebrated as the Corps of Discovery Expedition. But did Sacagawea view them as harbingers of a new age or a potential threat?

Being a Shoshone woman, Sacagawea was grounded in her own worldviews, values, and traditions. To her, the landscapes they traversed were not "unchartered territories"; they were the lands of her ancestors, spaces filled with stories and spirits. Yet, her interactions with Lewis and Clark were characterized by collaboration rather than conflict.

But why collaborate? Was it the allure of the unknown? Or the potential benefits of establishing diplomatic ties? Sacagawea's ability to act as a bridge was the real magic of this alliance. Her presence, often accompanied by her infant son on her back, was disarming: a sign of peace, an emblem of motherhood. Where language barriers existed, she was the translator; where cultural nuances were amiss, she provided clarity.

Her role in this expedition was transformative for both sides. For the indigenous tribes they encountered, Sacagawea was a familiar face in an unfamiliar crowd, a symbol that perhaps these outsiders could be trusted. She was an invaluable guide for the Americans, illuminating the mysteries of the lands they were so eager to incorporate into their national narrative.

As the expedition progressed, did Sacagawea ponder the implications of this American influx? Did she foresee the ripple effects it would set in motion: the expansion, the encounters, and the eventual erasure of many indigenous ways of life?

Such encounters are seldom one-dimensional. They're layered with hopes, apprehensions, and possibilities. Sacagawea's collaboration with the incoming Americans wasn't just about guiding them through physical terrains but navigating the intricate labyrinths of cultural understanding.

In the chronicles of history, the echoes of Sacagawea's story resonate powerfully. Her encounters with the Americans testify to the spirit of collaboration, the power of diplomacy, and the inevitability of change. As the pages of time continue to turn, her legacy remains, reminding us of that fleeting moment when the old world glimpsed the new... and nothing would ever be the same again.

Chapter 3

The Meriwether Lewis and William Clark Expedition

If we were to turn back the pages of history and let our fingers wander through the annals of American exploration, few episodes would pulsate with the same vibrancy and drama as the expedition led by Meriwether Lewis and William Clark. But what is it about this particular journey that leaves an indelible mark on our collective memory? What magic stirred when these two captains set out into the uncharted with their crew and the indispensable Sacagawea?

In the early 1800s, the vast western expanse of the United States was a siren song: a mysterious land filled with untold treasures and challenges. It beckoned the brave, the curious, and those hungry for adventure. Lewis and Clark, handpicked by President Thomas Jefferson, were tasked with a mission that sounds simple in theory but was monumental in practice:

- Explore the newly acquired Louisiana territory.
- Find a waterway to the Pacific Ocean.
- Strengthen American claims to the West.

Now, imagine setting foot in lands where no American had ventured before. Vast rolling plains, towering mountain ranges, and tumultuous rivers stretched endlessly. How does one even begin such an endeavour? And what challenges lie in wait?

It wasn't just the physical challenges—like navigating treacherous terrains or enduring harsh weather conditions—that made this journey legendary. The expedition was also about forging connections with the myriad of Indigenous tribes they encountered and with each other. And this is where Sacagawea's role becomes relevant and pivotal.

Sacagawea, a Shoshone woman, was more than just a guide. She was the bridge between two worlds. Her presence, often with her infant son in tow, was a beacon of peace, symbolising that these newcomers came without ill intent. With every gesture and every word she translated, she smoothed the path for Lewis and Clark. But did she ever wonder about the long-term ramifications of this journey? Did she foresee the waves of change it would bring?

Lewis and Clark, for their part, meticulously documented their findings: from detailed maps to descriptions of flora and fauna, from interactions with Indigenous tribes to personal reflections. These notes would prove invaluable, shedding light on areas of the continent previously shrouded in mystery.

But were there moments of doubt? Certainly. Moments when the weight of their task seemed too heavy when the path ahead was too daunting? Undoubtedly. Yet, with each sunrise, the expedition trudged on, fueled by the spirit of discovery.

As the duo and their team journeyed on, they uncovered more than just the lay of the land. They unveiled stories, cultures, and histories that had flourished there for centuries. The lands weren't 'wild' or 'untamed' as many believed; they were rich tapestries of life, tradition, and community.

When we reflect on the Lewis and Clark Expedition today, it's not just a tale of two men forging westward. It's a story of collaboration, resilience, and understanding. It reminds us of a time when the horizon was limitless, and the journey mattered just as much as the destination. And at the heart of it all was Sacagawea, navigating rivers and mountains and the delicate dance of cultures meeting for the first time...

So, as we ponder this iconic journey, let's ask ourselves: What does it truly mean to explore? To discover? And how do the ripples of these adventures shape the course of history? In the vast mosaic of America's past, the Lewis and Clark Expedition is a testament to the spirit of adventure, the bridges we build, and the legacies we leave behind.

Sacagawea: An Unexpected Asset

Who was Sacagawea? Was she merely a guide? A translator? To define her by these roles alone would be an injustice to her legacy. Instead, we ought to delve deeper into the myriad facets of her story, casting aside preconceptions and understanding her true significance in the tapestry of American exploration.

In the early 1800s, the American frontier remained a vast expanse of enigma. As the Lewis and Clark Expedition commenced its voyage into the unknown, few could have anticipated the pivotal role a young Shoshone woman would play. This wasn't just about trekking through treacherous terrains or mapping uncharted territories. It was about cultural navigation, about threading the fine line between respect and trespass.

Picture this: An expedition team, skilled yet unfamiliar with the ways of the land, encounters Indigenous tribes. Would a brigade of armed men not elicit suspicion, even hostility? Here, Sacagawea became more than a translator. Her presence, often accompanied by her infant son Jean Baptiste, signalled peace.

How invaluable must it have been for Lewis and Clark to have Sacagawea? A woman who could converse with Indigenous tribes, negotiate safe passages, and offer insights into the customs and practices of the people whose lands they trod upon. Despite being surrounded by strangers and often navigating challenges of her own, the respect she commanded speaks volumes.

But let's pause momentarily: How did Sacagawea find herself amidst such an expedition? Taken away from her Shoshone roots and integrated into the Hidatsa tribe, her life had been anything but straightforward. As fate would have it, her journey with the Hidatsa led to her crossing paths with Lewis and Clark.

Yet, it's essential to recognize that Sacagawea's value wasn't just in her skills as a guide or translator. The small acts—the way she identified edible plants, how she calmed tensions, the anecdotes she shared around campfires—these nuances enriched the expedition's experience immeasurably.

One might wonder: How did the members of the expedition view her? Records from the journey reflect admiration and respect. Whether it was her resourcefulness in rescuing essential items from a capsized boat or her calm demeanour amidst adversity, Sacagawea repeatedly proved herself indispensable.

However, as we celebrate her contributions, let's not romanticize her story entirely. She faced challenges, both personal and external. There must have been days of exhaustion, homesickness, and grappling with her identity amidst two clashing worlds. But isn't that the hallmark of truly extraordinary individuals? The ability to rise, endure, and leave an indelible mark?

So, as we reflect on the life of Sacagawea, let's remember her not merely as a guide but as a beacon. Amidst the wilderness, humans can still build bridges, demonstrating resilience. Sacagawea's story reminds us that sometimes, the most unexpected figures emerge as the most invaluable assets. And in the annals of American exploration, her name shines brightly, casting a luminous path for all who dare to venture into the unknown...

Setting Forth from Fort Mandan

As winter's grasp began to loosen and the first tendrils of spring crept across the land, Fort Mandan buzzed with activity. The fort, established by Lewis and Clark in present-day North Dakota, had been their shelter against the frigid winter months. But with the change of seasons, a new chapter awaited. And at the heart of this turning page was none other than Sacagawea.

Imagine being a young Shoshone woman, away from the comfort of her own tribe, thrust into the midst of an ambitious expedition that sought to map the vast, uncharted territories of the West. The world beyond Fort Mandan was unyielding, unpredictable, and teeming with opportunities and perils. But Sacagawea was no ordinary woman.

As preparations intensified, it wasn't just tools, supplies, or provisions that the expedition was counting on. It was also Sacagawea's unparalleled knowledge of the land, her linguistic skills, and her ability to foster peaceful interactions with the Indigenous tribes they would encounter. This expedition, aiming to reach the Pacific Ocean, was no mere adventure; it was an odyssey. And every odyssey needs its guiding star.

From the outset, Sacagawea's role transcended that of a mere guide or translator. The mere fact that she was present, cradling her infant son, Jean Baptiste, spoke volumes. Think about it: amidst the rugged explorers and vast landscapes, her calm demeanour and maternal aura painted a picture of peace, of familiarity. Wasn't it more comforting for the Indigenous tribes to see a mother among the explorers rather than just armed men?

Fort Mandan was more than just a protective shelter; it was a crossroads of cultures. It was where the explorers learned from the Mandan and Hidatsa tribes, absorbing stories, trade practices, and vital knowledge about the path ahead. And Sacagawea, with her foot in both worlds, became the bridge.

As the expedition set forth, navigating the intricate waterways, confronting treacherous terrains, and encountering diverse tribes, Sacagawea often took the lead. Can we even fathom the weight of responsibility she shouldered? With every step, every gesture, every word she spoke, she wasn't just guiding an expedition; she was shaping history.

Yet, it wasn't just the grand moments that defined her journey. It was also the subtle gestures: identifying edible plants, calming a spooked horse, or offering insights into tribal customs. Those moments, often overlooked in the grand narrative, were the stitches holding the fabric of the expedition together.

What drives a person to venture into the unknown, embrace challenges head-on, and be an ambassador of peace in potentially hostile territories? For Sacagawea, it was a mix of personal quest and a sense of duty. Maybe she saw this journey as a way to reconnect with her Shoshone roots. Or perhaps she realized that she had become an essential cog in the exploration wheel, and her unique position could foster understanding among diverse groups.

As the expedition left Fort Mandan, they weren't just embarking on a geographical journey. It was a journey of understanding, of discovery, and of unity. And while Lewis and Clark often take centre stage in this narrative, we must always remember the young Shoshone woman who made it all possible. The world beyond Fort Mandan was vast and daunting. Still, with Sacagawea leading the way, it felt a little more familiar, a tad less intimidating...

Chapter 4

Language as a Bridge

In the grand tapestry of history, certain individuals become the threads that hold disparate sections together. Sacagawea, a young Shoshone woman, emerged as a pivotal thread, binding cultures, aspirations, and destinies. How? Through the power of language.

Language, in its essence, isn't just a tool to communicate; it's a bridge. And in the vast expanse of North America, teeming with myriad tribes, languages, and customs, a bridge was sorely needed. Now, enter Sacagawea. Her understanding of Shoshone and Hidatsa not only helped Lewis and Clark converse with tribes they encountered but also afforded them a degree of legitimacy and peace.

Did Sacagawea realize the magnitude of her role? It's hard to say. But as they journeyed through the unpredictable terrains, each interaction with a new tribe became a testament to her irreplaceability. A simple gesture, a phrase, or an introduction could mean the difference between alliance and hostility. And time and again, she proved invaluable.

The Shoshone, her own people, proved a poignant example. For the explorers, securing horses for their onward journey was crucial. But how does one barter in a land where money holds no value? Through mutual respect and understanding. Sacagawea's reunion with her tribe and her ability to converse in their tongue played a key role in this diplomatic interaction. But more than just linguistic prowess, it was her identity – a woman from their own tribe who had seen the world beyond and returned – that spoke louder than words.

It wasn't just about knowing languages. It was about understanding the nuanced inflexions, the cultural underpinnings, the unspoken rules of conversation. Take, for instance, the tribes that the expedition encountered. Every tribe had its own customs, taboos, and ways of greeting. One misstep, one misunderstood word could spell disaster. Sacagawea navigated these intricacies easily, leaving many, including Lewis and Clark, in silent admiration.

But let's not romanticize the journey too much. It was fraught with its own challenges. There were days of frustration, moments where the weight of being the sole bridge might have felt overwhelming. Yet, Sacagawea carried on. Why? Perhaps she saw the bigger picture: a world where understanding could mitigate conflict, where different tribes and peoples could coexist and thrive.

Imagine being in her shoes: a young mother, traversing uncharted lands and knowing that your voice, your words, are often the only line of communication. Daunting? Absolutely! But the resilience and determination with which Sacagawea wielded her linguistic skills transformed her from being an interpreter to a diplomat in her own right.

In retrospection, as we delve into the annals of history, it becomes evident that language was not just a bridge but a lifeline. In the difficult journey of Lewis and Clark, Sacagawea emerged not just as a guide but as the linchpin, connecting worlds, fostering understanding, and crafting a legacy that still resonates today. Isn't it fascinating how words can shape destinies when wielded with intent and understanding?

The Crucial Shoshone Alliance

Deep deep in America's early expeditions lay tales of perseverance, bravery, and unexpected alliances. While the Lewis and Clark expedition is a monumental journey in America's history, one might ponder: what was the key to its success? Enter the Shoshone and, more importantly, Sacagawea, the linchpin connecting two divergent worlds.

It's hard to fathom the rugged terrain, the vast, uncharted wilderness confronting Lewis and Clark. And here's the clincher: the formidable Rocky Mountains couldn't be traversed without horses, and who had those horses? The Shoshone. But let's not get ahead of ourselves; securing horses wasn't merely a transaction; it required trust. And who better to sow seeds of trust than one of their own?

Sacagawea's encounter with the Shoshone wasn't just a chance meeting but a reunion. In an emotionally charged twist of fate, the chief of the Shoshone, Cameahwait, was Sacagawea's very own brother. Can you imagine? After years, during a daunting expedition, siblings reconnected in the wild's vast expanse. This personal bond became the bedrock upon which the Shoshone alliance was built.

The alliance wasn't merely about horses. The Shoshone shared knowledge – insights about the land, the rivers, and the places to seek shelter. Sacagawea emerged as more than just a translator in this trade of information. She became a beacon of hope, a bridge of understanding, transcending the mere words she spoke. It wasn't about the language she used but how she used it. Her presence humanized the expedition in the eyes of the Shoshone.

For Lewis and Clark, the Rocky Mountains posed a challenge, but the Shoshone alliance turned that challenge into an opportunity. Horses became the expedition's lifeline, allowing them to venture into territories otherwise out of reach.

And here's an analogy for you: think of the journey as a puzzle. Many pieces had to unite to craft the bigger picture and the Shoshone alliance? That was the corner piece. With it, the entire puzzle would have been complete and cohesive.

But what does this teach us? It's a lesson about the power of old and new connections. It's about understanding that relationships can bloom even in the most unpredictable circumstances, paving the way for unimaginable successes. And at the heart of it all was Sacagawea, a young Shoshone woman who bridged the gap between two cultures and cemented her place in the annals of history.

In a world riddled with misconceptions and apprehensions about the unknown, alliances like these remind us of the strength in unity and the magic that unfolds when diverse worlds come together.

Navigating Through Native Territories

Can you picture it? America is a canvas of uncharted territories, its landscape raw and untouched. To the modern mind, it's nearly unimaginable. But to Sacagawea, it was home. This land wasn't just geographical; it was cultural and spiritual. And as the Lewis and Clark expedition ventured forth, it was Sacagawea's insights into these native territories that made all the difference.

Let's pause for a moment and consider: How does one cross unfamiliar terrain in terms of land, culture, and language? It's a puzzle. And that's where Sacagawea, with her understanding of native traditions and languages, shined as an invaluable asset.

The Mandan village in present-day North Dakota was where her journey with the expedition began. But it wasn't merely physical terrain she helped navigate. It was the intricate web of relationships, the delicate dance of diplomacy. With tribes like the Hidatsa, the Nez Perce, and her own Shoshone people, she played a pivotal role. Her presence was a symbol, one that said, "We come in peace."

Her native roots provided credibility to Lewis and Clark. She wasn't just interpreting words but translating worldviews, mediating between two divergent universes. Think about it: How often do you feel understood even when speaking the same language? Sacagawea had the gift of empathy, allowing her to convey both words and sentiments.

Did you know that during their travels, the expedition had numerous encounters with native tribes? Some amicable, others fraught with tension. But Sacagawea's knowledge, instincts, and grace under pressure often tipped the scales in favour of peaceful interactions. She had an uncanny knack for understanding the nuances, the unstated rules, and the unspoken codes of conduct that varied from one tribe to another.

Navigating these native territories was no walk in the park. They encountered tribes who had never seen people of European descent. Tribes who approached them with caution, curiosity, and, at times, hostility. But with Sacagawea at their side, barriers melted. They weren't just explorers; they were guests in her homeland.

What makes her role so remarkable? It's the fact that she was not just a guide but a diplomat. A bridge between worlds. While Lewis and Clark documented landscapes, plants, and animals, Sacagawea was their compass in a vast ocean of cultural intricacies.

But let's not just celebrate Sacagawea as a guide. Let's celebrate her as a woman who became instrumental in one of America's most iconic journeys in a time and place where her voice could have easily been sidelined. It's a testament. To the strength of spirit, the power of understanding, the magic that happens when you truly know the lay of the land, both in the soil and the soul...

Chapter 5

Birth of Jean Baptiste

Picture this: The vast American wilderness, a tapestry of rolling hills, dense forests, and meandering rivers. Amidst the backdrop of this daunting yet magnificent terrain, a new life is introduced. A life that holds within it the hopes and aspirations of two worlds, harmoniously merging. Can you imagine the magnitude of that moment? This was the world into which Jean Baptiste was born.

The story of Jean Baptiste isn't merely a tale of birth but of convergence. Sacagawea, his mother, was at the crossroads of her life. Part of the famed Lewis and Clark expedition, she was instrumental in navigating the land and cultures that were so intrinsic to her yet so alien to the explorers she accompanied. And as this band ventured forth, she bore a child. But who exactly was Jean Baptiste?

Jean Baptiste, often fondly referred to as "Pomp" or "Pompey" by those who knew him, entered the world in February 1805. The circumstances of his birth, amidst an expedition fraught with challenges, were extraordinary. Amid natural obstacles and potential conflicts with native tribes, the expedition was on the verge of a medical crisis. Sacagawea was facing complications. How does one deal with childbirth in such circumstances?

In steps, Captain Lewis with a solution some might find surprising: using crushed rattlesnake tail as a remedy. Odd as it might sound, this traditional remedy was crucial in ensuring a safe birth. As dawn broke, the first cries of Jean Baptiste echoed across the plains. An emblem of hope, resilience, and the convergence of worlds.

But what does the birth of a child mean within the larger context of an expedition? To the members of this historic journey, Jean Baptiste was more than just a baby. He embodied the spirit of unity, collaboration, and mutual respect. His presence was a tangible testament to the bridge Sacagawea created between the explorers and the Native Americans. With every milestone he reached, the expedition was reminded of the importance of their mission and the hope for a unified future.

In the annals of history, Jean Baptiste is a potent reminder of Sacagawea's resilience, adaptability, and unmatched spirit. But beyond that, he stands as a symbol of a new America: diverse, integrated, and full of promise.

Isn't it astonishing how the birth of one child, in the heart of uncharted territory, could resonate with such profound implications? It challenges us to consider: What bridges can we build? What futures can we shape? And just as Sacagawea did over two centuries ago, how can we navigate the terrains of our lives, ensuring that future generations are beacons of hope and unity? For in the story of Jean Baptiste, we find not just a birth but the genesis of a legacy...

Motherhood in the Wilderness

Picture the vast American frontier: an untouched panorama of sprawling forests, unpredictable rivers, and open skies. Can you sense the ruggedness, the sheer intensity of it all? Yet, in the heart of this wild terrain, a delicate dance of motherhood was unfolding. Sacagawea, an indigenous woman in her late teens, navigated this demanding backdrop as a guide and a new mother. But what does it truly mean to embrace motherhood amidst such relentless adversity?

In 1805, in the stark midwinter, a newborn's cry echoed against nature's whispers. Jean Baptiste, Sacagawea's son, was introduced to the world. Now, childbirth is profound. A celebration of life, a beacon of hope. But in the untamed wilderness, it carried with it unparalleled challenges.

Sacagawea wasn't just feeding or comforting her child. She was doing so while crossing treacherous terrains, negotiating with diverse tribes, and assisting the Lewis and Clark expedition in their landmark journey. Does it astonish you? How could a woman so effortlessly balance the primal instincts of motherhood with the on-ground realities of an intense expedition?

Some moments seemed insurmountable. Like the time her boat nearly capsized on the turbulent waters. Sacagawea swiftly secured her infant with instincts honed sharp, ensuring his safety above all. These were not just acts of motherly love but fierce demonstrations of tenacity and presence of mind.

Her bond with Jean Baptiste was a constant wonder for the expedition members. They often observed her tending to him, singing lullabies in her native tongue, the soft melodies intertwining with the wild sounds. These gentle instances presented a contrast, a reminder of the tenderness that can exist amidst chaos.

But Sacagawea's role transcended the personal. Her child became a symbol of peace. Think about it: A party of explorers accompanied by a mother and her infant was less likely to be perceived as a threat by the native tribes. In many ways, Jean Baptiste's presence was a bridge of trust and understanding.

It's tempting to look at Sacagawea merely as a guide or translator. But, in essence, she was the heartbeat of the expedition. A resilient mother, carrying the weight of her child and the hopes of a developing nation, traversing the wild with unmatched grace. Motherhood in the wilderness wasn't just about survival; for Sacagawea, it was an act of unparalleled courage and love.

So, the next time the wind rustles through the trees or a river babbles over stones, pause for a moment. Think of a young mother, a symbol of strength and resilience, who showcased the profound depths of human endurance. Sacagawea's journey is a testament to all mothers who, in their ways, brave their own wildernesses every day... Isn't that truly remarkable?

Legacy of "Pompy"

Imagine being born amidst the wild, rugged embrace of nature, cradled by the sheer force and beauty of America's untamed lands. Jean Baptiste Charbonneau, affectionately known as "Pompy," began his life on a monumental journey: the Lewis and Clark expedition. But who was this child, and how did his beginnings, nestled in the shadow of his remarkable mother, Sacagawea, carve out a legacy that still resonates today?

In the simplest of terms, Jean Baptiste was not just Sacagawea's son. His very existence was a tapestry woven with threads of exploration, diplomacy, and hope. To the members of the expedition, he was an emblem of peace. After all, how could a party travelling with a mother and her baby intend any harm?

But beyond this initial journey, what became of this child of the wilderness? Pompy's life was as extraordinary as his beginning. Once the expedition concluded, he grew under the tutelage of none other than Captain William Clark. A bond formed, one that went beyond mere acquaintanceship. By recognizing the boy's potential, Clark ensured he received an education in St. Louis and later in Europe. Can you fathom that transition? From the American wilderness to European halls of learning...

As Pompy grew older, his wanderlust, perhaps inherited from his mother, took hold. He traversed the vast landscapes of Europe, mastering multiple languages and immersing himself in various cultures. His knowledge and experiences made him a valuable guide and diplomat, serving as a bridge between different worlds, much like his mother did years before.

However, the call of his homeland was too potent to ignore. Jean Baptiste returned to America, where he ventured into the Western frontiers. Using the skills and knowledge he'd amassed, he advocated for indigenous rights and played pivotal roles in various tribal negotiations. In essence, he continued the work his mother had inadvertently begun, fostering understanding between diverse communities.

There were tales, whispered among the tribes and settlers alike, of the child born amidst a journey of discovery. Tales of how he'd danced between worlds, holding onto his roots while embracing new horizons. These stories painted a picture of a man who was as much a part of the wilderness as he was of the civilized world.

Pompy's legacy isn't just about his adventures or accomplishments. It's a testament to the indomitable spirit of exploration and understanding. A person's beginnings can profoundly impact the trajectory of their life. The child of Sacagawea, born in the heart of a journey that shaped a nation, went on to shape his own narratives.

So, when the annals of history shine a light on the Lewis and Clark expedition, remember the young boy who started his life amidst it. Remember the legacy of "Pompy", a beacon of unity, exploration, and enduring hope... Isn't that something worth cherishing?

Chapter 6

The Great Falls Obstacle

Imagine a pristine landscape stretching as far as the eye can see. Majestic mountains punctuate the horizon and the land, untouched by industrial hands, beckons adventurers with its raw beauty. This is the American wilderness of the early 19th century. Into this tapestry of nature, the Lewis and Clark expedition weaves its thread with a narrative replete with challenges, discoveries, and moments of sheer human perseverance. And amidst this vast crew? Sacagawea, a young Shoshone woman, emerges as a guide and a beacon of hope and resilience.

Have you ever stood before a natural barrier so immense that it seems impossible? That's precisely the emotion that might've coursed through the veins of the expedition members upon their first encounter with the Great Falls of the Missouri River. Before them roared a cascade of water, deafening in intensity, spanning nearly a mile in width and dropping a staggering 400 feet in total descent. A formidable obstacle in their westward journey.

Now, imagine the collective sigh that must've echoed among the crew. This wasn't just a minor hiccup. The Great Falls presented not one but a series of waterfalls, each challenging the crew with its unique twist and turn. Portaging, or carrying their boats and equipment overland, around these falls became the only viable option. But this wasn't a mere day's work. The endeavour took almost a month, fraught with back-breaking labour and the constant drone of cascading waters as a reminder of the obstacle they faced.

Yet, amidst this challenge, Sacagawea's presence became invaluable. Familiar with the terrain, she assisted in identifying edible plants, providing sustenance to the weary men. The region, though picturesque, housed its fair share of dangers. Rattlesnakes slithered amidst the grass, their venomous bite a constant threat. But Sacagawea, with her indigenous knowledge, helped navigate these challenges.

Beyond her practical contributions, consider the emotional strength she lent to the expedition. Here was a young woman, a recent mother, showcasing resilience in adversity. If she, with her infant son on her back, could brave the daunting landscapes and the relentless roar of the falls, couldn't the rest of the crew muster the courage to move forward?

Lewis and Clark might've spearheaded the expedition, but individuals like Sacagawea lent it its heart and soul. The Great Falls, with its roaring waters and endless challenges, was but one chapter in their expansive journey. And while the waters of the Missouri River surged with wild abandon, the indomitable spirit of Sacagawea and the crew surged stronger, teaching us a timeless lesson in perseverance and the human spirit...

Isn't it fascinating how nature, in all its majesty, can bring forth challenges and stories of the undying human spirit? Sacagawea's journey alongside Lewis and Clark, especially during the trials of the Great Falls, serves as a testament to that very essence of humanity.

Navigating Nature's Fury

In all its glory, nature has a way of humbling even the most daring of souls. Sacagawea, young yet seasoned by life's challenges, faced her trials not just on personal fronts but also amidst the wild terrains of the American wilderness. One of the most harrowing chapters in her journey alongside the Lewis and Clark expedition took place in the Bitterroot Mountains, a mountain range known as much for its raw beauty as for its treacherous pathways.

Isn't it captivating how nature, while being a nurturing mother, can also pose as the fiercest adversary? The Bitterroots, with their jagged peaks and dense woods, stood as a testament to this dual face of nature. In September 1805, Sacagawea and the expedition ventured into this rugged terrain, hoping to find a westward passage. Little did they anticipate the series of challenges that lay ahead.

As days turned to nights and nights gave way to frosty mornings, the expedition, despite their collective might and wisdom, often found themselves at the mercy of the Bitterroots. Steep ascents, lack of food, and the onset of early winter snows added complexity to their journey. But was it just the physical hardships that tested their resolve?

Imagine the psychological battle they waged each day. With every step taken, the promise of reaching the Pacific seemed more distant. Hope, like a dwindling candle in a storm, seemed to waver. And yet, amidst this cloud of uncertainty, Sacagawea, a young Shoshone woman, displayed an innate sense of direction and an uncanny ability to spot game trails, which proved invaluable despite her unfamiliarity with the region.

Sacagawea's contribution went beyond navigation. Her calm demeanour amidst the chaos provided solace to the weary men. What's more, her very presence countered the threat posed by Native American tribes they encountered. A woman and a child? Surely, they're not here for conflict, the tribes surmised. This simple observation, rooted in the age-old respect for motherhood, often granted the expedition safe passage.

Stories of Sacagawea's bravery during this time are aplenty. On one particularly chilling day, when temperatures plummeted, and morale hit rock bottom, she foraged for edible roots and berries. With these humble findings, she prepared a modest meal that not only provided sustenance but lifted spirits, reminding the crew of the resilience of the human spirit.

The Bitterroots, for all their challenges, couldn't quell the indomitable spirit of Sacagawea and the Lewis and Clark expedition. When faced with nature's fury, they didn't just survive; they thrived, leaning on each other drawing strength from shared experiences and aspirations. In this treacherous chapter, Sacagawea's resilience shone the brightest, painting a vivid picture of a woman who was not just a guide but the very embodiment of hope...

And as they emerged from the Bitterroots, they carried with them not just tales of survival but lessons in camaraderie, perseverance, and the undying human spirit. In the face of nature's fury, these very qualities stand tall, don't they?

Establishing Peaceful Relations with Native Tribes

In the early 1800s, navigating the American wilderness was not just about nature's unpredictability. Still, it was also a dance of diplomacy. The Lewis and Clark expedition, ambitious and groundbreaking as it was, faced multifaceted challenges. Among these, establishing harmonious relations with the Native American tribes proved crucial. And in this complex tapestry of interactions, a young Shoshone woman named Sacagawea emerged as the unsung hero.

Think about it for a moment: How does one build bridges with communities, each with its rich tapestry of traditions, in lands where the white man was often viewed with suspicion? Sacagawea, being of Native American origin, seamlessly became the bridge between two worlds.

Her presence, often marked by a quiet strength, communicated a clear message to the tribes they encountered. This expedition was not of conquest but of curiosity and exploration. A woman with a baby on her back: what threat could she possibly pose? Such a simple yet profound image defused potential tensions time and again.

There's a particular incident that stands out. When the expedition reached the Shoshone territory, Sacagawea recognized the tribe's leader, Cameahwait, as her long-lost brother. Can you imagine the fate of such a reunion? This emotional bond facilitated trade for much-needed horses and cemented the trust between the two groups. It's moments like these that highlight the human side of historic expeditions, don't they?

But Sacagawea's influence wasn't just limited to her own tribe. Her ability to communicate, both verbally and through gestures, proved invaluable. She wasn't just translating words but cultures, emotions, and intentions. It's fascinating how communication, in its purest form, can break barriers and forge alliances.

Sacagawea's calm demeanour and genuine interactions created an atmosphere of mutual respect in regions where the mere sight of the expedition might have led to hostilities. It wasn't just about ensuring the safety of the expedition members but about planting seeds for future interactions between the natives and the settlers.

Remember, this was a time when misunderstandings could lead to unnecessary conflicts. A misplaced gesture, a misinterpreted word, and things could spiral out of control. With her nuanced understanding of both worlds, Sacagawea ensured that such faux pas were avoided.

In the grand narrative of the Lewis and Clark expedition, where tales of adventure and discovery dominate, fostering peaceful relations takes a backseat. But it's these very relations that allowed for the success of their journey. And at the heart of this diplomatic dance was Sacagawea, guiding, negotiating, and bridging gaps.

So, the next time we recount tales of treacherous terrains and discoveries, let's also remember the silent negotiations, the shared meals, the exchanged stories, and the bonds forged. In the vast American wilderness, it wasn't just about discovering lands and rediscovering humanity... And Sacagawea, with her grace and wisdom, was pivotal in that rediscovery.

Chapter 7

Gazing at the Pacific Ocean

The journey had been gruelling: unchartered territories, unpredictable weather, and constant encounters with the unknown. But amidst all the peril, there stood a beacon of hope, a young Shoshone woman named Sacagawea. Her spirit, as vast and indomitable as the land she traversed, was an integral part of what we now recognize as the Lewis and Clark expedition.

Imagine, if you can, reaching the edge of a continent. Before you lie, an expanse of water so vast and profound it seems to touch the sky. The Pacific Ocean: the end goal of the expedition. For many in the group, it was a moment of triumph, a testament to human endeavour. But for Sacagawea, what emotions did that endless horizon evoke?

Sacagawea, though a guide, was also a mother. With her infant son, Jean Baptiste, strapped to her back, every step she took was a dance between care and caution. The Pacific wasn't just a geographical milestone; it represented the culmination of countless days and nights during which she balanced the roles of guide, translator, and mother.

Could the vastness of the ocean mirror the depth of her thoughts? Was she reminiscing about the lands she had walked, the rivers she had navigated, the mountains she had seen? Or was she pondering over her place amidst these white explorers on a journey that was as much about discovery as it was about assertion?

There's a certain intimacy in the act of gazing. It's reflective and personal. While Lewis and Clark might have seen the Pacific as the triumphant endpoint of their expedition, Sacagawea's perception might have been painted with different shades. Perhaps she found a connection to her Shoshone roots in the rhythm of the waves. The vastness may have reminded her of the great plains and the stories of her ancestors.

With its endless horizon, the Pacific Ocean also presented a world of possibilities. With her intricate knowledge of the terrain, Sacagawea had proven she was not just a passive traveller but an active contributor to the expedition's success. Standing at the continent's edge, did she wonder about the future? About the world her son would inherit?

Engaging with these speculations allows us to appreciate the depth of Sacagawea's experience. The journey to the Pacific wasn't just a physical traversal of land; it was an emotional and psychological journey. In all its grandeur, the ocean wasn't just a sight to behold. For Sacagawea, it might have been a canvas upon which she painted her dreams, aspirations, and reflections.

As we delve into history, it's essential to recognize these moments: where the personal intersects with the monumental. Sacagawea's gaze upon the Pacific Ocean isn't just a point in a timeline. It's a testament to the human spirit, resilience, dreams, and endless quest for discovery. And as the waves kissed the shores, one could only wonder: what stories, hopes, and visions did they whisper to this remarkable woman?

Wintering at the Edge of the World

As winter's icy fingers began to stretch across the land, the expedition led by Meriwether Lewis and William Clark found themselves at the very fringe of the continent, where rivers met the sea and dense forests whispered ancient tales. On the west coast, they established a base they named Fort Clatsop.

What must it have been like for Sacagawea, standing at the threshold of such a juncture? The fort, situated near present-day Astoria, Oregon, wasn't merely a wooden outpost but a symbol of perseverance and a testament to human endurance. How did she cope with the winter chills and the homesickness that surely must have tugged at her heart in this remote locale?

The fort's log walls provided minimal relief from the relentless Pacific Northwest rain. Yet inside, there were sparks of warmth and camaraderie. Sacagawea, often the bridge between cultures, now played a pivotal role in fostering bonds within the group. Was her tales entertaining the men during the long, cold nights? Or her ability to find sustenance where others only saw wilderness?

This young Shoshone woman had been integral to the expedition's success. And as the days shortened and nights grew colder, Sacagawea took on another role: caretaker. Not just for her son, Jean Baptiste, but perhaps for the morale of the men around her. With her intricate knowledge of the land, she might have shown them which plants could be consumed or which held medicinal properties.

Fort Clatsop was a world away from the familiar terrains of the Shoshone territories. Did Sacagawea ever gaze at the vast Pacific and feel the weight of the distance she had travelled? Each droplet of rain might have whispered of her journey, and each gust of wind might have carried tales of the miles traversed.

Yet, challenges often birth opportunities. The interactions with the Clatsop and other local tribes presented a chance to trade and learn. Sacagawea's expertise in languages proved invaluable. How often did she step into negotiations, ensuring that the expedition procured elk meat or whale blubber staples during that wet winter?

And when spring teased its arrival, as the ice began its retreat and green buds emerged, the expedition readied to journey back. Fort Clatsop, that temporary haven, was left behind, but its memories were indelibly etched in the annals of history.

Sacagawea's time at Fort Clatsop encapsulates her spirit and resilience. While the fort was a mere stop in the journey, it is a testament to the power of collaboration, adaptation, and sheer human will. And isn't that the essence of exploration: discovering new lands and the boundless capacities of the human heart and spirit?

The Return Journey Begins

It's a pivotal moment in any expedition. There's that exhilarating instant when discovery reaches its climax and the inevitable need to return home. For Sacagawea, the Lewis and Clark expedition was not just a geographical voyage but a journey of personal evolution.

Can you imagine the tumult of emotions that might have surged within her as the group readied to embark on their return trip? The thrill of what lay ahead balanced with the pang of leaving behind lands that had grown familiar. There's a melancholy in farewells, even when the journey has been fraught with challenges.

While the route back might have felt like retracing steps, it was anything but. The landscapes that greeted them were familiar, but the context had changed. Remember those very waters and paths they had navigated before? They weren't the same. The season's shift had transformed them, and the journey's experiences had changed the travellers.

With Jean Baptiste nestled close, Sacagawea surely looked at the horizon with a different set of eyes. Where she once saw uncertainty, she now saw possibility. It's curious, isn't it, how one's perspective can alter so profoundly?

There were moments of joyous recognition as familiar territories emerged and times of reflection, especially for Sacagawea. The rivers whispered stories of their outbound journey, and the mountains stood tall, silently witnessing their remarkable feat. Did she find herself comparing her initial trepidations with the confidence she now felt?

One can't help but think: How did Sacagawea navigate these contrasting emotions? With each footstep echoing in rhythm with her heart, she aided the expedition with her knowledge and her spirit. Her presence was more than just a guide; it was a beacon of resilience and strength.

There were challenges, naturally. Nature has its rhythm and its unpredictability. Yet, with every setback, Sacagawea stood firm. The bonds she'd forged with the group only deepened. Together, they shared meals, laughter, concerns, and aspirations. What tales did they share around the campfire? How often did Sacagawea's insights or quick thinking steer them clear of potential hazards?

The return journey was not merely a geographic retracing. It was a testament to human endurance, adaptability, and the unbreakable spirit of collaboration. For Sacagawea, it might have been a road back to familiar terrains. Still, it also marked her emergence as an indomitable figure in history.

As the group moved, with each sunrise and sunset painting their path in hues of gold and crimson, a question lingered in the air: How will this epic journey be etched in the annals of time? Only time would tell, but one thing was clear: Sacagawea's legacy was destined to shine undimmed.

Chapter 8

Return to the Hidatsa and Mandan Villages

When one thinks of Sacagawea, images often suggest her courageously guiding the Lewis and Clark expedition. Yet, how often do we pause and wonder what it felt like for her when the journey led her back to the Hidatsa and Mandan villages? Isn't there something poignant about retracing steps to places once called home?

The vast plains, the whispering grasslands, and the majestic rivers were the landscapes Sacagawea grew up with. And as the expedition neared these villages, her heart must have swelled with nostalgia and trepidation. For isn't homecoming a bittersweet affair?

The air likely held a different scent, familiar yet tinged with change. The villages had remained stationary, but Sacagawea? She had traversed territories, faced innumerable challenges, and grown both in stature and spirit. How would the people she once knew now perceive her? And what tales did she bear for them?

The villages, rooted in the same land, had stories of countless sunrises and sunsets since her departure. Children who were toddlers during her time might now run around as young adults. Faces she remembered might have aged, and there would be new ones, curious and wide-eyed, hearing of her exploits.

It's fascinating. How places remain the same, yet the stories they encompass evolve. Sacagawea wasn't just returning as the young woman they once knew. She was now a mother, a guide, a symbol of resilience, and an integral part of an expedition that would reshape the nation's history.

Reuniting with the Hidatsa and Mandan people, Sacagawea found herself immersed in heartfelt conversations. Old friends and acquaintances would have approached, keen on sharing their stories and listening to hers. Did she recount tales of vast landscapes, snow-capped mountains and thick forests, moments that tested her resolve, and the new friendships she forged?

Yet amidst these narratives, one can't help but think of the moments of quiet introspection Sacagawea might have experienced. Gazing at the familiar sights of the villages, memories of her childhood might have played before her eyes. The joy, challenges, and lessons would have all culminated in a tapestry of emotions.

Such is the essence of a journey, especially one that brings you full circle. It doesn't merely chart a physical path but also maps the soul's evolution. And for Sacagawea, the return to the Hidatsa and Mandan villages wasn't just a geographical milestone. It was a testament to her enduring spirit and the rich tapestry of experiences she had woven.

As days turned into nights and the expedition prepared to move on, one wonders: did Sacagawea cast a final, lingering look at the villages? With a promise to return or with a silent acknowledgement that life's journeys are ever winding, ever new. Whatever her thoughts, one thing remains undeniable: her legacy, intertwined with these villages, continues to inspire. It serves as a beacon, illuminating the tales of a woman whose spirit was as vast and indomitable as the landscapes she traversed.

Life After Fame

When tales of exploration and adventure are recounted, it's easy to get lost in the glitz. To remember just the moments of triumph and not what follows. The shadows that succeed in the limelight are less talked about. But just as a coin has two sides, every story has its epilogue. What became of Sacagawea and Charbonneau once their expedition with Lewis and Clark was over?

The echoes of Sacagawea's courage and her essential role in the Lewis and Clark expedition reverberated across the lands. But as the noise of the expedition dimmed, life pressed on. With her husband, Toussaint Charbonneau, by her side, the world might have seen them as inseparable explorers. Yet, beyond their famed journey, their bond was not just about shared adventures but shared lives.

They moved to St. Louis after their famed journey. Isn't it curious how the bustling town, with its cacophony and vibrancy, might have felt to Sacagawea? Perhaps she yearned sometimes for the vast plains and open skies. Yet, amid the urban sprawl, a new chapter of their lives unfurled.

Sacagawea and Charbonneau were given a chance to settle in St. Louis, courtesy of William Clark. Clark, recognizing the invaluable contributions of the pair, ensured they were given land. Isn't that a testament to the deep bonds formed during the expedition? It was here, in this nurturing environment, that their son Jean Baptiste furthered his education.

While Charbonneau tried his hand at multiple ventures, Sacagawea became the bedrock of the family. The roles might have reversed: the woman once guiding explorers through wild terrains now navigated the challenges of daily life and parenthood.

And let's not forget: Sacagawea was a mother. Can you imagine the tales she would tell Jean Baptiste at bedtime? Would she recount the whispers of the wind over vast plateaus, the gentle rustle of leaves in dense forests, and the times when courage was the only companion? As her son embarked on his own adventures, did she see the echo of her younger self in him?

There's a melancholy note to their tale. The exact circumstances of Sacagawea's passing remain shrouded in mystery. Some say she left this world in her mid-twenties, while others claim she lived long, watching the world change around her. Charbonneau continued on his path, navigating the turbulence of loss and the weight of memories.

It's fascinating how lives that were once the stuff of legends slowly blend into the tapestry of the everyday. But that's life. Moments of fame are just that: moments. It's the quiet days, the uncelebrated routines, and the shared laughter and tears that truly define us.

Sacagawea and Charbonneau: their names might forever be intertwined with the great expedition, but beyond the pages of history, they were two souls forging their path together. A path that meandered through fame, love, challenges, and the simple joys of life.

The Mystery of Sacagawea's Later Years

Hasn't history always been tinged with a touch of the unknown? Like pieces of a puzzle left unsolved, certain chapters of Sacagawea's life remain shrouded in mystery. And while her journey with Lewis and Clark stands vividly etched in time, her later years seem to slip through the fingers of history.

By the time the expedition concluded, Sacagawea had already made an indelible mark on the pages of American lore. Her invaluable contributions, navigating unfamiliar terrains and establishing connections with indigenous tribes, elevated the expedition's success. But what of the woman behind the legend once the expedition's campfires dimmed?

Following the expedition, Sacagawea and her husband, Toussaint Charbonneau, settled in St. Louis. Here, their son, Jean Baptiste, received education and mentorship under

William Clark's watchful eye. But what paths did life beckon Sacagawea toward in this new chapter?

Rumours and tales weave intricate patterns about her subsequent years. One version suggests she lived a quiet life in St. Louis, tending to her family and perhaps reminiscing about her time among vast valleys and rushing rivers. Another theory suggests she journeyed westward, returning to the Shoshone roots from whence she came.

And then there are tales, whispered in hushed tones, that Sacagawea embarked on yet another expedition, her restless spirit leading her to places unknown. Could the same intrepid explorer who faced the wild terrains of America have set off on another adventure? An exciting notion to consider.

The details surrounding her eventual demise are as enigmatic as the tales of her later years. While some accounts place her passing in 1812 at the tender age of 24, others, perhaps more optimistically, claim she lived to see many more decades, passing away in the 1880s.

In our quest to unravel the mystery, we may stumble upon a larger truth: that life, much like rivers, seldom flows in predictable patterns. It's full of twists and turns, and sometimes, the waters run deep and silent, hiding their tales beneath serene surfaces.

While documents and diaries may offer glimpses, the full scope of Sacagawea's later years remains an enigma. And perhaps it's this very mystery that adds depth to her narrative.

Our imaginations bridge the gap, crafting stories, theories, and possibilities in the spaces between the known and unknown.

We might never know every detail of Sacagawea's life after the limelight. Still, in her mystery lies an invitation: to wonder, speculate, and imagine. Ultimately, isn't that what legends like her inspire in us all? A sense of wonder that lingers long after the tales are told.

Chapter 9

The Narrative of Lewis & Clark

As we delve into the annals of American history, the journey of Lewis and Clark stands out, casting a long shadow over the early 19th century. But what really brings colour to this canvas is the undeniable role of Sacagawea. Without her, would the narrative we've come to embrace be starkly different?

From the moment Sacagawea joined the Corps of Discovery, it became evident she wasn't merely another member but a beacon of hope. She forged ahead with her young child on her back and an insurmountable determination in her stride. Sacagawea bridged the divide in the heart of the wilderness, where language barriers might have proved formidable. The young Shoshone woman facilitated critical dialogues with indigenous tribes, ensuring the expedition's encounters with them were largely amicable. Can you imagine the weight of such a responsibility?

The terrain that Lewis and Clark set to navigate wasn't merely challenging; it was often treacherous. As the group confronted the imposing Rocky Mountains, Sacagawea recognized familiar landscapes from her childhood. And with every step, every whisper of the wind, she provided invaluable insights, redirecting the group when they veered off-course.

Beyond her expertise as a guide and interpreter, Sacagawea exuded an air of diplomacy. In an era of sparse cultural understanding, she acted as a living emblem of peace. Think about it: Would seeing a young woman and her child not quell any apprehensions or fears other tribes might harbour? Indeed, her presence announced that the expedition came in peace and not for conquest.

Yet, amidst these feats, the simplicity of her nature shone brightly. She remained humble, often gathering wild roots and berries to sustain the group. Can we overlook the day she salvaged essential journals and equipment when a boat capsized? Or the countless times she pointed out edible plants, ensuring the crew's sustenance in unfamiliar lands?

The culmination of the expedition and its triumphant success owed much to this incredible woman. While Lewis and Clark are often hailed for their leadership and bravery, it is imperative to recognize that Sacagawea was their compass in the truest sense. Without her, would the landscapes have been as navigable, the tribes as receptive?

As we revisit the narrative of Lewis and Clark, let's not merely recount the miles travelled or the challenges faced. Let's celebrate the spirit of Sacagawea: A woman who, amidst the vastness of untamed America, was the heart and soul of a journey that shaped a nation. Remember her name, for it is intertwined with the legacy of discovery and unity.

Representation in Art, Literature, and Media

Suppose you've ever ventured to understand the heartbeat of early America. In that case, you might have stumbled upon a name that rings with reverence: Sacagawea. More than a historical figure, she's a symbol, an inspiration woven into the very fabric of the nation's story. But how has our culture kept her memory alive through art, literature, and media?

Walk through an art museum's American history wing, and there's a high chance you'll be met with a painting that captures a moment from the Lewis and Clark expedition. Amidst the dramatic landscapes and depictions of rugged explorers, you'll often find a serene face, a young woman holding her baby. This is none other than Sacagawea. She's often represented in art as a beacon of hope, a guiding force amidst uncertainty. But more than that, she embodies the spirit of collaboration between the indigenous people and the early settlers.

Literature, with its beautiful penchant for diving deep, has etched Sacagawea's journey in myriad ways. Novels like "The Sacagawea of the Lewis and Clark Expedition" bring her story to life, giving voice to her thoughts, hopes, and fears. While these literary representations might take creative liberties, they keep the essence of Sacagawea intact: a woman of strength, wisdom, and resilience.

Children's books, too, have played their part. Isn't it wonderful that a young reader, while flipping through the pages of "Who Was Sacagawea?", can learn about the remarkable journey of this young Shoshone woman? It plants a seed, an idea that no matter the obstacles, one can leave an indelible mark on the pages of history.

And then there's media: a powerful tool in shaping perceptions. Throughout the years, films and documentaries have tried to piece together Sacagawea's story. Some stay true to historical accounts, while others venture into fiction. Yet, every portrayal has something in common: a woman whose spirit was unyielding, whose heart knew no bounds.

However, with representation comes responsibility. It's essential to ask: Have we always gotten it right? While many portrayals pay homage to Sacagawea's legacy, others may inadvertently overshadow her true essence. Amidst the vast canvas of interpretations, it's crucial to differentiate between the woman and the myth.

What does Sacagawea represent to you? To many, she remains a symbol of determination, bridging gaps between different worlds. To others, she's a testament to every mother's strength, navigating through uncharted territories for the promise of a better future.

As the sun sets on the horizon, casting golden hues on statues and monuments dedicated to Sacagawea, we are reminded of her enduring legacy. Through art, literature, and media, her story remains alive, reminding us, generation after generation, of the footprints she left on the sands of time. And as you take in her tale, always remember: stories like hers don't just belong to the past; they shape our present and inspire our future...

Symbolism and Controversy

When you hold a coin in your hand, what do you see? A piece of metal? A value? Or a story etched in miniature? For many, the Sacagawea Dollar is more than just currency; it's a symbol, a piece of history encapsulated in a palm-sized disk.

But why Sacagawea? And what tales and controversies surround this golden coin?

Introduced in the year 2000, the U.S. Mint aimed to replace the Susan B. Anthony dollar with something fresh, something meaningful. Sacagawea, the indigenous woman known for aiding the famed Lewis and Clark expedition, was their pick. On one side, the coin features a confident Sacagawea with her child, Jean Baptiste, wrapped snugly against her back. An image that evokes feelings of courage, resilience, and the spirit of adventure. An image that speaks to both the nation's history and its aspirations. But was this recognition overdue, or was it another act of tokenism?

To the admirers of Sacagawea, this coin was a long-awaited tribute. Here was a woman, a native at that, who played an indispensable role in one of the most challenging expeditions across America. Giving her a place on a currency elevates her from the footnotes of history books to a place of honour.

Yet, with recognition comes scrutiny. Critics asked: Does the coin represent Sacagawea, or is it a projection of what modern society wanted her to be? Her portrayal of a young, hopeful woman with a child might resonate with some. Still, others see it as an oversimplification, a move to fit her into a familiar narrative.

Another layer of controversy lay in the practicality of the coin. Accustomed to the paper dollar, many Americans needed more use for the coin in daily transactions. Was the Sacagawea Dollar then just a symbolic gesture devoid of utility in the real world?

And let's remember the artists and designers behind the coin. Whose interpretation of Sacagawea were we seeing? A rendition by Glenna Goodacre was chosen, but as with any piece of art, interpretations vary. Some believed her portrayal was noble, while others felt it amalgamated stereotypes.

So, as the coin glints in the sunlight, it doesn't just reflect rays but also the myriad views, beliefs, and feelings of the people who encounter it. Isn't it fascinating how something as ubiquitous as currency can evoke many emotions and discussions?

In the heart of it all, the Sacagawea Dollar remains an enigma: a blend of history, art, and economics. It forces one to ponder: Can any representation do justice to a life as multifaceted as Sacagawea's? In all its golden glory, the coin is a testament that some stories, some legacies, are too vast to be confined to a single narrative.

Chapter 10

Romanticizing the Guide

Have you ever gazed upon a painting or read an enthralling story and thought to yourself: how much of this is true? The life of Sacagawea is one such tale that has been painted with broad and sometimes embellished strokes throughout history. While her contributions to the Lewis and Clark expedition were remarkable, our collective memory often distorts the nuances of her role. So, what misconceptions loom large, and how did they come about?

Firstly, Sacagawea's contributions, while undeniably valuable, were often romanticized. The imagery of a lone indigenous woman leading a band of explorers through treacherous terrains, battling nature's whims, is compelling. Yet, Sacagawea was part of a larger ensemble of individuals, including her husband, Toussaint Charbonneau, who made the journey successful. The ensemble worked together, pooling their skills and knowledge.

Moreover, many narratives portray Sacagawea as the expedition's primary, if not sole, guide. But was she really the master navigator leading the way? Sacagawea undeniably had intimate knowledge of some regions, and her understanding of native languages and cultures proved invaluable. Yet, the vast journey stretched across territories unfamiliar even to her.

Then there's the subject of her age. Often, she's imagined as a mature, wise woman, drawing from decades of life experiences. The reality? Sacagawea was in her late teens during the expedition. Imagine a young woman, barely out of childhood, navigating a world of natural and artificial challenges. Does that make her contributions any less significant? Absolutely not. But it does provide a lens to view her achievements with a more grounded perspective.

Another misconception surrounds her relationship with the expedition team. Was she an equal partner, or was her involvement more nuanced? It's vital to remember the societal structures of the time. While she wasn't merely a passive participant, she wasn't calling the shots either. Her role oscillated between guide, interpreter, and diplomat, bridging the cultural gaps that the team frequently encountered.

But why this desire to romanticize? Well, tales grow taller over time, especially when they inspire. We crave heroes, figures we can look up to. And while that's not inherently wrong, we must tread cautiously. Over-romanticizing can overshadow genuine accomplishments with fanciful tales.

In essence, the life of Sacagawea offers us more than just an adventure story. It's a lesson in understanding the past, not through the tinted glasses of romance, but with the clarity of truth. After all, reality, with all its intricacies and shades, is often more captivating than the most imaginative fiction.

Indigenous Perspectives

In the tapestry of American history, few threads are as colourful and intricate as those representing its indigenous peoples. And within this vast weave, the story of Sacagawea stands out, shimmering with myths, truths, and half-understood narratives. But have we ever paused to consider: whose voice are we truly hearing? Is it Sacagawea's own, or is it an echo, reshaped and retold by generations far removed from her lived experience?

Diving deeper into indigenous accounts offers a more authentic insight. The native tales, passed down orally, often deviate from the popular narratives we've accepted. It's not just about setting records straight; it's about embracing the depth and diversity of indigenous perspectives.

Take, for instance, the idea of Sacagawea as the "Indian Princess," a stereotype that casts her as a noble savage. But from a native perspective, her journey with Lewis and Clark wasn't about exploration or conquest. It was about survival. Amidst unfamiliar terrains and unpredictable situations, her instincts and indigenous wisdom were crucial. But was she the guiding torch for the entire expedition? Or was she one among many contributors, her role sometimes amplified, other times minimized?

Furthermore, the tales often describe Sacagawea not as an isolated figure but as deeply rooted within her community. For the indigenous peoples, community and connection are paramount. While away from her birth tribe, she wasn't devoid of her cultural anchor. Her interactions with other tribes during the expedition were more than just transactions; they were reunions, moments of shared understanding in a journey fraught with uncertainties.

And what about her life after the expedition? Western narratives often fade her out post-journey, relegating her to a mere chapter in the Lewis and Clark saga. But indigenous tales bring her back to life, focusing on her later years, her eventual return to her people, and her role as a mother, sister, and community member.

The indigenous accounts remind us that history is multifaceted. We inadvertently place Sacagawea in a box by focusing only on the expedition. But her life was more than that single journey. It was a continuum, a series of experiences shaped by her indigenous identity.

So, why is it crucial to amplify these native perspectives? Well, for one, it's about justice. For centuries, indigenous stories have been sidelined, their voices muted. By centring their narratives, we enrich our understanding of history; we acknowledge and honour their rightful place in it.

The tales of Sacagawea are a testament to the resilience and brilliance of indigenous women throughout history. Reclaiming her story is more than just an academic exercise. It's an act of reverence, of coming full circle, and of paying homage to a legacy that, while sometimes overshadowed, remains unbroken.

In the end, history isn't just about facts and figures. It's about the people, their stories, and the myriad ways they're told. And when it comes to Sacagawea, perhaps it's time we listen more closely to the whispers of the wind, the murmurs of the rivers, and the songs of her people. After all, they've been singing her praises long before history books took notice. Don't you think it's time we joined the chorus?

Sacagawea's Final Resting Place

When you delve into the annals of history, it often feels like you're navigating a vast maze. Turn one corner and find clarity, but turn another, and you're greeted with many questions. And one of those intriguing, somewhat elusive questions revolves around Sacagawea's final resting place. Where did this emblematic woman, who once traversed mountains, rivers, and vast stretches of unknown territory, eventually lay her head for the last time?

A land as expansive as America holds many secrets, and in some corners, whispers about Sacagawea's final moments persist. Two places, in particular, claim to be her final resting place: one in Wyoming and another much farther north, in South Dakota.

Wyoming's Wind River Indian Reservation holds a gravesite with a headstone that reads: "Sacajawea, 1788-1884." Quite a leap in years. This would mean she lived to be nearly a hundred! A local narrative tells the tale of Sacagawea living out her days there, marrying a Shoshone man after losing her French-Canadian husband, Toussaint Charbonneau. The descendants of this community fiercely believe that she lived a long, fulfilling life amongst them. A touching sentiment, if you ask me: the idea of her returning to her roots and living a long life.

Yet, historians often lean toward another account. Many believe Sacagawea died on December 20, 1812, at Fort Manuel in what is now South Dakota. This version paints a more sombre picture: a young life, full of adventures and trials, cut short at age 25. It's hard to digest, right? To think of a fiery spirit, a guide and interpreter of one of America's most legendary expeditions, passing away so young...

But here's where it gets even trickier. The journals of John Luttig, a clerk at Fort Manuel, describe the passing of a "Shoshone woman" on that date. He never mentions Sacagawea by name. Could it have been another Shoshone woman? Or was it, indeed, the end of Sacagawea's journey?

The truth is suspended somewhere between these two narratives. The debate rages on, and maybe that's a fitting tribute. After all, Sacagawea's life was about discovery, pushing boundaries, and constantly seeking the horizon. Perhaps she'd appreciate the mystery that surrounds her even now.

While we may never have a definitive answer, this debate does more than ponder over a burial site. It emphasizes the mark Sacagawea left on the land and its people. Whether in Wyoming or South Dakota, her spirit lingers, reminding us of resilience, exploration, and the infinite power of human connection.

And isn't that the real takeaway here? Beyond the confines of graves and headstones, Sacagawea lives on. In the tales we share and the debates we engage in, her curiosity continues to ignite. So, where did Sacagawea really find her eternal rest? Maybe the answer isn't in a specific location. Maybe it's in the collective memory of a nation she once helped to chart. And that, my friends, is a resting place worthy of legends.

Chapter 11

Sacagawea's Enduring Legacy

It's intriguing. How do certain figures from our past manage to etch their legacies in stone, quite literally? Sacagawea is unique among the vast pantheon of historical icons, represented through statues, monuments, and memorials scattered across the land she once traversed. Why does she, above many others, hold such an esteemed position in the collective memory of a nation?

When you stroll through parks or visit historic landmarks across the United States, it's not uncommon to encounter a statue of Sacagawea. In these depictions, she often stands tall, with a baby strapped to her back and an expression that exudes determination. The artistry involved captures the very essence of a young Shoshone woman who, against all odds, played a pivotal role in the Lewis and Clark expedition. But beyond the art, what do these statues truly signify?

Monuments stand as silent witnesses to history, don't they? Every curve, every etching tells a story. For instance, in Bismarck, North Dakota, there's an impressive statue of Sacagawea with her child, Jean Baptiste. It reminds visitors of her vital role as an interpreter and guide during the westward expedition. It's not just a tribute to her contributions but an acknowledgement of the broader role of indigenous people in shaping the destiny of a nation.

Then there's Idaho's Sacajawea Interpretive, Cultural, and Educational Center. Isn't it fascinating that the soil beneath this memorial might have once felt her footsteps? The centre doesn't just pay homage to her but offers insights into the Agaidika Shoshone-Bannock tribes' cultures and traditions.

In Oregon, the Sacagawea Statue at Washington Park gives her a gaze that seems to be looking toward the horizon. A symbol of the new frontiers she constantly sought?

But let's pause and ponder a moment: Why need these memorials? Beyond the bronze and stone, they serve as a bridge. A bridge between generations. They allow stories of courage, resilience, and exploration to transcend time. Through Sacagawea's statues, both young and old are reminded of the indomitable spirit of a woman navigating uncharted terrains, not just geographically but also in a world dominated by male adventurers.

Yet, while these monuments celebrate Sacagawea, they also raise a subtle question. Are we doing enough to recognize and understand the depth of her contributions and the cultural heritage she represents? It's one thing to erect statues and quite another to genuinely honour her legacy by delving deep into indigenous people's stories, traditions, and struggles.

In essence, statues, monuments, and memorials do more than commemorate. They challenge, they inspire, and they beckon us to engage with the past in a meaningful way. Every time we pass by a monument dedicated to Sacagawea, it's an invitation to remember, to reflect, and most importantly, to continue the exploration she once began.

A Model of Curricular Representation

Imagine stepping into a classroom. The walls are adorned with posters of pivotal figures: scientists, writers, leaders, and among them, the familiar face of a young Shoshone woman with a baby on her back. Yes, it's Sacagawea. But how did she become a significant part of our educational fabric? And what does her inclusion signify for the broader educational community?

The narrative of Sacagawea is not just about a journey across uncharted terrains. It's a tale that transcends mere geography. The story weaves in themes of resilience, cultural exchange, and the power of collaboration. And that's why it resonates so deeply within educational circles.

Schools, colleges, and educational institutions have always been looking for inspiring narratives. In Sacagawea, they found a gem. Her life story offers many learning opportunities in history, culture, language, and even interpersonal dynamics. Consider what a young student can learn from Sacagawea's interactions with Lewis and Clark?

First, there's the obvious lesson of mutual respect. Even when indigenous people faced immense challenges and prejudices, Sacagawea's role was indispensable. Her ability to communicate with various tribes, her knowledge of the terrain, and her calming presence made her not just a guide but an ambassador of peace. Wouldn't we want our students to understand the importance of every individual's contribution, regardless of background or gender?

Moreover, her story provides an excellent platform for educators to discuss indigenous cultures, traditions, and histories. It's a gateway to dive deeper into the rich tapestry of Native American life, their beliefs, customs, and relationship with nature. How often do we encounter educational content that seamlessly melds history with anthropology?

The beauty of including Sacagawea in curricula isn't just about her journey but the undercurrents of those facts. She becomes a medium through which educators can tackle complex subjects: gender dynamics in historical contexts, the significance of cultural translators, and the idea of exploration as a collaborative effort.

But it's not just about the past. The implications of Sacagawea's story ripple into the present. In a diverse classroom, her story can serve as a touchstone for representation, identity, and belonging discussions. By showcasing how her unique skills and heritage played a crucial role in the expedition's success, educators plant the seed of an idea: every individual, with their distinct background and capabilities, brings something invaluable to the table.

When educators incorporate Sacagawea into their lessons, they aren't just teaching history. They are moulding minds to be more inclusive, more appreciative of diversity, and more understanding of the intricate dance between individual talents and collective efforts. Through her story, a simple classroom transforms into a space of exploration, not of lands, but of ideas, values, and perspectives.

So the next time you spot Sacagawea's face in a textbook or a classroom poster, remember: it's not just a nod to the past. It's a bridge to the future, where every student recognizes the potential within themselves and others.

Annual Celebrations and Festivals in Her Honor

In the heartland of America, as spring warms the soil and breathes life into the dormant trees, there's a palpable excitement in the air. Can you feel it? It's not just the promise of new beginnings that the season offers but the joyous anticipation of the annual celebrations and festivals dedicated to one remarkable individual: Sacagawea.

Isn't it fascinating that centuries after her journey with Lewis and Clark, we still gather in droves to honour Sacagawea? Her legacy has undoubtedly cemented its place in the American tapestry. Through the years, these festivals have emerged not merely as remembrances but as vibrant spaces of cultural amalgamation and communal harmony.

The Sacagawea Heritage Days, held yearly in Salmon, Idaho, is perhaps the most iconic of these events. It's the very soil where Sacagawea was born! Here, history enthusiasts, families, educators, and the curious converge. Through reenactments of key moments from her life, people are transported back in time. Picture this: young children, faces painted, running around tepees, and elders gathered around a fire, recounting tales of the Shoshone woman who changed the course of exploration in America.

And then, there's the Coin & Currency Festival in Missouri. Remember the golden dollar coin with Sacagawea's face imprinted on it? This festival celebrates that very coin's inception and Sacagawea's invaluable contributions. Numismatists, or coin collectors for those less familiar with the term, come from far and wide, showcasing their collections and trading stories of how this young Native American woman impacted economics and commerce.

Not far away, in North Dakota, the Three Tribes Museum holds an annual event emphasizing the rich confluence of cultures that Sacagawea represented. The festival is a blend of music, dance, and crafts, representing the Shoshone and the Hidatsa and Mandan communities she encountered. It's a day where barriers vanish, the language of unity and shared history is spoken, and Sacagawea's spirit dances in every tune and resonates in every drumbeat.

But why this collective memory? Why does this need to gather, year after year, in Sacagawea's name?

Perhaps it's because she embodies a unique blend of courage, wisdom, and resilience. In an era where women's voices were often marginalized, she stood out, carving a niche for herself and ensuring the success of an expedition that would reshape America. These festivals are powerful reminders of her journey, indomitable spirit, and the diverse cultures she brought together.

To partake in these festivals is to walk alongside Sacagawea, to momentarily live her experiences, and to be inspired. It's a message passed down through generations: that every individual, regardless of background, can make a mark and change the course of history.

So, the next time spring graces America with its warmth, and you hear the distant beats of drums or the excited chatter of festival-goers, know that it's Sacagawea's spirit, alive and thriving, beckoning you to join in, to celebrate a life well-lived and a legacy that continues to inspire.

Chapter 12

Sacagawea and the Women's Rights Movement

Sacagawea's journey is nothing short of legendary. A young woman navigating an uncharted world, playing an integral role in the renowned Lewis and Clark expedition, she represents more than just a historical footnote. She embodies resilience, tenacity, and a spirit that defied the norms of her era. But how does her story fit into the broader tapestry of the Women's Rights Movement?

In the early 1800s, women's roles were rigidly defined. The domestic sphere was their domain, while public life and import decisions belonged to men. Sacagawea, in this context, emerges as an anomaly. Guiding a group of men through challenging terrains, communicating with various tribes, and even saving precious journals and supplies from being lost to a capsized boat, can you imagine the audacity?

The significance of her actions becomes even more apparent when we juxtapose her story with the early rumblings of the Women's Rights Movement. In a time when women were fighting for a voice for representation, Sacagawea was out there, living that fight.

The famed Seneca Falls Convention in 1848, regarded by many as the inception of the Women's Rights Movement in

America, happened decades after Sacagawea's expedition. Yet, can't we see her journey as a precursor? While Elizabeth Cady Stanton and Lucretia Mott were vocal advocates, Sacagawea's story exemplified, in flesh and bone, the very ideals these women were championing.

She was not merely assisting the explorers but an active collaborator and decision-maker. Her insights were not just suggestions but crucial determinants that shaped the expedition's trajectory. This raises an interesting thought: While many women were confined to homes, there was Sacagawea, camping under open skies, forging through wilderness, setting up camps, and negotiating with tribal leaders. Isn't that the very essence of breaking barriers and redefining roles?

Of course, her narrative isn't free from challenges. Did she always have a choice? Were there moments of hesitation, of doubt? Perhaps. But that's the beauty of her story. In the face of adversity, she persevered.

However, let's not misconstrue. Sacagawea's life was not a deliberate statement on women's rights. She wasn't setting out to be a feminist icon. But sometimes, history has a peculiar way of finding its heroes. Through her actions and her resilience, she inadvertently became a symbol. A symbol for all women who dared to believe they could be more than what society prescribed.

To the modern reader, revisiting her story is an inspiration. It's a testament that the fight for women's rights started not just in convention halls or eloquent speeches but in the act of living defiantly. Sacagawea, with her baby on her back, navigating the vast expanse of America, serves as a vivid reminder: Change doesn't always begin with grand gestures. Sometimes, it starts with a single step into the unknown. And if she could do it, amid the wilderness and unknown challenges, what's stopping us?

So, as we delve into the annals of history and recount tales of women who've paved the way, let's ensure Sacagawea's story is told and retold. Not just as an explorer but as an emblem of indomitable spirit and a precursor to a movement that would change the world

The Real Feminine Strength

Have you ever paused to think about the tales of heroes and legends? Behind the glint of fame often lies a tapestry of trials, tribulations, and raw human spirit. And when it comes to Sacagawea, her story isn't just a chapter in an expedition logbook; it's an anthem of feminine resilience.

Born amidst the windswept plains of the Lemhi River Valley, Sacagawea's life wasn't one scripted for ease. As a young girl, her world was turned upside down when she was taken away from her Shoshone tribe by the Hidatsa. For a moment, imagine the profound loneliness she must have felt, the sheer disconnection from her roots. But within this young girl was a reservoir of strength waiting to be tapped.

Fast-forward to the encounter with Lewis and Clark. Here was Sacagawea, hardly in her late teens, roped into an expedition she didn't sign up for, traversing vast terrains. What made her not just another member but a cornerstone of the journey? The answer lies not just in her navigational skills or linguistic prowess, but in her indomitable spirit.

While the explorers came equipped with books and tools, Sacagawea brought along something far more precious: a life's worth of wilderness wisdom. The rivers whispered secrets to her, the mountains unveiled shortcuts, and the forests echoed memories of her past. In one harrowing incident, when the expedition's pirogue nearly capsized, Sacagawea's calm demeanour and quick thinking saved many crucial supplies and journals. This wasn't just skill but a testament to her grace under pressure.

But remember: she wasn't just a guide but a mother. How many tales tell of a young mother navigating the wild unknowns with a baby on her back? Each step she took was a dance between her dual roles. There's a tenderness to this image: A woman forging ahead, with the future nestled against her.

Isn't there a profound lesson in this for all of us? Sacagawea wasn't just a woman of her time but ahead of her time. In her journey, there's a symbolic representation of countless unnamed women who have, across eras and continents, showcased resilience that often remains unsung.

Perhaps it's time we ask: What makes strength? Is it just physical prowess or the ability to dominate? Or is it, like in Sacagawea's case, the fortitude to overcome, persist, and nurture simultaneously?

When viewed beyond the lens of just the Lewis and Clark expedition, her story emerges as a beacon for all women. It's not the grand moments but the smaller ones – a comforting lullaby sung at a campfire, a moment of solace offered in trying times, an intuition-driven nudge in the right direction.

In the grand narrative of history, tales of conquerors and kings often overshadow stories like Sacagawea's. But it's essential to realize that the bedrock of our past isn't just made of momentous battles or discoveries, but of people. Real people. People like Sacagawea carry the weight of the future on their shoulders and move forward with grace and grit.

In today's world, where discussions about feminine strength have taken centre stage, revisiting Sacagawea's life offers fresh perspectives. Her story, with its amalgamation of courage, care, and craft, showcases that real strength doesn't lie in overpowering but in empowering. And isn't that the essence of true feminine strength? It's high time we celebrate not just the legend but the woman, the mother, the guide, and the survivor. For in her tale, many will find their voice, strength, and path. Beyond the folklore, Sacagawea remains an epitome of real, raw, and resonating feminine power!

Modern-Day Reflections on Her Influence

Sacagawea is a name that resounds through the corridors of time. Yet, who was this formidable woman, and why, centuries later, does her tale continue to inspire and intrigue us?

Navigating a man's world in the early 19th century wasn't a walk in the park. So, when tales are recounted of a young

Indigenous woman who survived and thrived amidst challenges, it makes one pause and ponder. Sacagawea didn't just walk the earth; she treaded it, leaving imprints for future generations.

Today, in an era where the clamour for equal rights and female empowerment rings loud and clear, Sacagawea stands as a beacon. Think about it. How many teenagers do you know who could guide a monumental expedition, decipher the language of the wild, and bring different communities together, all while cradling a child? It's awe-inspiring.

Her influence isn't merely about physical endurance or knowledge. It's about resilience, adaptability, and the uncanny ability to bridge cultures. At a time when Indigenous peoples were often disregarded, Sacagawea's indispensable role in the Lewis and Clark Expedition shattered misconceptions.

Imagine a modern classroom, bustling with energy, where young minds are introduced to her story. As they lean in, eyes wide with curiosity, they learn more than historical facts. They absorb lessons of perseverance, cross-cultural respect, and the understated power of femininity.

Sacagawea's influence also ripples into the spheres of environmentalism and sustainable living. Her deep respect for nature, an integral part of Indigenous cultures, prompts a poignant question for today's world: How can we harmoniously coexist with nature, much like she did? Her life teaches us that nature isn't just a resource to exploit but a companion to converse with.

Moreover, Sacagawea's tale offers a rich canvas in the contemporary arts, from literature to film. Painters, writers, and filmmakers draw inspiration from her journey, and in doing so, they breathe new life into her legacy. These artistic interpretations make one wonder: What would Sacagawea make of today's world? Would she be proud of the bridges we've built or dismayed at the divides?

In community discussions, particularly amongst Indigenous groups, Sacagawea's life is a testament to their ancestors' strength and wisdom. Her story becomes a source of pride, a narrative that challenges stereotypes and rekindles a sense of identity.

To women worldwide, she remains a symbol of unyielding strength. She navigated literal and metaphorical terrains, challenging the gender norms of her era. Doesn't her life then offer a lens to view our struggles, a reminder that boundaries are often just illusions?

And so, as we reflect on Sacagawea's influence in our modern world, it's clear that her legacy isn't confined to the pages of history books. Her spirit, tenacity, and bridge-building ability serve as guiding lights. In a world teeming with challenges, from gender inequities to environmental crises, perhaps it's time to ask: What would Sacagawea do? Because in her story, we might find the inspiration to forge paths, build bridges, and leave our unique mark on history.

Chapter 13

The Charbonneau Bloodline

Imagine a family tree that intertwines itself with the very fabric of American history, its roots deeply embedded in the vast expanse of the unchartered West. That's the Charbonneau bloodline for you. A lineage that, thanks to its most famous member, Sacagawea, has woven itself into the tapestry of American folklore.

Toussaint Charbonneau, a French-Canadian trapper, is the figure at the centre of this familial web. Even before he met the young Shoshone woman, his life had been an interesting mosaic of adventures. Now, you might ask: How did this man, known more for his association with Lewis and Clark, earn such a prominent place in the annals of history? The answer: Through alliances and relations that shaped the West.

His partnership with Sacagawea was more than just marital. In many ways, their union symbolized the confluence of cultures: European traders seeking fortune in the wild terrains and Indigenous communities that had thrived on these lands for millennia. Their son, Jean Baptiste Charbonneau, aptly nicknamed "Pompy", became the living embodiment of this melding of worlds.

Born amidst the legendary Lewis and Clark expedition, Jean Baptiste's life was anything but ordinary. Jean Baptiste's early life read like an adventure novel, from being carried on his mother's back across treacherous terrains to being christened by William Clark himself. And this zest for life carried into his adulthood.

Did you know that as a young man, Jean Baptiste travelled to Europe, where he hobnobbed with royalty and learned languages that would later serve him in his various roles as a guide, trapper, and military scout? From the majestic courts of Europe to the vast plains of America, he truly was a bridge between two continents.

The Charbonneau line didn't end there. Through marriages and alliances, their descendants have spread across the land, each carrying a family legacy central to America's westward expansion. Each of them, in their own way, contributed to the vibrant mosaic that is today's America.

The most compelling aspect of the Charbonneau bloodline is its resilience. From facing the untamed wilderness of the West to navigating the complex socio-political landscapes of their times, they remained undeterred. Each generation, armed with tales of courage and adventure, passed down the line and pushed the boundaries further, making their mark and ensuring the Charbonneau name remained in history.

In modern times, the Charbonneau descendants remain proud bearers of their unique heritage. Whether it's in the realm of academia, the arts, or activism, traces of that indomitable spirit – which was so evident in Sacagawea – can be found. The strength of their lineage, its resilience and adaptability, serves as an inspiration. After all, isn't it fascinating how the actions of a few individuals in the past can echo so profoundly into the future?

Today, as we delve deeper into the Charbonneau bloodline, it's not just a study of genealogy. It explores passion, culture, and lineage that refuses to be confined by societal norms or geographical boundaries. It is a story of a family that, in essence, reflects the broader story of America: diverse, tenacious, and always evolving.

Modern-Day Ties to Sacagawea

Ah, Sacagawea. How many of us grew up listening to tales of this young Shoshone woman, her baby strapped to her back, guiding the famed Lewis and Clark expedition through the uncharted American wilderness? Her story, vivid and gripping, has been passed down through generations, and rightly so. But how does this ancient tapestry of bravery and exploration connect to our modern world? Let's dive in.

Today, in a world of technological marvels and skyscrapers, it might be easy to forget Sacagawea's journey's raw, visceral nature. But every now and then, we're reminded. Remember that coin jingling in your pocket? The one with the image of a woman and a child? That's the Sacagawea dollar coin, a tribute from the U.S. Mint. But why, you might ask, would a nation so forward-looking choose to commemorate a figure from the distant past?

Well, isn't that the beauty of history? Sacagawea represents timeless qualities: courage, resilience, and collaboration. In a world often divided, her story serves as a gentle reminder of the power of unity. It underscores the potential of what can be achieved when diverse backgrounds come together to pursue a common goal.

Our schools still resonate with her legacy. Across America, educational institutions proudly bear her name, instilling the spirit of adventure and exploration in young minds. Have you ever wondered why teachers still recount her story to eager children? It's more than just a history lesson. It's a tale of empowerment, of a young Indigenous woman making her mark in a male-dominated world.

In popular culture, too, Sacagawea has made her imprint. Her influence is palpable from literature to theatre, films to art installations. Inspired by her journey, artists often portray her as the embodiment of Mother Nature, guiding humanity through the literal and metaphorical wilderness. What's interesting is how different artists interpret her legacy. To some, she's the ultimate guide; to others, a symbol of motherhood. To many, she embodies the very essence of America: diverse, relentless, and full of potential.

Yet, the most profound modern-day ties to Sacagawea are found not in coins or classrooms but in the hearts of the Indigenous communities. For them, she isn't just a figure from the past but a beacon of hope, an emblem of the strength and tenacity inherent in their heritage. Celebrations and festivals in her honour are not just remembrances but affirmations of identity and cultural pride.

So, as we navigate our modern world, with its challenges and complexities, it's worth drawing inspiration from

Sacagawea's journey. In her story, we're reminded that with determination, collaboration, and a sense of purpose, we, too, can chart our own paths, even through the most uncharted terrains.

The Shoshone Legacy Today

The vast landscapes of North America echo with tales of its indigenous peoples. Among those whispers, the Shoshone stand out, resonating a potent legacy today. But how does a tribe with roots buried deep in the ancient soil find relevance in our contemporary setting? It all begins with a woman named Sacagawea. Let's explore, shall we?

Sacagawea, a Shoshone woman, bridged two worlds. Her journey alongside Lewis and Clark showcased the prowess, resilience, and knowledge of her people. Yet, as we navigate the bustle of the 21st century, the Shoshone legacy manifests in more ways than just this historical tapestry. The Shoshone today? They're a beacon of endurance, culture, and adaptability.

Visit any corner of the American West, and the Shoshone influence is undeniable. Their traditional lands, from the arid Great Basin to the craggy peaks of the Rockies, bear testimony to their profound connection with the environment. Think of it: A land where every river bend and mountain peak holds a story, a memory. Isn't that remarkable?

Modern-day Shoshone communities are bustling hubs of cultural revival. Powwows and celebrations aren't mere tourist attractions but a vibrant display of traditions being passed down, ensuring that Shoshone youths feel that pulse of their ancestry. Have you ever attended one of these gatherings? The beats of the drums, the colourful dance regalia, and the storytelling make time almost...stand still.

But it's not just about tradition. The Shoshone are forging ahead in education, governance, and sustainable development. They are working tirelessly to reclaim and protect their lands; in doing so, they're setting an example for the rest of us. How can we coexist with nature? How do we respect and honour the past while shaping a sustainable future? These are questions the Shoshone seem to answer with grace and action.

And who could forget their contributions to the culinary world? Native foods, cultivated and harvested by the Shoshone for centuries, now grace gourmet menus worldwide. Have you ever tasted a sunchoke or enjoyed a prickly pear drink? It's a nod to the Shoshone, a culinary journey through time.

Yet, beneath all these achievements, there's an underlying struggle, a battle against centuries of displacement, discrimination, and cultural erosion. Today's Shoshone narrative isn't merely about celebrating the past; it's about navigating challenges, asserting identity, and making their voices heard. It's a reminder: Never take our presence for granted. We share a piece of ourselves with the world in our stories, dances, and food.

The Shoshone legacy today is a dance between the ancient and the modern, the spiritual and the tangible, the challenges and the triumphs. As we look to the future, the Shoshone serve as a poignant reminder of the richness of heritage, the importance of community, and the sheer will to thrive in the face of adversity.

Chapter 14

Sacagawea's Place in American History

Sacagawea is a name that whispers tales of adventure, determination, and resilience. But who was she, really? And how did this Shoshone woman etch her name into American history?

Born in the cradle of the Rocky Mountains, Sacagawea's early life foreshadowed her indomitable spirit. Kidnapped from her Shoshone tribe, she found herself amongst the Hidatsa, far from her native land. Imagine, just for a moment, being whisked away from everything you've ever known. Intimidating. Yet, precisely, these challenges carved out the grit in Sacagawea.

The year 1804 brought with it a gust of change. Two explorers, Meriwether Lewis and William Clark, embarked on an expedition to traverse the wild and unpredictable American frontier. Now, you might wonder: where does a young Shoshone woman fit into this grand tapestry? Ah, that's where the narrative gets even more fascinating!

In a fortunate turn of events, Sacagawea found herself joining the famed Lewis and Clark Expedition. As an interpreter and guide, she became the bridge between the explorers and the myriad Native American tribes they encountered. Picture this: A vast expanse of unknown terrain stretches out, and amid this daunting landscape, a young woman confidently points the way, cradling her infant son, Jean Baptiste, on her back. A sight to behold, wouldn't you agree?

But Sacagawea's contributions were not limited to mere translations. As a woman and a mother, her presence offered the expedition an aura of peace. It signalled to the tribes they met that their intentions were non-hostile. Think about it: Her mere presence was a beacon of hope and trust in a land brimming with uncertainty.

However, her significance transcends the expedition. Sacagawea became a symbol. In a nascent America, she embodied the essence of unity, cooperation, and mutual respect between indigenous peoples and European settlers. Her journey, fraught with peril and challenges, showcased a shared quest for discovery and understanding.

Over the centuries, the legacy of Sacagawea has been celebrated and commemorated in countless ways. Statues honour her, coins bear her likeness, and stories recount her adventures. But isn't it more than just bronze and tales? It's a testament to the endurance of spirit, to the belief that collaboration can lead to enlightenment.

So, as we look back, we don't just see a Shoshone woman guiding two explorers. We witness an emblem of harmony, a torchbearer of unity, and a testament to the undying human spirit. Sacagawea's footprint in American history is profound, reminding us time and again of the potential that lies in understanding, mutual respect, and forging ahead together.

And as we step into the future, armed with tales of the past, we're compelled to ask: How can we emulate that spirit of unity and discovery today? How can we ensure that the legacy of Sacagawea continues to inspire generations to come? The answers, my friend, lie in the stories we choose to remember and the lessons we choose to imbibe. Sacagawea, though a figure from the past, remains a beacon for the future, guiding us towards a more inclusive, understanding, and unified America. What a legacy to leave behind.

The Enduring Fascination with Sacagawea

Have you ever found yourself captivated by a tale from the past? By a character so vivid and compelling that their story remains etched in the collective consciousness for centuries? Sacagawea, the intrepid Shoshone woman, stands tall among these captivating figures. But what is it about her that has ignited such enduring fascination?

Let's journey back to a young America, where untamed landscapes stretched as far as the eye could see. It was a land of boundless potential, yet equally abundant in perils. Into this dynamic, enter Sacagawea, a figure embodying resilience and spirit. Kidnapped from her Shoshone tribe, she faced adversity early on, didn't she? But it was precisely this grit that later made her a linchpin in the historic Lewis and Clark Expedition.

The vast American wilderness is daunting even to seasoned adventurers. For Lewis and Clark, navigating uncharted territory was like walking in the dark, only catching occasional glimpses of the path ahead. But Sacagawea? With her intimate knowledge of the terrain and the tribes, she was their guiding star. Can you imagine? In a time when women's voices often faded into the background, Sacagawea's guidance was paramount. She wasn't just a guide; she was a bridge between worlds. Her presence eased tense encounters with Native American tribes and conveyed a message of peace.

The tales of her voyages, with baby Jean Baptiste strapped to her back, evoke awe, don't they? It paints an image of a young mother navigating treacherous terrains, not just for her own survival but for the future of an entire nation. Quite a picture, right?

But let's go deeper. Beyond her exploits, it's Sacagawea's essence that captivates. Here was a woman who stood at the crossroads of cultures, a beacon of hope in an era of uncertainty. Her story is about adventure, unity, collaboration, and bridging divides.

In our modern age, when divides seem to be growing again, we look back to figures like Sacagawea. Why? Because she represents the possibilities that emerge when diverse worlds come together. When we learn from one another, share stories, and embark on collective journeys.

Today, statues, coins, and tales honour Sacagawea, but it's more than just material commemoration. Her legacy is a call to action: a nudge to explore, unite, bridge the divides, and embrace the unknown with the spirit of adventure.

Ultimately, the fascination with Sacagawea is not just about her but also about us. It reflects our yearning for unity, adventure, and understanding. Her story, echoing through the annals of history, reminds us that together, we can traverse the toughest terrains, bridge the widest divides, and pen tales that endure through the ages.

Keeping Her Story Alive

In an era where tales of pioneers mostly laud the actions of men emerges a beacon: Sacagawea. Her journey is so intrinsic to the fabric of America's past that it's as if the mountains and rivers whisper her name. How do we ensure that this formidable woman's legacy continues to inspire future generations?

Picture a young, fearless Shoshone woman navigating treacherous terrains. Sacagawea, a mere teenager, played a vital role in the Lewis and Clark Expedition. Their success might've hung in the balance without her. But beyond the expeditions, she embodied resilience, adaptability, and hope. Isn't it intriguing that she was the bridge in an age fraught with barriers?

The importance of teaching her story is clear: it's a testament to the human spirit, collaboration, and the belief that boundaries, whether geographical or societal, are meant to be overcome. But how do we keep such a story alive and resounding in the echoing chambers of the future?

First, it's about making her story accessible. Books for children and adults can unravel her tale in all its raw intensity.

We plant the seed of wonder by placing her narrative in classrooms, libraries, and homes. Imagine a child reading about her for the first time: the adventures, the challenges, the victories. A spark ignites.

Next, interactive experiences can bridge the gap between the past and the present. Virtual reality expeditions, following in her footsteps, can offer a firsthand experience of her journey. Museums dedicated to the expedition can put forth exhibits where Sacagawea is not just a side note but a focal point.

But beyond these tangible methods, it's crucial to engage in conversations. Discussions in classrooms, debates at family dinners, podcasts, and documentaries. Her spirit truly comes alive in these organic exchanges of thoughts and ideas. Consider this: every time her story is spoken aloud, she continues to live, breaking barriers and forging paths in hearts and minds.

Communities can also come together to celebrate her legacy. Annual events such as nature walks or youth exploration camps can testify to her indomitable spirit. What's better than walking a mile in her shoes to truly understand her mettle?

Moreover, in a digital age, her story can find wings on platforms where the youth congregate. Engaging animations, captivating podcasts, and interactive games can ensure she is not relegated to the dusty pages of forgotten history.

But, at the heart of it all lies a simple truth. To keep Sacagawea's story alive, we must recognize and champion the qualities she epitomized: resilience, unity, understanding, and exploration. As long as these ideals are celebrated and held aloft as virtues to aspire to, Sacagawea's spirit will continue to soar, inspiring countless more, generation after generation.

And isn't that the dream? For a story as timeless as hers to be the guiding light for many more pioneers to come. For future generations to look back and think: If Sacagawea could, so can I.

Literature and Resources

Sacagawea's life is nothing short of a tapestry woven with threads of resilience, tenacity, and spirit. To uncover the intricate details of her life, it is essential to delve into the sources that have worked painstakingly to narrate her journey. Here's an assemblage of references that have contributed to the painting of her full portrait:

1. Journals of the Lewis & Clark Expedition: Edited by Gary E. Moulton, these journals are a treasure trove of firsthand accounts. The explorers frequently mentioned Sacagawea, providing a window into their shared experiences and her invaluable role.

2. "Sacagawea's Nickname: Essays on the American West" by Larry McMurtry: An exploration of the western frontier, McMurtry adds depth to the understanding of Sacagawea's contributions.

3. "Sacagawea: The Life and Times of a Native American Interpreter" by Rosemary Entringer: This is one of the comprehensive biographies that extensively chronicles her life and significance during the expedition.

4. National American Indian Museum: Their exhibits and archives offer an in-depth perspective on Native American

history, including the pivotal roles played by figures like Sacagawea.

5. The Shoshone History and Culture Archives: As a member of the Lemhi Shoshone tribe, understanding their history and customs gives context to Sacagawea's upbringing and the skills she brought to the expedition.

6. "The Truth About Sacajawea" by Kenneth Thomasma: While catering to a younger audience, Thomasma's work is an enlightening account of her journey, emphasizing the respect she earned.

7. PBS Documentary - "Lewis & Clark: The Journey of the Corps of Discovery": Directed by Ken Burns, this documentary stitches together the tales from the journals with expert interviews, highlighting Sacagawea's impact.

8. "Bird Woman (Sacagawea): Guide of Lewis and Clark" by James Willard Schultz: An imaginative retelling, Schultz's narrative offers a glimpse into what Sacagawea might have felt and thought during her travels.

9. Lemhi County Historical Museum & Sacajawea Interpretive Center: Located in her native land, the centre holds artefacts, oral histories, and other resources that shed light on her early life and later years.

10. "Sacagawea Speaks: Beyond the Shining Mountains with Lewis and Clark" by Joyce Badgley Hunsaker: Drawing from various sources, Hunsaker crafts a potential first-person account, putting readers in Sacagawea's moccasins.

Printed in Great Britain
by Amazon

37602089R00059